Cultural Continuity in Mesoamerica

World Anthropology

General Editor

SOL TAX

Patrons

CLAUDE LÉVI-STRAUSS
MARGARET MEAD
LAILA SHUKRY EL HAMAMSY
M. N. SRINIVAS

MOUTON PUBLISHERS · THE HAGUE · PARIS
DISTRIBUTED IN THE USA AND CANADA BY ALDINE, CHICAGO

Cultural Continuity in Mesoamerica

Editor

DAVID L. BROWMAN

MOUTON PUBLISHERS · THE HAGUE · PARIS
DISTRIBUTED IN THE USA AND CANADA BY ALDINE, CHICAGO

General Editor's Preface

Ever since the Conquistadores first reported their discoveries of the Aztecs and Mayas in Mexico and the Incas in Peru, these civilizations have joined the great romantic mysteries of buried and forgotten history. The processes by which archaeologists have been unravelling these mysteries – processes often romanticized as much as the civilizations themselves – are well illustrated in this book and its companion volume, *Advances in Andean archaeology*. It is an endless story of the painstaking application of new techniques of discovery and the changing of theories interpreting the archaeology, history, and ethnology of a specific geographic and cultural area; each step in the process becomes a recognizable piece of a puzzle that can be fitted to other pieces. For one such area this extraordinary book puts some of the wide variety of particular new and disparate discoveries in useful perspective. The very variety of the individual papers is owed to their origin in an international Congress designed to bring together the widest possible variety of human scientists.

Like most contemporary sciences, anthropology is a product of the European tradition. Some argue that it is a product of colonialism, with one small and self-interested part of the species dominating the study of the whole. If we are to understand the species, our science needs substantial input from scholars who represent a variety of the world's cultures. It was a deliberate purpose of the IXth International Congress of Anthropological and Ethnological Sciences to provide impetus in this direction. The *World Anthropology* volumes, therefore, offer a first glimpse of a human science in which members from all societies have played an active role. Each of the books is designed to be self-contained; each is an attempt to update its particular sector of scientific knowledge and is written by specialists from all parts of the world. Each volume should be read and reviewed individually as a separate volume on its own given subject. The set as a whole will indicate what changes are in store for anthropology as scholars from the developing countries join in studying the species of which we are all a part.

The IXth Congress was planned from the beginning not only to include as many of the scholars from every part of the world as possible, but also with a view toward the eventual publication of the papers in high-quality volumes. At previous Congresses scholars were invited to bring papers which were then read out loud. They were necessarily limited in length; many were only summarized; there was little time for discussion; and the sparse discussion could only be in one language. The IXth Congress was an experiment aimed at changing this. Papers were written with the intention of exchanging them before the Congress, particularly in extensive pre-Congress sessions; they were not intended to be read aloud at the Congress, that time being devoted to discussions – discussions which were simultaneously and professionally translated into five languages. The method for eliciting the papers was structured to make as represen-tative a sample as was allowable when scholarly creativity – hence self-selection – was critically important. Scholars were asked both to propose papers of their own and to suggest topics for sessions of the Congress which they might edit into volumes. All were then informed of the suggestions and encouraged to re-think their own papers and the topics. The process, therefore, was a continuous one of feedback and exchange and it has continued to be so even after the Congress. The some two thousand papers comprising *World Anthropology* cer-tainly then offer a substantial sample of world anthropology. It has been said that anthropology is at a turning point; if this is so, these volumes will be the historical direction-markers.

As might have been foreseen in the first post-colonial generation, the large majority of the Congress papers (82 percent) are the work of scholars identified with the industrialized world which fathered our traditional discipline and the institution of the Congress itself: Eastern Europe (15 percent); Western Europe (16 percent); North America (47 percent); Japan, South Africa, Australia, and New Zealand (4 percent). Only 18 percent of the papers are from developing areas: Africa (4 percent); Asia-Oceania (9 percent); Latin America (5 per-cent). Aside from the substantial representation from the U.S.S.R. and the nations of Eastern Europe, a significant difference between this corpus of written material and that of other Congresses is the addition of the large proportion of contributions from Africa, Asia, and Latin America. "Only 18 percent" is two to four times as great a proportion as that of other Congresses; moreover, 18 percent of

2,000 papers is 360 papers, 10 times the number of "Third World" papers presented at previous Congresses. In fact, these 360 papers are more than the total of ALL papers published after the last International Congress of Anthropological and Ethnological Sciences which was held in the United States (Philadelphia, 1956).

The significance of the increase is not simply quantitative. The input of scholars from areas which have until recently been no more than subject matter for anthropology represents both feedback and also long-awaited theoretical contributions from the perspectives of very different cultural, social, and historical traditions. Many who attended the IXth Congress were convinced that anthropology would not be the same in the future. The fact that the next Congress (India, 1978) will be our first in the "Third World" may be symbolic of the change. Meanwhile, sober consideration of the present set of books will show how much, and just where and how, our discipline is being revolutionized.

In addition to the companion volume on Andean archaeology, the Editor of this book has edited for this series two others: *Pre-Columbian human biology* and *The earliest Americans: ecology, economics, and technologies.*

Readers will also be interested in reading others in *World Anthropology* on evolution and archaeology; on architecture and the arts; on Latin American topics; and on processes of cultural development in various parts of the world.

Chicago, Illinois   SOL TAX
September 9, 1977

Preface

Mesoamerican cultures have a minimum time depth of at least 25,000 years, and possibly at least twice that long. New evidence is beginning to suggest that man crossed the Bering Land Bridge into the New World between forty and fifty millennia ago; they had certainly drifted south to Mesoamerica by some twenty-five millennia ago. Dr. Irwin-Williams picks up the story here in her contribution, describing the evidence for reconstructing the lifeways of the earliest inhabitants of the Mexican highlands. By approximately 10,000 years ago, man in Mesoamerica had joined his compatriots world-wide in beginning to experiment with the manipulation and domestication of plants, and the consequent, concurrent technological innovations thus required. It is to the development of the agricultural basis of civilization, particularly in terms of the origins and modification of maize, that Dr. Beadle directs his attention.

Many of the papers in this volume are concerned with the cultural continuities formed upon an agricultural economic resource base. A major theme is the formation of exchange networks, including description of their functioning and constituent parts. Such networks were crucial not only for passing economic goods, but more importantly for the diffusion of ideas and concepts, and for the flow of prestige items which formed the basis of the hierarchical stratification and which were so necessary to the social fabric of Mesoamerica. Mesoamerican civilizations were shaped, kept in motion, and integrated by evolving patterns of trade.

Continuity is explored in other spheres and subsystems in addition to the economic; another important theme of this volume is the ideological continuity believed to persist between modern ethnographically documented ethnic groups and the prehistoric archaeological cultures. One approach is through the use of settlement pattern data and ceramic analysis to trace certain patterns persisting for more than two millennia. A second approach is the utilization of data furnished by the writing system, hieroglyphs, and stylized painting and pictographs to reconstruct artistic traditions from which it is possible to extract information on religious beliefs, political beliefs, and other ideational concepts which usually frustrate the prehistorian in attempting cultural reconstructions.

I would particularly like to thank Dr. Jane Pires-Ferreira, Dr. Ripley Bullen, and Dr. Malcolm Webb for the help they gave me in Chicago, particularly in stepping in and helping out when we had a simultaneous scheduling conflict.

I would like to thank Dr. Sol Tax and Ms. Karen Tkach and the other personnel of the IXth ICAES who helped track down missing contributions and generally to bring serenity out of confusion.

Washington University   DAVID L. BROWMAN
St. Louis, Missouri

Table of Contents

PART ONE

*Early Man in Mesoamerica
and the Agricultural Basis*

Introduction

Though somewhat separate in time and concern, the two papers by Irwin-Williams and Beadle summarize some important new data concerning the early residents of Mesoamerica, and the development of the economic base upon which the later cultural advances leading toward the high civilizations of Mesoamerica were predicated.

The series of localities in the Valsequillo region summarized by Irwin-Williams have presented us with some of the best available data for the lifeways of early man in the New World. It is particularly frustrating that the physical sciences cannot provide us with a firm date, that indeed the dating methods give us such widely different age determinations. Whether one accepts the approximately 20,000 B.P. determination of radiocarbon, the approximately 35,000 B.P. determination of tephrochronology, or the uranium-decay series estimates in the neighborhood of 200,000 years, it is still clear that Hueyatlaco and associated sites are some of the oldest in the New World. As we understand the sites archaeologically, the most recent date fits best with our other data, but final dating will depend on amino-acid racemization or some other method which can eliminate the disparities presently facing us.

The archaeological picture at Valsequillo is the same as we see at New World sites of comparable age – whether they be those of Old Crow Basin in the Yukon, or Paccaicasa in the Andes – that of nomadic hunters specializing in hunting elephants, giant ground sloths, and other now-extinct Pleistocene megafauna. The sites in the Hueyatlaco area include a number of such kill sites, the extinct megafauna including mammoth, horse, and camelid; along with the kill sites there are processing-activity areas as well, areas where the kills were butchered and processed. The site names vary, the exact kinds of megafauna at the kill sites differ, but the general level of technological proficiency and the pattern of nomadic hunting appear to be the same on both American continents at this time period. The question of man's antiquity in the New World is no longer one of guessing a first arrival date of ca. 11,000 B.C.; rather, we are now looking for evidence to determine whether the first nomads crossed the Bering Land Bridge into the Yukon some 45,000 years ago, or whether we must look back to 70,000 years ago.

The origin of corn has been a very confusing question both archaeologically and botanically. Though the most important New World food crop, and though corn is the third most important food crop in the world, there is yet little agreement on its origins; the four most noted botanists dealing with this problem (Beadle in this volume, Mangelsdorf 1974, Wilkes 1972, and Galinat 1971) have all come to slightly different evolutionary models for the development of maize. The question is compounded because of the fact that modern maize is so specialized that it requires man as an agent of dispersal for survival. While most other domesticated plants have logical ancestors, modern maize has developed to a point where we can find no simple, obvious wild relative.

In the 1930's, two of the best-known hypothetical reconstructions were posited. Beadle and Emerson suggested that maize was a derivative of teosinte, since they found cytological and genetic reasons to view the two as one species, while Mangelsdorf proposed a tripartite hypothesis involving Tripsacum, teosinte, and a yet undiscovered wild maize, possibly extinct. This debate has been going on for more than forty years now; though we do not yet have a final resolution, Beadle believes that we are beginning to approach one.

The tripartite hypothesis, developed and championed by Mangelsdorf through the 1960's, appears to have finally been abandoned. In his most recent book, Mangelsdorf's position (1974) is that there is an extinct wild maize from which both domestic maize and teosinte were derived. Tripsacum no longer is a viable part of the evolutionary schema. The close genetic relationship between maize and teosinte is recognized by Wilkes, Galinat, and Beadle as well, but there is no common agreement on what form is ancestral, nor any agreement on an exact developmental sequence. The final answer awaits further archaeobotanical and palynological research.

REFERENCES

GALINAT, W. C.
  1971   The origin of corn. *Annual Review of Genetics* 5: 447–478.
MANGELSDORF, P. C.
  1974   *Corn: its origin, evolution and improvement.* Cambridge, Mass.: The Belknap Press of Harvard University Press.
WILKES, H. G.
  1972   Maize and its wild relatives. *Science* 177: 1071–1077.

Summary of Archaeological Evidence from the Valsequillo Region, Puebla, Mexico

CYNTHIA IRWIN-WILLIAMS

The questions of the origin, age, and character of the earliest inhabitants of the western hemisphere are intriguing ones, and they present some of the major unsolved problems of New World prehistory. Scientific opinion has shifted dramatically in the past several decades from the belief that man in this hemisphere dated back no more than a few millennia. Modern estimates range from 11,000 to more than 30,000 years ago. Whatever the ultimate solution, it is apparent by now that the earliest Americans were few in number and left relatively little imperishable material culture. It is also evident that man in this remote period was only one of a large and varied fauna in a complex environment, that he should be studied in the context of available knowledge of contemporary geology and animal populations, and that the part played by man in faunal extinction is a basic problem in the study of the late Pleistocene.

The Valsequillo Reservoir area near Puebla, Mexico has long been known as an area that offered excellent opportunities for Pleistocene (and earlier) research. Professor Juan Armenta Camacho has carried out surficial reconnaissance in the region for many years and has amassed a large collection of archaeological and paleontological materials. His studies led him to conclude that certain bone and stone objects, possibly of human manufacture, had originated in the Valsequillo Formation, which had also produced an extensive extinct faunal assemblage featuring camel, horse, glyptodon, mastodon, mammoth, four-horned antelope, and dire wolf. If those objects definitely of human manufacture were in fact derived from this formation, and if it proved to be of the antiquity suggested by the fauna, research here might provide vital clues concerning the early inhabitants of the New World.

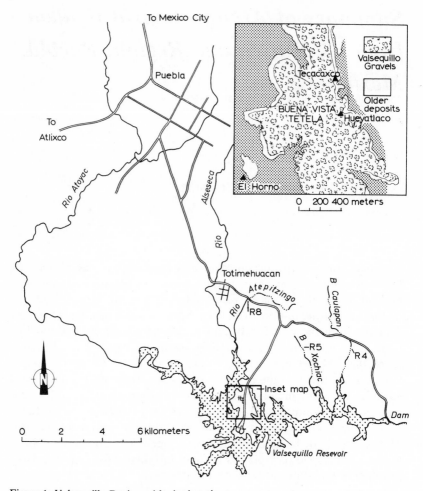

Figure 1. Valsequillo Region with site locations

In 1962 Professor Armenta and I conducted an intensive survey of the Valsequillo Formation. The goal was to investigate the possibility of the existence of fresh, unrolled artifacts of unquestionable human manufacture, *in situ* in the Valsequillo Formation. After a wide survey, four localities producing definite evidence of this association were identified and tested. A fifth locality was discovered in 1964. It was evident on the basis of the results of the 1962 pilot project that further research could profitably be done on the archaeology of the Valsequillo Formation. In addition, the character of the data indicated that an interdisciplinary approach, involving geology and paleontology as well as archaeology, was essential. Accordingly, the expanded

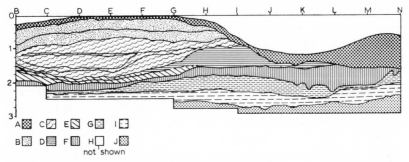

A▨ C▨ E▨ G▣ I▣
B▨ D▤ F▥ H☐ J▨
not shown

Figure 2. Stratigraphy of Hueyatlaco. *Unit A:* Recent dark soil. *Unit B:* Few fossils, no cultural materials. *Unit C:* Numerous fossils (e.g. horse, camel, mammoth); artifact assemblage including stemmed, basally thinned point; technology characterized by use of well made bifacial percussion flaking. *Unit D:* No fossils or cultural remains. *Unit E:* Numerous fossils (horse, camel, mammoth, mastodon); artifact assemblage including bipointed projectile point; technology characterized by use of well executed bifacial percussion flaking. *Unit F:* Rare fossils; no cultural remains. *Unit G:* Rare fossils; no cultural remains. *Unit H:* Local feature; fossils, and single, slightly retouched flake. *Unit I:* Numerous fossils (including horse, camel, mammoth, mastodon); artifact assemblage including edge-trimmed projectile points on blades or flakes; technology characterized by percussion and pressure edge trimming and complete absence of bifacial or total-coverage unifacial flaking. *Unit J:* Rare fossils; no cultural remains
Source: Irwin-Williams 1967.

project comprised full-scale investigations on the Pleistocene of the Valsequillo Region.[1]

The sites occur within the thirty meters of alluvial formation known as the Valsequillo Gravels (see Figure 1). Most of them lie near or on the Tetela Peninsula at the north end of the Valsequillo Reservoir, near Puebla. In descending relative stratigraphic position, the Tetela group includes the sites of Hueyatlaco, Tecacaxco, El Mirador, and El Horno. The fifth locality lies in a tributary arroyo, Barranca Caulapan, situated two kilometers to the east. The localities will be discussed in their relative chronologic order.

Hueyatlaco

The youngest of the group is the site of Hueyatlaco, located on a high outcrop of the Valsequillo Reservoir below the town of La Colonia

[1] Personnel contributing to the Valsequillo Program were as follows: Dr. C. Irwin-Williams, Eastern New Mexico University, Harvard University, archaeology, Principal Investigator; Professor Juan Armenta Camacho, Universidad de Puebla, archaeology; Dr. H. E. Malde, United States Geological Survey, geology; Dr. Clayton Ray, Smithsonian Institution, paleontology; Dr. Dwight Taylor, University of Arizona, malacology; Mrs. Virginia Steen-McIntyre, Washington State University, tephrochronology; Dr. Gordon Goles, University of Oregon, neutron activation analysis; Mr. Mario Pichardo del Barrio, Virginia Polytechnic Institute, paleontology.

Buena Vista de Tetela. It lies just south of the site of Tecacaxco, at an altitude of about 2,055 meters above sea level. It is situated about forty meters from a larger but more isolated outcrop of the Valsequillo Formation, near which Armenta (1959) reported finding the engraved fragment of proboscidean pelvis. This is the only site which produced an internal stratigraphic sequence (see Figure 2), and the only locality at which it was possible to excavate for more than one season. The composite picture is one of a long series of alluvial deposits, many of which are highly fossiliferous, and a few of which contain evidence of the hunting and butchering activities of early man. The units in this representative profile area are as follows:

Unit A, the uppermost recognized, was a recent dark loam, covering much of the earlier deposit. Culturally it yielded a few obsidian flakes, recent ceramics, and glass. It was obviously separated from the earlier deposits by a considerable hiatus marked by an erosional contact. Also belonging to Unit A were the silty deposits of a small recent arroyo cutting through one section of the site. These likewise produced pottery, tiny fragments of redeposited fossil bone, and glass.

The uppermost early deposit, Unit B, was a fine-grained, sandy silt within which two minor subdivisions were recognized. It contained a few fossils (principally horse and camel) but no cultural remains.

Deposit C at the south end of the site represented the effects of a small, shallow stream that cut a distinct southwest-trending channel in an earlier strata. The numerous recognizable divisions reflect the deposition of complexly bedded, silt-sized sediments within the chan-nel; the uppermost of these produced abundant fossils, principally horse and camel. Culturally it yielded the largest assemblage of artifacts available from any single deposit at the site (see Figure 3). These include a bifacially flaked stemmed projectile point, a large bifacial cutting tool, a scraping edge-and-perforator, a cutting edge on a blade or flake, a concave end scraper-and-perforator, and a gouge or scraper on an oblong flake, as well as a large number of crude blades and flakes. One of these artifacts, the concave scraper-and-perforator, was uncovered about one centimeter from a horse mandible. A tooth belonging to the mandible occurred about two centimeters from the parent fossil, illustrating the magnitude of displacement characteristic of the deposit. This association was removed *en bloc* to serve as a permanent exhibit. The correlative stratum at the north end of the site (Station 2) also yielded a crude percussion-flaked lanceolate object, probably a projectile point. Several of the other subdivisions of Unit C at both stations produced fossils but no cultural remains.

Unit D consisted of a very fine, clayey silt with a massive structure, light tan in color. It occurred principally as a thick deposit in the

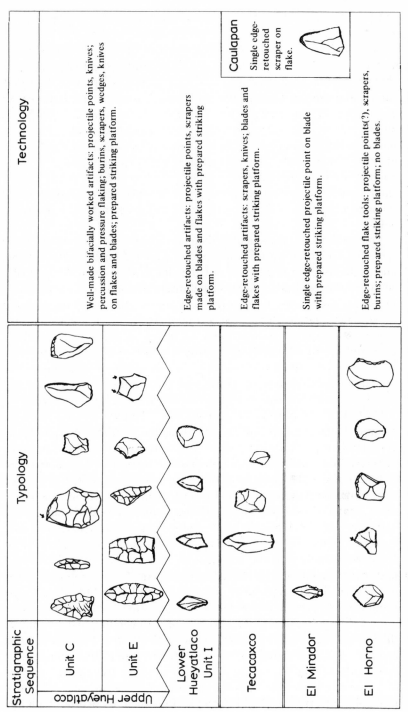

Figure 3. Technology and typology of artifacts from five Early Man sites in the Valsequillo Region. An unconformity at Hueyatlaco between Units I and E coincides with a change in the artifacts: from simple edge-retouched tools below, which were made on blades and flakes, to sophisticated bifacially worked tools above, which were made in a greater variety of forms. The artifacts are drawn at one-third natural size

southwest end of the trench between the two stations. It produced no artifacts or fossils.

Deposit E at Station 1 comprised a series of alluvial sediments in a shallow channel cut abruptly in earlier strata (see Figure 3). The channel represented was apparently considerably broader than that cut by the stream responsible for Unit C, and its orientation was distinct. That the current was occasionally somewhat stronger is shown by the lenses and layers of coarse sand and smally gravel. In mid-channel it was possible to recognize a maximum of eight minor internal stratigraphic divisions. The uppermost of these (1E1) was composed of a fine-bedded gray sand with a layer of pale yellow coarse sand, with fine gravel at its upper boundary. It contained fossil remains and one heavily calcinated chert flake, which will be described below.

The second of these subdivisions yielded very abundant fossil remains, including prominently horse, camel, four-horned antelope, and mammoth. In one section of the site was uncovered a part of a semi-articulated horse skeleton definitely associated with two artifacts, probably with two more; near the group of semi-articulated horse ribs and vertebrae was uncovered a well-made bifacial, bipointed projectile point. Directly under an associated vertebra occurred the tip of a well-made bifacial knife or point. Nearby were a fragment of a thick bifacial tool and a utilized core fragment. The remaining subdivisions of Unit E at the southern end of the site (Station 1) were fossiliferous but contained no cultural materials.

Unit 2E at the northern end of the site (Station 2) lay in a separate channel from the correlative stratum at the southern end, and was completely separated from the latter by arroyo cutting. The uppermost of these (2E1 and 2E2) was a thin layer at the base of 2E2, comprised of layers of variable, coarse yellowish-gray sand and grit. It contained very numerous fossils, principally mastodon, horse, camel, and mammoth. Many of the mastodon bones were concentrated in a small area, and may well be from the same animal, and were associated with evidence of human activities. The mandible and maxilla of the mastodon were finely split and fragmented. Two artifacts were discovered in direct association with these fragments. In 1962 a small wedge was discovered deeply imbedded in a fragment of mandible next to the tooth row. Nearby, a thin flake, with a burin-like spall removed from one edge, was recovered in 1964 *in situ* between the cusps of one of the molar teeth. A short distance away at the base of the channel, and probably not associated with the mastodon group, was recovered a well-made bifacial knife. Although occurring near fragmented remains of a juvenile mastodon, a horse jaw and peccary, this association is probably not primary. The bifacial knife is the only artifact with any sign of water wear in contradistinction to the absolutely fresh condition of the other artifacts.

Unit F consisted of a pale, yellowish-gray, sandy clay and silt conforming to what may have been a very broad, shallow channel cut abruptly and unconformably into older sediments. It contained relatively few fossils and no cultural remains.

Unit G comprised a pale yellow gravel and very coarse sand or grit, faintly bedded and locally displaying flow rolls at the base. Fossils were moderately abundant, including mastodon, mammoth, camel, and horse. No objects of cultural interest were recovered.

Deposit H was a very localized phenomenon occurring only at Station 2. It comprised a massive pale yellowish-gray sand, well sorted and peppered with dark grains. It evidently represented the fill of a narrow channel at the base of Deposit 2G, running in a general southwest-northeast direction. The numerous fossil remains of camel and horse concentrated in the channel were accompanied by a single lightly retouched flake scraper.

Below this occurred Unit I, a broad channel fill consisting of very fine, yellowish sand, gritty clay, and grit. Abundant fossil remains were recovered from Unit I including horse, camel, mastodon, four-horned antelope, etc. Of considerable interest were the several man-made objects: an edge-trimmed pointed object, probably a projectile point, found *in situ* underneath the rib of a large ungulate at Station 1; a second projectile point, found adjacent to and nearly touching a fragmentary proboscidean acetabulum at Station 2; a third probable projectile point, recovered underneath another ungulate rib a short distance from the second. Sparse unretouched flakes were also recovered.

Tecacaxco

The site of Tecacaxco is located about 100 meters north of Hueyatlaco, at a slightly lower altitude, 2,054 meters. Its relative stratigraphic position is likewise somewhat lower (earlier) than Hueyatlaco. The vertebrate fossils and cultural materials occurred in a shallow channel fill unit representing a small stream flowing into the Valsequillo Basin. No internal stratigraphic divisions were observed. Remains of mammoth, horse, and camel were recovered. The archaeological assemblage comprised fresh, unrolled flakes, crude blades, and retouched flake scrapers. The character of the assemblage and the technology are similar to those of the lowermost cultural deposit at Hueyatlaco, El Mirador and Tecacaxco, and are radically different from the later materials at Hueyatlaco.

El Mirador

The site of El Mirador is located about two kilometers east of the Tetela Peninsula. Preliminary investigations in 1962 yielded an assemblage of extinct fauna and one associated artifact. The association occurred in a coarse gravel lying stratigraphically well below Tecacaxco or Hueyatlaco (2,049 meters). A single artifact was recovered *in situ* in association with unarticulated remains of horse, camel, and mammoth. The artifact occurred about ten centimeters from a horse vertebrae, and proved to be an edge-trimmed projectile point made on a blade, similar to those from Unit I at Hueyatlaco. Full-scale excavations were not attempted because of local high water conditions in 1964–1966.

El Horno

Finally, the site of El Horno is located on the west bank of the old pre-reservoir Atoyac River on a low peninsula jutting out from the highland of the Tetela Peninsula, about one kilometer west of the town of La Colonia Buena Vista de Tetela. It is situated at an altitude of 2,040 meters above sea level, at the base of the earliest alluvial-channel fill of the Valsequillo Formation.

The association consists of a series of chipped-stone flakes and artifacts in direct association with the remains of a single butchered mastodon. The assemblage was recovered from a fine silt at the base of the Valsequillo Formation, representing one of the earliest events in the filling of the Valsequillo Basin. The site is situated more than fifteen meters stratigraphically below the latest Early Man locality, Hueyatlaco.

The fossil remains belonged largely to a single mastodon, comprising slightly less than one-third of the complete animal and included principally the articulated pelvic girdle minus the sacrum, several ribs, one tusk and fragments of the other, one tooth and numerous tooth fragments, and various fragments of long bones. In addition, a large number of fragmentary fossils representing long bones, ribs, cranium, and metapodials had eroded and been redeposited in the modern lake sediments. Fossils not pertaining to the mastodon were rare but included horse and small artiodactyl. Several of the mastodon bones exhibit evidence of butchering. Of the thirteen chipped-stone specimens recovered, six have been retouched, and two others show evidence of utilization. The artifacts are unifacial, manufactured on flakes (some with prepared striking platforms) and represent scrapers, perforators, cutting edges, and, probably, projectile points.

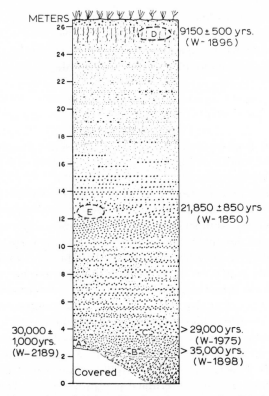

Figure 4. Schematic section of Valsequillo Gravels at Locality R4, in Caulapan Barranca, showing position of molluskan fossils (lettered sites) dated by radiocarbon method

Caulapan

The Caulapan Barranca is one of several tributaries flowing into the Valsequillo Reservoir east of the Tetela Peninsula. Although the group of deposits at Caulapan is separated from the Tetela group by about five kilometers, geologic mapping by H. E. Malde indicates that they may be of equivalent age, and represent all or part of the temporal range of the Valsequillo Formation. A series of molluskan fossils from the Caulapan section were submitted for radiocarbon dating (see Figure 4). A sample (B) from the base of the section was more than 35,000 B.P.; slightly above this, two samples were dated at more than 29,000 B.P. and 30,000 B.P. respectively. A sample collected midway up the section (E) was dated at about 21,850 B.P.; and, finally, a sample (D) from the uppermost part of the Valsequillo deposit yielded a date of 9150 B.P.

A single flake tool was recovered *in situ* in association with mollusks of Sample E, which was dated at 21,850 B.P. Accordingly, this association indicates the strong possibility of the existence of human culture in the Valsequillo Region at that date.

No extensive excavations were carried out due to the presence of ten to twelve meters of indurated overburden.

The Archaeological Assemblages

With this background, it is possible to discuss the character of the archaeological assemblages recovered, beginning with the latest, from Unit C of Hueyatlaco.

The assemblage from Unit C evidences a rather well-controlled bifacial percussion technique, employed to produce projectile points, cutting edges, scrapers, perforators, and possibly burins. Although most of the raw material is rather poor and full of irregularities, a few pieces indicate the existence of a blade industry, and the preparation of striking platforms. The character of the assemblage as a whole indicates the importance of hunting and processing game, specifically horse, camel, four-horned antelope, and mammoth. A brief hunting camp at or near a kill-site best fits these conditions.

The most diagnostic single item is a well-made projectile point, asymmetrical, broadly stemmed, with a concave base and abrupt shoulders. It was fashioned by well-controlled percussion with soft-hammer and occasional terminal-pressure retouch. The point is much thicker than the base, which was apparently deliberately thinned: the scars of wide, shallow, thinning flakes struck from the basal end are visible on both faces; they were evidently removed before the final point was formed, as all other visible flake removals postdate them. A burin-like but probably fortuitous removal at the tip of the piece completes the picture. Also recovered in the same group of artifacts and fossils at Station 1 was a thick bifacial piece with cutting edge likewise produced by well-controlled, soft-hammer percussion. It displays long, lateral-edge removals of a distinctly burin-like character. The concave scraper-perforator recovered adjacent to the horse mandible was made on a flake with a faceted striking platform and worked with soft-hammer percussion technique. Other artifacts from Unit C include a straight-end scraper on a stone-hammer-struck flake, a side scraper on a thick flake, a cutting edge made on a blade, and a small, crude, bifacially worked pointed object.

The next major group proceeds from Stratum 1E2 at Station 1. Outstanding is the large bifacial, bipointed point recovered in direct association with the partially articulated portion of a horse. The artifact was made by soft-hammer percussion with terminal-pressure retouch. It is strongly carinated on one face. In the same group the point of a projectile point or knife was recovered under a vertebra of the same horse. The specimen appears to have been made by percussion and pressure flaking, and it shows some secondary use and resharpening. Another bifacial fragment recovered nearby reflects a similar technology. It seems probable that this assemblage represents a single horse "kill." Also from Unit 2E are the two artifacts recovered with the group of fragmented mastodon bones: a simple wedge recovered *in situ* still embedded in a portion of the mastodon mandible and a burinated flake found in association with the mastodon molar. Finally, the single large, broken and rolled bifacial knife found in Unit 2E evidences a similar use of well-controlled percussion flaking.

Below this stratigraphic level, the technology of all earlier assemblages at this site and at the other four is radically different. At Hueyatlaco there is evidence of a well-controlled, blade-producing technique, including the ability to prepare the striking platform. At the same time, advanced percussion and pressure flaking extending across the entire surface of the artifact are entirely absent. Both points and scraping edges were prepared by simple edge trimming by pressure and percussion. Polishing was employed on one piece.

Deposit I at Hueyatlaco produced points made by these techniques. The first projectile point was recovered in direct association with a large ungulate rib at Station 1. The piece was made on a flake and has a roughly triangular form, with a short, asymmetrical basal projection on one side that may constitute a stem. The edges and base of the piece have been lightly trimmed by shearing and crude pressure retouch.

The second point recovered, adjacent to the proboscidean acetabulum, was made on a blade and is asymmetrically diamond shaped in overall form. The contracting stem has been formed by abrupt, coarse, probably stone-percussion flaking: the point, generally conforming to the outline of the original flake, has been lightly trimmed by shearing. All work is confined to the edges: none reaches far across either face. Of interest is the lower third of the stem, which has been heavily ground and polished both at the lateral edges and across the ventral face. The attitude of the polishing stroke is generally at right angles to the long axis of the piece.

The third point from Unit 2I was recovered beneath a large ungulate rib a short distance from the second and has numerous similarities. The piece was made on a thin blade, and the point has been lightly trimmed by pressure shearing. The existing base is formed by an abrupt hinge fracture. In addition, some simple edge-trimmed flake scrapers were recovered from this stratum. The artifacts indicate the existence of a technology and typology radically different from those of the succeeding levels.

The cultural materials from Tecacaxco were produced by a technology similar to that represented in Unit I of Hueyatlaco. Many of the blades exhibit a prepared striking platform. Several were retouched as scrapers, or show evidence of utilization for cutting or scraping.

The single point from El Mirador was manufactured on a small blade with a prepared striking platform. The base of the blade has been narrowed by steep, hard-hammer percussion to produce a "stemmed" appearance, and the point has been lightly trimmed by shearing. In general the character of the piece is not unlike the points from Unit I of Hueyatlaco.

The assemblage from El Horno differs from that of Hueyatlaco, Unit I, Tecacaxco and El Mirador in the absence of blades. Several of the flakes, however, have prepared striking platforms. One of these, recovered near a small group of mastodon ribs, is unifacially retouched to a blunt point, and may in fact represent a projectile point. Other artifacts include unifacial scrapers, perforators, and one implement, recovered directly under the mastodon acetabulum, appears to be a simple burin truncating a scraping edge.

Finally, the single specimen from Caulapan is a thick flake exhibiting a crudely prepared striking platform. The flake itself appears, like the specimens characteristic of El Mirador, Tecacaxco and Hueyatlaco, Unit I, to be one of a sequence of flakes removed from the same platform. It exhibits limited but regular pressure retouch along the distal end and adjacent lateral edges. It appears fresh and not obviously rolled. It was recovered in place by Irwin-Williams.

CHRONOLOGY OF THE VALSEQUILLO ARCHAEOLOGICAL LOCALITIES

Because of the premineralization characteristic of the fossil remains from the Tetela group (Hueyatlaco, Tecacaxco, El Mirador, and El Horno), and the absence of charcoal, it has been so far impossible to directly date these sites by the radiocarbon method. Accordingly, the only *direct* date on early archaeological material from the Valsequillo Region is 21,850 years for the mollusks recovered in association with the single flake scraper at Caulapan. Given the material used for dating (shell) and the scantiness of the archaeological remains, further dating is obviously desirable.

Several other avenues of approach have been explored, but these have, of necessity, relied upon essentially experimental and/or relatively new techniques whose reliability has yet to be confirmed. However, because of the potential significance of any early date for man in this hemisphere, a brief discussion of these attempts is included here.

1. Uranium-series dating, employing a technique not previously used on terrestrial fossils, was carried out by Barney Szabo on specimens from El Horno and Hueyatlaco. These yielded the apparently startling dates of 245,000±40,000 for Hueyatlaco and 280,000 years for El Horno. The discrepancy between these apparent ages and the indications of the archaeological materials was discussed in 1969 (Szabo, et al. 1969), but given the newness of the technique no obvious solutions were available. However, subsequent studies by Seitz and Taylor (1974) have provided a possible explanation of the problem. In their investigation of uranium variations in dated fossil bone from Olduvai Gorge, Tanzania, Seitz and Taylor examined uranium concentrations in a series of fossils as a function of age, and derived a predictive model for precipitation and leaching. From their study they concluded that "the Thorium and Protactinium excesses predicted by this model would explain the anomalously old ages obtained for fossil bones dated by the uranium-series method (Szabo, et al. 1969)" (Seitz and Taylor 1974: 133). Accordingly, on the basis of these new investigations, the apparent indications of great age suggested by Szabo's original study cannot at present be accepted as representing the true age of the Valsequillo deposits.

2. Virginia Steen-McIntyre has recently developed a new technique termed tephra hydration dating, which operates on basic principles generally similar to those employed for obsidian hydration dating. A series of tephra samples from deposits adjacent to the Hueyatlaco site (believed by Steen, Fryxell, and Malde to stratigraphically overlie the archaeological deposits) were analyzed by this technique. On the basis of comparisons with samples of known age from elsewhere in Mexico, Central America, and North America, Steen-McIntyre believes that these may reflect an age of about 250,000 years (Steen-McIntyre, et al. n.d.). Unfortunately, given our very limited control of the situation, this age does not seem acceptable at present. As noted, tephra hydration dating is a new technique which operates on general principles similar to those employed in obsidian hydration dating – that is, the glassy volcanic tephra (pumice-ash) take up water through time at a regular rate, given certain controls. As with obsidian hydration dating, the actual rate of hydration depends upon the composition of the glass and its internal irregularities and morphology, as well as on the environmental context, particularly temperature but also groundwater chemistry. In order to produce exact dates, it is essential to obtain a parallel series of independent, exact dates relating to the specific tephra (or obsidian) universe sampled. From these it is possible to derive a hydration rate stated in terms of degree of hydration per unit

of time. Reliable dates can then be obtained only on glass fragments of similar composition and morphology, and from similar temperature and ground water environments. Since, unfortunately, it was impossible to control any of these factors for the dated samples compared to the Valsequillo group, it is evidently not possible to derive a reliable estimate of the real age of the Valsequillo samples from them.

3. Using the fission track dating method, Charles Naeser obtained two dates from deposits near the Hueyatlaco archaeological locality (Steen-McIntyre, et al. n.d.). Steen-McIntyre, et al. believe the deposits to overlie the archaeological materials, although they were not present in the immediate area excavated by Irwin-Williams. The indicated ages are 600,000±340,000 years for one of these deposits (the *Tetela Brown Mud*) and 370,000±200,000 years for the second deposit (the *Hueyatlaco Ash*). The fission track method is based upon counting the tracks produced in a mineral crystal by the fast-moving particles resulting from radioactive decay. While it is certainly better understood than the other two techniques attempted, there exist numerous parameters, particularly with regard to environmental interaction with the sample, which have yet to be fully explored. In the current instance, the enormous statistical errors involved greatly reduce the utility of the method for the sensitive archaeological situation. In addition, the apparent stratigraphic relations between the two dated units are, in fact, *in reverse* of the ages indicated by this dating method. The *Tetela Brown Mud*, 600,000 years old, apparently *overlies* the *Hueyatlaco Ash*, 370,000 years old – a discrepancy of some 230,000 years. Here again, there are evident anomalies that cannot be dealt with successfully, and the dates obtained apparently do not reflect the true age of the deposits.

In brief, it appears that the chronology of the Valsequillo deposits remains at present uncertain and comments must be limited by the data. The character of the archaeological assemblages suggests that the upper units (C and E) at the latest site (Hueyatlaco) may well relate to other known early complexes in Mexico dating about 9–11,000 years ago (e.g., the Ajuereado Complex from nearby Tehuacan). A *terminus ante quem* of 8–9,000 years ago for the entire Valsequillo Formation is in accord with this possibility and also with the radiocarbon date of 9,150 from the uppermost Valsequillo deposit at Caulapan. The length of time represented by the stratigraphic hiatus within Hueyatlaco is unknown. However, it is certain that the technology and typology represented in assemblages below this hiatus is radically different. The technology employed in these assemblages and in those from other stratigraphically earlier localities is grossly similar to certain other early sites such as the early levels of Pikimachay Cave in Peru. If the scraper from Caulapan and the associated date of 21,850 is accepted as valid, there is evidence for the presence of man in the area at that time. A really firm chronology, however, should be based upon multiple reliable dates and associations, and must await the firm dating of the Valsequillo specimens and/or the location of comparable sites where local conditions permit direct dating.

SUMMARY

Archaeological investigations in the Valsequillo Region, Puebla, Mexico, were carried out from 1962–1966 by C. Irwin-Williams representing Harvard University and Juan Armenta Camacho representing the University of Puebla. These investigations yielded evidence at five localities of the direct association of man-made artifacts with an extensive late Pleistocene fauna including mammoth, mastodon, horse, camel, four-horned antelope, etc. Four of the archaeological localities occurred within the thirty-meter thick series of alluvial deposits known as the Valsequillo Gravels near the town of Colonia Buena Vista de Tetela on the north shore of the Valsequillo Reservoir. Their relative stratigraphic position is as follows:

Hueyatlaco – ten meters below the latest Valsequillo deposit
Tecacaxco
El Mirador
El Horno – at the base of the Valsequillo Gravels

A fifth archaeological locality was discovered in the correlative deposits of the tributary Caulapan Barranca about twelve meters above the base of the Valsequillo deposit.

The archaeological evidence from these localities may be summarized as follows: Hueyatlaco yielded stratigraphic evidence of three periods of occupation, each being represented by artifacts and vertebrate remains indicative of hunting activities. Artifacts of the two younger periods, as determined by Irwin-Williams, are similar and can be distinguished from those of the older period at Hueyatlaco, as well as assemblages at all the lower Valsequillo sites, by the presence of very well-made bifacial stone tools – namely, projectile points and knives. The hunters of these earlier periods also used scrapers and perforators, and they knew how to make blades (usually prismatic flakes that were struck from specially prepared stone cores). Artifacts of the older period of Hueyatlaco, which in places underlies an unconformity and more than a meter of archaeologically sterile deposits, lack bifacial tools. Like artifacts from the lower Valsequillo sites, they evidently express a different, less sophisticated method of working stone, which resulted in projectile points made on well-executed blades and flakes. By applying percussion and pressure, these blades and flakes were shaped into useful tools by simple edge trimming. In short, these artifacts are significantly distinct from the bifacial tools found in the younger layers of Hueyatlaco.

The sites lower than Hueyatlaco yielded archaeological material technologically similar to the older part of Hueyatlaco material, but they are nonetheless informative. Tecacaxco, in addition to some remains of the extinct fauna, produced several flakes and blades, some retouched to make scrapers. A projectile point from El Mirador resembles those from the lower part of Hueyatlaco and was made on an edge-trimmed blade that retains a prepared striking platform. El Horno contained the remains of a butchered mastodon associated with scrapers, perforators, and a possible projectile point, which together express the kind of technology represented by the other nonbifacial tool assemblages at Valsequillo, except that no blades were found. At the isolated locality of Caulapan, a single flake scraper was discovered in conjunction with mollusks which produced a single radiocarbon date of 21,850 years ago. Other attempts to derive an exact chronology for the Valsequillo deposits have so far proved inconclusive.

REFERENCES

ARMENTA CAMACHO, J.
   1959   *Hallazgo de un artefacto asociado con mamut en el valle de Puebla, México.* Instituto Nacional de Antropología e Historia, Dirección Prehistoria Publicación 7. Mexico City.
HAYNES, C. V.
   1968   Radiocarbon: analysis of inorganic carbon of fossil bone and enamel. *Science* 161: 687–688. Washington, D.C.
IRWIN-WILLIAMS, CYNTHIA
   1967   "Association of early man with horse, camel, and mastodon at Hueyatlaco, Valsequillo (Puebla, Mexico)," in *Pleistocene extinctions – the search for a cause.* Edited by P. S. Martin and H. E. Wright, 337–350. New Haven, Conn.: Yale University Press.
   1969   Comments on the associations of archaeological materials and extinct fauna in the Valsequillo region, Puebla, Mexico. *American Antiquity* 34(1): 82–83. Salt Lake City.
SEITZ, M. G., R. E. TAYLOR
   1974   Uranium variations in a dated fossil bone series from Olduvai Gorge, Tanzania. *Archaeometry* 16(2): 129–136.
STEEN-MCINTYRE, VIRGINIA, R. FRYXELL, H. E. MALDE
   n.d.   "Age of deposits at the Hueyatlaco archaeological site, Valsequillo area, Puebla, Mexico." Unpublished manuscript.
SZABO, B. J., H. E. MALDE, CYNTHIA IRWIN-WILLIAMS
   1969   Dilemma posed by uranium-series dates on archaeologically significant bones from Valsequillo, Puebla, Mexico. *Earth and Planetary Science Letters* 6(4). Amsterdam.

The Origin of Zea mays

GEORGE W. BEADLE

In pre-Columbian times *Zea mays* – common name: corn or maize – was by far the most important human food crop in the western hemisphere. It still continues to be so in all of Latin America. On a world basis it is the third most important human food crop, with an annual production of some two hundred million metric tons.

At the time of Columbus, whose men found great fields of this strange new plant on the island of Cuba, essentially all major races of maize – some two to three hundred – were already in cultivation and had been disseminated from its place of origin, probably southern Mexico, to mid-Chile in the south and to the mouth of the St. Lawrence River in the north.

Centuries before Columbus the three great cultural, religious, and trading centers of Teotihuacán in the Valley of Mexico, Dzibilchaltun in Yucatán and Chan Chan in Peru supported populations of some 75,000 to 200,000 each. Obviously storable food was needed in great quantities. Maize and beans were among the most important of these.

In the studies of teosinte-maize interrelations reported, the University of Chicago has generously provided laboratory, garden, greenhouse space, and technical assistance and time for experiments. The University of Illinois has provided space for growing hybrids as well as help in tending them. Space and help at the Botanic Garden of the Chicago Horticultural Society have been made available. The Rainbow Garden Association has provided plots for growing isolated hybrid populations. Facilities for growing hybrids plus help in harvesting and classifying have been provided by the International Maize and Wheat Improvement Center of Mexico, for my plantings there. Doctor Mario Gutiérrez has given me indispensable help in growing, harvesting, and classifying populations grown at the Center's El Batán Station. Professors Walton C. Galinat and H. Garrison Wilkes have helped in many ways. For help in collecting wild teosintes in Mexico and searching for mutant types among them the National Science Foundation has provided financial support.

Much of the substance of this account was presented as the Donald Forsha Jones Memorial Lecture at the Connecticut Agricultural Experiment Station on September 14, 1972.

Shortly before the conquest of the Aztecs by Cortés, Montezuma's tribute rolls indicate that the thirty-eight or so subdivisions of the empire were taxed an annual total of some 300,000 bushels of maize, an equal quantity of beans plus many other articles of food, clothing, ornamentation and other articles of value (Barlow 1949; Anderson and Barlow 1943).

Although modern plant breeders have greatly increased yields of maize through the development of new varieties and hybrid lines well adapted to various maize-growing regions and resistant to diseases and insect pests, this development of maize by the American Indian remains to this day man's most remarkable plant-breeding achievement (Kempton 1938).

CLOSEST RELATIVE OF MAIZE

For most cultivated plants, wild relatives are known from which they could reasonably have been derived. In fact, if one lists sixteen plant genera that include many of the world's most important food crops – maize, potatoes, sweet potatoes, beans, peanuts, manioc, cucurbits, and sunflower of New World origin, and wheat, rice, sugar cane, sugarbeets, barley, sorghum, soybeans, and oats of the Old World – for all except maize there are so many closely related wild species that it is difficult to determine just which one or more was ancestral to a given present-day crop plant. Bailey's *Manual of cultivated plants* (1949) lists for these sixteen crop-plant genera more than 500 species. Aside from the maize genus *Zea*, for which no wild species is recognized, not one of the other fifteen genera has less than six species assigned to it. It is thus no wonder that early plant explorers had great difficulty finding any wild relative that could conceivably have been the ancestor of maize. No other grass is known with a female inflorescence like that of an ear of modern maize. The reason is obvious, for this monstrous structure provides no effective means of seed dispersal, a must for any wild plant that depends on seeds for survival. If an ear of maize is left to its fate in nature, it will, under conditions favorable for germination, give rise to a group of seedlings so densely clustered that few are likely to produce mature "seeds." Thus all known living maize is dependent on man for survival.

Finally, however, early plant explorers found a candidate, a plant that grows in parts of Mexico, Guatemala, and Honduras, which natives in parts of Mexico called *teocentli*, or *teocintle*, from the Uto-Azteca language, meaning "God's corn." This is now anglicized to teosinte. Taxonomists assigned it to the new genus *Euchlaena* and gave it the specific name *mexicana*.

In 1790 teosinte was described by the botanist Hernández as a plant that "...looks like maize but its seed is triangular" (Wilkes 1967). Teosinte "seeds" (technically fruits) are arranged in a row, from five to ten, to form a somewhat flattened spike a few inches long and a quarter of an inch in width (Figure 1). This is teosinte's counterpart of an ear of maize. The triangularity of the individual fruits resides in the "fruitcases," which are dark, horny, cuplike segments of the rachis or axis of the spike closed on the outer long side by a lignified outer glume. On maturity the rachis segments fall apart through the development of abscission layers between adjacent fruits. Within each mature fruitcase is a single kernel much like that of maize (Figure 2).

In contrast to the one or a few ears produced by a modern plant of maize, a well-developed teosinte plant may produce a hundred or more ear equivalents, often many per node. As many as 9,000 "seeds" have been harvested from a single plant grown under cultivation in Mexico (Beadle and Gutiérrez, unpublished). Teosinte plants tend to be more highly tillered than most varieties of cultivated maize and each tiller produces female spikes at many nodes.

The most complete descriptions of races of teosinte are those of H. G. Wilkes (1967, 1972).

TEOSINTE AS AN ANCESTOR OF MAIZE

Is teosinte the ancestor of maize? A few botanists thought so. Vinson, for example, wrote in 1877, "Following the thinking of Darwin, teosinte is the ancestor of maize" (Wilkes 1967). But most of his contemporaries disagreed. The female inflorescences were so different they could not believe that one could have been transformed into the other in any plausible way.

Later a seemingly more likely candidate was found, a plant intermediate between teosinte and maize. Because of its small ear with partially exposed pointed kernels that resembled dogs' teeth, it was called *Zea canina*, dog maize or coyote maize. But this was soon found to be a naturally occurring hybrid between teosinte and maize, a hybrid that is easily made artificially and which is quite fertile. The fertility of this hybrid indicated that the genetic relation between teosinte and maize was much closer than previously assumed.

That was much the situation when the writer began graduate work at Cornell in 1927 with the late R. A. Emerson, who had shortly before demonstrated that teosinte is a so-called short-day plant, and that he could induce it to mature at the Cornell latitude by artificially shortening the summer day (Emerson 1924). This discovery made it practicable for him to use it in genetic studies. As a part-time graduate

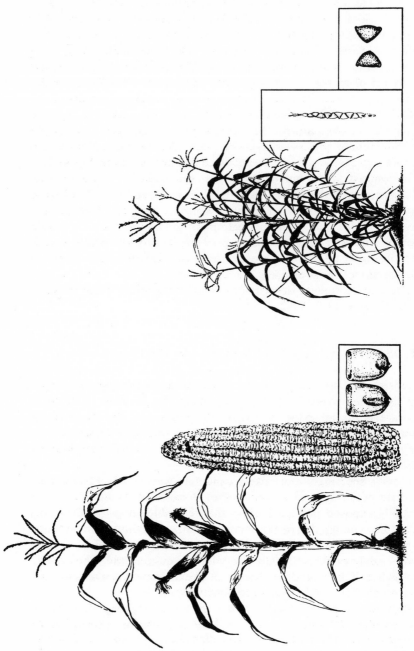

Figure 1.   Comparison of maize and teosinte plants, female spikes and individual fruits ("seeds")

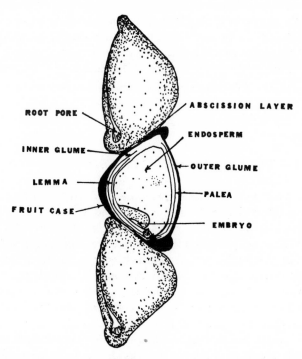

Figure 2. Segment of normal teosinte female spike including a diagrammatic section through a modified rachis segment, called the cupule, which forms the major component of the fruitcase. The suppressed lower floret is not clearly indicated. The fruitcase consists of the rachis segment plus the outer glume

student-assistant, the writer was assigned to study the cytology and genetics of maize-teosinte hybrids.

We confirmed the fertility of the hybrids and showed that the ten chromosomes of the Mexican teosintes pair normally with those of maize at appropriate stages of meiosis (Beadle 1932), and further, that in the eight chromosomes for which we had suitable genetic markers, crossing-over in the hybrids was essentially the same as that in pure maize controls (Emerson and Beadle 1932).

Our conclusion, perhaps not stated in so many words, was that cytologically and genetically maize and the Mexican teosintes can reasonably be regarded as one species. Now, forty years later this has been formally proposed on taxonomic grounds (Iltis 1972). The hypothesis that the wild form was the direct ancestor of its cultivated counterpart was thus entirely plausible in our way of thinking. We regarded the problem as essentially solved, that a relatively few major gene changes could and probably did convert the wild plant into a more useful cultivated one.

In discussions at this time Emerson pointed out that two mutants, a soft or reduced cupule and a non-shattering rachis, could make teosinte an easily usable food plant. It should be added that these postulated mutants are much the same as those that have played such significant roles in the evolution of the cultivated small grains of wheat, rye, barley, and oats, all of which are represented by varieties in which kernels can be threshed free of glumes, and in which the heads are non-shattering.

THE TRIPARTITE HYPOTHESIS

But there were skeptics. One was and still is, Professor Paul C. Mangelsdorf, formerly at Texas A. and M., then Harvard, and now at the University of North Carolina. In 1938 he and a colleague, R. G. Reeves, proposed that teosinte was not ancestral to maize, but instead was a relatively recent species resulting from hybridization of a wild maize, now extinct or undiscovered, and a species of the genus *Tripsacum* (Mangelsdorf and Reeves 1938, 1939; Mangelsdorf 1947). This hybrid is possible by special techniques. The evidence alleged to support this origin of teosinte was mainly that it is intermediate between the assumed parental species in many morphological traits.

Not everyone believed this evidence to justify the conclusion (Beadle 1939). The reasons were: first, that maize and *Tripsacum* have never been known to hybridize naturally, despite the fact that they grow in close proximity over millions of acres; second, that none of the eighteen chromosomes of *Tripsacum* pairs normally with any one of the ten chromosomes of maize; and third, that the hybrids produced artificially are completely male sterile. They produce offspring only in backcrosses in which the functional gametes of the hybrid carry the unreduced chromosome number, that is, ten from maize and eighteen from *Tripsacum*.

Nevertheless, this tripartite hypothesis has for a third of a century been supported by its proposers, with the result that it has thoroughly permeated genetic, botanical, plant-breeding, anthropological, and other literature. It is repeated in encyclopedias, in compendia, and in many text-books, sometimes being transformed from an hypothesis to an established fact.

More recently Walton C. Galinat, a former associate of Mangelsdorf, has shown that the fruitcase of teosinte, which the tripartite hypothesis must assume to have been contributed from *Tripsacum* as a block of closely linked genes, could not have arisen in that way for the simple reason that no such group of genes can be demonstrated in *Tripsacum* (Galinat 1970). In contrast to teosinte, the fruitcase of *Tripsacum* appears to be specified by genes that are not closely linked.

De Wet and Harlan (1972) and de Wet, Harlan, Lambert, and Engle (1972) of the University of Illinois, Urbana, have also argued against the tripartite hypothesis on the ground that, in their extensive studies of hybrids between maize and *Tripsacum*, they have never observed a segregant at all like teosinte.

It is of considerable importance to know that, contrary to the tripartite hypothesis assumption that teosinte is of relatively recent origin, teosinte has recently been reported to have existed some 7,000 years ago at a site about twenty miles southeast of Mexico City near the present town of Chalco. The two "seeds" recovered in an undisturbed Pre-ceramic Horizon are very much like the present most corn-like race of teosinte called Chalco (Lorenzo and González 1970). Could this race of teosinte have been the ancestor of maize? At this time one can do no more than speculate.

TEOSINTE AS A FOOD PLANT

One of the arguments against teosinte as an ancestor of maize has been that it is not obvious how its nut-like seeds with their heavy cases could have been used for food by primitive man. This view has persisted despite early Spanish evidence that teosinte seeds were indeed used as food. Wilkes (1967) referred to *Vatican Codex* 3738 in which it was said that in the tradition of the tribe ". . . in the old days [preconquest] they ate a wild plant called accentli [synonym of teosinte]." Young stalks of teosinte were undoubtedly chewed, as archaeological evidence indicates early maize was. Young spikes of teosinte can also be eaten before the cases become hardened.

In 1939, without knowledge of any documented use of teosinte as food, it occurred to me, as a boyhood lover of popcorn, that perhaps teosinte seeds would pop. A simple experiment demonstrated that they will. The popped kernels, exploded out of their cases, are indistinguishable from popped corn (Beadle 1939). That teosinte could have been used in this way in Pre-ceramic times has been well documented by Anderson and Cutler (1950). Maize kernels placed in a fire, on glowing embers, on hot rocks, or heated sand, pop very well and either pop free of the fire or can be retrieved by simple wooden sticks or tongs. Teosinte would surely behave similarly.

More recently, as a result of a friendly disagreement with Professor Mangelsdorf on the edibility of ground whole teosinte seeds in which he expressed doubt as to whether one could tolerate ingesting the fifty percent or more roughage contributed by the cases, the question was posed to Professor Nevin Scrimshaw, a biochemist-nutritionist of MIT, whom we both know and who has worked in the tropics with teosinte. Scrimshaw proposed that I do the following experiment:

Consume 75 grams of ground whole seeds of teosinte on each of two successive days. If no ill effects were experienced, increase the intake to 150 grams per day for two more days. If there were still no unpleasant consequences, the answer would be clear. There were no ill effects whatever.

Dry teosinte seeds have been ground with a pair of primitive grinding or pounding stones of a kind known to have been in use at least 8,000 years ago, with the conclusion that an energetic person inspired by extreme hunger could in one day, by a water flotation technique or in other ways, separate from the ground shell-kernel mixture enough shell-free meal of teosinte to feed a small family for one day or more (Beadle 1972). Whole, mature teosinte seeds can be eaten directly without great difficulty by first soaking them until they have been sufficiently softened to masticate. The shells can either be swallowed or selectively spit out.

RE-INVESTIGATION OF MAIZE-TEOSINTE HYBRIDS

Backing up a bit in the sequence of current interests in teosinte, shortly before I retired from academic administration I received a copy of Wilkes' monograph (1967), *Teosinte: the closest relative of maize.* It is by far the best and most useful document on the subject available and was read with great interest and admiration, qualified by a deeply felt reservation on noting in one passage his characterization of the maize-from-teosinte hypothesis as a "crude" attempt to explain the origin of maize, and in another as the "myth" that teosinte is maize's ancestor. Through correspondence the matter of the origin of maize was argued without coming to an agreement. The result, however, was that I decided to return to a study of the relation of teosinte to maize.

It should be added that Wilkes and I have become good friends, have collaborated in three teosinte-collecting trips in Mexico, and have influenced each other's thinking to some degree.

To supplement earlier small-scale studies indicating that near-equivalents to parental types could be recovered in second generation maize-teosinte hybrid populations, it was decided to grow large-scale populations of second generation and backcross populations in order better to estimate the magnitude of the genetic difference between the two.

As a first cross a primitive maize, the most teosinte-like that was clearly maize, and a maize-like teosinte that was unmistakably teosinte were chosen as parents. These choices could be expected to reduce the differences to those that are most essential. On the advice of Dr. Edwin J. Wellhausen of the International Center for Maize and

Wheat Improvement, headquartered in Mexico, Chapalote maize and Chalco teosinte were selected.

Mendel's laws say that in a second-generation segregating population with a one-gene difference each parental type will be recovered with a statistical frequency of one in four; with two independently segregating gene pairs, one in sixteen; and so on for more genes. For ten, the recovery will be somewhat less than one in a million, and for twenty, which is possible with a segregating gene pair located near each of the twenty chromosome ends, the recovery of a particular parental type will be less than one in a trillion plants – which is close to the total number of plants grown per year in the entire world. Thus if teosinte and maize differed by a large number of significant and unlinked differentiating genes, even as few as ten or a dozen, good types of maize and teosinte would be so rare as to be unrecoverable in any population that could reasonably be grown and classified.

It was decided to grow up to 50,000 second generation plants if necessary, for this would give a reasonable chance of recovering parental types with as many as six or seven major independently segregating genetic units. With the 1973 plantings, just about that many will have been grown and classified.

Since teosinte plants will not mature at United States corn-belt latitudes, there was a problem of where to grow the segregating populations. Fortunately arrangements were made with Dr. Wellhausen to grow them at the International Maize and Wheat Improvement Center's El Batán station near Texcoco, Mexico. Doctor Mario Gutiérrez of the Center has collaborated in planting, growing, harvesting, and classifying the plants grown there. Professor Walton C. Galinat of the University of Massachusetts also collaborated in the classification of the first large second generation grown in Mexico.

What have been the results? In the second generation cross of Chapalote maize and Chalco teosinte good maize and teosinte types were recovered with a frequency of about one of each in 500 plants. These frequencies are intermediate between those expected with four and with five independently segregating genes. This does not, however, take into account that the recovered parental types are not likely to be homozygous for all differentiating genes, or that not all genetic units involved are likely to be segregating independently. Furthermore, it is unlikely that the significant segregating genetic units are single genes, for we know that in more or less comparable situations there is a selective advantage in having differentiating genes closely linked in a manner that favors the recovery of parental types. This is not in disagreement with the findings of Mangelsdorf and Reeves (1938) in isolating differentiating genetic units through repeated backcrosses of hybrids to an unbred line of maize.

Second generation and backcross populations have been grown

involving other races of both maize and teosinte. They show that the frequency of recovered parental types may vary rather widely depending on the races involved.

In response to doubts expressed by Professor Mangelsdorf as to whether really "good" maize types were recovered a "cob quiz" was devised in which cobs from "pure" maize and those from hybrid populations were coded and presented separately to Professors Mangelsdorf and Galinat for classification. In both cases enough cobs of hybrids were judged to be those of good corn to confirm that "good" maize is indeed recovered in reasonable frequencies in second generation hybrids and in backcrosses of first generation hybrids to maize.

Despite the qualifications and reservations already mentioned, the genetic differences between maize and teosinte clearly cannot be so great as to render untenable the hypothesis of an ancestral relationship of teosinte to maize. When one considers that there are several hundred known genes for simple differing characters within varieties of maize in existence at the time of Columbus and almost surely as many or more for such qualitative ones as plant size, ear size and shape, number of ears, kernel size, response to day length, disease resistance, and other traits, it seems entirely reasonable to assume that pre-Columbian man could have discovered and preserved the far fewer mutants required to produce a useful plant from teosinte, that is, a primitive maize from which modern races of maize could subsequently have been selected. Two major differentiating traits, single versus double female spikelets and two-ranked versus four-ranked female spikes, are differentiated by single genetic units (Galinat 1971).

Archaeological Evidence

Beginning in the mid- to late forties many dry caves in southwestern United States and in Mexico have been explored by experienced archaeologists. Among the many recovered materials that reveal much about the lives of the peoples who occupied these sites are remains of maize, the most revealing of which are cobs. In zones of increasing depth and age in some caves, sequences of cobs are found that clearly indicate changes under domestication. The oldest cobs are found, on radioactive carbon dating, to have grown something like 7,000 years ago. Cobs of this age are very small, an inch in length, more or less, and are estimated by Mangelsdorf, MacNeish, and Galinat (1964), who have studied a great many of them in detail, to have each borne about fifty to sixty small kernels.

These cobs reveal a great deal about the evolution of cultivated maize over the past seven millennia. With respect to the origin of maize, Mangelsdorf and his associates allege the oldest of them to be the remains of a truly wild maize, this on the basis of the reported uniformity of the oldest cobs, plus the fact that they occur at earlier levels than other plant remains unmistakably known to have been cultivated. If there had been such a wild maize growing independently of teosinte, it is now extinct, or as yet undiscovered despite extensive searches for it. While it is logically impossible to prove that such maize never existed as a wild plant, one can seriously question whether the available evidence compels or even suggests such a conclusion.

Let us examine the alternative, and to some a more plausible interpretation, namely, that these oldest cobs represent stages in the transition of teosinte to maize through human selection.

First, early cobs are obviously much closer morphologically and genetically to teosinte than is modern maize, this for the very simple reason that cobs closely matching them are readily recovered in second and later generations of maize-teosinte hybrids, as Mangelsdorf (1958a) has shown and as has been abundantly demonstrated in the more recent hybrid populations.

Second, if the earliest archaeological types are indeed genetically closer to teosinte, as expected on the hypothesis that they were directly derived from teosinte, this should be evident in second and backcross generations of hybrids of recovered archaeological types with teosinte. Experiments now in progress indicate that the genetic differences are indeed reduced in number in this way.

Third, the earliest alleged wild maize is said to have fragile cobs. This is the equivalent of the fragile rachis of teosinte and could reasonably be expected to have persisted for some time after teosinte was deliberately cultivated.

Fourth, some of the earliest cobs are two-ranked, another teosinte trait.

Fifth, the earliest maize cobs are reported to have longer glumes than has modern maize, which Mangelsdorf suggested could well be the genetic equivalent of the tunicate character of modern maize. In fact, Mangelsdorf (1958b) has used tunicate types of modern maize in reconstructing a close approximation of the earliest archaeological specimens.

Elaborating on this suggested role of tunicate, there is reason to believe this character to have had a far more important bearing on the origin of maize than has previously been recognized, for it suggests how in a simple and plausible way teosinte could have been converted into a more useful food plant and a logical precursor of maize.

Professor Galinat has generously provided me with a number of lines of teosinte to which an intermediate allele of the dominant

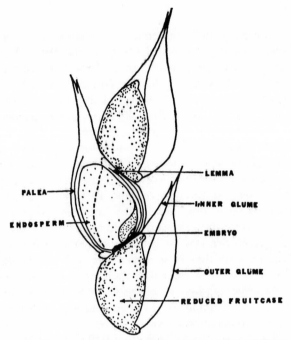

Figure 3. Segment of a tunicate teosinte spike corresponding to Figure 1, showing membranous outer glumes and moderate reduction of cupule. Kernels only partially enclosed in cupules

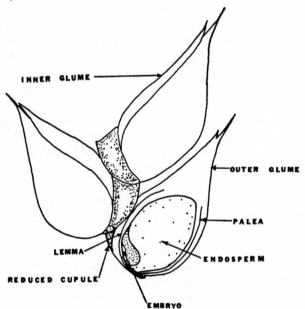

Figure 4. Segment of a tunicate teosinte spike corresponding to Figures 1 and 2, but with greater reduction in cupule such that kernels can be readily threshed free of smaller softer fruitcases and less indurated outer glumes

tunicate gene has been introduced from maize. With these many additional lines have been produced by further backcrossing to teosintes. These modified teosintes have just the characteristics Emerson postulated as the first steps in the transformation from teosinte to maize. The fruitcases of tunicate teosintes are reduced to shallow, less indurated cupules with enlarged but membranous outer glumes (Figures 3 and 4). In addition, as de Wet, et al. (1972) have pointed out, the abscission layers of the rachis are less well developed, with the result that there is much less tendency of the spikes to shatter upon ripening. Thus a single tunicate mutation can convert teosinte into a plant from which naked kernels can be threshed with ease. Furthermore, the yields of such plants can approximate those of wheat.

Had the tunicate mutant change been an early step in evolution of maize from teosinte, the presence of the tunicate trait in the archaeological maize would be accounted for. The plausibility of this interpretation would seem further increased by the fact that tunicate alleles are dominant and, in the heterozygous state, most useful for the purposes suggested. This means that if in early stages of cultivation a tunicate mutant of teosinte had been selected for planting, it would not have seemed to disappear in the next generation through out-crossing, as would a recessive mutant. Furthermore, there would have been an advantage in getting rid of it in subsequent stages of evolution under domestication for exactly the same reasons that tunicate types of modern corn are less useful to man than their non-tunicate counterparts.

If the earliest archaeological specimens of maize were in fact wild maize, rather than a transitional form, it seems highly improbable that it and teosinte could have shared the same habitat, or overlapping ones, for teosinte, with its many attributes of a successful wild plant (well-protected kernels, an effective mechanism for seed dispersal, a built-in dormancy system that helps maximize the chance of germination under favorable circumstances, plus a remarkable ability to reproduce in the wild under a variety of circumstances), would surely have competitively replaced the wild maize.

If, on the other hand, teosinte and wild maize had occupied different habitats, as has been postulated, it is difficult to believe they could have remained as completely inter-fertile as the evidence shows they have been for thousands of years.

Pollen Evidence

Barghoorn, Wolfe, and Clisby (1954) have claimed to have established beyond reasonable doubt the existence of maize in the Americas prior to the arrival of man, this by the discovery of fossil pollen of maize in samples from a construction drill core taken at the Bellas Artes site in Mexico City at a depth of more than 200 feet. This would indicate an age of from forty to eighty thousand years.

The identification of these pollen grains as maize was at first based on size, most modern pollen of maize being larger than modern pollen of teosinte. Kurtz, Liverman, and Tucker (1960) challenged this conclusion on the grounds that maize pollen varies markedly in size depending on environmental conditions and that therefore size alone is not clearly diagnostic, nor is the ratio of long axis of the grains to pore diameter, which character had been said to be a more reliable criterion. Galinat (1971) believes the fossil pollen to be too large for primitive maize and has suggested, as have others, that conditions of preservation of fossil pollen and methods of preparation may affect its size and thus invalidate this as a basis for identifying fossil pollen as maize or teosinte.

As a result of these uncertainties, a re-examination of the Bellas Artes pollen was later made by Irwin and Barghoorn (1965). They concluded that the two pollens could be reliably distinguished by exine characteristics revealed by phase-contrast microscopy, and again judged the fossil pollen to be that of maize. But still more recently, Banerjee, a graduate student of Barghoorn, has used a superior method of electron microscopy which shows the two pollen exines to be indistinguishable (Banerjee and Barghoorn 1972). Grant (i.p.) confirms this.

Soil engineers experienced in drill-core sampling have expressed the opinion that without special precautions it is not possible, beyond reasonable doubt, to exclude contamination of core samples with material from higher levels, even in the interior of cores. It should be added that the upper horizons of the Bellas Artes site contained modern maize pollen.

For these several reasons it seems clear that the fossil pollen evidence is at best inconclusive.

Linguistics

Such linguistic evidence as exists is consistent with the teosinte ancestry of maize. Why otherwise would teosinte be called "God's maize" or "God's grass"? As pointed out by Wilkes (1967), in the Nobogame area of Chihuahua teosinte is known as *madre de maíz* [mother of maize], presumably from an earlier native designation. Do these terms represent a kind of cultural memory? With many other existing native names for teosinte in the various parts of its range, this would appear to be a rewarding area for further linguistic study (Wilkes 1967).

Ecological Considerations

In addition to its highly successful mechanism of seed dispersal as compared with the apparently far less effective one of postulated wild maize, teosinte has other characteristics favorable to its survival in the wild.

Contrary to a statement by Wilkes (1967), teosinte "seeds" have a dormancy or mechanism of delayed germination which favors their germination in circumstances suitable for survival (Beadle, unpublished). In addition, the fruitcase of teosinte provides significant protection to the enclosed kernels, as compared with their naked or less well-protected counterparts in maize. Controlled experiments with mice, rats, squirrels, other rodents, and pigeons indicate this, for given a choice maize kernels are strongly preferred to teosinte "seeds" by these animals (Beadle and Fox, unpublished materials).

The colors and patterns of the heavily indurated protective fruit-cases of teosinte vary from grey to brown to black, often with mottling, spotting, or striping. In this and in shape they may very effectively mimic the pebbles and particles of the soil surface on which they fall. They are remarkably well camouflaged (Wilkes 1967).

Teosinte responds adaptively to the conditions under which it grows. In fertile soil with optimum moisture plants are large, well tillered and produce abundant "seed." Under adverse conditions, they respond by producing few or no tillers, restricting growth, and by producing no more "seed" than resources permit. In the extreme, this may be a single mature "seed." In contrast maize gambles on at least one whole ear and thus produces no "seed" at all if this fails.

Folklore

Regional folklore would seem also to contribute to further understanding of the role of teosinte in prehistoric times. The Wilkes monograph clearly indicates this. It records that Lumholz, who travelled extensively in Mexico at the turn of the century and reported his observations in considerable detail, noted that in the Nobogame area teosinte growing in or near fields of maize was said to be "good for the maize." It is easy to minimize the significance of such an assertion by assuming it to be an excuse for not making the effort to rogue the interloper out of the maize plantings. In fact, there is good evidence that teosinte can be "good for the maize" under primitive conditions of culture in which maize is grown in small areas, often relatively isolated from other maize. Under these conditions, with seed saved for successive generations, inbreeding is intensified. This we know reduces vigor and yields.

If teosinte grows adjacent to or in such isolated plots, hybrids between it and maize occur with a frequency that depends on a good many factors such as relative times of pollination and spatial relations (Wilkes 1972). When corn is pollinated by teosinte, the hybrid kernels are usually indistinguishable from pure corn and thus may be planted. The resulting first-generation hybrid plants exhibit marked hybrid vigor. Like those of *Zea canina*, however, their ears are small and undesirable and therefore will not be chosen in selecting seed for the succeeding crop.

These hybrid plants will, however, have previously shed abundant pollen which will be widely disseminated because of their height and vigor. Thus backcrosses to maize as the female parent will appear in the next generation. Some of these will be acceptable maize showing marked hybrid vigor. Second and later generation backcrosses to maize result in an even higher frequency of high-yielding good maize plants. In this way the maize will be rejuvenated according to the same principles used in producing modern high-yielding corn hybrids.

That such rejuvenation will indeed occur has been demonstrated in a well-controlled experiment by Lambert and Leng (1965) of the University of Illinois, Urbana. These investigators hybridized a well adapted, high-yielding, inbred line of maize with four races of teosinte and made several successive backcrosses to the inbred maize parent. Yields in the second and third backcrosses were increased as much as 100 percent.

As both Mangelsdorf (1961) and Wilkes (1967) have shown, such hybridization is not infrequent in parts of Mexico where maize and teosinte grow in close proximity, thus creating sympatric populations in which genes of teosinte and maize are exchanged regularly at a rather low frequency. As has often been pointed out in more or less comparable situations, the selective advantage of getting back the parental types well adapted to the two habitats – maize fields and areas occupied by teosinte – will in time result in clustering of genes differentiating the two partners in the sympatric relation (Galinat 1971). That this has in fact taken place is indicated by several of the genetic studies previously mentioned.

Comparative Cytology

Another important line of evidence bearing on the maize-teosinte relationship comes from studies of supernumerary B-type chromosomes, an "abnormal" chromosome 10, and of heterochromatic knobs of varying sizes and positions that are found on both maize and teosinte chromosomes. These have been extensively studied by Longley and Kato (1965), and others (Galinat 1971). Most knobs in teosintes, as identified by position, are found in one or another of the many races of maize. Position, sizes, and frequencies of knobs also reveal much about centers of distribution and paths of dissemination of maize relative to teosinte. They confirm that the two species have had a close and long-continuing association and, insofar as the results are available, I judge them to be consistent with the view that maize is a direct descendant of teosinte. More extensive data, now in preparation for publication by McClintock, Kato, and Blumenschein, will undoubtedly add importantly to the total evidence bearing on this relation.

Biochemical Evidence

Seed storage proteins of maize and teosinte have been compared by a number of investigators. As an example, Waines (1972) and Gray, Grant, and de Wet (1972) have shown by electrophoretic techniques that there is little or no qualitative difference in the two. Several enzyme systems have been investigated with no indication of significant differences in the two forms. Although the known sharing of a large gene pool by the two species would suggest few such differences, additional studies are clearly needed and are in fact under way or proposed in a number of laboratories.

THE TRIPARTITE HYPOTHESIS RECONSIDERED

At a conference held at Harvard in June 1972, Mangelsdorf conceded that the evidence against the tripartite hypothesis was substantial and persuasive. But consistent with his firm conviction that the earliest archaeological specimens of maize represent wild maize, he has since proposed an alternative hypothesis on maize and its relatives (1974). He kindly permitted me to see relevant excerpts in manuscript form. In his new proposal he assumes that maize, as represented by the earliest archaeological specimens, antedated the teosintes, which he now proposes were derived from wild maize by mutation. This indeed represents a reversal of position since he previously maintained that teosinte and maize were so different that teosinte could not have been ancestral to maize.

If maize could have given rise to teosinte, the reverse must also be both possible and far more probable, for teosinte is a highly successful wild plant and maize is not. Postulated wild maize, as represented in the earliest archaeological specimens, is assumed by Mangelsdorf, et al. to have dispersed its seeds in part by virtue of a fragile cob. In this there seems to be a curious inconsistency. If the earliest archaeological specimens were wild maize and had brittle cobs, how could they have survived harvesting, transportation to the caves, shelling of kernels, mixing with other debris on the cave floors, plus being tramped on prior to their being covered with protecting layers? If the cobs were fragile, this would indicate teosinte as an ancestor. If they were not fragile, it is difficult to believe they could have been wild maize, for how then would they have disseminated their seeds?

Regardless of how the question of the fragile cob is rationalized, the fruitcase-cupule relation seems overridingly persuasive as evidence that the direction of change was from teosinte to maize. How else can one account for the cupule of the corncob, clearly present in the earliest archaeological specimens? As Galinat (1970, 1971) has pointed out the cupule indicates that corn must have evolved from an ancestor with a cupulate fruitcase. With *Tripsacum* excluded, teosinte remains the sole candidate. There is no other living or known extinct species that so logically satisfies all criteria.

REFERENCES

ANDERSON, E., R. H. BARLOW
1943   The maize tribute of Moctezuma's empire. *Annals of the Missouri Botanical Garden* 30: 413–418.
ANDERSON, E., H. C. CUTLER
1950   Methods of corn popping and their historical significance. *Southwestern Journal of Anthropology* 6: 303–308.
BAILEY, L. H.
1949   *Manual of cultivated plants.* New York: Macmillan.
BANERJEE, U. C., E. S. BARGHOORN
1972   Fine structure of pollen grain exine of maize, teosinte and *Tripsacum. Thirtieth Annual Proceedings of the Electron Microscopy Society of America, Los Angeles, California* 226–227.
BARGHOORN, E. S., M. K. WOLFE, K. H. CLISBY
1954   Fossil maize from the Valley of Mexico. *Botanical Museum Leaflets, Harvard University* 16: 229–240.
BARLOW, R. H.
1949   The extent of the empire of the cultura Mexica. *Ibero-Americana* 28: 1–141.

BEADLE, G. W.
1932   *Euchlaena* and its hybrids with *Zea*, I: Chromosome behavior in *E. mexicana* and its hybrids with *Zea mays*. *Zeitschrift für Abstammungs- und Vererbungslehre* 62: 291–304.
1939   Teosinte and the origin of maize. *The Journal of Heredity* 30: 245–247.
1972   The mystery of maize. *Field Museum of Natural History Bulletin* 43: 2–11.

DE WET, J. M. J., J. R. HARLAN
1972   Origin of maize: the tripartite hypothesis. *Euphytica* 21: 271–279.

DE WET, J. M. J., J. R. HARLAN, R. J. LAMBERT, L. M. ENGLE
1972   Introgression from *Tripsacum* into *Zea* and the origin of maize. *Caryologica* 1: 25–31.

EMERSON, R. A.
1924   The control of flowering in teosinte. *The Journal of Heredity* 15: 41–48.

EMERSON, R. A., G. W. BEADLE
1932   Studies of *Euchlaena* and its hybrids with *Zea*, II: Crossing-over between the chromosomes of *Euchlaena* and those of *Zea*. *Zeitschrift für Abstammungs- und Vererbungslehre* 62: 305–315.

GALINAT, W. C.
1970   *The cupule and its role in the origin and evolution of maize.* University of Massachusetts Bulletin 585.
1971   The origin of corn. *Annual Review of Genetics* 5: 447–478.
1973   Preserve Guatemalan teosinte, a relict link in corn's evolution. *Science* 180: 323.

GRANT, C. A.
i.p.   A scanning electron microscopy survey of some Maydeae pollen. *Grana*.

GRAY, J. R., C. A. GRANT, J. M. J. DE WET
1972   Protein electrophoresis as an indicator of relationship among maize, teosinte and *Tripsacum*. *Illinois State Academy of Science Newsletter* 4: 5.

ILTIS, H.
1972   The taxonomy of *Zea mays* (Gramineae). *Phytologia* 23: 248–249.

IRWIN, H., E. S. BARGHOORN
1965   Identification of the pollen of maize, teosinte and tripsacum by phase-contrast microscopy. *Botanical Museum Leaflets, Harvard University* 21: 37–57.

KEMPTON, J. H.
1938   Maize – our heritage from the Indian. *Smithsonian Report for 1937*, 385–408.

KURTZ, E. B., J. L. LIVERMAN, H. TUCKER
1960   Some problems concerning fossil and modern corn pollen. *Torrey Botanical Club Bulletin* 87: 85–94.

LAMBERT, R. J., E. R. LENG
1965   Backcross response of two mature plant traits for certain corn-teosinte hybrids. *Crop Science* 5: 239–241.

LONGLEY, A. E., T. A. KATO
1965   Chromosome morphology of certain races of maize in Latin America. *International Center for Maize and Wheat Improvement Research Bulletin* 1: 1–112.

LORENZO, J. L., L. GONZÁLEZ
1970   El más antiquo teosinte. *INAH Boletín* 42: 41–43.

MANGELSDORF, P. C.
1947   The origin and evolution of maize. *Advances in Genetics* 1: 161–207.
1958a   The mutagenic effect of hybridizing maize and teosinte. *Cold Spring Harbor Symposium on Quantitative Biology* 23: 409–421.
1958b   Reconstructing the ancestor of corn. *Proceedings of the American Philosophical Society* 102: 454–463.
1961   Evolution at a single locus in maize. *Science* 133: 1366.
1974   *Corn, its origin, evolution and improvement.* Cambridge, Mass.: Harvard University Press.
MANGELSDORF, P. C., R. S. MACNEISH, W. C. GALINAT
1964   Domestication of corn. *Science* 143: 538–545.
MANGELSDORF, P. C., R. G. REEVES
1938   The origin of maize. *Proceedings of the National Academy of Science* 24: 303–312.
1939   The origin of Indian corn and its relatives. *Texas Agricultural Experiment Station Bulletin* 594: 1–315.
WAINES, J. G.
1972   Protein electrophoretic patterns of maize, teosinte and *Tripsacum*. *Maize Genetics Cooperation News Letter* 46: 164–165.
WILKES, H. G.
1967   *Teosinte: the closest relative of maize.* Cambridge, Mass.: The Bussey Institution of Harvard University.
1972   Maize and its wild relatives. *Science* 177: 1071–1077.

PART TWO

Exchange Networks

Introduction

Long-distance exchange of certain exotics has long been understood to be a crucial factor in the validation of the polities in pre-Hispanic Mexican states. So important has trade been viewed by archaeologists that a theory of "trade-determinism" has become very popular as the prime hypothesis for the origin of the Mayan empire, and to a lesser extent, other polities. Such one-variable models can never be adequately explanatory; they are primarily a result of the neofunctionalism in "new" or "scientific" archaeology. While ideally not limited to economic questions, in many respects the data recovered by archaeologists allow more complete and useful reconstructions of economic activity than for other cultural spheres. Thus it is not surprising that some of the best contributions deal with economic interaction spheres.

Reconstruction of trade networks is necessarily limited by our control of the data. Until recently we have been restricted to generally detailing the items exchanged; but thanks to a variety of new elemental analytical techniques, increasingly fine distinctions can be made of interaction spheres, with the dispersal of individual trade items detailed at each step of the way. Recent papers, such as that of Parsons and Price (1971), with its commentary by Chapman (1971), on Mesoamerican trade and its role in the emergence of civilization, have gone a long way toward producing new and more meaningful cultural reconstructions.

The series of papers in this section by Pires-Ferreira are particularly important for constructing models for the Formative Period of Mesoamerican civilization. What is exceedingly useful is the fact that we have three different prestige items detailed, each with slightly different, though overlapping, exchange networks. These papers summarize the better part of the work of Dr. Pires-Ferreira's dissertation (1973) on Formative Period exchange networks. In contrast to the shell exchange network and the iron ore mirror exchange network, the obsidian network appears to be quite complicated – complicated in part because the obsidian used comes from a variety of different sources in a mosaic pattern throughout Mesoamerica, and complicated because in some areas distribution appears to be by reciprocity, while in others it appears to be through redistributive patterns.

For the Early Preclassic, trade was undertaken by some groups still basically egalitarian in organization, while other members of the network were chiefdoms or incipient states, with power based on differential status among individuals. In the chiefdoms, distribution of obsidian or other exotic or "non-utilitarian" items served as status validators. Since they reaffirmed power, they have been found archaeologically in these areas unequally distributed through redistributive patterns, with concentrations found at political nodes of the system, and with relatively little exotica found at the level of the individual household. On the other hand, in the more egalitarian systems, such exotica or non-utilitarian items served more as systemic regulators which helped to keep the system functioning at times of economic or demographic imbalance. Archaeologically in these zones long-distance trade items of this sort are found rather more equally distributed throughout the settlements.

In the analysis of the obsidian exchange networks linking villages, Pires-Ferreira is able to detail some important shifts and patterns. In the distribution of obsidian, a distinct shift from reciprocal patterns to redistributive patterns is observed between the Early and Middle Formative. Obsidian increased in value as a trade regulator and status validator, such that while some areas like Oaxaca were dependent on outside sources during the Early Formative, each of the major settlement areas apparently achieved control of a local obsidian source by the Middle Formative. The power shift between San Lorenzo and La Venta in the Olmec heartland, which previously has been observed in the shift of a variety of ceramic trains in the highlands by Grove, Coe, and others (see, for example, papers in Hammond 1974 and Benson 1968), can now also be documented in the shifts and changes of the obsidian exchange network, in dissolution of traditional exchange ties with San Lorenzo, and in greater importance in direct obsidian exchange between the Central Highlands and the Gulf Coast areas.

Dissolution of obsidian trade networks and establishment of new networks between the Gulf Coast area and the Central Mexican Highlands area is mirrored in the trade in iron ore mirrors as well. During the Early Formative, San José Mogote in Oaxaca appears to have been the center of manufacture of small, thumbnail-size, flat, hematite or magnetite mirrors; these were traded in an area about 350 km. in radius, from San Pablo in Morelos in the northwest to San Lorenzo in Veracruz to the southeast. The realignment of trade patterns following the shift from San Lorenzo to La Venta in political dominancy in the Olmec area is noted in the mirror exchange network as well, as verified by Dr. Barbara Evans's Mössbauer analyses. Oaxaca thumbnail mirrors are replaced by large concave mirrors made only on the Gulf Coast in the Olmec area; mirror production apparently came to an end in the Valley of Oaxaca, and is directly correlated with the development of a local obsidian source and exchange network in the Oaxaca area. This regionalization and concomitant decrease in long-distance exchange between the Early and Middle Formative is clearly identifiable for the obsidian and iron-ore mirror interaction spheres; for the shell exchange networks it is less clear, but it can still be observed.

The importance of trade continues through the evolution of Mesoamerican states. Webb argues that Mesoamerican civilization was shaped, kept in dynamic motion, and integrated by evolving patterns of trade. There are certain state-inducing factors, above all a resource distribution, which require extensive, centralized exchange, such as best provided in state polities. For Webb, commercially inspired militarism is the social dynamic which determined the overall social development of the region. The Epiclassic, for example, is marked by a shift in patterns of long-distance trade from the theocratic importation of highly exotic ritual and prestige goods toward movement of more secular luxury goods for the consumption of the elite (particularly warriors). In a state consciously dependent upon controls such as wealth, the transformation from theocratic chiefdoms to the more secular state frees a large portion of the social surplus from religious usages and permits a less restricted choice among alternative courses of actions. The Epiclassic is thus argued by Webb to be a time of major reworking and expansion of trade spheres, accompanied by increased warfare, for rivalry over trade is seen as the major cause of war among Mesoamerican states.

The strong economic-commercial organization of Mesoamerican states had its impact on the political structure of the immediate pre-Conquest Aztec state as well. Berdan reexamines Chapman's (1957) ports-of-trade model in terms of more recent evidence; he concludes that rather than intentionally neutral locales, as posited during the earlier formulation, the ports of trade during the Postclassic were actually controlled locales, maintained by the major polities deliberately, for the convenience of the economic guilds such as the *pochteca* of the Aztec and the *ppolom* of the Mayans. Investigation of mercantile guilds and ports of trade gives us a powerful tool for understanding the Postclassic empires. While we cannot yet extend these institutions back in time, further consideration of ports of trade will prove to be useful, for they certainly appear to be evolutionary developments of the yearly trade fairs which were held in pre-Hispanic times from Kettle Falls and Mandan in the Rocky Mountain area to the north, to Tiwanaku in the Andes to the south.

REFERENCES

BENSON, E. P., *editor*
  1968   *Dumbarton Oaks Conference on the Olmec.* Dumbarton Oaks
         Research Library and Collection, Washington, D.C.
CHAPMAN, A. M.
  1957   "Ports of trade enclaves in Aztec and Maya civilizations," in *Trade
         and market in the early empires.* Edited by K. Polanyi, C. M.
         Arensberg, and H. W. Pearson, 114–153. Glencoe, Ill.: The Free
         Press.
  1971   Commentary on "Mesoamerican trade and its role in the emergence
         of civilization," in *Observations on the emergence of civilization in
         Mesoamerica.* Edited by R. F. Heizer, J. A. Graham, and C. W.
         Clewlow, Jr., 196–211. University of California Archaeological
         Research Facility Contribution 11. Berkeley.
HAMMOND, N., *editor*
  1974   *Mesoamerican archaeology: new approaches.* Austin: University of
         Texas Press.
PARSONS, L. A., B. J. PRICE
  1971   "Mesoamerican trade and its role in the emergence of civilization,"
         in *Observations on the emergence of civilization in Mesoamerica.*
         Edited by R. F. Heizer, J. A. Graham, and C. W. Clewlow, Jr.,
         169–195. University of California Archaeological Research Facility
         Contribution 11. Berkeley.
PIRES-FERREIRA, J. W.
  1973   "Formative Mesoamerican exchange networks." Unpublished
         Ph.D. dissertation, University of Michigan, Ann Arbor.

Obsidian Exchange Networks: Inferences and Speculations on the Development of Social Organization in Formative Mesoamerica

JANE WHEELER PIRES-FERREIRA

Speculation concerning the origin of exotic or nonlocal materials found in archaeological sites has been important in shaping the history of archaeological theory. Traditionally "import" items have been seen as evidence of diffusion or migration, or they have become the basis of trade and "trade route" hypotheses. While the former propositions have come under critical review (Renfrew 1969), trade hypotheses have become a universal device for explaining the presence of apparently unusual materials in archaeological sites. Often, however, the postulated origin of such material is a result of speculation or educated guessing on the part of the excavator. And occasionally, as in the Olmec "jade trade route" example, untested reconstructions explaining the role of trade in directing cultural development have come to be considered established facts. The critical examination of such trade hypotheses has only recently become possible through the application of various petrographic, chemical, and isotopic analytical techniques which make possible accurate determination of the origin of import items.

I wish to thank the following persons for their generous assistance in the realization of this research: J. B. Griffin, E. N. Wilmsen, J. R. Parsons, H. T. Wright, P. L. Cloke, and J. T. Meyers of the University of Michigan, C. Sheffer of Temple University, J. D. Speth of Hunter College, W. O. Payne of Orange Coast College, C. DiPeso of the Amerind Foundation, M. Spence of the University of Western Ontario, J. L. Lorenzo of the Departamento de Prehistoria, C. Renfrew of Southampton University, D. C. Grove of the University of Illinois, E. B. Sisson of the R. S. Peabody Foundation for Archaeology, J. Aufdermauer and H. Walter of the Proyecto Puebla-Tlaxcala Fundación Alemana para la Investigación Científica, M. C. Winter of the University of Arizona, G. Lowe and T. Lee of the New World Archaeological Foundation, and J. Michels of the University of Pennsylvania, for supplying obsidian samples from Formative Period sites. Special thanks go to R. H. Cobean and M. D. Coe, Yale University, for the exchange of obsidian source samples and information on Mesoamerican sources, and finally to K. V. Flannery of the University of Michigan for his encouragement and support of this research.

One of the most frequently studied import-export items has been obsidian. Due to its widespread distribution in archaeological sites and the finite number of geological sources, it can provide clear evidence of prehistoric exchange. Optical spectroscopy (Renfrew, Dixon, and Cann 1966; Cobean, et al. 1971), X-ray fluorescence (Weaver and Stross 1965; Jack and Heizer 1968; Stross, et al. 1968), and neutron activation analysis (Gordus, et al. 1967; Gordus, Wright, and Griffin 1968; Wright 1969) have been successfully utilized to characterize obsidian sources and thus to determine the origin of obsidian artifacts found in archaeological sites in the Near East, Europe, North America, and Mesoamerica. The present study reports the results of neutron activation analysis of some 600 samples from 20 geological sources in Mesoamerica and 422 archaeological samples of Early and Middle Formative (1200–600 B.C.) dates in Mesoamerica.

ANALYTICAL TECHNIQUE

The automated method of Na and Mn neutron activation analysis has previously been described in detail (Gordus, et al. 1967). In brief, twenty-five samples of approximately fifty milligrams each are weighed, sealed in polyethylene tubing and irradiated together with Na and Mn standards for sixteen seconds. They are then placed in an automatic sample changer which is connected to a $2'' \times 2''$ welltype NaI(Tl) scintillation detector as well as to a single channel analyzer. One-minute counts of the Na and Mn activity in each sample are taken every two hours and twenty-five minutes over a period of twenty-four hours and the information is recorded on both teletype printout and punch paper tape. Actual Na and Mn percentages are calculated by comparison to the irradiated standards. Although certain refinements in technique have been made in order to obtain more accurate results (J. T. Meyers, personal communication), sampling and analysis procedures remain quite similar to those previously published.

Selection of Na and Mn as the elements for analysis was made by Gordus, et al. (1967) in accordance with the capabilities of his analytical equipment. Certain criticism has been leveled at the use of Na percentage to differentiate between geological sources. This element, one of the most common on earth, does exhibit considerable variability within any given geological source of obsidian and, among the twenty Mesoamerican sources examined, serves to differentiate only four sources. Clearly, though not so conveniently, a more diagnostic element could have been chosen.

But despite the X-ray fluorescence suggestions (Stross, et al. 1968) that the percentage of Mn varies widely within discrete obsidian

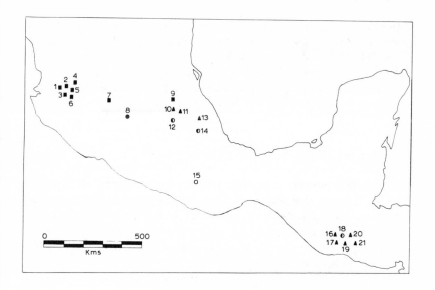

■   Sources not utilized: Early or Middle Formative
●   Primary source : Early Formative
○   Primary source : Early and Middle Formative
○   Primary source : Middle Formative
▲   Secondary source: Middle Formative

Figure 1.   Location of Mesoamerican obsidian sources

Legend
 1. Ixtlán del Río, Nayarit, Mexico.
 2. Magdalena, Jalisco, Mexico.
 3. Teuchitlán, Jalisco, Mexico.
 4. Di Peso Source, Jalisco, Mexico.
 5. Tequila, Jalisco, Mexico.
 6. Santa Teresa Quarry, Jalisco, Mexico.
 7. Penjamo, Guanajuato, Mexico.
 8. Zinapécuaro, Michoacán, Mexico.
 9. Metzquititlán, Hidalgo, Mexico.
10. Cerro de las Navajas, Hidalgo, Mexico (also called Rancho Guadjolote, Las
    Minillas, Cruz del Milagro, El Ocote, and Pachuca).
11. Tulancingo, Hidalgo, Mexico (also called Pizzarín and Rancho Tenango).
12. Barranca de los Estetes, Mexico, D.F., Mexico (also called Otumba, TA-79, Teoti-
    huacán and Malpais).
13. Altotonga, Veracruz, Mexico.
14. Guadalupe Victoria, Puebla, Mexico.
15. Unknown"Oaxacan" source, Oaxaca, Mexico (source known from archaeological
    sites in the Valley of Oaxaca and Nochixtlán. A source is reported to exist in the
    Tlaxiaco-Yolomecatel area.)
16. Aldea Chatalun, Departamento de Chimaltenango, Guatemala.
17. San Bartolomé Milpas Altas, Departamento de Sacatapequez, Guatemala.
18. El Chayal, Departamento de Guatemala, Guatemala.
19. Media Cuesta, Departamento de Santa Rosa, Guatemala.
20. Jalapa, Departamento de Jalapa, Guatemala.
21. Ixtepeque Volcano, Departamento de Jutiapa, Guatemala (also called
    Papalhuapa).

sources, the results obtained through neutron activation analysis indicate the opposite to be the case. Utilizing the improved technique on samples from eleven geological sources, a maximum variation of 0.01 percent at a 0.95 confidence level was found to exist. The percentage of Mn in Mesoamerican obsidian is thus demonstrated to be a most useful element for distinguishing sources.

THE GEOLOGICAL SOURCES

Obsidian is a volcanic glass created by rapid cooling of extrusive volcanic lava. Its distribution is generally restricted to areas of recent vulcanism. Mesoamerican obsidians occur primarily in the east-west neovolcanic chain of central Mexico and in the highlands of Guatemala. Samples collected from twenty of these sources were examined in this study (see Figure 1).

Geological source samples were obtained through field surveys by the author and other members and associates of the University of Michigan Neutron Activation Analysis Laboratory and through the assistance of several individuals and institutions. An attempt was made to obtain a representative series of samples for each source. However, lack of time and funds made this an impossibility and extensive testing of five sources was substituted in order to examine the range of Na and Mn variability within sources. Each of the five sources, Barranca de los Estetes, Cerro de las Navajas, El Chayal, Guadalupe Victoria, and Penjamo, was extensively collected with samples being taken at intervals across the surface exposure of the source. Thirty or more samples from each of these sources were analyzed.

Every geological source and archaeological sample was irradiated and counted a minimum of five times and the final Na and Mn percentage calculations represent an average of the five results. Multiple analyses insure an accuracy of better than ± 2.0 percent at a 0.95 confidence level. The calculated percentages are plotted against each other with the percentage Na scaled from 2.00 to 4.12 along the abscissa and the percentage $Mn \times 10^2$ scaled from 0.00 to 14.40 along the ordinate. The percentage $Mn \pm 10^2$ is utilized in plotting to facilitate visual differentiation between clusters while reducing the plot size to conform with computer format specifications. The plotting parameters represent the observed range of variations in Na and Mn for Mesoamerican obsidian sources. All sources thus analyzed and plotted produced a roughly elliptical cluster of data points.

Definitions of boundaries for each source cluster were standardly calculated. Utilizing a computer-controlled digital plotter a confidence ellipse with a probability level of 0.95 was drawn, based on the

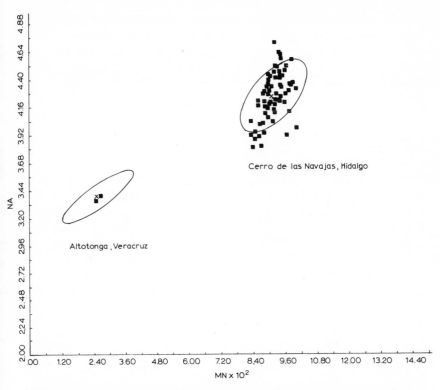

Figure 2. Confidence ellipses drawn at 0.95 probability. For Cerro de las Navajas the ellipse is calculated directly from the data points. For Altotonga the estimate of the ellipse is based in part on the known maximum variation for Na and Mn in Meso-american obsidian sources

distribution of data points for each source containing twenty or more samples (see Figure 2, Cerro de las Navajas). When fewer than twenty samples were available for a source, the ellipse was determined from the degree of inclination and spread of the available points and the known *maximum* variations in Na and Mn content for Mesoamerican obsidians (see Figure 2, Altotonga). While such ellipses are not wholly satisfactory because they tend to cover a larger range of variation than is characteristic of the source, they do provide a plausible basis for defining a source until such time as more samples can be analyzed. Adoption of the 0.95 probability level ellipse provides a standardized definition of source boundaries, elimination of erroneous data points, and an accurate tool for distinguishing between sources. Of the twenty geological sources analyzed, only nine were found to have been utilized during the Early and Middle Formative Periods of Meso-american prehistory. The ellipses for these nine sources are illustrated in Figure 3.

In one instance, the existence of a geological source not sampled

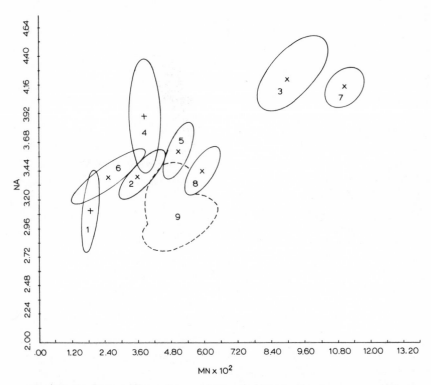

Figure 3. Confidence ellipses drawn at 0.95 probability for the nine sources which were exploited in prehistoric Mesoamerica: 1. Zinapécuaro, Michoacan, 2. Barranca de los Estetes, Mexico, 3. Cerro de las Navajas, Hidalgo, 4. Tulancingo, Hidalgo, 5. Guadalupe Victoria, Puebla, 6. Altotonga, Veracruz, 7. Unknown Oaxacan, 8. El Chayal, Guatemala, and 9. Other Guatemalan, including Aldea Chatalun, Ixtepeque Volcano, Media Cuesta, San Bartolomé Milpas Altas, and Jalapa

in the survey was documented. When all the archaeological samples which could not be assigned to a source were plotted together, one distinctive elliptical cluster was noted. Samples from Early and Middle Formative Period sites in the states of Oaxaca, Puebla, and the Valley of Mexico made up the cluster. The greatest number of samples in the cluster were from sites in the Valley of Oaxaca. In addition, twenty-one samples of uncertain date from the Valley of Nochixtlán, Oaxaca (these samples are not included in the statistics given in this paper), also fall in this cluster. Given the persistent reports of an obsidian source in the Tlaxiaco-Yolomecat area of the Mixteca Alta region, Oaxaca (John Paddock, personal communication), the indication of a small zone of recent volcanic activity on geological maps of the area and the primary concentration of archaeological artifacts from this source in Oaxacan sites, it is tentatively suggested that these samples do indeed represent an unknown Oaxacan source. The probable location of this source is recorded as number 15 in Figure 1.

THE ARCHAEOLOGICAL SAMPLES

Although more than 72,000 Mesoamerican obsidian artifacts have been analyzed by the University of Michigan Laboratory, only 988 of them could be assigned to a dated archaeological context. Among these 988 samples are 255 datable to the Early Formative and 167 from the Middle Formative which provide the data for this paper. The remaining 566 samples dating to the Late and Terminal Formative, Classic, and Postclassic Periods will be considered in a future paper. Approximately 1,150 undated samples will be disregarded, for, while the examination of artifacts of uncertain provenience may be of interest in testing the analytical technique, such results will not contribute to an understanding of prehistoric exchange systems.

Obsidian artifacts were obtained for analysis through the kindness of numerous individuals and institutions. When the total collection of obsidian from a site was available for analysis, an unbiased selection of samples for each provenience unit was made by mixing the obsidians in a bag and blindly selecting those which would be sampled for analysis. No attempt was made to visually select samples according to color variation in the obsidian in order to avoid a bias in the statistics. Occasionally, selection of the artifacts to be analyzed was made by the excavator; this has perhaps introduced bias into the results.

Archaeological samples were analyzed and plotted as outlined above. Transparent overlays on which the source ellipses had been drawn to the standard plot scale were used to determine the source origin of archaeological samples. Those artifacts which did not fall within the area of any source ellipse were recorded as indeterminate and set aside for re-analysis. Where two ellipses overlapped a cluster of archaeological data points, as for example the Barranca de los Estetes and Tulancingo ellipses, it was found that the samples would generally be distributed throughout the entire area of one or the other ellipse. Seventy-five samples from the site of Moyotzingo, Puebla, were densely packed within the Barranca de los Estetes ellipse including the Tulancingo overlap zone, but not one sample fell in any other part of the Tulancingo ellipse. Though obviously we cannot be 95 percent confident of the ascription, in such cases all samples were recorded as having come from the one ellipse which was completely filled. Where the sample size was too small or the distribution of points indicated that both sources were being utilized, samples falling in the overlap zone were recorded as being from either one source or the other. Table 1 lists by time period, state, site and source results of the 422 analyses. In Table 2, the sites are grouped by geographic area, and the percentage of obsidian from each source is calculated.

Table 1. Early and Middle Formative Mesoamerican obsidian samples analyzed by the University of Michigan Neutron Activation Analysis Laboratory listed by time period, state and region, site, and obsidian source origin

Period	State and Region	Site	Zinapécuaro, Michoacan	Barranca de los Esteres, Mexico	Cerro de las Navajas, Hidalgo	Tulancingo, Hidalgo	Guadalupe Victoria, Puebla	Altotonga, Veracruz	Unknown Oaxacan	El Chayal, Guatemala	Other Guatemalan	Indeterminate to be re-analyzed	Total sample size
Early Formative	CHIAPAS	Altamira								7			7
		Angostura el Carmen								2			2
	MORELOS	San Pablo		42					2		2	4	50
	OAXACA	Huitzo								1			1
		San José Mogote	14	19			5	2	1	1	2		44
		Tierras Largas	8	20			26	6	6				66
	PUEBLA	Las Bocas		7									7
	TABASCO	Campo Nuevo					49			2	1		52
		Gamas					3						3
		Nerio Hernandes					7						7
		Rancho Guadalupe					10			3	1		14
	VALLEY OF MEXICO	Tlapacoya		2									2
		Sub-Total											255
Middle Formative	MORELOS	Cerro Chacaltepec		3							2		5
	OAXACA	Huitzo		1	1	3							5
		Tierras Largas	4	8	1	1	7		8		2		31
	PUEBLA	Acatepec		9				1	1			1	12
		Moyotzingo		75								17	92
	VALLEY OF MEXICO	El Arbolillo	1	7	2	1			1		1		13
		Zacatenco		3		1			2		3		9
		Sub-Total											167
		TOTAL											422

Table 2. Early and Middle Formative obsidian sample percentages listed by time period, state and region, and obsidian source origin

Archaeological period and geographical region	1. Zinapécuaro, Michoacan	2. Barranca de los Estetes, Mexico	3. Cerro de las Navajas, Hidalgo	4. Tulancingo, Hidalgo	5. Guadalupe Victoria, Puebla	6. Altotonga, Veracruz	7. Unknown Oaxacan	8. El Chayal, Guatemala	9. Other Guatemalan
	%	%	%	%	%	%	%	%	%
Early Formative									
Chiapas								100.00	
Morelos		90.70				4.65	4.64		
Oaxaca	20.60	36.50			28.50	8.40	2.00	2.00	2.00
Puebla		100.00							
Tabasco					90.80			6.60	2.60
Valley of Mexico		100.00							
Veracruz[a]		4.82	4.82[b]		62.64			21.70	6.02
Middle Formative									
Morelos	14.30	85.70							
Oaxaca	11.10	25.00	2.80	11.10	19.50	2.80	22.20		5.50
Puebla		79.60	1.20				1.20		
Valley of Mexico	4.50	45.40	9.10	9.10			13.70		18.20
Veracruz[ac]		26.32	5.26		10.53	5.26		31.58	5.26

Calculated from the analyses of Cobean, et al. (1971 and personal communication) eliminating all obsidians attributed to possible or probable source origins and to unknown obsidian source groups. The possibility that these samples are intrusive from more recent levels should be considered. Add 15.79% from the Gueretaro obsidian source.

DEFINITION OF PREHISTORIC OBSIDIAN EXCHANGE NETWORKS

One of the most interesting uses of prehistoric obsidian exchange data is Renfrew, Dixon, and Cann's linear regression analysis (1968) of the relationship between quantity traded and distance to the source. Utilizing optical spectroscopic analysis, they identified twelve Neolithic villages in the Near East whose obsidian came from the Çiftlik flow in central Turkey. The percentage of obsidian or locally available flint and chert in the lithic inventory was recorded and the distance to Çiftlik from each site was calculated. This was then recorded on log-normal graph paper, with percent of obsidian on the logarithmic (Y) axis and distances from sources on the arithmetic (X) axis. A linear regression line relating distance from source to percentage of obsidian was plotted.

The figures suggest that somewhat more obsidian was moving (and over greater distances) in the Neolithic Near East than in Formative Mesoamerica. Within 100 to 300 kilometers of Çiftlik, most chipped stone found at Neolithic sites is obsidian: at least 80 percent, as against 20 percent flint or chert. Outside this "supply zone," the proportion of obsidian falls off exponentially with distance. At Tabbat al-Hammam, 400 kilometers away, the percentage of obsidian is down to 5 percent; at Beidha, almost 900 kilometers away, the percentage is only 0.1 percent. In another paper, the authors suggest such a pattern would result if, for example, "villages were spaced at 90 kilometers apart, and . . . each village would pass to its neighbors down the line one half of the total it received " (Renfrew, Dixon, and Cann 1968: 329). Of course, there are many more villages than that, and a good deal of variation to either side of the regression line; but the model – percentage of obsidian is a function of (1) reciprocal exchange and (2) distance to the source – is useful.

The model works for the Neolithic East because (1) there we are dealing with reciprocal exchange, and (2) because there are sources only in the north, so the percentage of obsidian decreases as one moves south. In Formative Mesoamerica, however, the situation becomes more complicated because (1) obsidian appears to have been exchanged both under conditions of reciprocity and redistribution, and because (2) the obsidian sources form a mosaic pattern.

Consideration of the first variable, social organization, on the distribution of obsidian in Formative Mesoamerica necessitates examination of exchange under conditions of reciprocity and redistribution. Rappaport's study (1967) of the Maring of New Guinea illustrates the mechanisms of exchange under conditions of reciprocity. Trade among the Maring is effected through direct exchanges between individuals on a reciprocal basis, and each trader or local group acts as one link in a "chain-like " structure (Rappaport 1967: 106–107). The producers and consumers of a particular commodity may be separated from each other by so many links that they are unknown to each other, just as the village of Beidha probably had no knowledge of the Çiftlik obsidian source, and the village of Tierras Largas no knowledge of the Barranca de los Estetes source (see below). In such a situation, the material passes from kinsman to kinsman, or from valley to valley, through "trade partnerships " established by fictional kin ties. These ties are necessary because, as Sahlins (1972) points out, at a prestate level people generally do not like to trade with (and do not deal fairly with) non-relatives. As yet, however, we do not have convincing ways of demonstrating trade partnerships archaeologically.

In the Maring system, the two main locally produced exchange items are salt (from saline springs in the Simbai Valley) and stone axes (from quarries in the Jimi Valley). Both are "subsistence" items in the sense that they relate to eating on the one hand and felling trees for agriculture on the other. They are, however, circulated in the same "sphere of conveyance" (Bohannan, quoted in Rappaport, 1967: 106) with "non-utilitarian" goods such as ornamental feathers (from bird-of-paradise, parrot, and eagle), shells, and animal furs (used to decorate shields, headbands, and loincloths). The ascription of "non-utilitarian" status is questionable because these items are used as bridewealth by the Maring and hence are of great economic importance.

Bird-of-paradise plumes and fur enter the Simbai Valley from the north. The locals keep some, and trade some south to the Jimi Valley, along with Simbai Valley salt. Shells of three types (gold-lip, sea-snail, and cowrie) enter the Jimi Valley from the south. The locals keep some, and trade the rest north to the Simbai Valley, along with Jimi Valley axes.

Such a chain-like reciprocal exchange structure, as Rappaport points out, has a number of weaknesses. First, the number of axes produced by the Jimi quarries is a function not of the demand for axes but of the Jimi Valley's need for salt. And if the Simbai Valley people have an adequate supply of axes, they may simply say, "we don't want any more," whereupon the Jimi Valley suffers a salt shortage. So many links separate the quarries from the salt springs that the Jimi axe makers cannot shame, cajole, or wheedle the Simbai salt makers into making more salt. Second, trade in "subsistence" items is related to population density anyhow; if population in the Jimi Valley drops, it will need less salt and the Simbai will probably be left with an axe shortage. Thus, "it may be questioned whether a direct exchange apparatus that moves only two or three items critical to subsistence would be viable" (Bohannan, quoted in Rappaport 1967: 106).

For these weaknesses, Rappaport (1967: 106) offers a tentative solution: "It may be suggested that the inclusion of both the non-utilitarian valuables and utilitarian goods within a single 'sphere of conveyance'. . . stimulated the production and facilitated the distribution of the utilitarian goods." Bird-of-paradise plumes fade, fur perishes, and the pressure for spectacular generosity in bridewealth is so great that demand for these items is constant, and they "could be freely exchanged for stone axes and native salt" (1967: 106). Thus, so-called "non-utilitarian" or "exotic" exchange might act as a systematic regulator which keeps trade in subsistence products going even when the balance of trade or demographic stability is in doubt. If this is the case, it may be no accident that, in the case of Formative Mesoamerica, such exotic items as magnetite mirrors moved north from Oaxaca through the Valleys of Nochixtlán and Morelos, along the same chain-link route through which Barranca de los Estetes obsidian blades probably moved south.

In a reciprocal economy where individual households negotiated for their own obsidian, we would expect a great deal of variability between households, both in the sources used and the proportions of obsidian from various sources. The source for this variability would be differences from one household or kin group to another in terms of their trade partnerships or contacts in areas nearer the sources. This kind of variability is what the data for Early Formative obsidian flakes and chunks seem to show.

As Rappaport points out, such systematic regulators are needed because of the unsophisticated nature of reciprocal exchange and of "chain-like" structures. In redistributive economies, where trade is co-ordinated by a chief or some managerial agency, "supralocal authorities may demand production and enforce deliveries" (Rappaport 1967: 108). In this case, exchange might continue even with demographic shifts in chain-like systems. "They might even work in 'reciprocal systems' in which the parties to the transactions are groups in which production might be commanded by a local authority who might, conceivably, take into consideration the requirements of other groups" (1967: 108).

In redistributive economies, materials coming into a valley might be "pooled" by some administrative authority – either a paramount chief at the largest village, or a "headman" or high-status family at smaller villages. He might then redistribute the material to his kinsmen or followers according to their needs and the amount of pressure they are able to put on him. In the case of obsidian in Formative Mesoamerica, the introduction of prismatic blades imported from the Barranca de los Estetes and Zinapécuaro source areas beginning around 1000 B.C. is associated with a reduction of variation in source usage by households suggesting that some form of pooling, probably precipitated by the demand for prismatic blades, was being practiced. For the Early Formative evidence of such pooling comes only from the largest sites, but by the Middle Formative it has spread even to small hamlets.

Further, if the redistribution of "subsistence" items were based on chiefly power, we would expect the authorities to "demand production and enforce deliveries" as Rappaport suggests. In this case, the exchange system would not need the "exotic" or "non-utilitarian" items as regulators. One would expect long-distance trade in exotic ores, shells, and plumes to diminish, except insofar as the elite needed these to enhance their status. The administration of a highly developed chiefly redistributive system should have been able to demand levels of production which would make it possible to derive most "utilitarian" items from within their sphere of influence or negotiate for them with the elites of other regions. One would therefore expect *more regionalization and less long-distance trade in exotica on the level of the individual household.*

While some Mesoamerican Formative societies were egalitarian, others were complex chiefdoms or emergent chiefdoms with redistributive economies (Flannery 1968). Whereas in egalitarian society most goods are equally available to all members of the community, at the chiefdom level some goods are amassed by paramount chiefs for redistribution according to a hereditarily defined rank order (Service 1962; Sahlins 1972). The position of chief is an institutionalized office conferred by birth order within the ruling lineage, and often associated with the concept of divine descent from the gods. This exclusive chief-god relationship serves to legitimize the right of chiefly stewardship over the land, its people, and their produce. But concomitant with the chiefly right to demand community support and tribute is chiefly responsibility for accumulation, storage, and redistribution of the produce. Negligence of these responsibilities may lead to the overthrow of a chief. Exclusive control over the exploitation and distribution of rare resources, insured by the power of chiefly taboo, further underwrites the position of the paramount chief in relation to his followers. Transformation of such rare resources into luxury goods is usually accomplished by craft specialists attached to the chiefly household, and their products, together with the raw material itself, provide the paramount with a basis for negotiating exchange with other chiefs. Such exchanges lead to the acquisition of both utilitarian and exotic sumptuary goods which again are used to reinforce and legitimize chiefly status and power. Abstractly then, a chiefdom can be pictured as a sphere where lines of redistribution radiate out from the central paramount according to social rank order to integrate dependent centers. Two or more such spheres may be linked together in an exchange network as a result of exchange between the respective paramounts. In Formative Mesoamerica, magnetite mirrors and possibly obsidian blades may have been so traded.

Archaeologically it is a difficult matter to identify chiefdoms. The La Venta basalt-column tomb containing the skeletons of two children accompanied by numerous sumptuary goods is often cited (Flannery 1968) as evidence of ascribed status and, thus, of ranked society. Both the Valleys of Mexico and Oaxaca have also produced infant burials with sumptuary goods, although not on the scale of the La Venta discovery. Such evidence of hereditary ranking is diagnostic of chiefdoms, but since many chiefdoms have a redistributive economy, we can look also for differences in artifact distributions in chiefdoms. The

Table 3. Summary of Early and Middle Formative Period obsidian versus flint data available **f** testing the Renfrew trade model in Mesoamerica

	Distance in kilometers to primary source	% Total obsidian from all sources versus flint	% Barranca de los Estetes obsidian in total obsidian	% Barranca de los Estetes obsidian versus flint	References
Middle Formative sites					
El Arbolillo I-II	30 (1)	80.20	53.84*	43.31	Vaillant 1935
Zacatenco	30 (1)	86.60	30.00*	28.90	Vaillant 1935
Las Canoas	100 (1?)	50.00	100.00?	50.00	Flannery 1964
Cerro Chacaltepec	135 (1)	?	60.00*	±56.00	Grove 1970
Huitzo	230 (3)	15.00	20.00*	3.00	Pires-Ferreira 1973
Tierras Largas	400 (1) ±60 (4)	16.00	25.80	4.10	Pires-Ferreira 1973
Early Formative sites					
Tlapacoya	40 (1)	?	100.00*	?	Tolstoy & Paradis 197
Gualupita	90 (1)	57.60	100.00?	57.60?	Vaillant 1935
Las Bocas	120 (1)	?	100.00*	?	
San Pablo	130 (1)	?	90.70	±80.00	Grove 1970
Tierras Largas	245 (2)	15.00	30.30	5.00	Pires-Ferreira 1973
San José Mogote	390 (1)	18.50	43.18	6.80	Pires-Ferreira 1973

Primary sources: 1. Barranca de los Estetes
2. Guadalupe Victoria
3. Tulancingo
4. Unknown Oaxacan
* This percentage is based on a small number of analyzed samples

Renfrew-Dixon-Cann model has provided one way of documenting egalitarian society through analysis of the distribution of obsidian. Although it is difficult, due to lack of data, to test the Formative Mesoamerican data in the same way, in one case a reversed regression line is suggested. If it is indeed shown to be the case that San Lorenzo had more Guadalupe Victoria obsidian than other sites closer to the source, a correlation between a reversed regression line and redistribution may be suggested.

Turning to the second variable in the Renfrew-Dixon-Cann model, the mosaic distribution of obsidian sources in Mesoamerica complicates verification of "percentage of obsidian is a function of distance to source." As one moves south, away from the Valley of Mexico sources, one comes gradually closer to the Guatemalan sources. Moreover, there are some coastal areas – such as, for example, the Ocos region of Guatemala (Coe and Flannery 1967) – where there is no available chert source, and thus 100 percent of the chipped stone is traded obsidian in any case. In order to obtain figures truly comparable to Renfrew's, we would have to calculate the percentage of obsidian from one specific source within the total chipped stone industry at many different sites in areas where flint is an available alternative; however, no one has yet had the money or patience necessary to effect neutron activation on sufficient samples. All these problems, coupled with the fact that most excavators have not published the percentage of obsidian in their total chipped stone assemblage, make application of the Renfrew-Dixon-Cann model difficult, if not impossible, in Mesoamerica at present.

The few figures we have, however, suggest that it might be applicable if sufficient data were available. For example in Table 3, we give the percentage of obsidian from all sources versus flint, and the distance in kilometers to the nearest *primary* obsidian source known to have been used by each site. Data on the percentage of obsidian versus flint is inadequate for the Early Formative. For the Middle Formative, the sites of El Arbolillo and Zacatenco, only thirty kilometers from the source, have obsidian percentages of 80 percent and 86 percent relative to "quartz." Las Canoas, at approximately 100 kilometers distance, has 50 percent obsidian to flint, while Huitzo and Tierras Largas, at about 240 kilometers, have 15 percent and 16 percent respectively. These figures seem sufficient basis to suggest that Mesoamerica may also have "supply areas" within which the obsidian percentage is close to 80 percent, and beyond which the proportion drops exponentially with distance.

Some problems in constructing Table 3 should be pointed out. In order to provide a point of reference, columns three and four providing data on the percentage of Barranca de los Estetes obsidian in relation to the total obsidian and to the flint fraction have been calculated. At least limited neutron activation analysis results are available for all but two other sites, Gualupita, and Las Canoas. In both cases the early appearance of obsidian prismatic blades, a phenomenon directly associated with the utilization of Barranca de los Estetes obsidian (see below), suggests that Barranca de los Estetes was the primary source.

Because of the mosaic pattern of obsidian source location in Mesoamerica, the major concern in analysis of the Formative Period exchange systems becomes how much obsidian from each source relative to all other sources was moving in what direction and at what time.

In order to determine the areas of Mesoamerica which utilized each obsidian source and to suggest some of the sites in the network of exchange for each source, a series of Q-type, sample-to-sample correlation matrices were calculated utilizing the raw data counts presented in Table 1. (The University of Michigan Statistical Research Laboratory Midas statistical package was used in calculation of the matrices.) Each separate geological source observation was computed against the archaeological site variables, and cells of high correlation, defining the degree of participation in the exchange sphere for the source under consideration, were noted. Subsequently the archaeological site data were grouped according to geographical area (as in Table 2) and matrices including all the obsidian source observations were calculated. The composition of exchange networks determined by the grouped data matrix (see Figures 4a-b and 5a-b) matches exactly the composition of the spheres which had been previously determined through the individual source/archaeological site matrices.

Definition of obsidian exchange networks through correlation matrix analysis is only as accurate as the data is complete. Where large samples from the major excavated sites for a given time period are available (as, for example, in the case of Early Formative Morelos, Oaxaca, Tabasco, and Veracruz), we can be certain that an outline of the major exchange linkages within a network is accurately identified, although the exact boundaries of the network cannot be known. Where the data are incomplete due to insufficient sample size or the lack of archaeological work in a given area, correlation matrix analysis will not produce results. Three cases in the Early and Middle Formative data involve the utilization within a sphere of significant quantities of obsidian from sources located in archaeologically unknown or unrepresented regions. These cases suggest either: (1) direct exploitation of the obsidian controlled by the sphere; or (2) the presence of undiscovered archaeological sites in the area of the source which constitute a second sphere in an exchange network. Although distance between the sites and sources in question relates directly to the possibility of direct exploitation, provisional definition of an exchange network can be made based on the relative importance of the source within the sphere where it is represented. Where obsidian from a given source amounts to more than 20 percent of the total obsidian supply for a given site, some degree of regularity in the supply, possibly involving an exchange network, is suggested. On a provisional basis, the 20 percent minimum is utilized in hypothesizing exchange network linkages between sites and archaeologically unrepresented source areas.

The Early Formative: Obsidian Exchange Networks Linking Villages

Four obsidian exchange networks have been identified for the Early Formative (see Figures 4a and 4b). San Lorenzo is involved in only two of these networks: the Guadalupe Victoria source network and the El Chayal source network. The two other networks, based on the Barranca de los Estetes and Zinapécuaro sources respectively, are

Correlations

7 observations = obsidian sources

Variable	Valley of Mexico	Puebla	Morelos	Oaxaca	Tabasco	Veracruz	Chiapas
Valley of Mexico	1.0000						
Puebla	1.0000	1.0000					
Morelos	0.9982	0.9982	1.0000				
Oaxaca	0.6789	0.6789	0.6616	1.0000			
Tabasco	−0.1862	−0.1862	−0.2069	0.4173	1.0000		
Veracruz	−0.1686	−0.1686	−0.1963	0.3445	0.9633	1.0000	
Chiapas	−0.1667	−0.1667	−0.1851	−0.3804	−0.1005	0.1554	1.0000

"Barranca de los Estetes exchange network"

"Guadalupe Victoria exchange network"

* = Local exchange sphere.

Figure 4a. Q-type correlation matrix for Early Formative obsidian samples

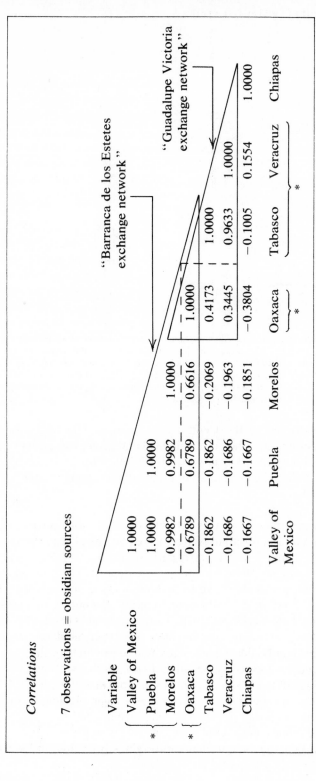

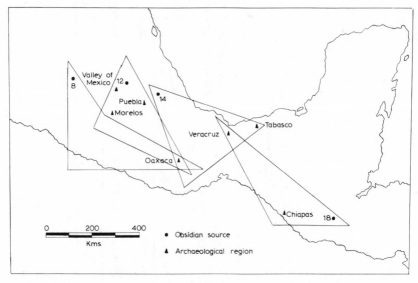

Figure 4b. Early Formative obsidian exchange systems as determined through correlation matrix analysis. The large triangles enclose the sites and sources linked by exchange systems and do not represent actual geographical boundaries. The sites which make up each archaeological region are listed in Table 1. The obsidian sources on which the exchange systems were based are: 8 = Zinapécuaro, 12 = Barranca de los Estetes, 14 = Guadalupe Victoria, and 18 = El Chayal

virtually restricted to the Central and Oaxacan Highlands. In the following paragraphs, the archaeological and geological evidence for each of the four networks, as well as the implications of this evidence for understanding the mechanics of prehistoric exchange systems, will be examined.

THE GUADALUPE VICTORIA EXCHANGE NETWORK. The Guadalupe Victoria obsidian source is located adjacent to the village of the same name in the eastern part of the state of Puebla. It is characterized by an extensive, stream-laid deposit of weathered obsidian boulders, which may have eroded out of associated ash deposits. No obsidian flows or deposits were found by the author in a survey of the immediate region in 1970. Cobean, et al. (1971) and J. L. Lorenzo (personal communication) have suggested that the Guadalupe Victoria obsidian boulders may be extrusive products of the Pico de Orizaba, which is located immediately to the southeast. Whatever the ultimate origin of the obsidian, analysis of more than 100 samples from across the entire deposit characterizes it as a single and unique source.

Guadalupe Victoria obsidian ranges from semi-transparent to banded and cloudy gray with abundant white inclusions. It is quite brittle, and experimental attempts to produce prismatic blades from

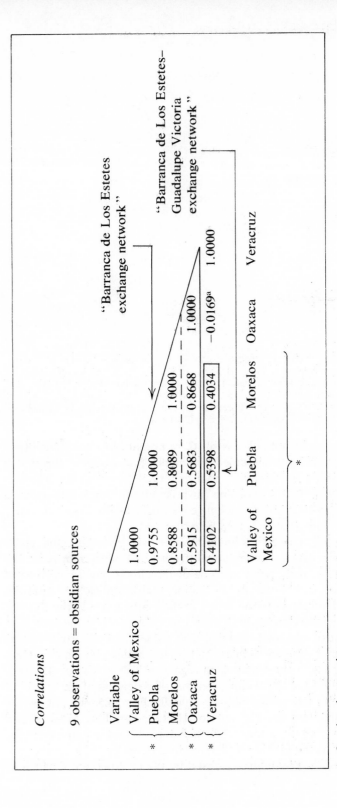

Correlations

9 observations = obsidian sources

Variable	Valley of Mexico	Puebla	Morelos	Oaxaca	Veracruz
Valley of Mexico	1.0000				
Puebla	0.9755	1.0000			
Morelos	0.8588	0.8089	1.0000		
Oaxaca	0.5915	0.5683	0.8668	1.0000	
Veracruz	0.4102	0.5398	0.4034	−0.0169[a]	1.0000

"Barranca de Los Estetes exchange network"

"Barranca de Los Estetes–Guadalupe Victoria exchange network"

* = Local exchange sphere.

[a] – Note the change from 0.3445 in the Early Formative indicating a realignment in obsidian exchange networks which isolated Oaxaca from Veracruz.

Figure 5a. Q-type correlation matrix for Middle Formative obsidian samples

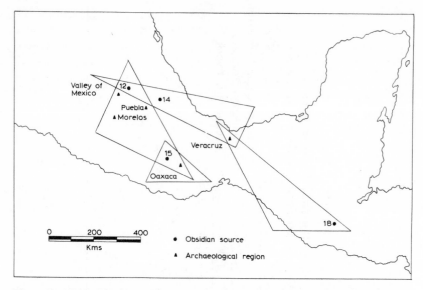

Figure 5b. Middle Formative obsidian exchange systems as determined through correlation matrix analysis. The large triangles enclose the sites and sources linked by
exchange systems and do not represent actual geographical boundaries. The sites which
make up each archaeological region are listed in Table 1. The obsidian source on which
the exchange systems were based are: 12 = Barranca de los Estetes, 14 = Guadalupe
Victoria, 15 = Unknown Oaxacan, and 18 = El Chayal

the boulders were not successful. Core preparation was difficult, as
the flakes consistently assumed anomalous and irregular forms due
to the inclusions and generally poor quality of this obsidian. The fact
that this source was a poor one for prismatic blades is important in
understanding the shifts in exchange networks beginning in the Early
Formative about 1000 B.C. (see below).

    No Early Formative sites have so far been discovered in the region
of Guadalupe Victoria. Our sample from Las Bocas, approximately
100 kilometers to the west and one of the closest known early sites
to the source, contained no Guadalupe Victoria obsidian. Approximately 300 kilometers to the south, at the major Early Formative site
of San Lorenzo, Guadalupe Victoria was found to be the source of
62.2 percent of the total obsidian (see Table 2). At the four smaller
sites of Campo Nuevo, Gamas, Nerio Hernandez and Rancho Guadalupe, located in the Chontalapa region of Tabasco some 450 kilometers southeast of Guadalupe Victoria, 90.8 percent of the obsidians
sampled came from that source. And finally, 36.5 percent of the
obsidian examined for the sites of Huitzo, San José Mogote, and
Tierras Largas in the Valley of Oaxaca were found to come from the
approximately 200-kilometer-distant Guadalupe Victoria source.

    An interesting possibility is raised by the 62.2 percent Guadalupe

Victoria obsidian at San Lorenzo and the 90.8 percent frequencies at the four small Chontalapa sites. If we assume that these small hamlets were dependencies of larger ceremonial and administrative centers like San Lorenzo or La Venta, it may be that obsidian was channeled to them by the larger centers. In this case, it would appear that San Lorenzo was holding on to larger amounts of the higher-quality El Chayal obsidian (which is suitable for blade manufacture) and passing on larger amounts of the lower-quality Guadalupe Victoria obsidian to dependent hamlets. This possibility could be checked by analysis of the distribution of obsidian on house floors (see below).

THE EL CHAYAL EXCHANGE NETWORK. Of the Early Formative San Lorenzo obsidian samples, 21.7 percent were found to have come from the El Chayal source in Guatemala, some 580 kilometers to the southwest (see Table 2). This source, located in the Central Highlands near Guatemala City, is noted for its extensive deposits of high-quality grey obsidian and associated prehistoric workshop areas (Coe and Flannery 1964). Early Formative sites are known from nearby highland areas and Shook and Proskouriakoff (1956: 96) report Middle Formative (Las Charcas phase) obsidian workshops from Kaminaljuyu, approximately thirty-five kilometers southwest of El Chayal. Unfortunately, however, no analysis of obsidian from Formative Guatemalan sites is available, and the routes of exchange through which San Lorenzo obtained El Chayal obsidian are not known.

Grove (1974) has suggested a Pacific coastal exchange route for the El Chayal obsidian. In fact, the presence of only El Chayal obsidian at the Ocós period sites of Altamira and Angostura el Carmen (see Table 1) suggests that this source may have been the only supply of obsidian serving the abundant Early Formative sites of the Guatemalan and Chiapas estuary systems. These sites frequently contain 100 percent obsidian lithic industries, a reflection of the total absence of flint sources in the Pacific Coastal Plain. It is possible that these coastal sites were linked to other sites in the movement of El Chayal obsidian and local marine and estuary shells towards the isthmus of Tehuantepec and the Gulf Coast area. For the period prior to 1200 B.C. there is little evidence of direct contact between the two areas. Coe (personal communication) notes that the Ojochi and Bajio phases at San Lorenzo look like "country cousins" of the Ocós sites on the Pacific Coast. For the 1200 to 850 B.C. period, there is even less evidence to suggest a coastal contact route between the two areas, but the hypothesis must be considered.

A second possible conformation of the El Chayal exchange network may involve the direct movement of obsidian northward along the major rivers to the coastal area. Although the recent work of Hammond (1972) suggests this route may have been in use as early as the Middle Formative Period, no Early Formative sites have ever been reported for the area. Evaluation of this hypothesis must await further fieldwork and analysis.

Secondary distribution of El Chayal obsidian after it reached San Lorenzo is of interest because it follows the linkages of the Guadalupe Victoria exchange network. El Chayal obsidian represents 5.6 percent of the total at the small Tabasco sites and 2.0 percent of the total in Oaxaca. No El Chayal obsidian has been identified from any site located outside the linkages of the Guadalupe Victoria and El Chayal exchange networks.

THE BARRANCA DE LOS ESTETES EXCHANGE NETWORK. The Barranca de los Estetes obsidian flows are located in the Teotihuacán Valley, near the village of Otumba in the state of Mexico. These deposits, in an area locally referred to as Malpais, are extensive and contain a highly silicified grey obsidian of uniform quality. Experimental knapping with Barranca de los Estetes obsidian shows that its flaking properties are ideally suited for controlled-pressure flaking and blade production. The distribution of Barranca de los Estetes obsidian during the Early Formative is densest in the Central Highlands region of Mexico. Although no Early Formative Period sites have been reported from the Teotihuacán Valley, they are numerous elsewhere in the Valley of Mexico, and David Grove (1972) has recently suggested that re-analysis of the ceramics from W. T. Sanders' survey of the Teotihuacán Valley will reveal the presence of Early Formative pottery.

When the percentage of Barranca de los Estetes obsidian in the total obsidian sample (setting aside the percentage of flint) is calculated, it suggests a "supply zone" extending up to 130 kilometers from the source and including the sites of Tlapacoya (with 100 percent Barranca de los Estetes obsidian), Las Bocas (with 100 percent Barranca de los Estetes obsidian), and San Pablo (with 90.7 percent Barranca de los Estetes obsidian). Beyond the "supply zone," Early Formative sites in the Valley of Oaxaca, approximately 375 kilometers to the south, contained 36.5 percent Barranca de los Estetes obsidian. Similar proportions of Barranca de los Estetes obsidian in the Central Highlands continue during the Middle Formative and indeed are characteristic of all periods except, perhaps, the Aztec (unpublished data). The reason for this almost unique homogeneity in obsidian exploitation patterns during Central Highlands prehistory lies in the fact that it is an obsidian rich area; abundant supplies of high-quality obsidian were locally available for use and export.

Direct exchange between the Central Highland and Oaxaca spheres is indicated by the presence of 36.5 percent Barranca de los Estetes obsidian found in the Early Formative Oaxacan samples. Barranca de los Estetes obsidian was also found at San Lorenzo, but comprised only 4.8 percent of the total obsidian industry. A −0.17 average correlation between San Lorenzo is therefore probably best understood as a product obtained through the established Guadalupe Victoria exchange linkages with Oaxaca. The position of Oaxaca as a critical point of overlap between the Central Highland-Barranca de los Estetes and the Gulf Coast-Guadalupe Victoria exchange networks suggests that it may have played a pivotal role in the transmission of some Gulf Coast materials to the Central Highlands.

Increasing shipment of Barranca de los Estetes obsidian to distant regions in subsequent periods reflects the increasing demand for prismatic blades. The earliest evidence of manufacture of obsidian blades comes from the Valley of Mexico where they were found in association with the Iztapan mammoth (Ayeleyra, et al. 1952). In Morelos, Oaxaca, and along the Gulf Coast the earliest blades date to about 1000 B.C. and are made of Barranca de los Estetes obsidian. The rare blade cores found at these sites were insufficient in size and number to have produced the quantities of blades which were recovered. This permits the hypothesis that much of the Barranca de los Estetes obsidian was exported from the Central Highlands in the form of finished blades. Certainly this was the case in later periods; MacNeish (personal communication) reports finding obsidian blades wrapped in bark cloth, presumably to prevent breakage during transportation, in one Tehuacán cave.

THE ZINAPÉCUARO EXCHANGE NETWORK. The Zinapécuaro obsidian flows, located in the state of Michoacán, produce a cloudy gray obsidian of high quality. The area surrounding the source is archaeologically unknown, so that the network through which Oaxaca obtained 20.2 percent of its total obsidian supply from this source (located at a distance of approximately 530 kilometers) cannot be determined. The only other piece of Zinapécuaro obsidian identified from the sites considered in this paper is one artifact from mixed levels at the site of San Pablo, Morelos (not included in the statistics). Considering Grove's suggestion (1974) that the Central Highland "Tlatilco culture" contains "West Mexican influences," it is surprising that more Zinapécuaro obsidian was not found there, but the explanation may lie in the readily available Barranca de los Estetes source. It is suggested by this author that the absence of Zinapécuaro obsidian at San Lorenzo may be an analytical anomaly. (See Table 4 for a comparison of the results of duplicate samples analyzed by Cobean at Yale and the University of Michigan Neutron Activation

Table 4. Comparative results of eight archaeological samples from Tierras Largas, Oaxaca, analyzed by optical emission spectroscopy (Yale University) and neutron activation analysis (University of Michigan)

Samples	Sample number	Analysis of Yale University (Cobean, et al.)	Analysis of the University of Michigan laboratory
1. Tierras Largas B74C/feature 151/depth 75–95/N Small unused flake	OB–3861	Guadalupe Victoria, Puebla	Guadalupe Victoria, Puebla
2. Tierras Largas B74B/feature 152/depth 90–120 small unused flake	OB–3862	Guadalupe Victoria, Puebla	Guadalupe Victoria, Puebla
3. Tierras Largas B74B/feature 116/depth 100 small unused flake	OB–3863	Guadalupe Victoria, Puebla	Guadalupe Victoria, Puebla
4. Tierras Largas B74B/feature 130/depth 70–90/W blade fragment	OB–3864	possibly El Parariso, Queteraro	Zinapécuaro, Michoacán
5. Tierras Largas B74/square 3796/feature 112/depth 50–90 blade fragment	OB–3865	possibly El Parariso, Queteraro	Barranca de los Estetes, Mexico
6. Tierras Largas B74A/house 1/square C13 small unused flake	OB–3866	probably Barranca de los Estetes, Mexico	Zinapécuaro, Michoacán
7. Tierras Largas B74A/house 1/square E15 small unused flake	OB–3867	unknown source	Barranca de los Estetes, Mexico
8. Tierras Largas B74A/house 1/square D14 blade fragment	OB–3868	possibly El Parariso, Queteraro	Zinapécuaro, Michoacán

Analysis Laboratory.) A suggestion of the possible importance of the Zinapécuaro source areas as a second center of prismatic blade manufacture and export is seen in the equal proportions of Barranca de los Estetes and Zinapécuaro prismatic blades in Oaxaca.

The Middle Formative: Obsidian Exchange Networks Linking Villages

The partial destruction of San Lorenzo around 900 B.C. (Coe 1968) marks the beginning of the Middle Formative Period. This destruction, followed by the rise of La Venta, is probably the first of a cycle of such political readjustments which characterize the Formative Periods. The effects of political realignment after this event were felt throughout Mesoamerica. Some of the existing obsidian exchange networks broke down, others were modified, and new ones were established as new villages rose to prominence. The "pan-Mesoamerican" aspect of the Early Formative long-distance exchange patterns disappeared; the frequency and intensity of long-distance exchange were reduced; and a period of increasing insularity and regionalization followed. Perhaps paradoxically, this regionalization took place during a period of great political evolution in the highland regions of Mexico.

For example, despite the premier position of La Venta as the dominant center succeeding San Lorenzo (a position reflected in amassed luxury items), La Venta remains a regional site. The excavators have suggested that the bulk of the raw material found at La Venta was probably obtained within 100 miles of the site (Heizer 1961). A similar trend towards regionalization is noted for Middle Formative sites in the Valley of Mexico (Tolstoy and Paradis 1970), Morelos (Grove 1970), and the Valley of Oaxaca (Winter 1973). Four obsidian exchange spheres have been identified for this period (Figures 5a and 5b).

THE GUADALUPE VICTORIA-BARRANCA DE LOS ESTETES EXCHANGE NETWORK. The most significant modification of exchange network patterns from the Early Formative to the Middle Formative Periods centers on the breakdown and realignment of the Early Formative Guadalupe Victoria exchange system. The dissolution of traditional exchange ties between the San Lorenzo site and La Venta is accompanied by the rise of the latter to political dominance. The San Lorenzo-Oaxaca Q-type matrix correlation drops from the Early Formative +0.38 average to a −0.01 average during the Middle Formative, clearly indicating the dissolution of ties between these spheres. Unfortunately, obsidian percentage data for the major Gulf Coast site of this period, La Venta, are not available.[1] We can only guess what its role in the Middle Formative obsidian exchange networks might have been.

The second important change in obsidian exchange system connections during the Middle Formative involves an increase of direct obsidian exchange between the Central Highland and Gulf Coast areas. Barranca de los Estetes obsidian jumps from 4.8 percent to 26.3 percent of the total at San Lorenzo, and the coefficient between the two areas changes from −0.17 average to +0.47 average. The increase of direct contact between these two areas probably reflects the breakdown of the Oaxaca-San Lorenzo network; but another contributing factor is that, by the time of the Middle Formative, well-made pris-

[1] Only twelve excavated obsidian samples from La Venta have been analyzed (Jack and Heizer 1968). Three of the samples were identified as Cerro de las Navajas obsidian, two as unknown source B, six as unknown source C and one as possibly coming from El Chayal. Unknown sources B and C are grey obsidians and may possibly represent the Barranca de los Estetes and Guadalupe Victoria sources found in the Middle Formative samples from San Lorenzo (see Table 2).

matic blades were in great demand throughout Mesoamerica, thus increasing the importance of Barranca de los Estetes. Our first Middle Formative obsidian exchange network thus links the Gulf Coast (San Lorenzo and probably La Venta) and the Guadalupe Victoria and Barranca de los Estetes sources. The Guadalupe Victoria-Barranca de los Estetes exchange network involved a one-way movement of obsidian from Barranca de los Estetes to the coast; consequently, while it greatly changed the patterns of obsidian utilization on the coast, the Central Highland pattern remained essentially unchanged.

THE EL CHAYAL EXCHANGE NETWORK. The percentage of El Chayal obsidian at San Lorenzo increased from 21.7 percent to 31.6 percent during the Middle Formative. At La Venta one of the twelve excavated obsidians analyzed by Jack and Heizer (1968) was identified as coming from this source. Although a series of Pacific Coast sites such as Aquiles Serdán, Izapa, and Pijijiapán reflect a strong Gulf Coast influence at this period, this network is poorly understood because no obsidians from Middle Formative sites in the Guatemalan Highlands or from the Pacific Coast are included in this sample.

THE BARRANCA DE LOS ESTETES EXCHANGE NETWORK. The Central Highlands-Barranca de los Estetes exchange system remained essentially unchanged during the Middle Formative Period. The predominant importance of Barranca de los Estetes obsidian in the Central Highlands continued; 85.7 percent of the obsidian at Cerro Chacaltepec, Morelos, and 97.6 percent of that found at Acatepec and Moyotzingo, Puebla, came from this source. In the Valley of Mexico, however, a tendency to diversify sources is seen at El Arbolillo and Zacatenco. Although of all the sites analyzed these are the closest to the Barranca de los Estetes source, they contain only 45.5 percent Barranca de los Estetes obsidian. Small amounts of obsidian from other sources comprise the balance: Zinapécuaro 4.5 percent, Cerro de las Navajas 9.1 percent, Tulancingo 9.1 percent, unknown Oaxacan 13.7 percent, and other Guatemalan 18.2 percent. This apparent diversification may, however, be a function of the small sample sizes.

Twenty-five percent of the obsidian samples from the Middle Formative levels in Oaxaca were of Barranca de los Estetes obsidian, indicating a continuity of exchange ties with the Central Highlands from the Early to the Middle Formative Periods. The average coefficient between the two areas changes from +0.58 to +0.50. A diversification of source utilization, similar to that in the Valley of Mexico, is also seen in Oaxaca at this time. Obsidian from six of the eight sources represented in Middle Formative deposits in Oaxaca was also present in the Valley of Mexico. It is in this period that the pooling of obsidian, begun at the major villages during the Early Formative Period, spreads to include even the small hamlets.

THE UNKNOWN OAXACAN EXCHANGE NETWORK. Although obsidian from eight geological sources is found in the Middle Formative of Oaxaca, five of the sources could have been obtained within the established Barranca de los Estetes exchange system, two suggest some continued contact with the Gulf Coast, and one source is a local one. Definition of the unknown Oaxacan source has been discussed above. The obsidian is consistently green in color and the irregular shape of the artifacts suggests it may not be of very high quality. It represents 22.2 percent of the total Oaxacan obsidian, 13.7 percent of the Valley of Mexico obsidian, and 1.2 percent of the Puebla Middle Formative obsidian. The source was known during the Early Formative (1.1 percent in Oaxaca and 4.6 percent in Morelos), but was not extensively exploited. The reason for this may lie partly in the presumed poor quality of the source and partly in the position of Oaxaca as middleman in the Central Highland–Gulf Coast obsidian blade exchange. The use of this Oaxacan source is further evidence for the Middle Formative regionalization already mentioned.

Indeed, during the Middle Formative, for the first time, each of the major settlement areas – the Central Highlands, the Gulf Coast, Guatemala, and Oaxaca – apparently controlled a local obsidian source. Individually negotiated long-distance trade, a form of foreign relations characteristic of simpler societies like those of Melanesia, was gradually replaced by intensive regional exploitation and by regional specialization in blade making. In the latter, Barranca de los Estetes and El Chayal rose to prominence. In later times, Teotihuacán and Kaminaljuyu were to monopolize blade making in those areas.

SUMMARY

The Early Formative Period in Mesoamerica was characterized by four major obsidian exchange networks. The first, referred to as the Barranca de los Estetes network, linked the Central Highlands of Mexico with the Oaxacan Highlands. This network brought to Oaxaca prismatic blades of Barranca de los Estetes obsidian, some of which were probably passed on to Veracruz via the second major network. The latter, referred to as the Guadalupe Victoria network, linked the Oaxaca Highlands to the Gulf Coast. This network circulated a poor-quality obsidian from the Guadalupe Victoria, Puebla, source, little or none of which was passed on by Oaxaca to the obsidian-rich Central Mexican Highlands. A third network, based on the El Chayal source, linked the Gulf Coast with the Guatemalan Highlands, most probably by a Chiapas-Guatemalan Pacific Coast route. The fourth or Zinapécuaro network also involved the movement of prismatic blades from Michoacan to the Oaxacan Highlands.

The partial destruction of San Lorenzo about 900 B.C., combined with political evolution in Oaxaca and the Central Highlands, resulted in the breakdown and realignment of the Early Formative exchange networks.

A growing demand for well-made prismatic obsidian blades increased the importance of the Barranca de los Estetes and El Chayal sources, while Guadalupe Victoria faded into the background. The demand for blades also led increasingly to the pooling of imported obsidian for distribution by local elites, a phenomenon directly associated with the consolidation of power in the respective regions.

REFERENCES

AYELEYRA ARROYO DE ANDA, LUIS, MANUEL MALDONADO-KOERDELL
  1952 Asociación de artefactos con mamut en el Pleistoceno superior de la Cuenca de Mexico. *Revista Mexicana de Estudios Antropológicos* 8(1): 3–29.
COBEAN, ROBERT H., MICHAEL D. COE, EDWARD A. PERRY, JR.,
  KARL K. TUREKIAN, DINKAR P. KHARKAR
  1971 Obsidian trade at San Lorenzo Tenochtitlán. *Science* 174(4010): 666–671.
COE, M. D.
  1968 "San Lorenzo and the Olmec civilization," in *Dumbarton Oaks Conference on the Olmec*. Edited by Elizabeth Benson, 41–78. Washington, D.C.: Dumbarton Oaks.
COE, MICHAEL D., KENT V. FLANNERY"
  1964 The pre-Columbian obsidian industry of El Chayal, Guatemala. *American Antiquity* 30(1): 43–49.
  1967 *Early cultures and human ecology in south coastal Guatemala*. Smithsonian Contributions to Anthropology 3. Washington, D.C.
FLANNERY, KENT V.
  1964 "The Middle Formative of the Tehuacán Valley." Unpublished Ph.D. dissertation, Department of Anthropology, University of Chicago.
  1968 "The Olmec and the Valley of Oaxaca: a model for interregional interaction in Formative times," in *Dumbarton Oaks Conference on the Olmec*. Edited by Elizabeth P. Benson, 79–117. Washington, D.C.
GORDUS, A. A., et al.
  1967 Identification of the geologic origins of archaeological artifacts: an automated method of Na and Mn neutron activation analysis. *Archaeometry* 10: 87–96.
GORDUS, A. A., GARY A. WRIGHT, JAMES B. GRIFFIN
  1968 Obsidian sources characterized by neutron activation analysis. *Science* 161(3839): 328–384.

GROVE, DAVID C.
1970   The San Pablo pantheon mound: a Middle Preclassic site in Morelos, Mexico. *American Antiquity* 35(1): 62–73.
1972   Review of "Materiales para la arqueología de Teotihuacán" by José Luis Lorenzo. *American Anthropologist* 74(1/2): 122–123.
1974   "The Highland Olmec manifestation: a consideration of what is and what isn't," in *Mesoamerican archaeology: new approaches*. Edited by N. Hammond, 109–128. Austin: University of Texas Press.

HAMMOND, NORMAN
1972   Obsidian trade routes in the Mayan area. *Science* 178: 1092–1093.

HEIZER, ROBERT F.
1961   "Inferences on the nature of Olmec society based upon data from the La Venta site," in *Kroeber Anthropological Society Papers* 25: 43–57.

JACK, R. N., ROBERT F. HEIZER
1968   Finger-printing of some Mesoamerican obsidians. *Contributions of the University of California Archaeological Research Facility* 5: 81–99.

PIRES-FERREIRA, JANE WHEELER
1973   "Formative Mesoamerican exchange networks." Unpublished Ph.D. dissertation, Department of Anthropology, University of Michigan, Ann Arbor.

RAPPAPORT, ROY A.
1967   *Pigs for the ancestors*. New Haven: Yale University Press.

RENFREW, A. COLIN
1969   Trade and culture process in European prehistory. *Current Anthropology* 10(2/3): 151–169.

RENFREW, A. COLIN, J. E. DIXON, J. R. CANN
1966   "Obsidian and early culture contact in the Near East," *Proceedings of the Prehistoric Society* 32: 30–72.
1968   "Further analysis of Near Eastern obsidians," *Proceedings of the Prehistoric Society* 34: 319–331.

SAHLINS, MARSHALL D.
1972   *Stone Age economics*. Chicago and New York: Aldine/Atherton.

SERVICE, ELMAN R.
1962   *Primitive social organization*. New York: Random House.

SHOOK, EDWIN, TATIANA PROSKOURIAKOFF
1956   "Settlement patterns in Mesoamerica and the sequence in the Guatemala Highlands," in *Prehistoric settlement patterns in the New World*. Edited by Gordon Willey. Viking Fund Publications in Anthropology 23. New York.

STROSS, F. H., *et al.*
1968   Analysis of American obsidian by X-ray fluorescence and neutron activation analysis. *Contributions of the University of California Archaeological Research Facility* 5: 59–79.

TOLSTOY, PAUL, LOUISE I. PARADIS
1970   Early and Middle Preclassic culture in the Basin of Mexico. *Science* 167: 344–351.

VAILLANT, C. G.
1935   Excavations at El Arbolillo. *Anthropological Papers, American Museum of Natural History* 35(2). New York.

WEAVER, J. R., F. H. STROSS
1965   Analysis by X-ray fluorescence of some American obsidians. *Con-*

tributions of the University of California Archaeological Research Facility 1: 89–103.

WINTER, MARCUS C.
1973   "Tierras Largas: a Formative community in the Valley of Oaxaca, Mexico." Unpublished Ph.D. dissertation, University of Arizona.

WRIGHT, GARY A.
1969   *Obsidian analysis and prehistoric Near Eastern trade: 7500 to 3500* B.C. Anthropological Papers 37. Museum of Anthropology, University of Michigan.

Shell Exchange Networks in Formative Mesoamerica

JANE WHEELER PIRES-FERREIRA

Shells: Methodology and Raw Data

The identification of shell materials from Early and Middle Formative Mesoamerican sites was completed by Dr. Joseph R. Morrison of the Smithsonian Institution, Washington, D.C., and the author. The extensive collections of Mesoamerican mollusks at the Smithsonian Institution provided comparative material for the analysis of archaeological material from the following sites: San José Mogote, Tierras Largas, Huitzo, Abasolo, and Laguna Zope, Oaxaca; Gamas, Tabasco; Santa Marta rockshelter, Chiapas; Nexpa and San Pablo, Morelos; and El Arbolillo East and West in the Valley of Mexico. Additionally, the excavation reports for Early and Middle Formative sites were reviewed; and data on the shell material from the following sites was added to the list: La Victoria (Coe 1961), and Salinas la Blanca (Coe and Flannery 1967) in Guatemala; and Zacatenco (Vaillant 1930) and El Arbolillo (Vaillant 1935) in the Valley of Mexico.

As the analysis proceeded, it became clear that only two significant categories of shell material were to be found in Early and Middle Formative sites, namely, Pacific Coast marine and estuary shells and Atlantic drainage freshwater shells. Only one Atlantic marine shell has been reported in the Mexican Highland sites of these periods, a fragment of *Cassis* sp. or cameo shell identified from Vaillant's excavations at El Arbolillo (Vaillant 1935: 249). Table 1 lists the shells so far identified from Formative Period Mesoamerican sites. The table is divided according to time periods and geographic origins of the shells.

The Early Formative: Shell Exchange Networks Linking Villages

Precise identification of shell exchange networks is not possible due to the limited amount of data available from Early Formative sites and the general nonspecific nature of information regarding shell species origin. In the first case, the lack of preservation of shell material at San Lorenzo and other Gulf Coast sites leaves a large gap in our understanding of shell exchange networks. In the second case, the wide natural distribution of the shell species which were exchanged makes identification of specific points of origin impossible. We are limited to generalizations such as "Pacific marine" or "Atlantic drainage." Despite these limitations, however, certain patterns of shell-species distribution do appear in the available data which admit the preliminary definition of two distinct exchange networks: one based on the exchange of unworked Pacific Coast shells for ornament production by highland craftsmen, and one based on the more generalized distribution of Atlantic drainage freshwater shells.

THE PACIFIC COAST SHELL EXCHANGE NETWORK. Twenty-nine species of Pacific Coast shells (including marine and estuary forms) have been recovered from six Early Formative sites (see Table 2). Three of these sites, Abasolo, San José Mogote, and Tierras Largas, are located in the highland Valley of Oaxaca; the remaining three, Laguna Zope, La Victoria, and Salinas la Blanca, are located on the Pacific Coast. Eleven of the species represent food animals found only at the coastal sites, thirteen others are found only in highland sites, and five are found at both highland and coastal sites (see Table 2).

Of the five shell species found at both Pacific Coast and Highland Early Formative sites, *Pinctada mazatlantica*, or the Pacific pearl oyster, is the most frequent. Commonly found in shallow offshore water from lower California to Peru (Keen 1958: 58), these shells were the principal material used by Early Formative shell workers in the highlands. The shells of an adult animal are sufficiently thick and resistant to permit cutting, grinding, and drilling into elaborate forms. The shape of these shells provides a relatively large, flattish working surface with waste limited to the marginal valve area. These characteristics are the opposite of those exhibited by the fragile Atlantic drainage shells which could not be cut or ground into decorative forms. At San José Mogote and Tierras Largas in the Valley of Oaxaca, abundant evidence of the working of *Pinctada mazatlantica* shells was found, and at nearby Abasolo a finished pendant was recovered from a burial.

The exchange links through which the unworked shell reached the Oaxacan craftsmen are not known. A tenuous suggestion that they may have passed through the Tehuantepec region comes from surface shell material identified at the site of Laguna Zope near Juchitán. This large Early and Middle Formative site was first reported by Delgado (1961, 1965). A surface survey of the site in 1968 located quantities of shell in association with Early and Middle Formative ceramics (Flannery, personal communication). Included among the shells were both worked and unworked *Pinctada mazatlantica* fragments. The most frequent worked form was a shell with the heavy valve section cut away. This indicates either the existence of local shell working and/or the preparation of shell "blanks" for long-distance exchange. Examination of this hypothesis must await future excavation of Laguna Zope and other Early Formative Pacific Coast sites.

Two other Pacific marine shells found less frequently at both Highland Mexican and Pacific Coast sites are *Spondylus calcifer* and *Strombus galeatus*. Both species are commonly found just below the low-tide line on beaches from California to Peru (Keen 1958: 336). The spiny oyster or *Spondylus calcifer* was found among the shells at Laguna Zope and in association with shell-working areas of Early Formative houses at San José Mogote. Unlike the *Pinctada mazatlantica*, however, it appears that these shells were exchanged and used whole for pendants and were not cut or worked into ornaments. Also exchanged whole were the conch shells of *Strombus galeatus*. Incised fragments of presumed shell trumpets have been found on house floors and in association with public buildings at San José Mogote and Tierras Largas. Fragments of this gastropod have also been found at Abasolo in the Valley of Oaxaca and at Laguna Zope, La Victoria, and Salinas la Blanca on the Pacific Coast.

Two Pacific estuary shells have also been found in Early Formative sites of the Valley of Oaxaca and the Pacific Coast. A fragment of *Agaronia testacea* from Tierras Largas is matched by one from La Victoria, and *Anomalocardia subrugosa* is reported from San José Mogote, Tierras Largas, Laguna Zope, and La Victoria. Utilization of these shells was apparently restricted to the grinding or drilling of holes for suspension.

In addition to the five Pacific Coast species found at both highland and coastal sites, thirteen other Pacific species have been identified at Highland Mexican sites (see Table 3). The mechanics of the exchange which brought such a variety of shell into the Mexican Highland area are not understood. Surface materials from Laguna Zope contain abundant shells, including four of the five shell species found at both highland and lowland sites. Future excavations here and at other sites in the Tehuantepec region may show this area to be a crossroads or origin point for the Pacific Coast shell exchange networks. Access to the imported raw shell appears to have been limited, especially for *Pinctada mazatlantica* (see below), to shell-working sites or portions of sites, which in turn passed on their finished shell ornaments to other smaller sites. Pacific shell may have moved through the same "sphere of conveyance" which brought El Chayal obsidian to the Pacific and Gulf coasts, but full evaluation of this hypothesis must await both future Pacific Coast excavations and the discovery of preserved Early Formative shell at Gulf Coast sites.

THE ATLANTIC DRAINAGE SHELL EXCHANGE NETWORK. While Atlantic drainage freshwater shells were widely exchanged during the Early Formative Period, Atlantic marine and estuary shell resources were not utilized. The only identified marine remains come from the Tabasco coastal site of Gamas, where some thirty fragments of *Crassostrea virginica* presumably represent meal refuse. Two estuary clams, *Rangianella* sp. and *Rangianella flaxuosa petitiana*, were also identified among the Gamas shells and likewise were exploited for food.

Of the six species of Atlantic drainage shells identified, all but one are found at sites outside the drainage area (see Tables 1 and 4). The one exception is *Orthalicus decolor*, an edible gastropod found only in Early Formative levels at the Santa Marta rockshelter in Chiapas. The most widely distributed of the five freshwater clams found at sites outside the Atlantic drainage area are *Baryonaias* sp. and *Baryonaias* cf. *pigerrimus*. Found in the large river systems from Tampico to the Laguna de Terminos (Morrison, personal communication), shells of these clams have been identified at the sites of San José Mogote and Tierras Largas in the Valley of Oaxaca, at Laguna Zope on the Pacific coast of the Isthmus of Tehuantepec, at El Arbolillo in the Valley of Mexico and San Pablo in Morelos. Apparently because of their fragility, these shells were not imported for ornament production; rather they were, when utilized, perforated for suspension as pendants. The three other species also found at the sites in the Valley of Oaxaca include *Actionaias* sp., *Anadara incongrua*, and *Anadonta globosa*. The distribution of these species is the same as for *Baryonaias*.

The exchange of Atlantic drainage freshwater clam shells is poorly understood due to the widespread distribution of these five species and the total absence of shell data from Early Formative Gulf Coast sites. It is possible that these shells were moved into the highlands along the Guadalupe Victoria obsidian exchange network linkages. Evidence from the house floors at San José Mogote and Tierras Largas (see below) suggests that distribution of this shell may have been similar to the distribution of obsidian flakes and chunks during the

Early Formative Period at Tierras Largas. In comparison to the distribution of the Pacific *Pinctada mazatlantica* which was restricted to the shell craftsmen and their clients, Atlantic drainage freshwater clams were more generally available. But the mechanisms of this exchange will only be elucidated by future excavations.

The Middle Formative: Shell Exchange Networks Linking Villages

Among the shells identified for seven Middle Formative sites, forty-four species were recorded (see Table 2). A total of thirty-seven Pacific marine and estuary species were found, compared to twenty-nine for the Early Formative. In contrast, the Atlantic drainage total drops from six species to one for the Middle Formative.

THE PACIFIC COAST SHELL EXCHANGE NETWORK. Thirty-seven species of Pacific Coast shells have been recovered from seven Middle Formative sites. Five of the sites are located in the Mexican Highlands (Huitzo and Tierras Largas in the Valley of Oaxaca, El Arbolillo and Zacatenco in the Valley of Mexico and Nexpa, Morelos), and two on the coast of Guatemala (La Victoria and Salinas la Blanca). Thirteen marine and fifteen estuary species were found only at the coastal sites and are largely related to subsistence activities. Four marine and two estuary species were found only at highland sites, while one marine and two estuary forms were found at both coastal and highland sites (see Table 5).

Only three of the seventeen Pacific Coast shell species found at highland Early Formative sites were identified in the Middle Formative material. *Strombus galeatus*, found at La Victoria, Salinas la Blanca, and Tierras Largas, is the only marine species found at both coastal and highland sites during the Early and Middle Formative Periods. Other Pacific marine species exchanged during both periods include *Pinctada mazatlantia*, found at Middle Formative Zacatenco, Nexpa, and Tierras Largas, and *Spondylus* sp. found at Huitzo. The sample size for this period is small and no evidence concerning the relation between shell import and shell craft production is available.

Two new Pacific estuary species are identified at highland sites during the Middle Formative. Shells of *Amphrichaena kindermanni*, a marsh clam found in the estuary systems of the Pacific Coast (Clench, in Coe 1961) have been found both at La Victoria and Salinas la Blanca as well as at Huitzo in the Valley of Oaxaca. A second estuary form, the snail *Neritina (Theodoxus) luteofasciata*, was found at both Salinas la Blanca and Zacatenco. This species is found from the Gulf of California to Panama (Keen 1958: 266).

Thirty-seven species of Pacific Coast shells have been identified

from Middle Formative sites, compared to twenty-nine for the preceding period; but twenty-eight of the thirty-seven are found only at
coastal sites and the number of species found at highland sites drops
from seventeen to nine. Although this decrease is probably related to
the regionalization process and associated drop in long-distance
exchange demonstrated by obsidian exchange patterns (Pires-Ferreira
1973), the mechanisms of the exchange remain unknown.

THE ATLANTIC DRAINAGE SHELL EXCHANGE NETWORK. A
decrease, corresponding to that in the number of Pacific Coast species,
is also recorded for Atlantic drainage shells during the Middle Formative Period (see Table 6). Only four shells of *Baryonaias* sp. from
Huitzo and Tierras Largas are identified from all seven Middle Formative sites. This reduction in the movement of freshwater clam shell
is not replaced by other species, for only one fragment of Atlantic
marine shell, *Cassis* sp. or cameo shell from El Arbolillo, has been
identified. The cause of the drop-off in the exchange of Atlantic
drainage shell is likewise to be found in the trend towards centralization characteristic of the Middle Formative. The mechanism of this
exchange, however, is unknown.

The Distribution of Shell in Formative Mesoamerican Households

Evidence from three house floors of the Tierras Largas Phase at
Tierras Largas indicates that the importation of Pacific marine shell
goes back to 1500 B.C. (Winter 1973: 181). The shell appears to be
evenly distributed among all the houses, and no Atlantic drainage
shells are found (Winter 1973: 181; see Table 7, which summarizes
Winter's data).

The importance of Pacific Coast shell, marine and estuary, continues and grows during the San José phase (1200 to 850 B.C.). Data
from thirteen house floors at San José Mogote illustrates that Pacific
Coast shell was the primary material of local shell ornament production
(see Table 8). Twenty Pacific Coast shell ornaments and finished pieces
are compared to two Atlantic drainage ornaments, and eighteen Pacific
Coast shell unfinished pieces or waste products are compared to three
Atlantic drainage shells in this category from the houses. Twenty-three
unworked Pacific Coast shells and twenty-six unworked Atlantic
drainage shells are also found. Examination of the worked shell
indicates that *Pinctada mazatlantica*, or the Pacific pearl oyster, was
the preferred raw material for ornament production at San José
Mogote. This shiny shell not only presents a relatively large and
flattish working area, but is also resistant to cutting, grinding, and

drilling, the basic ornament production procedures. Experiments in working both *Pinctada mazatlantica* and the freshwater clam shells by these techniques showed the latter to be too brittle for ornament manufacture.

At San José Mogote, shell ornament manufacture appears to be limited to certain houses in one section of the site. Concentrations of unfinished pieces or shell waste products are found in houses 2, 4, 5, and 8 of Area C (OS62C) at the site, while only two such fragments were found on the floors in Area A (OS62A) (see Table 8). Area C houses contrast with those in Area A in that house architecture is less elaborate (no "painted shrines" are found) and in the absence of magnetite mirror manufacturing for "elite" exchange; but in comparison with those of Tierras Largas, they cannot be defined as low status (Flannery, personal communication). The distribution of artifacts on the Area C house floors (unpublished data) suggests that their occupants were part-time craft specialists who also practiced agriculture. The concentrations of Pacific shell and ornament manufacture suggest that specific exchange ties existed for obtaining the raw material. The mechanisms of such an exchange are not understood, but clearly contrast with those previously described for obsidian.

Evidence of household and *barrio* specialization in shell ornament production was not found at the smaller site of Tierras Largas. Winter (1973: 181) notes an even distribution of shell and shell-working evidence among the three house "clusters" he excavated (see Table 9). It is difficult to relate this finding to the dichotomy in Pacific Coast and Atlantic drainage shell distribution seen at San José Mogote, because Winter has not subdivided his worked-shell categories according to the origins of the shells. However, this situation may be analogous to the change from one period to another in evidence of obsidian pooling at the two sites. The more specialized importation of Pacific Coast shells seen at San José Mogote may not occur until the Middle Formative at Tierras Largas.

That the relation between Pacific Coast shell import and shell ornament manufacture seems clear is further suggested by the association of finished Pacific shell products and Atlantic drainage shell in houses containing no evidence of Pacific shell ornament manufacture. House 9 in Area C of San José Mogote provides such an example. Two elaborate finished Pacific shell products, including a pendant with a paw-wing motif, were found together with two unworked Pacific shell fragments and twelve Atlantic clam shells.

The mechanism by which finished ornaments were distributed both at San José Mogote and to other sites in the Valley is not understood. Nor is it clear whether the distribution of Atlantic clam shells is a function of technical unsuitability for ornament manufacture, or a question of status, or both. It may be that the freshwater clam shells were obtained from the Papaloapan River in the nearby Canada Tomellin and used in imitation of higher-status marine-shell ornaments. A similar situation involving the manufacture from wood of imitation stone axes by Mt. Hagen natives in New Guinea has been reported by Strathern (1969: 327). Conversely, however, these shells may have been obtained through exchange with Gulf Coast sites. If the shell was imported through the same "sphere of conveyance" in which the Guadalupe Victoria obsidian and magnetite mirrors moved, a far different value may have been attached to them. But full understanding of the value of Atlantic drainage shell and the way in which it was obtained in Early Formative Oaxaca will only come with future excavations.

Data from only one Middle Formative house floor are available. The total of six shells recovered from house "cluster" G-3 at Tierras Largas include four Pacific marine, one Atlantic drainage, and one Atlantic or Pacific drainage shell. Winter (1973: 181) has suggested that this reflects a reduction in exchange contacts with the Gulf Coast area. If this is indeed the case, it would agree well with evidence for the reduction of the number of Atlantic drainage shell species in highland sites, the breakdown of the Guadalupe Victoria obsidian exchange network (see "Obsidian exchange networks. . ." this volume) and the end of Oaxacan magnetite mirror manufacture and exchange with the Gulf Coast (see "Mössbauer Spectral Analysis. . ." this volume).

ble 1. Shells identified at Formative Period Mesoamerican sites

ollusk	Site	Provenience or Period	Total	Reference*
LANTIC MARINE – EARLY FORMATIVE				
assostrea virginica emlin	Gamas	Excavation 1, pit 1	±30	P-F 1973
LANTIC ESTUARY – EARLY FORMATIVE				
ngianella flaxuosa etitiana Dall	Gamas	Excavation 1, pit 1	6	P-F 1973
ngianella sp.	Gamas	Excavation 1, pit 1	6	P-F 1973
LANTIC DRAINAGE – EARLY FORMATIVE				
tionaias sp.	San José Mogote	62C/H4	1	P-F 1973
	Tierras Largas	B74B Feat 141, D35	1	P-F 1973
	Tierras Largas	San José phase	6	P-F 1973
adara incongrua	San José Mogote	62C/H4	1	P-F 1973
adonta globosa Lee	Tierras Largas	San José phase	1	P-F 1973
ryonaias cf. *piger-* nus Closse and scher	San Pablo	H 17	1	P-F 1973
ryonaias sp. Quadula sp.)	El Arbolillo	Trench C	2	V 1935
	San Pablo	G 11	1	P-F 1973
	San Pablo	G 13	1	P-F 1973
	San José Mogote	62A/C2	1	P-F 1973
	San José Mogote	62A/C3	3	P-F 1973
	San José Mogote	62A/C4	3	P-F 1973
	San José Mogote	62A/D1	2	P-F 1973
	San José Mogote	62A/B2 (redeposited San José phase)	1	P-F 1973
	San José Mogote	62C/H2	6	P-F 1973
	San José Mogote	62C/H4	1	P-F 1973
ryonaias sp. Quadula sp.)	San José Mogote	62C/H8	2	P-F 1973
	San José Mogote	62C/H9	12	P-F 1973
	Tierras Largas	San José phase	2	P-F 1973
	Laguna Zope	Surface		

Throughout Table 1, the following key is used:
1961 = Coe (1961)
1967 = Coe and Flannery (1967: 78–80)
1973 = Pires-Ferreira (1973: 99–142)
1930 = Vaillant (1930: 49–50)
1935 = Vaillant (1935: 249)

Table 1. Shells identified at Formative Period Mesoamerican sites (continued)

Mollusk	Site	Provenience or Period	Total	Reference
Pachychilus indiorum Morelet	Santa Marta rockshelter	$\dfrac{\text{N 1} - \text{E 2}}{1}$	2	P-F 1973
	Santa Marta rockshelter	$\dfrac{\text{W 3.5}}{2}$	9	P-F 1973
	Santa Marta rockshelter	$\dfrac{\text{W 2}}{3}$	8	P-F 1973
	Santa Marta rockshelter	Level 4	1	P-F 1973
	Santa Marta rockshelter	$\dfrac{\text{N 1} - \text{E 2}}{2}$	2	P-F 1973
	Santa Marta rockshelter	$\dfrac{\text{Tr W 3}}{3}$	11	P-F 1973

PACIFIC MARINE – EARLY FORMATIVE

Anachis sp.	San José Mogote	62C/H4	1	P-F 1973
Anadara grandis Broderip and Sowerby 1829	La Victoria	Ocós phase	1	C 1961
Anadara perlabiata Grant and Gale 1931	La Victoria	Ocós phase		C 1961
Arca cf. *labiata* Sowerby	Tierras Largas	74D feature 160 (San José phase)	1	P-F 1973
Busicon cf. *columella*	Tierras Largas	Early Tierras Largas phase	1	P-F 1973
Chione sp.	San José Mogote	62A/C3	1	P-F 1973
Chione gnidia Broderip and Sowerby 1829	La Victoria	Ocós phase		C 1961
Iphigenia alitor Sowerby 1817	La Victoria	Ocós phase		C 1961
Mulinia pallida Broderip and Sowerby 1829	La Victoria	Ocós phase		C 1961
Mytella falcata Orbigny 1846	La Victoria Salinas la Blanca	Ocós phase Ocós phase	1 (?)	C 1961 CF 1967
Neritina cassiculum Sowerby	San José Mogote	62C/H4	1	P-F 1973

Table 1. Shells identified at Formative Period Mesoamerican sites (continued)

Mollusk	Site	Provenience or Period	Total	Reference
Pinctada mazatlantica Hanley 1856	Abasolo	B153, burial 1, pendant from chest	1	P-F 1973
	San José Mogote	62A/C1	1	P-F 1973
	San José Mogote	62A/C3	2	P-F 1973
	San José Mogote	62A/D1	3	P-F 1973
	San José Mogote	62A/D2	4	P-F 1973
	San José Mogote	62A/Platf.II, S.II-III, redep. San José phase	3	P-F 1973
	San José Mogote	62A/B3 (redeposited San José phase	2	P-F 1973
	San José Mogote	62C/H1	1	P-F 1973
	San José Mogote	62C/H2	10	P-F 1973
	San José Mogote	62C/H4	19	P-F 1973
	San José Mogote	62C/H5	1	P-F 1973
	San José Mogote	62C/below H6	2	P-F 1973
	San José Mogote	62C/H7	1	P-F 1973
Pinctada mazatlantica Hanley 1856	San José Mogote	62C/H8	8	P-F 1973
	San José Mogote	62C/H9	4	P-F 1973
	San José Mogote	62C/H10	1	P-F 1973
	Tierras Largas	Early Tierras Largas phase	2	P-F 1973
	Tierras Largas	Late Tierras Largas phase	5	P-F 1973
	Tierras Largas	San José phase	6	P-F 1973
	Laguna Zope	Surface		P-F 1973
Spondylus calcifer Carpenter 1856	San José Mogote	62A/Platform II, Stage II-III, redeposited San José phase	2	P-F 1973
	San José Mogote	62C/H5	2	P-F 1973
	San José Mogote	62C/H8	1	P-F 1973
	Laguna Zope	Surface		P-F 1973
Spondylus cf. *pictorem*	Tierras Largas	C15, San José phase	1	P-F 1973
Strombus galeatus Swainson 1823	La Victoria	Ocós phase		C 1961
	Salinas la Blanca	Ocós phase		CF 1967
	Abasolo	B153-E12/D170-180	1 (?)	P-F 1973
	San José Mogote	62A/C4	1 (?)	P-F 1973
Strombus galeatus Swainson 1823	San José Mogote	62A/platform I, stage II E, redeposited San José phase	1	P-F 1973
	San José Mogote	62C/H4	1	P-F 1973
	Tierras Largas	San José phase	1	P-F 1973
	Laguna Zope	Surface		P-F 1973
Strombus cf. *galeatus* Swainson	Tierras Largas	San José phase	2	P-F 1973
Pyrene sp.	San José Mogote	62A/C3	1	P-F 1973

Table 1. Shells identified at Formative Period Mesoamerican sites (continued)

Mollusk	Site	Provenience or Period	Total	Reference
Thais biserialis	San José Mogote	62A/E complex base of wall, redeposited San José phase	1	P-F 1973
Tivela cf. *gracilior* Sowerby	Tierras Largas	74C feature 159, San José phase	1	P-F 1973
PACIFIC ESTUARY – EARLY FORMATIVE				
Agaronia testacea Lamark 1811	La Victoria Tierras Largas	Ocós phase B74D/feature 160/S	1	C 1961 P-F 1973
Amphrichaena kinder-manni Philippi	La Victoria	Ocós phase		C 1961
Anomalocardia sub-rugosa Wood 1828	La Victoria San José Mogote	Ocós phase 62A/platform I, stage II E, redeposited San José phase	1	C 1961 P-F 1973
	San José Mogote	62A/platform I, stage II-III, redeposited San José phase	1	P-F 1973
	San José Mogote	62C/H1	1	P-F 1973
	San José Mogote	62C/H2	1	P-F 1973
	San José Mogote	62C/H7	1	P-F 1973
	Tierras Largas	San José phase	2	P-F 1973
	Laguna Zope	Surface		P-F 1973
Cerithidea mazatlantica Carpenter 1856 (*Cerithium hegewischii* Philippi)	San José Mogote San José Mogote	62C/H2 62C/4	2 2	P-F 1973 P-F 1973
Cerithium stercus-muscarum Valen-ciennnes 1838	San José Mogote	62A/platform II, stage II-III, redeposited San José phase	2	P-F 1973
	San José Mogote	62C/H4	1	P-F 1973
	San José Mogote	62A/C3	1	P-F 1973
	Tierras Largas	74D/feature 160/S, San José phase	1	P-F 1973
Ostera columbiensis Hanley 1846	La Victoria Salinas la Blanca	Ocós phase Ocós phase		C 1961 CF 1967
Ostera chilensis Philippi	Tierras Largas	Late Tierras Largas phase	1	P-F 1973
Polymesoda radiata Hanley 1844	La Victoria	Ocós phase		C 1961
Ptotothaca asperrima Sowerby 1835	La Victoria	Ocós phase		C 1961
Trachycardium proce-rum	Laguna Zope	Surface		C 1961

ble 1. Shells identified at Formative Period Mesoamerican sites (continued)

•llusk	Site	Provenience or Period	Total	Reference
LANTIC OR PACIFIC MARINE – EARLY FORMATIVE				
rdata sp.	San José Mogote	62A/C2	1	P-F 1973
igilla sp.	San José Mogote	62C/H9	1	P-F 1973
	Tierras Largas	Late Tierras Largas phase	1	P-F 1973
LANTIC OR PACIFIC ESTUARY – EARLY FORMATIVE				
vella sp.	San José Mogote	62C/H8	1	P-F 1973
ritella sp.	San José Mogote	62C/H8	1	P-F 1973
LANTIC OR PACIFIC DRAINAGE – EARLY FORMATIVE				
adonta sp.	San José Mogote	62C/H2	1	P-F 1973
	Tierras Largas	San José phase	1 (?)	P-F 1973
ND SNAILS – EARLY FORMATIVE				
ymaeus sp.	San José Mogote	62C/H9	1	P-F 1973
glandina sp.	San Pablo	G 15	1	P-F 1973
	Santa Marta rockshelter	N 1 – E 2 / 3	1	P-F 1973
	San José Mogote	62C/H1	1	P-F 1973
	San José Mogote	62C/H9	1	P-F 1973
	Tierras Largas	74D/2530	1	P-F 1973
thalicus decolor rebel	Santa Marta rockshelter	138 B/6	1	P-F 1973
	Santa Marta rockshelter	114E-6/2	1	P-F 1973
	Santa Marta rockshelter	N 1 – E 2 / 1	1	P-F 1973
	Santa Marta rockshelter	W 3.5 / 2	1	P-F 1973
	Santa Marta rockshelter	N 1 – E 2 / 2	1	P-F 1973
IDENTIFIED – EARLY FORMATIVE				
identified	San José Mogote	62A/C1	1	P-F 1973
	San José Mogote	62A/C2	2	P-F 1973
	San José Mogote	62A/C3	2	P-F 1973
	San José Mogote	62A/C4	2	P-F 1973
	San José Mogote	62A/D1	2	P-F 1973
	San José Mogote	62A/D2	6	P-F 1973
	San José Mogote	62A/platform I, stage II E, redeposited San José phase	1	P-F 1973
	San José Mogote	62C/H1	1	P-F 1973
	San José Mogote	62C/H2	1	P-F 1973
	San José Mogote	62C/H9	2	P-F 1973
	Tierras Largas	B74C/feature 151, #48	1	P-F 1973
	Tierras Largas	B74D/feature 160 S	1	P-F 1973

Table 1. Shells identified at Formative Period Mesoamerican sites (continued)

Mollusk	Site	Provenience or Period	Total	Reference
ATLANTIC MARINE – MIDDLE FORMATIVE				
Cassis sp. Scopoli 1777	El Arbolillo	Bead with adult female skeleton 141, trench C	1	P-F 1973
	El Arbolillo	Skeleton 129, necklace	1	V 1935
ATLANTIC DRAINAGE – MIDDLE FORMATIVE				
Baryonaias sp. (Quadula	Huitzo	B46A/house 1	2	P-F 1973
sp.	Huitzo	B46A/feature 1	1	P-F 1973
	Tierras Largas	Guadalupe phase	1	P-F 1973
PACIFIC MARINE – MIDDLE FORMATIVE				
Anadara aequatorialis	La Victoria	Conchas I phase		C1961
Orbigny 1846	Salinas la Blanca	Cuadros phase	5	CF 1967
Anadara grandis	La Victoria	Conchas II phase		C 1961
Broderip and Sowerby 1829	Salinas la Blanca	Jocotal phase	1	CF 1967
Anadara obesa Sowerby	La Victoria	Conchas I phase		C 1961
Anadara perlabiata Grant and Gale 1931	La Victoria	Conchas I and II phases		C 1961
Cardita laticostata	La Victoria	Conchas I and II phases		C 1961
Sowerby 1833	Salinas la Blanca	Cuadros phase	5	CF 1967
Chione pulicaria Broderip 1835	La Victoria	Conchas I phase		C 1961
Harvella elegans Sowerby 1825	Salinas la Blanca	Cuadros phase	2	CF 1967
Iphigenia alitor	La Victoria	Conchas I and II phases		C 1961
Sowerby 1817	Salinas la Blanca	Cuadros phase	10	CF 1967
	Salinas la Blanca	Jocotal phase	1	CF 1967
Lunarca brevifrons Sowerby 1833	La Victoria	Conchas I phase		C 1961
Malea cf. ringens	Huitzo	B46C/zone D2	2	P-F 1973
Melogena cf. patula	El Arbolillo	(West) E172N1	1	P-F 1973
Mulinia pallida Brode-	Salinas la Blanca	Jocotal phase	2	CF 1967
rip and Sowerby 1829	Salinas la Blanca	Cuadros phase	2	CF 1967
Mytella falcata	La Victoria	Conchas I phase		C 1961
Orbigny 1846	Salinas la Blanca	Jocotal phase	1	CF 1967
	Salinas la Blanca	Cuadros phase	5	CF 1967

able 1. Shells identified at Formative Period Mesoamerican sites (continued)

Mollusk	Site	Provenience or Period	Total	Reference
Pinctada mazatlantica Hanley 1856	Zacatenco	E Trenches	1	V 1930
	Zacatenco	Middle Period	1 (?)	V 1930
	Nexpa	Burial NA-2 female with unworked "Pectoral"	1	P-F 1973
	Tierras Largas	Guadalupe phase	3	P-F 1973
Pitar (Pitar) consanguineus C. B. Adams 1852	Salinas la Blanca	Cuadros phase	1	CF 1967
Pitar (Hysteroconcha) lupanaria Lesson 1830	Salinas la Blanca	Jocotal phase	1	CF 1967
Spondylus sp.	Huitzo	B46A/zone F1	1	P-F 1973
Strombus galeatus Swainson 1823	La Victoria	Conchas I and II phases		C 1961
	Salinas la Blanca	Jocotal phase	1	CF 1967
	Salinas la Blanca	Cuadros phase	2	CF 1967
	Tierras Largas	Guadalupe phase	1	P-F 1973

PACIFIC ESTUARY – MIDDLE FORMATIVE

Mollusk	Site	Provenience or Period	Total	Reference
Agaronia testacea Lamark 1811	La Victoria	Conchas I and II phases		C 1961
	Salinas la Blanca	Jocotal phase	27	CF 1967
	Salinas la Blanca	Cuadros phase	3	CF 1967
Amphrichaena kindermanni Philippi	La Victoria	Conchas I and II phases		C 1961
	Salinas la Blanca	Jocotal phase	5	CF 1967
	Salinas la Blanca	Cuadros phase	10	CF 1967
	Huitzo	B46C/zone D2, Guadalupe phase	3	P-F 1973
Anomalocardia subrugosa Wood 1828	La Victoria	Conchas I and II phases		C 1961
Cerithidia mazatlantica Carpenter 1856 (*Cerithium hegewischii* Philippi)	Salinas la Blanca	Jocotal phase	7	CF 1967
	Salinas la Blanca	Cuadros phase	41	CF 1967
Cerithidea valida C. B. Adams 1852	La Victoria	Conchas I phase		C 1961
	Salinas la Blanca	Cuadros phase	2	CF 1967
Melampus tabogensis C. B. Adams 1852	Salinas la Blanca	Cuadros phase	2	CF 1967
Natica (Natica) chemnictzii Pfeiffer 1840	La Victoria	Conchas I phase		C 1961
Neritina (Theodoxus) luteofasciata Miller 1879 (*Neritina pieta*)	Salinas la Blanca	Jocotal phase	1	CF 1967
	Salinas la Blanca	Cuadros phase	2	CF 1967
	Zacatenco	E Trenches, Middle Period	1	V 1930

Table 1. Shells identified at Formative Period Mesoamerican sites (continued)

Mollusk	Site	Provenience or Period	Total	Reference
Neritina usnea Roedina	El Arbolillo	(East) L28-N1, La Pastora phase	1	P-F 1973
Noetia (Noetia) reversa Sowerby 1833	Salinas la Blanca	Cuadros phase	4	CF 1967
Olivella (Pachyoliva) semistrata Gray 1839	Salinas la Blanca	Cuadros phase	1	CF 1967
Ostera columbiensis Hanley 1846	La Victoria Salinas la Blanca	Conchas I and II phases Cuadros phase	4	C 1961 CF 1967
Polinices (Polinices) bifasciatus Gray 1834	La Victoria	Conchas I phase		C 1961
Polymesoda radiata Hanley 1844	La Victoria Salinas la Blanca Salinas la Blanca	Conchas I and II phases Jocotal phase Cuadros phase	2 486	C 1961 CF 1967 CF 1967
Sanguinolaria bertini Pitsbry and Lowe 1932	Salinas la Blanca	Jocotal phase	1	CF 1967
Thais (Thaisella) kios-quiformis Duclos 1832	La Victoria	Conchas I phase		CF 1967
Thais (Vasula) melones Duclos 1832	Salinas la Blanca	Jocotal phase	1	CF 1967
Trachycardium senti-cosum Sowerby 1833	La Victoria	Conchas I phase		C 1961
Turritella jewettii	Huitzo	B64A, cleaning profile at 4 m. depth, zone E	1	P-F 1973
ATLANTIC OR PACIFIC ESTUARY – MIDDLE FORMATIVE				
Neritina sp.	El Arbolillo	Skeleton 129, female adult, necklace of 20 shells		V 1935 (see also pp. 169, 238)
ATLANTIC OR PACIFIC DRAINAGE – MIDDLE FORMATIVE				
Anadonta sp.	Tierras Largas	Square 3796, feature 112, Guadalupe phase	1	P-F 1973
Nephronais sp.	Salinas la Blanca	Jocotal phase	4	CF 1967
LAND SNAILS – MIDDLE FORMATIVE				
Euglandina sp.	Tierras Largas	Guadalupe phase	1	P-F 1973
Orthalicus zebra	Zacatenco	E Trenches, Middle Period	1	V 1930
UNIDENTIFIED – MIDDLE FORMATIVE				
Unidentified	Huitzo	B46A	4	P-F 1973

Table 2. Total number of identified shell species by geographic origin: Middle and Early Formative Sites

Place of origin	Early Formative	Middle Formative
Atlantic marine	1	1
Atlantic estuary	2	—
Atlantic drainage	6	1
Pacific marine	19	18
Pacific estuary	10	19
Pacific drainage	—	—
Atlantic or Pacific marine	2	—
Atlantic or Pacific estuary	2	1
Atlantic or Pacific drainage	1	2
Land snail	3	2
Total	46	44

Table 3. Pacific coast shells found at highland sites: Early Formative

Mollusk	Site
1. *Agaronia testacea*	Tierras Largas, Oaxaca
2. *Anachis* sp.	San José Mogote, Oaxaca
3. *Anomalocardia subrugosa*	San José Mogote, Oaxaca
	Tierras Largas, Oaxaca
4. *Arca* cf. *labiata*	Tierras Largas, Oaxaca
5. *Busicon* cf. *columella*	Tierras Largas, Oaxaca
6. *Cerithidia mazatlantica*	San José Mogote, Oaxaca
7. *Cerithium stercus-muscarum*	San José Mogote, Oaxaca
	Tierras Largas, Oaxaca
8. *Chione* sp.	San José Mogote, Oaxaca
9. *Neritina cassiculum*	San José Mogote, Oaxaca
10. *Ostera chilensis*	Tierras Largas, Oaxaca
11. *Pinctada mazatlantica*	Abasolo, Oaxaca
	San José Mogote, Oaxaca
	Tierras Largas, Oaxaca
12. *Spondylus calcifer*	San José Mogote, Oaxaca
13. *Spondylus* cf. *pictorem*	Tierras Largas, Oaxaca
14. *Strombus galeatus*	Abasolo, Oaxaca
	San José Mogote, Oaxaca
	Tierras Largas, Oaxaca
15. *Strombus* cf. *galeatus*	Tierras Largas, Oaxaca
16. *Pyrene* sp.	San José Mogote, Oaxaca
17. *Thais biserialis*	San José Mogote, Oaxaca
18. *Tivela* cf. *gracilior*	Tierras Largas, Oaxaca

Table 4. Atlantic drainage shells found at sites outside the Atlantic drainage area: Early Formative

Mollusk	Site
1. *Actionaias* sp.	San José Mogote, Oaxaca
	Tierras Largas, Oaxaca
2. *Anadara incongrua*	San José Mogote, Oaxaca
3. *Anadonta globosa*	Tierras Largas, Oaxaca
4. *Baryonaias* sp.	Laguna Zope, Oaxaca
	San José Mogote, Oaxaca
	Tierras Largas, Oaxaca
	San Pablo, Morelos
	El Arbolillo, Valley of Mexico
5. *Baryonaias* cf. *pigerrimus*	San Pablo, Morelos

Table 5. Pacific coast shells found at highland sites: Middle Formative

Mollusk	Site
1. *Amphrichaena kindermanni*	Huitzo, Oaxaca
2. *Malea* cf. *ringens*	Huitzo, Oaxaca
3. *Melogena* cf. *patula*	El Arbolillo West, Valley of Mexico
4. *Neritina* (*Theodoxus*) *luteofasciata*	Zacatenco, Valley of Mexico
5. *Neritina usnea*	El Arbolillo East, Valley of Mexico
6. *Pinctada mazatlantica*	Zacatenco, Valley of Mexico
	Nexpa, Morelos
	Huitzo, Oaxaca
	Tierras Largas, Oaxaca
7. *Spondylus* sp.	Huitzo, Oaxaca
8. *Strombus galeatus*	Tierras Largas, Oaxaca
9. *Turitella jewettii*	Huitzo, Oaxaca

Table 6. Atlantic drainage shells found at sites outside the Atlantic drainage area: Middle Formative

Mollusk	Site
1. *Baryonaias* sp.	Huitzo, Oaxaca Tierras Largas, Oaxaca

Table 7. Sources of Early and Middle Formative shell found at Tierras Largas, By number of specimens

Time period	Pacific marine	Pacific man-grove	Pacific estuary	Atlantic drainage fresh-water	Atlantic or Pacific drainage fresh-water	Atlantic or Pacific marine	?Marine	?	Total
Mixed Formative	11	1		2			1	3	18
Monte Alban I-A	2							1	3
Guadalupe phase	4			1	1				6
Late San José phase	16		1	13	2			1	33
Early San José phase	2			3					5
Late Tierras Largas phase	7					1		1	9
Early Tierras Largas phase	2								2
Total	44	1	1	19	3	1	1	6	76

Table 8. Sources and utilization of shells: Early Formative, San José Mogote, house floors

San José Mogote Early Formative House floors	Ornaments and finished pieces, including fragments			Unfinished pieces and waste products			Unworked shell fragments			Unworked whole shells			Shell tools			Subtotal			Tot
	P	A	U	P	A	U	P	A	U	P	A	U	P	A	U	P	A	U	
OS62A																			
House C1	1		1													1		1	
House C2							1	3								1	3		
House C3	2	1	1	1	1		3	1								6	3	1	
House C4			2				1	3								1	3	2	
OS62C																			
House 1	2						1		1							3		1	
House 2	6			5	1			6	2	2						13	7	2	
House 4	3	1		10			7	2		4			1			25	3		
House 5				1			2									3			
House 6							2									2			
House 7	1									1						2			
House 8	2		1	1			5	2				1	1			9	2	2	
House 9	2		1		1	1	2	11	2							4	12	4	
House 10	1															1			
Total	20	2	6	18	3	1	23	26	8	7		1	2			70	31	16	1

P = Pacific marine and estuary
A = Atlantic drainage
U = Unidentified

Table 9. Utilization of shells: Early and Middle Formative Tierras Largas house floors

Time period	Ornaments and finished pieces, including fragments	Unfinished pieces and waste products	Unworked fragments	Unworked whole shells	Tools	Total
Mixed Formative	6	4	7	1		18
Monte Alban I-A	1	2				3
Guadalupe phase	2	1	2		1	6
Late San José phase	12	5	13	3		33
Early San José phase	1	2	1	1		5
Late Tierras Largas phase	4	2	2		1	9
Early Tierras Largas phase	2					2
Total	28	16	25	5	2	76

Summary

Two distinct shell exchange networks have been outlined for the Early and Middle Formative Periods. The first, based on Pacific Coast marine and estuary shells, involves the movement of raw material from the coast to craftsmen in the highlands who manufactured ornaments for local distribution. The links in this network cannot be identified due to lack of excavated Pacific Coast sites, nor are the mechanisms by which the finished products were distributed understood. By contrast, unworked Atlantic drainage shell appears to have been generally more available, suggesting it may have been obtained directly in much the same manner as Early Formative Tierras Largas obtained obsidian. Reduction in the availability of this shell, as well as of Pacific forms, during the Middle Formative suggests a period of centralization and associated reduction in long-distance exchange.

REFERENCES

COE, MICHAEL D.
  1961 *La Victoria, an early site on the coast of Guatemala.* Papers of the Peabody Museum of Archaeology and Ethnology 53. Cambridge, Mass.
COE, MICHAEL D., KENT V. FLANNERY
  1967 *Early cultures and human ecology in south coastal Guatemala.* Smithsonian Contributions to Anthropology 3. Washington, D.C.
DELGADO, AUGUSTÍN
  1961 "La sequencia arqueológica en el Istimo de Tehuantepec," in *Los Mayas del Sur y sus relaciones con los Nahuas meridionales.* Mexico City: Sociedad Mexicana de Antropología.

1965   Archaeological research at Santa Rosa, Chiapas and in the region of Tehuantepec. *Papers of the New World Archaeological Foundation* 12/13. Provo, Utah: Brigham Young University.

KEEN, A. MYRA

1958   *Sea shells of tropical west America.* Stanford: Stanford University Press.

PIRES-FERREIRA, JANE WHEELER

1973   "Formative Mesoamerican exchange networks." Unpublished Ph.D. dissertation, University of Michigan, Ann Arbor.

STRATHERN, MARILYN

1969   Stone axes and flake tools: evaluations from New Guinea. *Proceedings of the Prehistoric Society* 35: 330–344.

VAILLANT, GEORGE C.

1930   Excavations at Zacatenco. *Anthropological Papers of the American Museum of Natural History* 32(1). New York.

1935   Excavations at El Arbolillo. *Anthropological Papers of the American Museum of Natural History* 35(2). New York.

WINTER, MARCUS C.

1973   "Tierras Largas: a formative community in the Valley of Oaxaca, Mexico." Unpublished Ph.D. dissertation, University of Arizona, Tucson.

Mössbauer Spectral Analysis of Olmec Iron Ore Mirrors: New Evidence of Formative Period Exchange Networks in Mesoamerica

JANE WHEELER PIRES-FERREIRA
and BILLY JOE EVANS

The nature of Preclassic Olmec society has been an object of speculation and study by Mesoamerican archaeologists for more than a hundred years. The Olmec were first known from the lowland Gulf Coast sites of Tres Zapotes (Melgar and Serrano 1871; Stirling 1942), La Venta (Blom and LaFarge 1926; Stirling 1943) and San Lorenzo (Tenochtitlán) (Stirling 1955). At these sites the earth-mound complexes (oriented 7–12° west of true north, associated *inter alia* with sculptures, colossal heads, buried serpentine, and carved jade offerings as well as concave mirrors made of iron ore) made up the corpus of what came to be called the Olmec culture or art style. From 1928 to 1933, ceramics and jades clearly related to the lowland Olmec tradition were excavated in the Central Highlands of Mexico (Vaillant 1935). However, when Vaillant demonstrated a greater antiquity for this material than was previously suspected, the error of naming the art style after the historic Olmec of the Gulf Coast became obvious ("Mayas y Olmecas" 1942). Thus the question of origin for the apparently elaborate Olmec society was removed from history into

We wish to thank J. T. Meyers, Museum of Anthropology, University of Michigan, for writing the data-plotting program. The Mössbauer measurements were supported by grants to B. J. Evans from the Petroleum Research Fund, which is administered by the American Chemical Society, and a basic research grant from the Alfred P. Sloan Foundation. We wish to thank the following persons and organizations for their kind assistance with regard to the field survey: Ing. Rubén Pesquera Velázquez, Gerente de Exploración, Consejo de Recursos Naturales no Renovables, Mexico City; Ing. Eleizer Ortiz García and Ing. James Elwell of Plan Oaxaca; Drs. Michael and Anne Kirkby of the Valley of Oaxaca Prehistoric Human Ecology Project and Leeds University, England; Sr. Cecil Welte, Director, Oficina de Estudios de Humanidad del Valle de Oaxaca, Oaxaca de Juarez, Mexico; Dr. William O. Payne, Orange Coast College, Costa Mesa, California; Mr. Richard Drennan, Museum of Anthropology, University of Michigan, Ann Arbor; and Srs. Edmundo Chávez and Eligio Martínez S. of Mitla, Oaxaca, Mexico.

prehistory; and the explanation of its pervasive influence in Mesoamerica became the focal point of "Olmec" research.

The Olmec have been explained away as being the descendents of
a now-extinct Negro race, descendants of Alexander the Great's
seamen, survivors of Atlantis, or members of the lost tribe of Israel
who arrived in the Gulf Coast area with an already highly evolved
culture. Although the exact origin of the Olmec is still unknown, few
archaeologists today would propose it to be anything but an indigenous
development. Because of the widespread pattern of Olmec objects,
much of the theorizing concerning origin and spread of this culture
has involved migration and trade route explanations. A west Mexican
origin, based on the frequency distribution of Olmec jades, was
proposed by Covarrubias (1956). Others have seen the Gulf Coast area
as the "homeland" or "metropolitan center" from which missionaries and/or commercial traders and/or armies (Bernal 1968: 122–123;
Coe 1965a: 112–113; Coe 1965b: 764, 771; Jiménez Moreno 1966: 14)
spread out in search of certain luxury goods. But only with the recent
excavations at San Lorenzo (Coe 1968) and La Venta (Drucker,
Heizer, and Squier 1959) on the Gulf Coast, at San José Mogote,
Tierras Largas, and Huitzo in the Valley of Oaxaca (Flannery, editor
1970) and at San Pablo in the state of Morelos (Grove 1970) has it
become possible to examine these hypotheses and formulate new ones
on a scientific basis. This paper is directed both to the examination
of one of these recent hypotheses concerning the exchange of iron
ore mirrors (Flannery 1968) and the study of Olmec iron ore mirrors
in general.

THIS INVESTIGATION

The simultaneous discovery of a production site for iron ore mirrors
in the Valley of Oaxaca during 1966 (Flannery 1968) and the recovery
of almost identical mirrors of the same age at San Lorenzo (Coe 1968)
have led to the suggestion of an exchange relationship between the
two sites based *in part* on San Lorenzo's (presumed) importation of
Oaxacan mirrors (Flannery 1968). The mirrors (see Plate 1) at both
sites date to the Early Formative Period, 1200–850 B.C. (that is, the
San José phase in Oaxaca and the San Lorenzo A and B phases at
San Lorenzo), thus predating the well-known mirrors from La Venta
which come from construction phases II–IV of the 850–600 B.C.
Middle Formative Period (Drucker, Heizer, and Squier 1959: 177–186).
Throughout the rest of this paper the unfortunate misnomer "Olmec"
will be eliminated in favor of the chronological expressions "Early
Formative" and "Middle Formative."

Plate 1. Magnetite mirrors and mirror fragments from Early Formative San José phase house floors, San José Mogote, Oaxaca

In order to examine both the origin and distribution of the mirrors, samples were obtained from possible geological sources in the Valley of Oaxaca and the Sierra Madre del Sur, as well as from the archaeological sites. The locations of the various geological sources and archaeological sites are shown in Figure 1.

The previous physicochemical measurements which had been made on the La Venta iron ore mirrors (Curtis 1959: 284–288) had determined only their gross petrologic characteristics. No quantitative measurements of the relative amounts of hematite, ilmenite, and magnetite, or of the composition of individual mineral phases in the different specimens were made. Such data are necessary in order to determine the geologic origin of the ores used in mirror production and to distinguish between mirrors derived from different ores. Attempts at obtaining this information through neutron activation analysis and X-ray fluorescence produced intractable results (Pires-Ferreira 1973) and sample preparation for the electron microprobe proved to be rather difficult. Wet chemical analysis is not desirable because the destruction of the mirrors necessary to obtain sufficient material for analysis could not be tolerated.

Recent developments in the instrumentation for Mössbauer spectroscopy, and the large number of carefully executed fundamental studies of magnetites (Evans 1968), ilmenites (Gibb, Greenwood and Twist 1969; Shirane, et al. 1962), and hematites (Artman, et al. 1968) using this technique, made conditions propitious for the application of Mössbauer spectroscopy to a study of the iron ore sources and mirrors from archaeological sites in Mesoamerica. Crucial to the

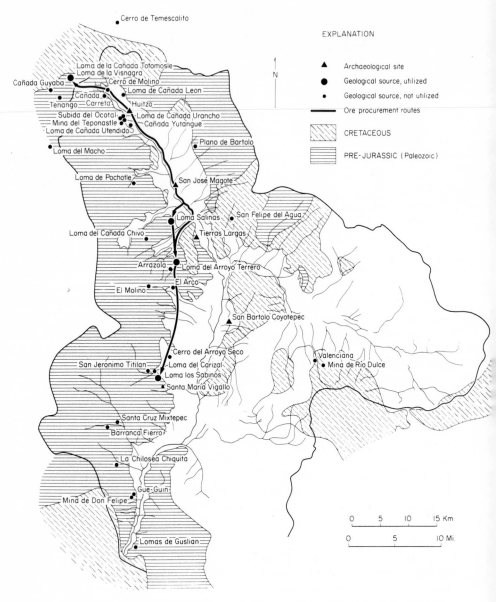

Figure 1. Location of iron ore sources and archaeological sites in the Valley of Oaxaca, Mexico

undertaking of the present investigation was the hope that correlations between various probable source materials and the mirrors could be reached by a *visual inspection of the primary data*, thus eliminating the complex data-reduction programs necessary to other techniques, which often remove the non-physicochemically trained archaeologist from participation in reading and interpreting the results of the analyses at all stages.

MÖSSBAUER SPECTROSCOPY

General Considerations

For extended discussions on nuclear gamma-ray resonance spectroscopy, commonly known as Mössbauer spectroscopy in honor of its Nobel Prize-winning discoverer (Mössbauer 1958) and more recently as NGR spectroscopy, the reader is referred to the abundant reviews (Greenwood and Gibb 1971; Goldanskii and Herber 1968). Only those aspects having direct pertinence to the present investigation are summarized here.

But for one important exception, the physics of NGR spectroscopy are very similar to those of atomic resonance spectroscopy for which the classical illustration is the absorption of the D lines of a sodium vapor lamp or of common salt placed in the flame of a Bunsen burner by sodium vapor contained in an appropriately placed tube. Mössbauer spectroscopy differs from atomic resonance absorption, however, inasmuch as the ratio of the recoil energy, E_R, to the energy breadth, Γ_γ of the emitted or absorbed radiation, i.e. E_R/Γ_γ, is much larger in the former case than in the latter. In order for there to be resonant emission and absorption of the nuclear gamma rays, the recoil process must be suppressed and this is done by incorporating the atoms into a solid substance; therefore, this technique is not generally applicable to liquids. On the other hand, the solid need not be crystalline, and glasses can also be studied.

For iron-containing specimens, such as the mirrors of Mesoamerica, nuclear gamma-ray resonance can be observed for the Fe^{57} isotope, which has a natural abundance of 2.19 percent. The resonance absorption corresponds to the nuclear transition from the ground state to the lowest-lying excited state, which has an energy of 14.4 kev. This lowest-lying excited state is populated by the electron capture decay of Co^{57} ($t_{\frac{1}{2}} = 270$ days).

The experimental set-up is depicted in Figure 2. A radioactive source of Co^{57} is used to provide the 14.4 kev gamma rays; this source is usually in the form of cobalt metal plated onto another metal, such

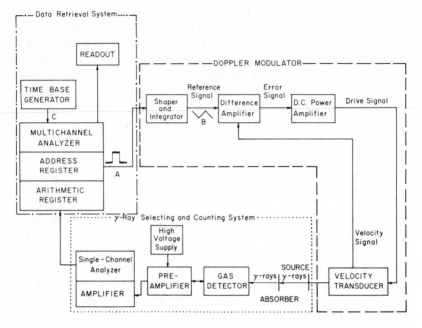

Figure 2. Experimental set-up for Mössbauer spectral analysis

as Cu, Cr, or Pd. Because of the very narrow emission lines of the source and the absorber, nuclear gamma-ray resonance is possible only if the absorber is identical to the source. If this condition is fulfilled, the resonance absorption is indicated by the decrease in count rate (below that expected for mass absorption) when the absorber is placed between the source and the detector. The detector is usually a proportional counter, but scintillation and semiconductor detectors are also used. As in other spectroscopic techniques, it is desirable to obtain the absorption or transmission as a function of energy or wave length; and for this purpose there must be some means of changing the energy of the gamma ray emitted by the radioactive Co^{57} source. The energy of the gamma ray is varied by means of the Doppler effect, that is, the source is moved *relative* to the absorber. The same result can be accomplished by moving the absorber relative to the source. The energy change, ΔE, as a function of velocity is given by the equation $\Delta E = E_o V/C$, where E_o is the energy of the emitted gamma ray, V is the velocity of the source, and C is the velocity of light. The spectra are constructed by plotting the count rate at the detector as a function of the Doppler velocity of the source. Such a spectrum is illustrated schematically in Figure 3. For thin absorbers, the line shapes are Lorentzian, that is, $I(V) = I(O)/[1+(v-V_o)/(\Gamma/2)^2]$ where $I(V)$ is the absorption at Doppler velocity V, $I(O)$ is the maximum

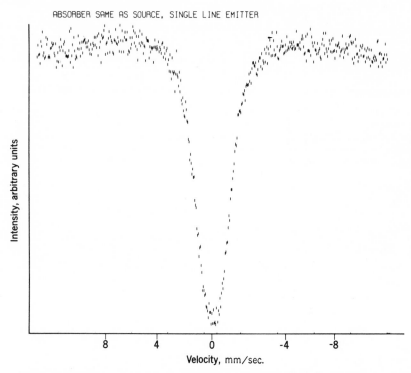

Figure 3. Mössbauer spectrum, absorber same as source, single line emitter

absorption, V_o is the Doppler velocity at maximum absorption, and Γ is the width of the absorption line, e.g. full-width-at-half-maximum intensity.

The spectrum can be obtained point-by-point using a *constant velocity* Doppler shifter and counting for a sufficiently long time (on the order of 5–10 minutes) at a given velocity setting, manually changing the velocity setting and counting at the new velocity until a complete spectrum has been obtained. These operations can also be automated. At the present time, it is more usual to have a *constant acceleration* Doppler shifter and to synchronize the motion of the Doppler shifter (or velocity transducer) with the address of a multi-channel analyzer operating in the multi-scaling mode; this mode of operation is illustrated schematically in Figure 4.

The Mössbauer spectra of most iron-containing materials do not resemble that in Figure 3. In general, the spectrum will show a shift of the absorption maximum from zero velocity and/or various splittings of the single line into many absorption lines. These shifts and splittings arise from the hyperfine interactions of the nuclear charge and electric quadrupole and magnetic dipole moments with the

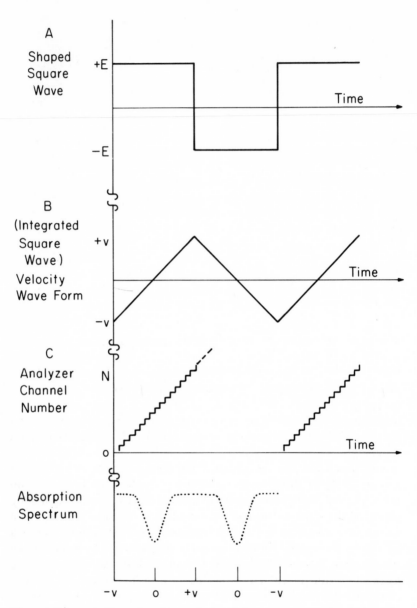

Figure 4. Schematic illustration of an analysis utilizing a *constant acceleration* Doppler shifter to obtain Mössbauer spectra

electronic charge and the electric and magnetic fields, respectively. A particular combination of magnitudes and signs of these hyperfine interations is sometimes unique to a given material. The hyperfine interactions include the following:

1. *Electrostatic interaction between the electronic charge density at the nucleus and the nuclear charge distributions in the ground and first excited states.* The Fe^{57} nucleus has different radii in its ground and first excited states. Consequently, its charge density is different in these two states and so is its interaction with the electronic charge density at the nucleus. This leads to a shift in the energy of the excited state relative to the ground state. Furthermore, since the electronic charge density at the nucleus depends upon the electronic structures of the atom and its neighboring atoms, the relative shift in the energy of the excited state will be different for various materials. Therefore, when the source and absorber are not identical, the center of gravity of the spectrum does not occur at zero Doppler velocity. The centers of gravity of Fe^{57} Mössbauer spectra in different materials and/or at inequivalent sites in the same material will not, in general, be the same. The shift of the center of gravity of the spectrum from zero velocity, known as the *isomer shift*, is usually referred to a single, standard absorber such as iron metal, stainless steel, or sodium nitroprusside. The isomer shifts of Fe^{2+} oxides are in general different from those of Fe^{3+} oxides, typical values for the former being 1.1 mm/sec and for the latter 0.5 mm/sec with respect to an iron metal absorber.

2. *Interaction between the gradient of the electric field at the nucleus and the electric quadrupole moment of the nucleus.* Since the spin quantum number of the ground state of Fe^{57} is less than 1, its electric quadrupole moment is zero and so is its interaction with the electric field gradient. However, the 14.4 kev excited state of Fe^{57} has a nuclear spin quantum number of 3/2 and a non-zero value for its electric quadrupole moment. The spin degeneracy of the excited state is partially lifted by the electric quadrupole interaction, and the excited state is split into two levels. Any time the symmetry of the site occupied by the iron atom is less than cubic, it is *possible* for there to be a non-zero electric field gradient.

3. *Magnetic dipole interaction.* In magnetically ordered materials there is a further splitting of the nuclear levels resulting from the interaction between the nuclear magnetic dipole moment and the *internal* magnetic fields generated by the electronic spin and orbital moments. For Fe^{57} the magnetic dipole interaction splits the ground state ($I = 1/2$) into two levels and the excited state ($I = 3/2$) into four levels. If the Fe^{57} atom occupies a lattice site with less than cubic symmetry in a magnetically ordered material, then both the electric

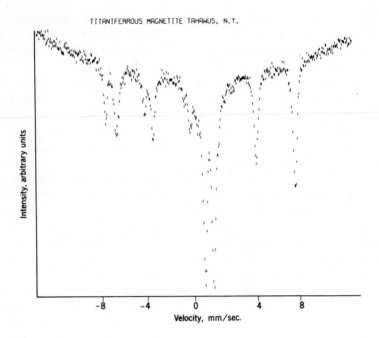

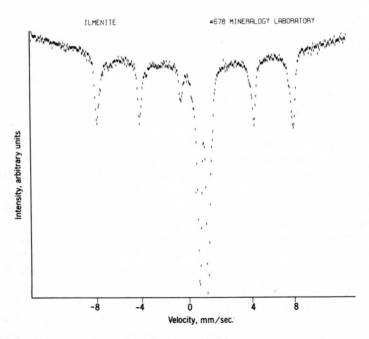

Figure 5. Mössbauer spectra of relatively pure iron oxides

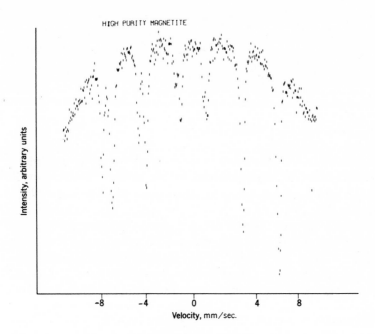

HIGH PURITY MAGNETITE

Intensity, arbitrary units

Velocity, mm/sec.

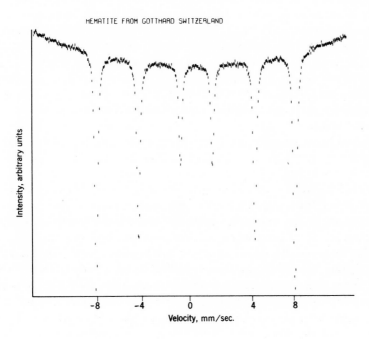

HEMATITE FROM GOTTHARD SWITZERLAND

Intensity, arbitrary units

Velocity, mm/sec.

quadrupole and magnetic dipole interactions can have non-zero values; and further shifts in the energies of different levels will take place. As in the case of the isomer shifts, the magnetic dipole interaction is different, in general, for various materials and also for inequivalent atoms in the same material.

Mössbauer Spectra of Selected Iron Oxides

The predominant iron oxides in the mirrors of Early and Middle Formative sites in Mesoamerica are magnetite (Fe_3O_4), ilmenite ($FeTiO_3$) and hematite (αFe_2O_3); there may also be some titano-magnetite ($Fe_{3-x}Ti_xO_4$) and titano-hematite ($Fe_{2-x}Ti_xO_3$) phases contained in the mirrors. The Mössbauer spectra of these materials are shown in Figure 5 (Evans 1968; Gibb and Greenwood 1969; Shirane, et al. 1962; van der Woude 1966). Ilmenite has a rhombohedral structure with Fe and Ti atoms being located in sites having six oxygen nearest neighbors; and even though the sites have approximately octahedral symmetry, the site symmetry is less than cubic. Above 55 °K ilmenite is not magnetically ordered, and the magnetic dipole splitting of the Fe^{57} nuclear levels is expected to be absent at 300 °K. The spectrum in Figure 5, exhibiting only an isomer shift and an electric quadrupole interaction, is in accord with the structural and magnetic properties. αFe_2O_3 has a structure very similar to that of ilmenite but differs from $FeTiO_3$ inasmuch as the Ti sites of $FeTiO_3$ are occupied by Fe in αFe_2O_3. However, hematite is magnetically ordered at 300 °K, being antiferromagnetic and having a magnetic ordering temperature of 950 °K (Schieber 1967). As expected, its spectrum exhibits all three interactions with values characteristic of an Fe^{3+} oxide.

Titano-hematites will have Fe^{57} Mössbauer spectra intermediate between those of hematite and ilmenite (Shirane, et al. 1962). For small values of x in $Fe_{2-x}Ti_xO_3$, the Mössbauer spectra will resemble that of αFe_2O_3, with the separation between the outermost lines decreasing more rapidly than any of the other line separations with increasing x. The width of the outermost lines and the relative intensity of the innermost pair of lines will also increase with increasing x.

Magnetite has the spinel structure and contains three inequivalent iron atoms: (1) 8 Fe^{3+} ions in tetrahedral oxygen coordination; (2) 8 Fe^{3+} ions in 6-coordinated oxygen polyhedra; and (3) 8 Fe^{2+} ions in 6-coordinated oxygen polyhedra. The 6-coordinated polyhedra are only approximately octahedral. There is a reduction in the number of time-averaged, inequivalent iron atoms in magnetite due to rapid electron exchange among the 6-coordinated Fe^{2+} and Fe^{3+} ions at

300 °K. The rapid electron exchange has the effect of reducing the two inequivalent 6-coordinated ions to a single, time-averaged species during the characteristic measurements time of the Fe^{57} Mössbauer measurement. The doublet structure in the absorption peaks in the negative velocity region of Figure 5 (magnetite) is due to the two different spectra arising from the tetrahedrally coordinated Fe^{3+} and the time-averaged $(Fe^{3+} - Fe^{2+})$ 6-coordinated ions. The more intense member of the doublets is due to the time-averaged $(Fe^{2+}-Fe^{3+})$ species.

Titano-magnetites will exhibit spectra having a relationship to pure Fe_3O_4 in a manner similar to that expected for hematites and titano-hematites (Banerjee, et al. 1967).

From the Mössbauer spectra in Figure 5, it is clear that a straight-forward distinction can be made between materials that consist of different amounts of $FeTiO_3$, αFe_2O_3, and Fe_3O_4. For the massive iron oxide deposits from which the source materials for the mirrors were extracted, the relative amounts of the different iron oxides are not expected to vary greatly over regions the sizes of the finished mirrors. Therefore, a determination of the relative amounts of the iron oxides might serve to distinguish between mirrors from different sources. Because the spectra of each of these iron oxides are also sensitive to impurities, especially to titanium, the character of each of the individual spectra in a multiphase mirror can also be used as an indicator of differences and similarities between the source materials of different mirrors. The present technique differs from the traditional chemical methods since differences in both chemical composition and structure are employed in characterizing the mirrors. It is also obvious from the spectra presented that conclusions can be drawn concerning the mirrors and their possible source materials by visual inspection of the primary data.

EXPERIMENTAL

A systematic survey of all potential iron-bearing geologic zones in the Valley of Oaxaca was completed during a five-month period in 1967. Surveys of the Isthmus of Tehuantepec, highland Chiapas, and More-los were also completed in 1968 and 1970 (Pires-Ferreira 1973). A sampling procedure designed to test physical variation within the iron ore at each source was used for all fifty-four sources examined. The thirty-six major surface exposures of iron ore discovered in the Valley of Oaxaca (see Figure 1) are described in Table 1, and the eighteen sources sampled outside the valley are described in Table 2. Archaeo-logical samples were obtained from the collections of museums and various individuals. A summary of the samples tested to date is presented in Table 3 (see Appendix for Tables).

Material for the Mössbauer analysis was obtained with a diamond or tungsten stylus from a 1 cm^2 area. For the highly polished mirrors absorber material was removed from the unpolished surface. Absorbers were prepared by mixing 50 milligrams of the powdered sample with thinned Duco cement, forming a one-inch disc of the slurry on a 0.005-inch mylar backing and permitting it to air dry.

The Mössbauer spectra were obtained with a constant acceleration, electromechanical drive which is similar in design to those in use at the United States National Bureau of Standards (DeVoe 1970). The 14.4 kev gamma rays were detected with a proportional counter filled with a 90 percent argon–10 percent CO_2 gas mixture. The 14.4 kev pulses were selected using a single-channel analyzer and stored in a 1024 channel analyzer operating in the multi-scaling mode; only 256 or 512 channels of the analyzer memory were used to store the spectrum. A seven millicurie source of Co^{57} in a copper matrix was employed as the Mössbauer source and typically a spectrum with an off-resonant count per channel of 5×10^5 was obtained in 12 hours.

The counts per channel were obtained using a teletype printer/punch and were plotted without further data analysis on a computer-controlled digital plotter. The plots of the *primary data* for some of the geological sources and archaeological samples are presented in Figures 6 to 21.

RESULTS

On comparison of the Mössbauer spectra of both the ore source and archaeological samples (Figures 6 to 21) with those of pure magnetite, hematite, and ilmenite (see Figure 5), it is readily observed that these are the dominant mineral phases in the samples. Further, it is clear that in most cases one of these mineral phases predominates, thereby facilitating the division of the samples into generalized groups according to the type of dominant iron oxide: I, samples composed principally of magnetite; II, samples of relatively pure hematite; III, samples of ilmenite; IV, samples containing a mixture of magnetite and ilmenite; and V, samples containing a mixture of magnetite and hematite. In the case of the archaeological samples, these groups were further subdivided according to the probable geologic origin.

One question of particular interest in the study of geological sources was just how widely the Mössbauer spectra of samples collected from different parts of a source would vary. Two series of five samples each from the Loma los Sabinos and Cerro de Temescalito sources were analyzed. The results (see Figure 10) showed in both cases that there

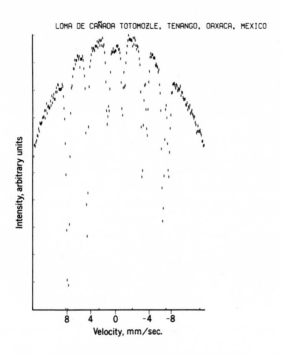

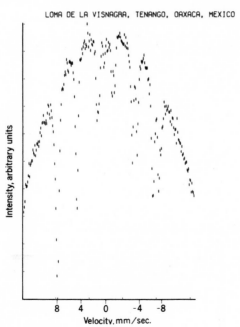

Figure 6. Mössbauer spectra: Group I–A, Magnetite. Loma de Cañada Totomosle, Loma de la Visnagra sources

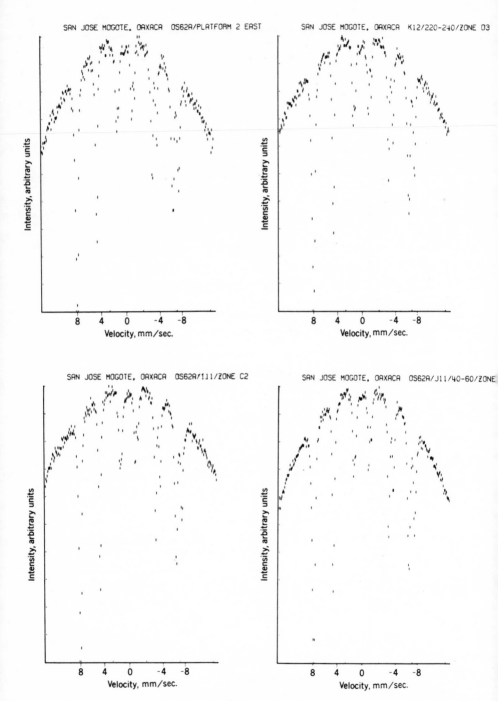

Figure 7. Mössbauer spectra: Group I–A, Magnetite. Archaeological samples matching the Loma de Cañada Totomosle-Loma de la Visnagra source

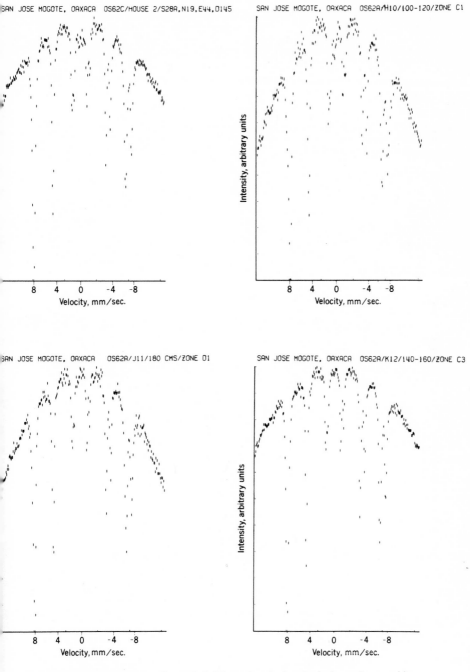

Figure 8. Mössbauer spectra: Group I–A, Magnetite. Archaeological samples matching the Loma de Cañada Totomosle-Loma de la Visnagra source

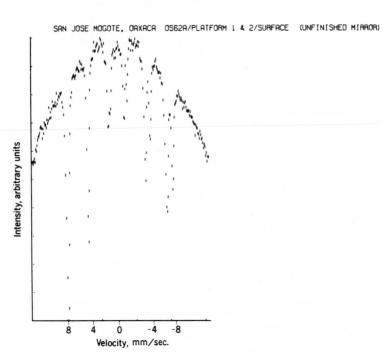

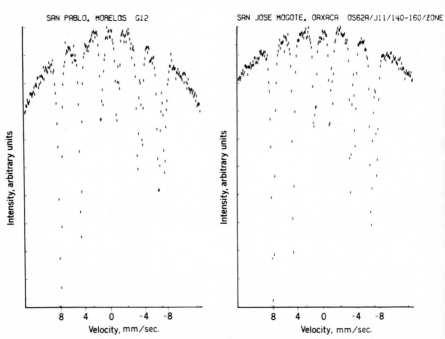

Figure 9. Mössbauer spectra: Group I–A, Magnetite. Archaeological samples matching the Loma de Cañada Totomosle-Loma de la Visnagra source

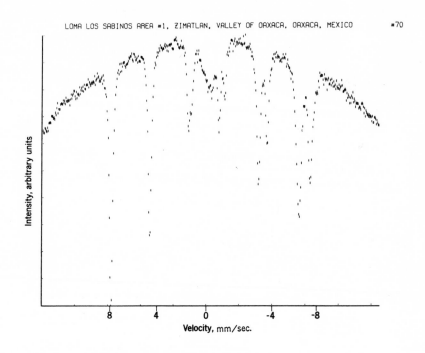

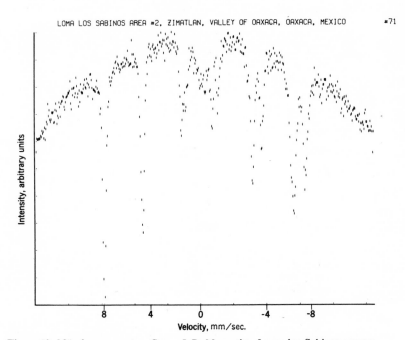

Figure 10. Mössbauer spectra: Group I–B, Magnetite. Loma los Sabinos source

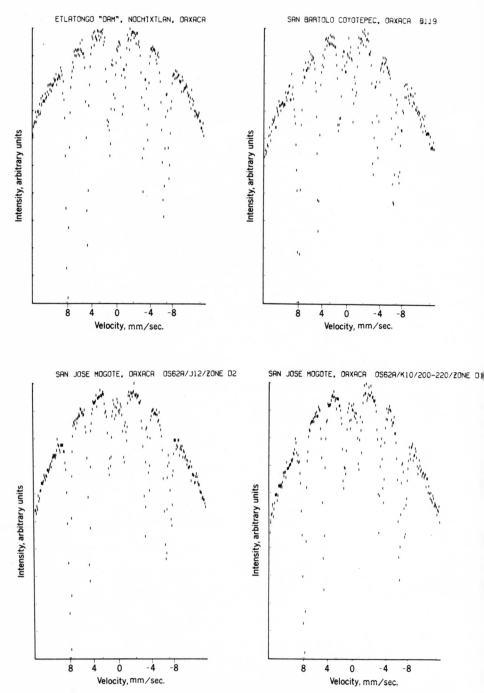

Figure 11. Mössbauer spectra: Group I–B, Magnetite. Archaeological samples matching the Loma los Sabinos source

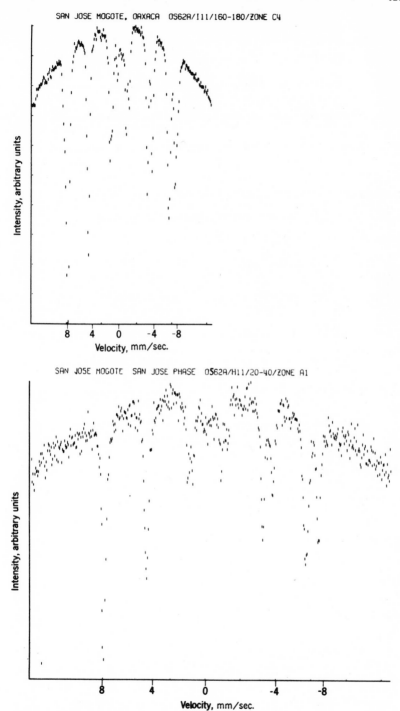

Figure 12. Mössbauer spectra: Group I–B, Magnetite. Archaeological samples matching the Loma los Sabinos source

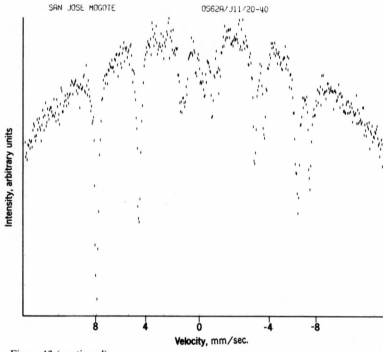

Figure 12 (continued)

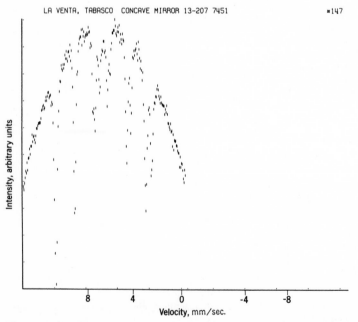

Figure 13. Mössbauer spectra: Group I–C, Magnetite. Unmatched magnetite source

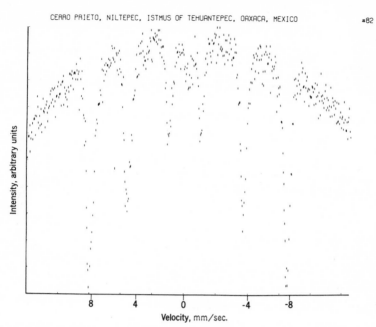

Figure 14. Mössbauer spectrum: Group II–A, Hematite. Cerro Prieto, Niltepec source

was no appreciable variation in composition and structural details of the major phases throughout the ore source. Once this was established, the probability of *accurately* identifying the geologic origin of the ores used for the mirrors was greatly increased.

Several spectral details were used in matching the archaeological and source samples. For the magnetite samples, the relative intensity and separation of the doublet structure of the peaks in the extreme negative velocity region were used to distinguish between the various sources which make up this group. For mirrors containing hematite and ilmenite, the spectra are so distinctive that the choices are obvious. For the mixed magnetite–ilmenite group the presence of magnetite is evidenced by the doublet structure in the negative velocity region. In some cases a significant amount of Ti has been dissolved in the magnetite and the doublet structure has been reduced to a strong outer peak and a weak inner peak. The relative intensity of these two peaks of the doublet, however, serves to distinguish between different sources.

The largest number of archaeological samples are magnetites (Group I). Utilizing the spectral details outlined above, we have subdivided this group according to three probable geologic source origins. A summary of the archaeological samples, divided into the probable source groups, is presented in Table 3. Group I-A included

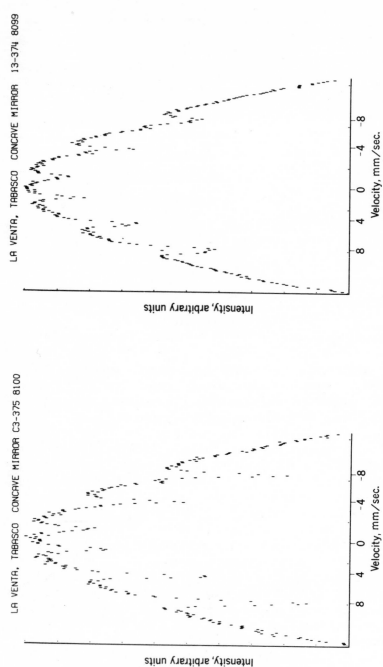

Figure 15. Mössbauer spectra: Group II–A, Hematite. Archaeological samples matching the Cerro Prieto, Niltepec source

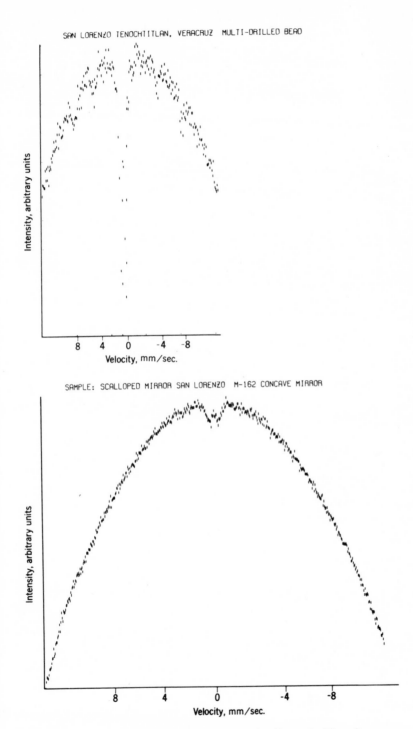

Figure 16. Mössbauer spectra: Group III–A, Ilmenite. Unmatched ilmenite source

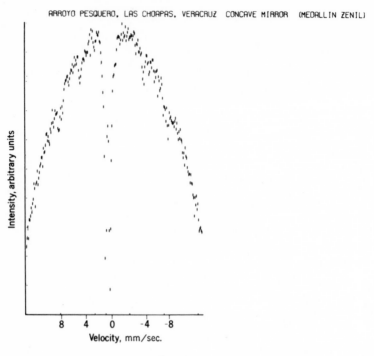

ARROYO PESQUERO, LAS CHOAPAS, VERACRUZ   CONCAVE MIRROR   (MEDALLIN ZENIL)

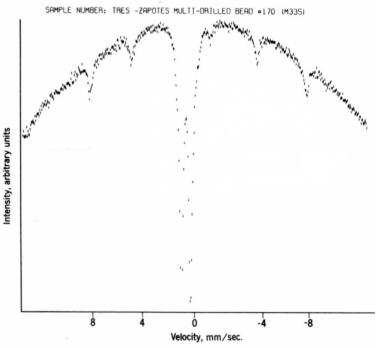

SAMPLE NUMBER: TRES –ZAPOTES MULTI–DRILLED BEAD =170 (M335)

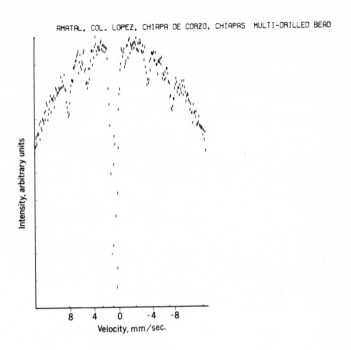

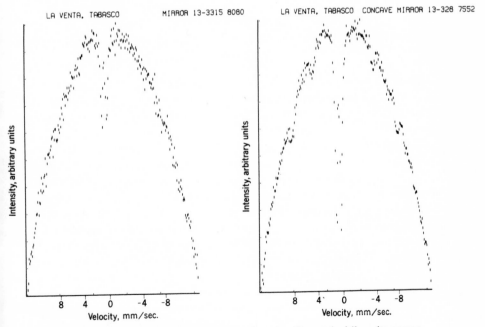

Figure 17. Mössbauer spectra: Group III–A, Ilmenite. Unmatched ilmenite source

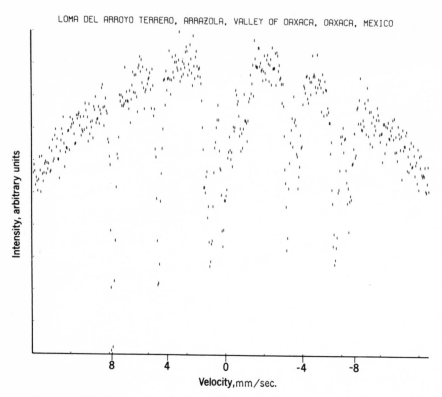

Figure 18. Mössbauer spectrum: Group IV–A, mixed magnetite and ilmenite. Loma del Arroyo Terrero source

ten Early Formative San José phase samples from the Oaxaca Valley site of San José Mogote, and one Early Formative San Pablo–La Juana phase sample from the site of San Pablo in the state of Morelos. These nearly identical spectra of a quite pure magnetite, free from any ilmenite contamination, closely match the spectrum obtained for the source of Loma de Cañada Totomosle in the *municipio* of Santiago Tenango, located two kilometers to the northwest of the headwaters of the Río Atoyac and just outside the Valley of Oaxaca. This source is located on the side of a mountain which has been cut through by a stream. A similar ore deposit called Loma de la Visnagra was encountered on the mountain side directly opposite the Loma de Cañada Totomosle source and yielded a spectrum very similar to it. The geographical proximity and spectra similarity point toward a probable common origin of the two ore deposits, and so they will be referred to as the Loma de Cañada Totomosle–Loma de la Visnagra source. The ore found here is compact and non-friable. In section it presents inclusion-free surfaces quite suitable for mirror making.

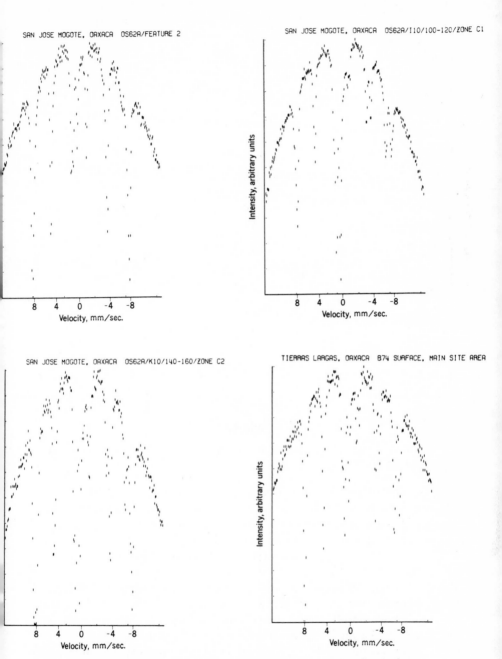

Figure 19. Mössbauer spectra: Group IV–A, mixed magnetite and ilmenite. Archaeological samples matching the Loma del Terrero source

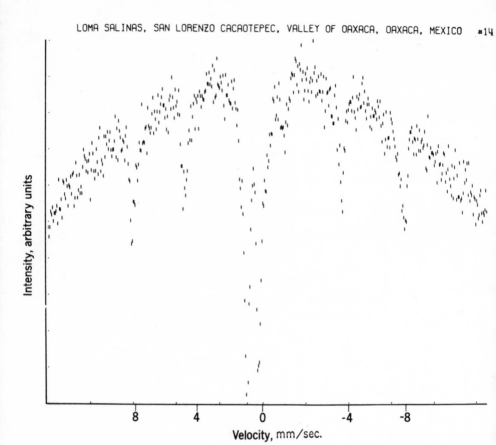

Figure 20. Mössbauer spectrum: Group IV–B, mixed magnetite and ilmenite. Loma Salinas source

   The second sub-group of magnetite samples, Group I-B, includes five Early Formative San José phase samples from San José Mogote, one San José phase sample from San Bartolo Coyotepec, a second site in the Valley of Oaxaca, and one sample of similar age from Cruz phase levels at the site of Etlatongo in the neighboring Valley of Nochixtlán. The spectra are similar to those of Group I-A, but here a significant amount of ilmenite contamination serves to distinguish between the two sub-groups. The spectra of these archaeological samples closely match those from the Loma los Sabinos and Cerro de Temescalito sources. Although it is difficult to visually distinguish between these two sources without resorting to spectrum-stripping techniques, we feel that there are other considerations which make the ore at Cerro de Temescalito an unlikely source. On the one hand, the Loma los Sabinos, Zimatlán, source is located in the Valley of Oaxaca in an area where there is archaeological evidence of Early

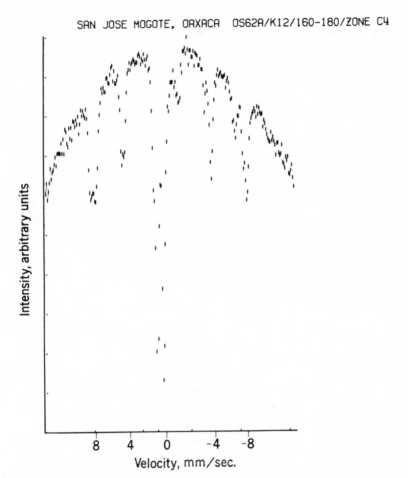

Figure 21. Mössbauer spectrum: Group IV–B, mixed magnetite and ilmenite. Archaeological sample matching the Loma Salinas source

Formative occupation (Flannery 1970). The ore, which occurs on the surface in quite large lumps, is very compact, having few large fissures and fractures and exhibiting little or no weathering. In section it presents essentially inclusion-free regions which could be used for mirror making. On the other hand, however, the Cerro de Temescalito source is located outside the Valley of Oaxaca in a mountainous area known from archaeological survey not to have been occupied until the Classic Period (Drennan, personal communication). Furthermore, the ore at this source, whether from the surface or sub-surface, contains severely weathered zones along both external fractures and fissures and freshly exposed internal surfaces which would cause the ore to be too friable for mirror making.

The third sub-group, Group I-C, consists only of one Middle Formative Period sample, a scalloped-edged, concave mirror from La Venta. The spectrum of this mirror does not match any of the sources we have examined to date.

Only two of the archaeological samples examined proved to be of hematite. The two samples which will be referred to as Group II-A are concave mirrors from the Middle Formative Period site of La Venta. They present nearly identical spectra and are tentatively identified as being made of ore from the source of Cerro Prieto, located at Niltepec on the Isthmus of Tehuantepec. Although this is the source suggested by Williams and Heizer (1965: 12) as the probable origin of La Venta mirror ore, more iron ore sources are known to exist in the region than were sampled in this survey and for this reason the identification must be considered tentative. However, the Cerro Prieto ore is dense and compact, showing little weathering and containing few fissures or fractures, and would have served well for mirror making.

Seven of the archaeological samples examined produced such closely identical ilmenite spectra that they are almost certainly made of ore from a single geologic source. Although the spectra do not match any of the sources we examined, we will refer to them as Group III-A. Three of the samples are concave mirrors; one from the Middle Formative site of La Venta, one from Middle Formative levels at San Lorenzo, and one from an undated deposit at Arroyo Pesquero, Las Choapas, Veracruz (Figures 16 and 17). One of the samples is a flat, poorly polished mirror from La Venta, and the remaining three samples are unique multi-drilled beads. One of the beads comes from Early Formative levels at San Lorenzo, the second from probable Middle or Late Formative associations at Tres Zapotes, and the third from an undated cache at Amatal, near Chiapa de Corzo.

The mixed magnetite–ilmenite samples are subdivided into two different source groups. Group IV-A consists of three Early Formative San José phase pieces from the site of San José Mogote and one probable San José phase piece from Tierras Largas which is also in the Valley of Oaxaca. The spectra matched that obtained for the Loma del Arroyo Terrero source which is located on lands of the *municipio* of Arrazola, just off the western slope of Monte Alban in the Valley of Oaxaca. The surface exposure of the ore is slight, and the small lumps found are probably not of adequate quality for mirror making.

Group IV-B contains a single sample of Early Formative age from San José Mogote. The spectrum matches one obtained for the Loma Salinas sources at San Lorenzo Cacaotepec in the Valley of Oaxaca. Although the ore at this source is found over a fairly large area, it occurs only in small fragments – generally too small for mirror making.

DISCUSSION

The Early Formative

All but one of the archaeological samples of the Early Formative Period (1200–850 B.C.) were either magnetites or mixed magnetite–ilmenites from geological sources in the Valley of Oaxaca. The majority of the samples examined came from San José Mogote, the largest site in the Valley of Oaxaca during this period, situated on a localized, non-iron-bearing zone of ignimbrite tuff. A surface survey of the site revealed a heavy concentration of iron ores, more than 600 pieces in a single area approximately 25×25 meters, which had been collected from various iron sources in the valley. Excavations adjacent to this area unearthed a series of four house floors and associated midden deposits. Whole and broken magnetite mirrors, unfinished mirrors, and worked and unworked lumps of iron ore were found together on these floors. Comparative examination of the finished and unfinished mirrors reveals a similarity in size, shape, and grinding technique which indicates that mirrors were being produced. The typical products are thumbnail-size, flat-surface mirrors of various geometric forms and highly polished on one or two sides (see Plate 1). Traces of multi-directional grinding are discernible on the unfinished and rough-finished sides of the mirrors. Closer examination of the mirror surfaces revealed some traces of ocher in surface irregularities, indicating that this substance may have been used in order to obtain the high polish of the finished products.

Analysis of the ore lumps and unfinished mirrors from the San José Mogote house floors indicates that ore was collected from at least four sources. The Loma de Cañada Totomosle–Loma de la Visnagra magnetite source, 27 kilometers by air northwest of the site, is represented by ten samples. This source, located in the mountains just outside the valley, was exploited throughout the entire period of mirror production at San José Mogote. Although it is located beyond the present known geographical limits of Early Formative settlements in the Valley of Oaxaca (Flannery, personal communication), it may have become known as the result of exploitation of the pine trees which grow both at the site of this probable source and on the high mountains surrounding the valley. Ample evidence of importation of pine charcoal and logs was obtained in the Early Formative levels at San José Mogote (Flannery 1970: 41). The second major source of magnetic ore was Loma los Sabinos, located on the edge of the valley floor, 33 kilometers by air south of San José Mogote, within an area of known Early Formative occupation (Flannery 1970). The ore obtained from these two sources is the most inclusion-free and unweathered, and gives spectra most closely approximating those of pure magnetite of all the sources collected in and around the valley. Clearly there was a demand for high-quality magnetite ore, for many ore sources of lower quality were passed over in order to reach these sources.

In one case, however, ore lumps from such an intermediate source of titano-magnetite were collected but apparently never worked into finished mirrors. Three samples from the source of Loma del Arroyo Terrero, 14 kilometers by air from San José Mogote and 17 kilometers following watercourses along the most probable route to the Loma los Sabinos source (see Figure 1), were found on two separate house floors. It seems probable that ore from this source may have been collected while *en route* to or from the Loma los Sabinos source. The final ore source represented is a titano-magnetite ore of poor quality from the Loma Salinas source only 6 kilometers south-southwest of San José Mogote. It is not surprising to find ore from this source at the site, for it is located adjacent to the major source of ceramic clay (W. O. Payne, personal communication) and near a large mica outcrop which may also have been exploited.

Despite the large number of ore sources in the Valley of Oaxaca, distribution of iron ores and iron ore products in archaeological sites of the Early Formative is very limited. At San José Mogote, the ores are essentially limited to one mirror-making "neighborhood" or area where they are associated with luxury items and imported trade goods. Ore products have been found only at two other smaller sites in the valley. The ore lump from San José phase association at the site of San Bartolo Coyotepec was probably obtained directly from the Loma los Sabinos source which is only 16 kilometers to the southwest across the flat valley floor. At Tierras Largas, an ore lump of probable Early Formative date was found to come from the Loma del Arroyo Terrero source, which at 8 kilometers distance is the closest source to that site. We see, perhaps, the domination which San José Mogote held over the main sources particularly in the cases of Tierras Largas and Huitzo (which despite extensive excavation produced no iron ore material) located on the direct routes from San José Mogote to the two major magnetite sources (Figure 1). These smaller sites contain a few unworked lumps of ore of inferior quality from local sources probably collected in imitation of the restricted goods which were collected and processed at San José Mogote.

Considering the restricted distribution of San José Mogote mirrors within that site and valley, and their association with other luxury and import items, it was proposed (Flannery 1968) that the mirrors were part of an exchange system which probably linked Oaxaca to San Lorenzo as well as to other regions of Mexico. Although in the present study we have not been able to examine any of the Early Formative San Lorenzo mirrors, we have been able to demonstrate that Oaxaca ores were traded or exchanged towards the northwest, presumably from the site of San José Mogote. One ore lump whose Mössbauer spectrum is very similar to that of the Loma de Cañada Totomosle–Loma de la Visnagra ore (see Figures 6 and 9) was found in Early Formative levels at the site of San Pablo in the state of Morelos, 320 kilometers northwest of San José Mogote, in association with Delfina fine gray pottery also imported from the Valley of Oaxaca (W. O. Payne, personal communication). A second export piece of probable Early Formative date came from a Cruz phase association at the site of Etlatongo in the Valley of Nochixtlán, 50 kilometers north of San José Mogote. The spectrum of this sample matches the Loma los Sabinos source (see Figures 10 and 11). Although the eastern extension of San José Mogote mirror distribution has not been examined in the current study, it seems possible, based on evidence of other Oaxacan and Veracruz exchange links (Pires-Ferreira 1973), that studies now in progress may find the San Lorenzo mirrors to have a Oaxacan origin.

Turning to a consideration of the Valley of Mexico, where no magnetite mirrors of certain Early Formative date have been recovered as yet (Pires-Ferreira 1973), it is noted that small, worked, natural parting fragments of crystalline hematite are found in association with Early Formative ceramics at Tlatilco. These roughly formed "mirrors" are probably made from locally available crystalline hematite sources (José Luis Lorenzo, personal communication). The placement of these mirrors on the chest of figurines is an Early Formative tradition, and a similar placement of the pieces of crystalline hematite on figurines in the Valley of Mexico suggests that they are used in imitation of the magnetite mirrors. Because of the distinctive physical appearance of these "mirrors" and their restricted distribution, it was not necessary to use the Mössbauer technique to define this tradition of "mirror making."

The Middle Formative

Between approximately 900 and 850 B.C., mirror production came to an end in the Valley of Oaxaca. Extensive excavation of Middle Formative Guadalupe phase levels at the sites of Huitzo, San José Mogote, and Tierras Largas have failed to recover even one lump of ore. This is correlated with both the "fall" or "overthrow" and eventual abandonment of San Lorenzo and the rise of La Venta. The small flat thumbnail-size magnetite mirrors disappear from the archaeological inventory of the Gulf Coast and are replaced by large concave mirrors which are most frequently made of ilmenite and hematite.

Samples of four of the La Venta concave mirrors in the collections of the Museo Nacional de Antropología were obtained. One of these mirrors, from mound A-2 fill of Stirling's 1942 excavations (Drucker, Heizer, and Squier 1959: Figure 50c), was made of magnetite. The Mössbauer spectrum of this sample (see Figure 13) did not match any of the sources or other archaeological samples examined in the study. Technologically, however, it did match a Group III-A ilmenite mirror of similar form from Middle Formative Nacaste phase levels at the site of San Lorenzo. Both mirrors have concave reflecting surfaces surrounded by scalloped edges. The mirror from La Venta is a fragment, one edge of which has been reworked. The position of these scalloped-edge mirrors in relation to the larger plain concave mirrors from La Venta is unclear, but a possible developmental sequence might be suggested, as these mirrors form the only common link in mirror form between the sites of San Lorenzo and La Venta.

The two hematite concave mirrors from La Venta (see Figure 15) are tentatively identified as being made of ore from the Cerro Prieto source which is located at Niltepec in the Isthmus of Tehuantepec. It has been noted (Heizer 1961: 44) that Niltepec was the source of approximately 5,000 tons of serpentine found at the site of La Venta, and Williams and Heizer (1965: 12) have suggested that Niltepec is also the probable source of "ilmenite" for mirror making. As tempting as it is to make a positive identification of this source, the knowledge of other sources extant in the isthmus which were not sampled in the survey (Ojeda Rivera, et al. 1965) is a strong inhibition against doing so. The two mirrors in question are the one found in Offering 9, construction phase IV, of Drucker's 1955 excavation (Drucker, Heizer, and Squier 1959: Figure 49a) and the second also from Drucker's 1955 excavation but not illustrated in the 1959 report. In form, both mirrors utilize the natural outline of the ore lump with the concavity fitted to the size of the piece. Both are highly polished across the entire concave surface and roughly ground and shaped on the reverse side. The second mirror has a groove running diagonally across the back side. These two mirrors differ from the other La Venta mirrors in the Museo Nacional de Antropología collections in that they are the only two which utilize the natural form of the ore lump from which they were made. The other La Venta mirrors are artificially shaped on all surfaces.

The other La Venta mirrors are found to come from an ilmenite source which was not among the sources examined in this study. One of these samples, excavated by Drucker in 1955 and not illustrated in the 1959 report of Drucker, Heizer, and Squier, represents a fragment of a flat, poorly polished (unfinished?) mirror. The second is a concave mirror perforated for suspension from Offering 1943-F (Drucker, Heizer, and Squier 1959: Figure 50a). A third concave mirror from Arroyo Pesquero at Las Choapas in the collections of the museum of the Universidad Veracruzana is made from the same ilmenite ore and is so technologically similar to the La Venta mirrors that it may have been produced in the same workshop.

Three multi-drilled beads from the sites of San Lorenzo, Tres Zapotes, and Amatal were found to have been made from this same ilmenite ore. The function, widespread distribution, and date of these unique objects remain something of a mystery. Only at San Lorenzo, where they were found in a cache associated with Monument 21 in San Lorenzo phase zone C fill, are they firmly dated. The Tres Zapotes sample coming from unmarked collections in the United States National Museum would tentatively be dated as Middle–Late Formative. The Amatal samples come from an undated cache found near the site of Chiapa de Corzo.

Despite the widespread distribution in time and space of both the mirrors and multi-drilled beads made from the ore of this single, still-unlocated ilmenite source, it may be that they were all produced at a single site or workshop. Our results suggest that the location of such a workshop may be in Veracruz (La Venta?) or the Isthmus of Tehuantepec because: (1) the spectra do not match the local Chiapas sources of La Mina and Cerro Gracias a Dios, and further (2) other possible ore sources which could not be reached in the survey are known to exist in the Isthmus of Tehuantepec.

CONCLUSIONS

First of all, we have demonstrated that Mössbauer spectroscopy can be a uniquely useful technique in archaeological investigations of iron-containing artifacts. While we have limited our present study to materials with substantial amounts of iron and to a transmission spectroscopic geometry which requires removal of material from the specimens, this technique can be extended to other archaeological elements, namely tin and antimony, and can also be adapted to a scattering geometry which is completely non-destructive of both the material and physical form of the artifact. However, it is felt that the success of the present study may be unique and not attainable in other applications for which very similar Mössbauer spectra are obtained for the different phases. Difficulties can also arise in cases for which there have not been a sufficient number of fundamental Mössbauer investigations of the materials contained in the artifacts. Such an unfavorable situation appears to have existed in a recently reported Mössbauer study of ancient pottery (Cousins and Dhwarmawardena 1969).

Second, with regard to the substantive and archaeologically relevant conclusion of this study, we have demonstrated that during the Early Formative Period (1200–850 B.C.), magnetite mirrors being produced at the site of San José Mogote in the Valley of Oaxaca were made from ore obtained at two different local sources and that ores from these sources were exchanged or traded at least as far as the Valley of Nochixtlán and the state of Morelos. We have outlined reasons suggesting that this exchange system reached at least as far as the Gulf Coast. We have discussed the disappearance of the Oaxacan mirror industry around 900–850 B.C. and have documented the more diverse basis of the subsequent Gulf Coast mirror industry which utilized magnetite, ilmenite, and hematite. We have tentatively identified the Cerro Prieto, Niltepec, hematite source as the raw material for two La Venta mirrors and have shown two others, as well as a third from Arroyo Pesquero, Las Choapas, to have been made of ore from a single, although unidentified, ilmenite source.

APPENDIX

Table 1. Valley of Oaxaca iron ore sources

1. Arrazola   Sample 59

Arrazola (Etla). A small surface scatter of iron ore is found on the lower slopes of the southwest side of Monte Alban. The source is located on the north side of the road, halfway between Arrazola and Hacienda San Francisco Javier.

Hardness: 6.5
Specific gravity: 4.0
Streak: black
Luster: metallic
Fracture: irregular
Magnetism: strong

Thanks are expressed to the following persons who have assisted us in obtaining archaeological samples for analysis: Arql. Roman Piña Chan, Museo Nacional de Antropología, Mexico City; Arql. José Luis Lorenzo, Departamento de Prehistoria, Mexico City; Arql. Robert García Moll, Museo Nacional de Antropología, Mexico City; Arql. Alfonso Medellin Zenil, Museo de Antropología, Universidad Veracruzana, Xalapa; Drs. Gareth Lowe and Thomas Lee, New World Archaeological Foundation, Tuxtla Gutierrez, Chiapas; Dr. David C. Grove, Department of Anthropology, University of Illinois, Champaign-Urbana; Dr. Michael D. Coe, Department of Anthropology, Yale University, New Haven; Dr. Clifford Evans, Department of Anthropology, Smithsonian Institution, Washington, D.C.; and finally to Kent V. Flannery, Director, Valley of Oaxaca Prehistoric Human Ecology Project, whose interest and support were vital to this study.

Table 1. Valley of Oaxaca iron ore sources (continued)

2. Barranca Fierro

Barranca Fierro, ranchería of San Miguel Mixtepec, approximately one-and-one-half kilometers west of Santa Cruz Mixtepec. Surface scatter of ore sparse but extensive. Ploughed up in fields and in arroyos. In an area of typical weakly metamorphosed quartz-granite.

Hardness: 5.5
Specific gravity: 5.0
Streak: black
Luster: metallic
Fracture: irregular
Magnetism: strong

3. Cañada Carreta   Samples 18, 163

San Francisco Telixtlahuaca. Referred to as Cañada Peras in old publications. 2,300 meters at 20° northwest of the Telixtlahuaca church. Surface exposure 20 meters by 15 on a spur above the Cañada Carreta stream, a tributary of the Río Atoyac. Fairly pure ore in rotting gneiss matrix.

Hardness: 5.5
Specific gravity: 3.9–6.0
Streak: black
Luster: metallic
Fracture: irregular along crystal faces
Magnetism: strong

4. Cañada Guyaba

Santiago Tenango. 75° northwest at one kilometer's distance from the *municipio* of Santiago Tenango on the hillside of Cañada Guyaba. Fairly pure pieces of ore coming out of rotting gneiss and quartz bedrock.

Hardness: 5.5
Specific gravity: 4.9
Streak: cherry red
Luster: earthy
Fracture: crumbles
Magnetism: absent

5. Cañada Yutangue

Santa María Tenexpán. 20° southwest of the church of Tenexpán and due south approximately one-and-one-half kilometers from the archaeological site of Barrio del Rosario Huitzo (OS64). Small crystals of ore found in pockets in a pegmatite formation. Plan Oaxaca assay: TiO_2 29.90%; Fe 26.90%; CaO 13.05%; SiO_2 8.32%; and P 3.40%.

Hardness: 5.5
Specific gravity: indeterminate
Streak: brown-red
Luster: earthy
Fracture: irregular along crystal faces
Magnetism: absent

Table 1. Valley of Oaxaca iron ore sources (continued)

6. Cerro del Arroyo Seco   Sample 62

La Ciénaga. 40° northeast of the Zimatlán church at eight kilometers' distance. Located at the end of the road to Santa Inez del Monte on a southerly hill demarcated by two branches of the Arroyo Seco, one-and-one-half kilometers at 60° northwest from the end of the road. Small crystals of ore embedded in a quartz feldspar gneiss, compact and fairly pure ore.

Hardness: 5.5
Specific gravity: 5.0
Streak: black
Luster: metallic
Fracture: irregular
Magnetism: strong

7. Cerro de Molino   Sample 44

San Francisco Telixtlahuaca. 30° north of the Telixtlahuaca church at approximately two kilometers' distance. Leave Telixtlahuaca on the road to the Cañada Tomellin (north); just beyond the second bridge the red talus from the mines can be seen on the hillside to the left of the road. Surface scatter samples eroding from gneiss bedrock.

Sample 1.
Hardness: 5.5
Specific gravity: 4.8
Streak: black
Luster: metallic
Fracture: irregular along crystal faces
Magnetism: strong

Sample 2.
Hardness: 5.5
Specific gravity: 5.1
Streak: black
Luster: sub-metallic
Fracture: irregular
Magnetism: strong

Sample 3.
Hardness: 5.5
Specific gravity: 4,4
Streak: red
Luster: metallic
Fracture: irregular
Magnetism: absent

Table 1. Valley of Oaxaca iron ore sources (continued)

8. Cerro de Temescalito   Sample 45

San Francisco Telixtlahuaca. 12.3 miles from the Pan-American Highway on the road to Telixtlahuaca and San Sebastián Sedas (2.3 miles beyond the Monumento la Carbonera crossroads). The deposit covers three large hills just to the right of the road when facing north. Rotting gneiss bedrock, pure ore.

Hardness: 5.5
Specific gravity: 5.0
Streak: black
Luster: metallic
Fracture: irregular
Magnetism: strong

9. El Arco   Sample 60

Cuilapán. Located on the road from Zimatlán to Zachila at the junction of the Arroyo El Arco. Small pieces of ore are found eroding out of gneiss bedrock on the Cerro El Arco on the north side of the Arroyo El Arco and approximately two kilometers west of the road.

Hardness: 5.5
Specific gravity: indeterminate
Streak: black
Luster: metallic
Fracture: irregular
Magnetism: weak

10. El Molino   Sample 65

Cuilapán. Located approximately twelve kilometers due west of the convent at Cuilapán adjacent to the remains of a colonial hacienda. Surface scatters of small iron crystals are found on the southern bank of the Arroyo Cuilapán in gneiss bedrock.

Hardness: 5.5
Specific gravity: indeterminate
Streak: reddish brown
Luster: metallic
Fracture: irregular
Magnetism: weak

11. Gue-Guin

Santa Mará Ayoquezco. On the south slope of Loma Ayoquezco 30° southeast of the Loma Ayoquezco archaeological site and 40° southwest at two kilometers' distance from the church of Ayoquezco. Bedrock is weakly metamorphosed quartz-granite, surface scatter small.

Hardness: 5.5
Specific gravity: 3.4
Streak: red
Luster: metallic
Fracture: irregular
Magnetism: absent

12. La Chilosea Chiquita   Sample 26

Guegovela de Tlapacoyan. Three kilometers west of Agua Blanca between the
Arroyos Aguacate and Chilosea Chiquita. A vein deposit of more or less pure ore
sticking up from poorly metamorphosed quartz-granite bedrock. Surface exposure
of 5 by 5 meters.

Hardness: 5.5
Specific gravity: 5.0
Streak: black
Luster: metallic
Fracture: irregular
Magnetism: strong

13. Loma del Arroyo Terrero   Sample 67

Arrazola (Etla). On the road from Tiracoz to Arrazola, approximately 700 meters
before entering Arrazola, a small surface scatter of ore is found to the north of
the road. This is due south of the main pyramid on Cerro de Azompa. Rotten gneiss
bedrock and pure ore.

Hardness: 5.5
Specific gravity: 5.1
Streak: black
Luster: metallic
Fracture: irregular
Magnetism: strong

14. Loma del Cañada Chivo

San Felipe Tejalapam (Etla). 37° west-northwest of Jalapa at approximately four
kilometers' distance and 55° southwest of Tejalapam at approximately five kilometers' distance. A sparse scatter of ore is found on the lower slopes of the Loma
del Cañada Chivo, below the mica mine. Rotten gneiss bedrock.

Hardness: 5.5
Specific gravity: 4.5
Streak: black
Luster: metallic
Fracture: irregular
Magnetism: weak

15. Loma de Cañada Leon

San Francisco Telixtlahuaca. At the junction of the Ríos Verde and Rosa above
the Telixtlahuaca dam. The source is exactly due north of Telixtlahuaca and
approximately one kilometer north-northeast of the dam. An abundant surface
scatter of very large pieces of ore.

Hardness: 5.5
Specific gravity: 3.2
Streak: brown
Luster: earthy
Fracture: irregular
Magnetism: absent

Table 1. Valley of Oaxaca iron ore sources (continued)

16. Loma de Cañada Totomosle

Santiago Tenango. Two-and-one-half kilometers from Tenango to the northeast, above the Río Grande. The Mogote del Sol is 10° east of magnetic north from the source. A surface scatter of 350 by 200 meters containing very high-quality ore eroding out of rotting gneiss.

Hardness: 5.5
Specific gravity: 5.0
Streak: black
Luster: metallic
Fracture: irregular
Magnetism: strong

17. Loma de Cañada Urancho

Santa María Tenexpán. One-half kilometer at 65° southwest of the church of Tenexpán on the west side of the Cañada Urancho and approximately 150 meters above the river bed. A small scatter of iron crystals on the surface associated with a pegmatite formation. Plan Oaxaca assay: TiO_2 29.90%; Fe 26.90%; CaO 13.05%; SiO_2 8.32%; P 3.40%.

Hardness: 5.5
Specific gravity: 4.0
Streak: black
Luster: non-metallic to sub-metallic
Fracture: irregular
Magnetism: weak

18. Loma de Cañada Utendido

Santiago Suchilquitongo. Follow the road to Tenexpán west from Suchilquitongo, turn south up the Cañada Utendido river bed for approximately one kilometer to the first hill due south of the end of the road. The source is located on the second flank up the hill. This is approximately two kilometers due west of the Suchilquitongo church. The small iron crystals are found in a pegmatite feldspar, quartz, mica, and ilmenite deposit.

Hardness: 5.5
Specific gravity: indeterminate
Streak: grey
Luster: sub-metallic
Fracture: irregular
Magnetism: absent

19. Loma del Carizal   Sample 68

San Jerónimo Titilán. Located on the road from Zimatlán to San Jerónimo, 10° northwest and seven kilometers' distance from the Santa María Vigallo church. A small surface exposure of heavy, high-quality ore associated with gneiss bedrock.

Hardness: 5.5
Specific gravity: 4.8
Streak: black
Luster: metallic
Fracture: irregular along crystal faces
Magnetism: absent

Table 1. Valley of Oaxaca iron ore sources (continued)

20. Loma del Macho

Tejocotes, Santiago Tenango. 30° northwest of El Poleo at kilometer 489.5 of the Pan-American highway. Approximately one-half kilometer from the house of Rubén Vivas at El Poleo along the trail adjacent to the house to the north. A surface scatter of high-quality iron ore associated with rotting gneiss bedrock. *In situ* veins of ore can be seen.

Hardness: 5.5
Specific gravity: 5.5
Streak: black
Luster: metallic
Fracture: irregular along crystal faces
Magnetism: strong

21. Loma de Pochotle

Santo Tomás Mazaltepec. 1.4 miles at 80° southwest of the Mazaltepec church and 47° southwest of Zautla. A very small scatter of ore in association with gneiss and quartz bedrock.

Hardness: 5.5
Specific gravity: 5.1
Streak: grey
Luster: sub-metallic
Fracture: irregular
Magnetism: weak

22. Loma de la Visnagra   Sample 54

Santiago Tenango. 55° southwest at three kilometers' distance from the *municipio* of Santiago Tenango on the Loma de la Visnagra facing the Mogote del Sol and above a tributary of the Río Grande. Pure, heavy ore weathering out of rotting gneiss on surface. The ore is dense with no inclusions or interior weathering along crystal faces.

Hardness: 5.8
Specific gravity: 5.0
Streak: black
Luster: metallic
Fracture: irregular
Magnetism: strong

Table 1. Valley of Oaxaca iron ore sources (continued)

23. Loma Los Sabinos   Samples 70, 71

Zimatlán. Located adjacent to the road from Zimatlán to San Jerónimo Titilán, approximately four kilometers at 60° northwest of the Zimatlán church. This extensive source consists of a surface ore exposure covering approximately one square kilometer. The ore is eroding out of a quartz-gneiss formation which is deeply cut by three arroyos. The size of the ore lumps ranges from boulders, the largest approximately 30 by 20 centimeters, to small fragments. The ore is dense, compact and of high quality, with very little evidence of surface or interior oxidation.

Hardness: 5.5
Specific gravity: 5.4
Streak; black
Luster: metallic
Fracture: irregular
Magnetism: strong

24. Loma Salinas   Samples 14, 164

San Lorenzo Cacaotepec. One-and-one-half kilometers southwest of the Cacaotepec church at 35°. Small pieces of ore are scattered across the surface of the hill and pockets of ore are exposed in gneiss bedrock where arroyo cutting has occurred. A Monte Alban IA (Late Formative) site covers part of the source area. The arroyo bed below the source provided part of the clay utilized in the ceramic industry at San José Mogote (W. O. Payne, personal communication).

Hardness: 5.5
Specific gravity: 5.2
Streak: black
Luster: metallic
Fracture: irregular
Magnetism: strong

25. Lomas de Guslián   Sample 69

Ranchería Río Y. On the east bank of the Río Atoyac at the Ranchería. A vein of ore can be seen running from the river to the top of the hill, and an abandoned mine is located on the lower slope of the hill. Large lumps of ore mixed with quartz and feldspar are eroding from the exposed vein. The ore is impure.

Hardness: 5.5
Specific gravity: 5.2
Streak: black
Luster: metallic
Fracture: crumbles irregularly
Magnetism: strong

Table 1.   Valley of Oaxaca iron ore sources (continued)

26.   Mina de Don Felipe   Sample 74

Loma de Ayoquezco, Santa María Ayoquezco. Above the Arroyo de la Cucharita
on the south flank of the Loma Ayoquezco, 20° and approximately twelve kilometers northeast of San Andrés Zabache. In a typical poorly metamorphosed
quartz-granite deposit, the deposit of ore has largely been removed by mining. A
few fragments of ore found in the mine and on the surface of fields immediately
below the entrance. Impure ore.

Hardness: 3.0
Specific gravity: indeterminate
Streak: red
Luster: earthy
Fracture: crumbles
Magnetism: absent

27.   Mina de Río Dulce

Magdalena Tetipac. One-and-one-half kilometers at 30° east of Magdalena Tetipac
in the Cañada de Río Dulce. Follow the road through Tetipac to Río Palasalina
and turn there on the road to the left immediately after crossing the river. Follow
the road for one-half kilometer along the Río Dulce, cross the river again, and
proceed 500 meters up the hill to the mine. The mine was operated in the 1930's
by an American company and is very large. Deposits of ocher occur on the surface
adjacent to the mine, but it is impossible to determine if the ore found in and around
the mine occurred on the surface.

Sample 1.
Hardness: 3.5
Specific gravity: 3.3
Streak: cherry red
Luster: earthy
Fracture: crumbles, uneven
Magnetism: absent

Sample 2.
Hardness: 5.0
Specific gravity: 4.0
Streak: red
Luster: earthy
Fracture: uneven
Magnetism: absent

28.   Mina del Teponastle

Santiago Suchilquitongo. Approximately two-and-one-half kilometers due west of
the church of Suchilquitongo. Magdalena Apasco is due east of the source and
Tenexpan is due north. Small crystals of ore found in a pegmatite deposit with
feldspar, quartz and mica. Plan Oaxaca assay: TiO_2 29.90%; Fe 26.90%; CaO
13.05%; SiO_2 8.32%; P 3.40%.

Hardness: 5.5
Specific gravity: 3.0
Streak: red-brown
Luster: earthy
Fracture: irregular
Magnetism: absent

Table 1. Valley of Oaxaca iron ore sources (continued)

29. Plano de Bartolo

San Juan Bautista Guelache. A one-hour walk north from the village of Guelache up the Cañada Plano de Bartolo. The mines of La Undida and Mina del Agua, reported by González Reyna (1962) as iron ore mines, are located here, but survey of the mines recovered no ore. The Plano de Bartolo is a third mine located one-half kilometer north of the others along the course of the river bed. Lumps of poor-quality ore were found here adjacent to the mine entrance. The bedrock is a rotting gneiss with quartz.

Hardness: 5.5
Specific gravity: 4.5
Streak: cherry red
Luster: earthy, sub-metallic
Fracture: irregular
Magnetism: absent

30. San Felipe del Agua   Sample 57

San Felipe del Agua. In the grounds of the State of Oaxaca plant nursery located on the northern edge of the village of San Felipe del Agua. Lumps of dense ore are found in association with iron-oxide-stained earth adjacent to the stream bed. The surface scatter is small and widely scattered.

Hardness: 5.6
Specific gravity: 4.2
Streak: red
Luster: earthy
Fracture: irregular
Magnetism: absent

31. San Jerónimo Titilán   Sample 75

San Jerónimo Titilán. Lumps of ore were found eroding from gneiss deposits exposed in the main street of this village. Follow the road from Zimatlán to the northwest, past the Loma los Sabinos source to the village. The surface scatter is small and the ore pieces are also small.

Hardness: 5.5
Specific gravity: 4.5
Streak: black
Luster: metallic
Fracture: irregular
Magnetism: strong

32. Santa Cruz Mixtepec

Santa Cruz Mixtepec. A mine is located one-half kilometer due west of the Santa Cruz church. A few ore lumps were found inside the mine but no surface scatter of ore was found outside the mine. The bedrock is typical poorly metamorphosed granite.

Hardness: 5.5
Specific gravity: 5.2
Streak: red
Luster: metallic
Fracture: irregular
Magnetism: absent

Table 1. Valley of Oaxaca iron ore sources (continued)

33. Santa María Vigallo   Sample 77

Santa María Vigallo. A sparse surface scatter of ore covers the hills between one
and two kilometers northwest of the *municipio* of Santa María. The ore is mixed
with the gneiss bedrock.

Hardness: 5.5
Specific gravity: indeterminate
Streak: red
Luster: sub-metallic
Fracture: irregular
Magnetism: absent

34. Subida del Ocotal   Sample 58

Santa María Tenexpán. 60° southwest of the Tenexpán church at one-half kilometer's distance on the east side of the Cañada Urancho. Small crystals of ore
are exposed in the gneiss bedrock. Plan Oaxaca assay: TiO_2 29.90%; Fe 26.90%;
CaO 13.05%; SiO_2 8.32%; P 3.40%.

Hardness: 5.5
Specific gravity: indeterminate
Streak: black
Luster: sub-metallic
Fracture: irregular
Magnetism: weak

35. Tenango   Sample 24

Santiago Tenango. Outcrop on the road from Santiago Tenango to La Carbonera
(on the Pan-American highway), three-fourths of a mile after leaving the *municipio*
of Tenango. A very low-grade ore is found in rotting gneiss.

Hardness: 5.0
Specific gravity: indeterminate
Streak: red
Luster: earthy
Fracture: uneven, crumbly
Magnetism: absent

36. Valenciana

Magdalena Tetipac. Located in the *barrio* of Valenciana of the village of Tetipac,
ore deposits are exposed in the roads of the *barrio*. Ore lumps are found in the
gneiss bedrock and are mixed with the gneiss.

Hardness: 6.5
Specific gravity: 3.5
Streak: red
Luster: sub-metallic
Fracture: irregular
Magnetism: absent

Table 2. Iron ore sources outside the Valley of Oaxaca sampled for Mössbauer spectral analysis

1. Cerro del Mercado
   Durango
2. Cerro Estaquio
   La Ventosa, Isthmus of Tehuantepec, Oaxaca
3. Cerro Gracias a Dios   Sample 81
   Hacienda La Razón, Chiapas
4. Cerro Peñela
   San Juan Guichicovi, Isthmus of Tehuantepec, Oaxaca
5. Cerro Prieto   Sample 82
   Niltepec, Isthmus of Tehuantepec, Oaxaca
6. El Encino
   Pihuamo, Jalisco
7. El Norillo
   Tamaulipas
8. El Tamarindo   Sample 25
   Jalapa del Marquez, Isthmus of Tehuantepec, Oaxaca
9. La Huerta
   Jalisco
10. La Mina   Sample 84
    Colonia Lopes, Chiapas
11. La Negra
    Chihuahua
12. La Perla
    Chihuahua
13. LaVentosa
    Isthmus of Tehuantepec, Oaxaca
14. Las Cuevas   Sample 83
    Jalapa del Marquez, Isthmus of Tehuantepec, Oaxaca
15. Las Truches
    Michoacán
16. Nizaduga
    Salinas, Isthmus of Tehuantepec, Oaxaca
17. Peña Colorada
    Colima
18. Rincón Moreno
    Isthmus of Tehuantepec, Oaxaca

Table 3. Summary of tested iron ore samples

Site	Provenience	Period	Sample number	Description	Reference
Group I-A: Loma de Cañada Totomosle–Loma de la Visnagra magnetite source, Tenango, Oaxac					
San José Mogote, Valley of Oaxaca	OS62A/Platforms 1 and 2, surface	San José phase, Early Formative	8	Unifinished mirror	
San José Mogote, Valley of Oaxaca	OS62A/Platform 2, east	San José phase, Early Formative	133	Ore lump	
San José Mogote, Valley of Oaxaca	OS62A/J 11/40–60, zone B1	San José phase, Early Formative	103	Ore lump	
San José Mogote, Valley of Oaxaca	OS62A/H 10/100–120, zone C1	San José phase, Early Formative	7	Ore lump	
San José Mogote, Valley of Oaxaca	OS62A/I 11/zone C2	San José phase, Early Formative	105	Unfinished mirror	
San José Mogote, Valley of Oaxaca	OS62A/J 11/140–160, zone C3	San José phase, Early Formative	2	Ore lump	
San José Mogote, Valley of Oaxaca	OS62A/K 12/140–160, zone C3	San José phase, Early Formative	4	Ore lump	
San José Mogote, Valley of Oaxaca	OS62A/J 11/180 CMS, zone D1	San José phase, Early Formative	108	Ore lump	
San José Mogote, Valley of Oaxaca	OS62A/K 12/220–240, zone D3	San José phase, Early Formative	12	Ore lump	
San José Mogote, Valley of Oaxaca	OS62C/House 2/S28 A	San José phase, Early Formative	5	Ore lump	
San Pablo, Morelos	G 12	San Pablo phase, Early Formative	93	Ore lump	
Group I-B: Loma los Sabinos sources, Zimatlán, Valley of Mexico					
San José Mogote, Valley of Oaxaca	OS62A/H 11/20–40, zone A1	San José phase, Early Formative	6	Ore lump	
San José Mogote, Valley of Oaxaca	OS62A/J 11/20–40, zone A2	San José phase, Early Formative	11	Ore lump	
San José Mogote, Valley of Oaxaca	OS62A/I 11/160–180, zone C4	San José phase, Early Formative	1	Ore lump	
San José Mogote, Valley of Oaxaca	OS62A/K 10/200–220, zone D1	San José phase, Early Formative	10	Ore lump	
San José Mogote, Valley of Oaxaca	OS62A/J 12, zone D2	San José phase, Early Formative	13	Ore lump	
San Bartolo Coyotepec, Valley of Oaxaca	Surface	Eroded San José phase level	96	Ore lump	
Etlatongo, Valley of Nochixtlán, Oaxaca	Platform	Cruz phase (?), Early Formative	97	Mirror	
Group I-C: Unmatched magnetic source					
La Venta, Tabasco	Mound A2 fill 1942 (Museo Nacional de Antropología e Historia, 13–207 7451)	Construction phase I–IV, Middle Formative	147	Reworked concave mirror fragment with scalloped edge	Drucker, Heizer, Squier 1 182, Fig 50

able 3. Summary of tested iron ore samples (continued)

ite	Provenience	Period	Sample number	Description	Reference
roup II-A: Cerro Prieto Hematite source, Niltepec, Isthmus of Tehuantepec					
a Venta, Tabasco	Drucker 1955 (Museo Nacional de Antropología et Historia, 13–375 8100)	Middle Formative	144	Concave mirror fragment illustrated	Drucker, Heizer, and Squier 1959.
a Venta, Tabasco	Offering 9, 1955 (Museo Nacional de Antropología e Historia, 13–374 8099)	Construction phase IV, Late-Middle Formative	143	Complete concave mirror perforated for suspension	Drucker, Heizer, and Squier 1959: 180, Figure 49
roup III-A: Unmatched ilmenite source					
a Venta, Tabasco	Drucker 1955 (Museo Nacional de Antropología e Historia, 13–355 8080)	Middle Formative	146	Fragment of flat, poorly polished mirror perillustrated	Drucker, Heizer, and Squier 1959
a Venta, Tabasco	Offering 1943-F (Museo Nacional de Antropología e Historia, 13–328 7552)	Middle Formative	148	Fragment of concave mirror perforated for suspension	Drucker, Heizer, and Squier 1959: 182, Figure 50
as Choapas, Veracruz	Arroyo Pesquero	Middle Formative	92	2 fragments of concave mirror	Museo de Xalapa, Veracruz
an Lorenzo, Veracruz	Cache associated with colossal head, Monument 17	Early Formative	141	Multi-drilled bead	
matal (near Chiapa de Corzo), Chiapas	Isolated cache	?	94	Multi-drilled bead	
an Lorenzo, Veracruz	SL PNW St. Ia 00820	Nacaste phase, Middle Formative	162	Scalloped-edge, concave mirror	
res Zapotes, Veracruz	?	Middle-Late Formative	170	Multi-drilled bead	
roup IV-A: Loma del Arroyo Terrero mixed magnetite and ilmenite source, Arrazola, Valley of axaca					
an José Mogote, Valley of Oaxaca	OS62A/I 10/ 100–120, zone C1	San José phase, Early Formative	3	Ore lump	
an José Mogote, Valley of Oaxaca	OS62A/K 10/ 140–160, zone C2	San José phase, Early Formative	9	Ore lump	
an José Mogote, Valley of Oaxaca	OS62A/feature 2, zone C2	San José phase, Early Formative	109	Ore lump	
ierras Largas, Valley of Oaxaca	B 74 main site area surface	San José phase?, Early Formative?	144	Ore lump with quartz inclusions	
roup IV-B: Loma Salinas mixed magnetite and ilmenite source, San Lorenzo Cacaotepec, Valley f Oaxaca					
an José Mogote, Valley of Oaxaca	OS62A/K 12/ 160–180, zone C4	San José phase, Early Formative	107	Ore lump, worked	

REFERENCES

ARTMAN, J. O., A. H. MUIR, JR., H. WIEDERSICH
1968   Determination of the nuclear quadrupole moment of Fe^{57m} from αFe_2O_3 data. *Physical Review* 173(2): 337–343.
BANERJEE, S. K., W. O'REILLY, C. E. JOHNSON
1967   Mössbauer-effect measurements in FeTi spinels with local disorder. *Journal of Applied Physics* 38(3): 1289–1290.
BERNAL, I.
1968   *El mundo Olmeco*. Mexico City: Porrua.
BLOM, F., O. LA FARGE
1926   *Tribes and temples*, volume one. New Orleans.
COE, M. D.
1965a   *The jaguar's children: Pre-classic central Mexico*. New York: The Museum of Primitive Art.
1965b   "The Olmec stule and its distributions," in *Handbook of Middle American Indians*, volume three, 739–775. Austin: University of Texas Press.
1968   "San Lorenzo and the Olmec civilization," in *Dumbarton Oaks Symposium on the Olmec*, 41–71. Washington, D.C.
COUSINS, D. R., K. G. DHWARMAWARDENA
1969   Use of Mössbauer spectroscopy in the study of ancient pottery. *Nature* 223(5207): 732–733.
COVARRUBIAS, M.
1956   *Mezcala, ancient Mexican sculpture*. New York.
CURTIS, G. H.
1959   "The petrology of artifacts and architectural stone at La Venta," in *Excavations at La Venta, Tabasco, 1955*. Edited by P. Drucker, R. F. Heizer, and R. J. Squier, 284–289. Bureau of American Ethnology Bulletin 170. Washington, D.C.
DE VOE, J. R., *editor*
1970   *Radiochemical analysis section: Mössbauer spectroscopy, nuclear chemistry, nuclear instrumentation, and radioisotope techniques*. National Bureau of Standards, Technical Note 501. Washington, D.C.
DRUCKER, P., R. F. HEIZER, R. J. SQUIER, *editors*
1959   *Excavations at La Venta, Tabasco, 1955*. Bureau of American Ethnology Bulletin 170. Washington, D.C.
EVANS, B. J.
1968   "Order, disorder and hyperfine interactions in spinel ferrites." Unpublished Ph.D. dissertation, University of Chicago.
FLANNERY, K. V.
1968   "The Olmec and the Valley of Oaxaca: a model for inter-regional interaction in Formative times," in *Dumbarton Oaks Symposium on the Olmec*, 79–110. Washington, D.C.
FLANNERY, K. V., *editor*
1970   *Preliminary archaeological investigations in the Valley of Oaxaca, Mexico, 1966–1969*. A report to the National Science Foundation and the Instituto Nacional de Antropología y Historia.
GARG, V. K., S. P. OURI
1971   Quadrupolar hyperfine anisotropy in ilmenite. *Physica Status Solidi B: (Basic Research)* 44(1): K45–K47. Berlin.

GIBB, T. C., N. N. GREENWOOD, W. TWIST
1969   The Mössbauer spectra of natural ilmenites. *Journal of Inorganic and Nuclear Chemistry* 31(4): 947–954.

GOLDANSKII, V. I., R. H. HERBER
1968   *Chemical applications of Mössbauer spectroscopy.* New York: Academic Press.

GONZÁLEZ REYNA, J.
1962   *Reseña geológica del Estado de Oaxaca.* Consejo de Recursos Naturales no Renovables, No. 7E. Mexico City.

GREENWOOD, N. N., T. C. GIBB
1971   *Mössbauer spectroscopy.* London: Chapman and Hall.

GROVE, D. C.
1968   "The Pre-classic Olmec in central Mexico: site distribution and inferences," in *Dumbarton Oaks Symposium on the Olmec,* 179–185. Washington, D.C.
1970   The San Pablo pantheon mound: a Middle Preclassic site in Morelos, Mexico. *American Antiquity* 35(1): 62–73.

HEIZER, R. F.
1961   Inferences on the nature of Olmec society based upon data from the La Venta site. *Kroeber Anthropological Society Papers* 25: 43–57.

JIMÉNEZ MORENO, W.
1966   "Mesoamerica before the Toltecs," in *Ancient Oaxaca.* Edited by J. Paddock, 3–82. Stanford, Calif.: Stanford University Press.
1942   *Segunda Reunión de Mesa Redonda.* Sociedad Méxicana de Antropología.

MELGAR, J. M., J. MARÍA SERRANO
1871   Estudio sobre la antigüedad y el orígen de la cabeza colosal de tipo etiopico que existe en Hueyapán del cantón de los Tuxtlas. *Boletín de la Sociedad Mexicana de Geografía y Estadística,* época 2, 3: 104–109.

MÖSSBAUER, R. L.
1958   Kernresonanzfluoreszenz von Gammastrahlung in HIr[191]. *Zeitschrift für Physik* 151(2): 124–143.

OJEDA RIVERA, J., *et al.*
1965   *Geología regional y yacimientos minerales de la porción meridional del Istmo de Tehuantepec, México.* Mexico City: Consejo de Recursos Naturales No Renovables.

PIRES-FERREIRA, J. W.
1973   "Formative Mesoamerican exchange networks." Unpublished Ph.D. dissertation, University of Michigan, Ann Arbor.

SCHIEBER, M. M.
1967   *Experimental magnetochemistry.* New York: Interscience.

SHIRANE, G., D. E. COX, W. J. TAKEI, S. L. RUBY
1962   A study of the magnetic properties of the $FeTiO_3$–αFe_2O_3 system by neutron diffraction and the Mössbauer effect. *Journal of the Physical Society of Japan* 17(10): 1598–1611.

STIRLING, M. W.
1942   An initial series from Tres Zapotes, Veracruz, Mexico. *Contributed Technical Papers, Mexican Archaeology Series* 1(1). Washington: National Geographic Society.
1943   *Stone monuments of southern Mexico.* Bureau of American Ethnology Bulletin 138. Washington, D.C.

1955 *Stone monuments of the Río Chiquito, Veracruz, Mexico.* Bureau of American Ethnology Bulletin 157. Anthropological Papers 143: 1–23.

VAILLANT, G. C.
1935 Early cultures in the Valley of Mexico: results of the stratigraphical project of the American Museum of Natural History in the Valley of Mexico 1928–1933. *Anthropological Papers of the American Museum of Natural History* 35(3).

VAN DER WOUDE, F.
1966 *Mössbauer spectra and magnetic properties of iron compounds.* Rotterdam: Bronder-Offset.

WILLIAMS, H., R. F. HEIZER
1965 *Sources of rocks used in Olmec monuments.* Contributions of the University of California Archaeological Research Facility 1: 1–39. Berkeley.

The Significance of the "Epiclassic" Period in Mesoamerican Prehistory

MALCOLM C. WEBB

In a recent book written to introduce students to anthropology as a profession, Fried (1972: 12–23) points out that the irreducible core of our discipline is the comparative analysis of human societies. The normative nature of this view is indicated by a comparison with Kroeber's observation (1948: 4) that "anthropology looks for such general and recurrent processes as may occur in the multifarious events of history and in the diverse societies, institutions, customs and beliefs of mankind" and with Kluckhohn's characterization of anthropology (1949: 2) as "the science of human similarities and differences." These statements appear in *Anthropology* and in *Mirror for man*, respectively, two texts which have undoubtedly contributed significantly to the intellectual background of the majority of currently active North American anthropologists. Indeed, such comparativist principles are essentially an echo and elaboration of the view of the great anthropological pioneer, E. B. Tylor, who, in 1881, began the first general anthropology text in English with the declaration that the scientific student of mankind is one "who seeks to understand how mankind came to be as they are and to live as they do. . ." (Tylor 1930: vol. 1, p. 1).

It is, then, not surprising that, as it enters the second century of its existence, anthropology is increasingly characterized by a concern with the cross-cultural investigation of social process, a concern revealed in such movements as cultural ecology, the new archaeology, and a modernized cultural evolutionism, or by the widespread interest in certain aspects of the work of Lévi-Strauss and of Chomsky (among others). The study of the ancient Mesoamerican high civilizations is no exception to this trend; recent years have witnessed a tendency for scholarly interest to move away from older concerns with temporal, spatial, and artifactual definitions of archaeological periods toward a concern with the growth (and decay) through time of specific societies or cultural traditions, with the factors, environmental and otherwise, that shaped them, with their interactions, and with the effects which such interactions had upon all the parties involved (e.g. Wolf 1959; Coe 1962a, 1966; Sanders and Price 1968; Willey 1966; Weaver 1972; Tourtellot and Sabloff 1972; Sabloff and Willey 1967; Webb 1973; Culbert 1973).

Equally important in bringing about this shift in approach has been the obvious but rather overwhelming consideration that the same rich accumulation of data during the past two decades which has made possible the investigation of process has also strikingly demonstrated that the traditional grand periodization of Mesoamerican history – the division into Preclassic or Formative, Classic, and Postclassic periods – has serious flaws. Two ultimately related aspects of these deficiencies are particularly outstanding. In the first place, it is increasingly doubtful whether it is appropriate to divide an essentially continuous developmental process into segments (either in each subarea or throughout Mesoamerica as a whole), implying, thereby, that the Middle and Late Preclassic have more in common with the Early Preclassic than they have with the Early Classic, and that the Early and the Late Classic resemble each other more in terms of developmental stage than either resembles, respectively, earlier or later periods. This question was raised, although not entirely answered, by Coe and by Wolf more than a decade ago (Coe 1957; Wolf 1959: 270–274). In the second place, the traditional interregional alignment of local sequences – and, more importantly, of developmental stages – has completely dissolved. This is, of course, not because of any lack of both short- and long-distance ceramic and archaeometric links (e.g. Dumond and Muller 1972; Weaver 1972; MacNeish, Peterson, and Flannery 1970; Johnson and MacNeish 1972); on the contrary, it is precisely as our knowledge of these matters has become more abundant that the difficulties have become serious. The very concept of a Pan-Mesoamerican Classic Period becomes problematic indeed when one considers that, at the time of the Petén Maya collapse, Teotihuacán and, to a lesser extent, Monte Albán had been in decay for two centuries while many of the Classic Period centers of the Gulf Coast and Yucatán would continue to be quite prosperous for some time (Armillas 1964; Wauchope 1964). Our present awareness that full Classicism crystallized considerably earlier in the great highland basins than it did in the lowlands (notably the Petén) has perhaps generated less concern over interregional correlations. This is undoubtedly due in large part to the fact that this issue has been utterly swallowed up in the larger question of the division between the Preclassic and Classic Periods.

Of course, it is possible to adopt the view that these problems are essentially mechanical and superficial, and that the expectation of approximately coeval period boundaries is merely a survival from an earlier stage of scholarship, a relic of the time when the only available absolute dates for pre-Hispanic Mesoamerica were those provided by the Maya calendar and when the Maya themselves were considered to be the region's greatest cultural innovators. Thus, the traditional "Classic" Period was, really, the time of the Long Count and Period Ending dates, more or less crudely extended to other regions. Even the realization that Teotihuacán was not the protohistoric Tula at first resulted only in a shift of the highland column from a location on top of the Maya Classic to a parallel position. Our present conceptual embarrassment arose precisely because the availability of carbon dates shifted the so-called Protoclassic and the Classic throughout most of Mesoamerica outside of the Petén backward by two centuries, transforming the Maya Classic into an example of conservatism, or even retardation, and leaving a gap before the protohistoric Toltec Period. One might, indeed, question whether the concept of a Classic Period does, in fact, add to our understanding. There is certainly nothing sacred about heavy horizontal lines on chronological charts.

However, considerably more is really at stake than this. The older view did make a crude sort of sense in that the presumed temporal and developmental equivalencies were explained in terms of real cultural forces, such as diffusion, migration, invasion, the spread of theocratic cults, and common militaristic tendencies, which linked together societies on the same temporal horizon, however overworked or inadequately conceived these mechanisms may have been. That we have not yet achieved a similar synthesis which would take advantage of our currently more refined knowledge is suggested by the continued interest in the Petén Maya collapse (or, what comes to the same thing, their prolonged survival [Willey and Shimkin 1971; Culbert 1973]), by the renewed interest in the temporal placement of the Puuc and of the Mexican Late Classic Gulf Coast sites (Pollock 1970; Thompson 1970; Rands 1967a, 1967b; Rathje and Sabloff 1972; Brainerd 1958; Andrews IV 1960, 1962), and by the historical void which prevails in the Valley of Mexico at the end of the Classic, notwithstanding the existence of ceramics which bridge the gap stratigraphically (Hicks and Nicholson 1964; MacNeish, Peterson, and Flannery 1970; Dumond and Muller 1972; Blanton 1972). I would, moreover, suggest that it is the examination of generally recurrent social processes which offers our best hope of achieving a new synthesis that will again demonstrate the necessary interconnection of developments in all of the major subregions of Mesoamerica.

The processes with which I shall deal are those associated with the rise, expansion, and decline of archaic state systems. Although, due to limitations of space, I will concentrate upon a major shift in the patterns of state control and of interstate relationships which I believe occurred in Mesoamerica during the eighth to tenth centuries A.D., it is important to note that the temporal and spatial pattern of development up to that period had been such as would be expected on general theoretical grounds. Carneiro (1961, 1970) has argued for many years that states arise where a sharply segmented environment causes heavy population pressure on limited agricultural land, hence, increasing war, while Dumond (1965), and also Harner (1970), have suggested in similar fashion that a strong relationship exists between population size and density, and the centralization and concentration of social control. Sahlins (1958), Service (1962), and Wolf (1959) have shown the importance in several areas of the world, including Mesoamerica, of exchange between the environmentally diverse portions of a region for generating and concentrating wealth and power so that chiefdoms may emerge from tribes, and states from chiefdoms. Coe (1968: 105–115), working in Veracruz, and Flannery (Flannery 1968; Flannery, Kirkby, Kirkby, and Williams 1967; Flannery and Coe 1968), working in Oaxaca, have suggested that control both of limited areas of good land and of trade wealth were the bases of early chiefly – or even state – authority in these areas. Sanders (1957; Sanders and Price 1968) has also applied both theories in combination to state origins in Mesoamerica as a whole. This is essentially my own view, although I see agricultural competition and war as more important for the generation of that differential wealth which Fried (1960, 1967), among others, regards as essential in the formation of pristine states, and I view commerce as more vital in the spread of states into secondary state areas as essentially described by Friedrich Engels many years ago (Engels 1942; Webb 1965, 1968). Chiefdoms appear to occur when state-inducing factors – above all, a resource distribution that requires extensive, centralized exchange – are present to only a moderate degree.

The widespread development of Late Formative cult centers throughout Mesoamerica, but with the Gulf Coast Olmec heartland (whose generally lower agricultural carrying capacity would lead to earlier population pressure and scattered settlement) taking the lead at this chiefly stage, fits this scheme quite well, as does the tendency for the semiarid highland basins (whose rich but areally restricted agricultural land would in time give rise to extreme population pressure, settlement nucleation, and resource competition) increasingly to take the lead in state formation during the Protoclassic and Classic (Palerm and Wolf 1957; West 1965; Sanders and Price 1968; J. Parsons 1968; Coe 1968; Flannery 1968; Blanton 1972). In the same way, noting the relatively regular distribution of resources, only moderately productive subsistence base, relatively homogeneous land, and low population (prior to the Late Classic) of the Petén, it is not surprising that current evidence indicates that substantial populations first moved into that area from the southwestern and southeastern margins after 1000 B.C. (Willey, Culbert, and Adams 1967; Gifford 1968; Adams 1972), that the beginnings of Classicism enter in Chicanel and, in later times, from a (perhaps ultimately Olmecoid) Guatemalan and Salvadoran highland base (Willey and Gifford 1961; L. Parsons 1966, 1967; Sharer 1968, 1969; Sharer and Gifford 1970; Andrews V 1969), and that subsequent developments took place at a slow rate.

I have suggested elsewhere that the Mesoamerican Protoclassic and Early Classic periods may fruitfully be regarded as an unusually rich and protracted transitional stage in which fully evolved states, consciously dependent upon secular controls such as wealth and overt force, first emerged from ancestral theocratic chiefdoms (Webb 1968, 1973). Wherever it has occurred in the world, this transformation offers the advantage of freeing a large portion of the social surplus from religious uses and of generally permitting a less restricted choice among alternate courses of action. It is not without its problems, however. Since chiefdoms lack a fully effective control of coercive force, they must typically depend upon obedience "freely" secured through shared values, spiritual sanctions, and ceremonial feasting and redistribution (this explains the largely religious ends towards which monumental and luxury production are normally directed in such societies). In consequence, the size and durability of a chiefdom is restricted by the credibility of its public cult, a credibility which is subject to stress precisely as increased size and diversity divert resources and open additional options. Their reliance on shared beliefs and their inability to handle internal confict and stress severely limit the capacity of chiefdoms for social differentiation and innovation – as long as they remain chiefdoms. Therefore, as chiefdoms approach statehood, both instability and overly rigid adherence to existing organizational and conceptual patterns present real dangers.

In reality, of course, the true bases of support for such hierarchical societies are the real benefits provided by their leadership: dispute resolution, allocation of resources, organization of labor, protection, sociability, bestowal of desired status, and, particularly, access to desired goods. For this reason, chiefdoms typically depend on a steady flow of commerce and are much concerned with both long- and short-distance trade (Webb 1964, 1965, 1968, 1973; Rathje 1971). Because of their concern with status indicators and sumptuary customs, however, much of their long-distance trade in particular consists of exotic, rare, and striking objects of no utilitarian value (Tourtellot and Sabloff 1972). States, in contrast, have a vastly increased appetite for, and ability to secure over a wide area, goods which are more pragmatically useful, although perhaps nevertheless designed primarily for luxury consumption (cf. Rands 1967a, 1967b). The ability of such societies to develop higher levels of economic specialization (impossible without reliable mechanisms of conflict resolution) and to undertake innovative policies (impossible without systemic flexibility) may produce an almost explosive surge of social expansion. This greater complexity and freedom of action characteristic of states implies, therefore, that the transition from chiefdom to state should be accompanied by a change and rationalization of trade patterns, a shift in which the greatest beneficiaries should be the most secular groups. The desire to secure foreign goods on the most favorable terms quite commonly gives rise to large-scale commercial warfare, itself a major factor leading to secularization.

When one bears these points in mind, the period of A.D. 750 to 950, in other words, the later Classic, assumes great significance. As Jiménez Moreno (1966), Paddock (1966), and Nicholson (1960) have long suggested, it was during this era that the basic patterns of Postclassic history were established. Its opening is marked by the effective demise of Teotihuacán, the most dominant Classic site not only of the Mexican central highlands but of all of Mesoamerica. The great size and complexity of this center along with its widespread influence do leave very little doubt that state controls were effectively operative within it (Armillas 1950, 1964). On the other hand, the largest public works there seem to be devoted to nonmilitaristic duties, and there are relatively many fewer indications of warfare than in later sites. Outside of its metropolitan territory, evidence for trade, although found over a wide area, seems, except for obsidian, to consist of a relatively small number of especially fine products and of examples of iconography, neither of which appears to be strongly associated with obvious routes of trade. This pattern seems, then, to still retain much essential continuity with ancient, chiefly "Olmec," patterns of trade (Willey and Shimkin 1971). The fifth-century Teotihuacán occupation of Kaminaljuyu as a military trade colony (a development greatly clarified by Sanders' recent work at the latter site) indicates, however, that basic changes were taking place.

That these developments had gone much further by the end of the Classic is suggested by the emergence then of a zone of persistent architectural, sculptural, iconographic, and ceramic intercontact linking together a number of highland and Gulf Coast centers – Cholula (at first alone, then both Cholula and Tula), Xochicalco, Tajín, Remojadas, Cerro de las Mesas, Cerro Montoso, coastal Tabasco, the Río Bec area, the Puuc sites, and (less clearly) the lower Usumacinta –

and having more diffuse connections with the highlands of Chiapas and Guatemala and with lower Central America (Noguera 1945, 1950, 1954; Marquina 1951: 116–129, 143–145; 1968; Acosta 1956–1957; Du Solier 1945; Spinden 1933; García Payón 1943, 1950, 1951a, 1951b, 1953; Medellin Zenil 1960; Drucker 1943; Berlin 1953, 1956; Brainerd 1958; Rands 1967a, 1967b; Barthel 1964; Sanders 1960; Sáenz 1963, 1968; Piña Chan 1964; Butler 1935; Vaillant 1927; Proskouriakoff 1951, 1953, 1963: 44, 48, 52, 72; Robertson 1963: 26, 30; Foncerrada de Mólina 1962; Thompson 1952, 1966a, 1970; McVicker 1967; Morley 1935: 137–140; Kubler 1962: 17–19, 92, 99, 138, 158, 212–217; Von Winning 1965; Coe 1962b; Brockington 1970; Seler 1904a, 1904b). It probably is significant that this intercontact zone is characterized by fairly numerous resemblances which connect neighboring areas rather than the previous quite widespread but scattered diffusion of a smaller number of outstanding traits from a few dominant centers. The result is a kind of overlapping chain, each link of which – highlands to central Gulf Coast, central Gulf Coast to Tabasco-Campeche, Tabasco-Campeche to Puuc, Tabasco-Campeche to Guatemalan highlands – is closely similar to a corresponding stage in a major Gulf Coast-Yucatán-highland-Guatemalan trade network which we know existed at the time of the Spanish Conquest (Chapman 1957; Thompson 1970; Wauchope 1964). Among the more valuable items exchanged on a large scale in the sixteenth century along these routes were cacao and slaves, which moved from Tabasco, Yucatán, and Soconusco to central Mexico, and salt, which moved from both central Mexico and Yucatán to salt-deficient areas. The México Conquest period, as well as the peoples who ruled immediately before them, were much concerned about control of this trade route and directed war and diplomacy to this end (Kelly and Palerm 1952: 14–24; Barlow 1949: 51–53, 83). The generally similar geographic pattern of the Toltec expansion suggests that an analogous motivation existed earlier in the Postclassic (Diehl 1971; Cobean 1972). It seems quite possible, therefore, that these terminal Classic contacts represent the essential shift in patterns of long-distance trade from theocratic importation of highly exotic ritual and prestige goods toward movement of more secular luxury goods for elite consumption.

While really hard evidence for trade goods is scanty in the ninth and early tenth centuries A.D., much of the material traded in the Postclassic obviously would not leave clear traces in the archaeological record (Thompson 1957). In pottery, such trade wares as do exist generally point to our postulated trade network (Paddock 1966; MacNeish, Peterson, and Flannery 1970: 206–210; Willey, Culbert, and Adams 1967; Pendergast 1967a, 1967b, 1969). This is notably true in regard to the early fine paste wares of Tabasco and Campeche, which foreshadow the later spread of the Altar and Silho fine-orange trade wares (Rands 1967a, 1967b). Along the Oaxacan coast, Brockington (1970, 1972) reports a widespread Late Classic ceramic which, although manufactured locally, resembles Tabascan and Puuc types such as Balancán fine orange in such great detail as to indicate very intense contact with those areas. It was presumably this contact which carried the Maya traits (which appear to be *western* Maya traits) to Xochicalco and highland Oaxaca. Paddock (Paddock, Mogor, and Lind 1968) has found at Lambityeco less abundant but nevertheless unmistakable connections with Balancán fine orange in a Monte Albán IV context, along with figurines strongly resembling the contemporary Valley of Mexico Coyotlatelco type. Altar fine orange appears in terminal Classic–Early Postclassic contexts in the Tehuacán Valley, and at Tajín and Isla de Sacrificios (I), followed by Silho fine orange at a later date; Cholula *Policroma laca* occurs in Tehuacán, Monte Albán IV, the Gulf Coast, and Pacific Coast Guatemala during this transitional period as well (MacNeish, Peterson, and Flannery 1970: 209–210). In addition, a prominent pottery type of the Late Classic central Gulf, *Rojo sobre blanco* [red-on-white], is markedly similar to the Tehuacán type Coxcatlan Red-on-orange, which begins at this time and which is a close relative to a common Cholutecan ware (MacNeish, Peterson, and Flannery 1970: 199–203; Medellin Zenil 1960: 55–59).

The strong stylistic resemblances, not only in pottery but also in sculpture and architecture, which join together all the areas in question at this time, in fact suggest the kind of extensive (although not necessarily intimate), enduring, and, at least, occasionally friendly contacts that are quite likely to have been caused by trading relationships. Working from a quite different point of view, Sharp (1972) has recently come to precisely the same conclusion as a result of her studies of the *greca* [Greek Key] motif which especially links the Puuc, Oaxaca, and Tajín at this period. I have, in fact, previously pointed out that artistic representations of items associated with merchants, merchant gods, or wealth, such as fans, staves, tumplines, specialized headdresses, packs, and bags, are concentrated along the western border of the Maya zone from Verapaz to Chichén Itzá, and also up the Gulf Coast to Tajín. These representations first become common in the eighth and ninth centuries but continue down until the Late Postclassic, thus demonstrating a marked continuity with Conquest period trading systems (Webb 1970, 1973). The same continuity is demonstrated by ceramic distributions in that, with the passage of time, Balancán fine orange is replaced in these regions by Silho fine orange and Plumbate, and these in turn by Late Postclassic wares.

The period in which these patterns of interaction presumably crystallized also accords well with the regional sequences. It is becoming clear that the Mixteca–Puebla complex, particularly the "Cholutecan" ceramic sequence, took shape in and about Puebla–Tlaxcala out of Classic Teotihuacán sources immediately after the collapse of Teotihuacán itself, but before the rise of Tula (Noguera 1950; Nicholson 1960, 1966; Snow 1969; Dumond and Muller 1972). Although the great site of Cholula itself may have suffered some interruption of occupation during this period, the continuance of considerable building activity about the south side of the Great Pyramid into the terminal Classic Period along with the rapid recovery of the site suggests that the region maintained its dynamism throughout the period (Marquina 1970; MacNeish, Peterson, and Flannery 1970: 209–210, 236–237; Dumond and Muller 1972). Considering the key role which the Mixteca–Puebla complex was soon to play in the formation of later Postclassic states and the strong ties to both Tajín and the Mixtec region which are indicated by the prominence of *greca* and interlaced volute motifs in terminal Classic constructions at the Great Pyramid, it seems reasonable to place the expansive activity and the "tyranny" of the Historic Olmecs in this period, a view long held by Jiménez Moreno (1954–1955, 1966; cf. Vaillant, 1938; Acosta 1956–1957).

I would assign the same terminal Classic–initial Postclassic date to the Puuc florescence, a view which returns to Brainerd's original position (Brainerd 1954: 25, 35–39, 80–81; 1958; Covarrubias 1957: 235–238; Pollock 1967). It also reconciles the views of Andrews who, on the basis of his work in Yucatán, favored the Spinden correlation (Andrews IV 1960) with that held by the majority of Mayanists, who feel that the GMT correlation accords much better with the situation in the Petén. The placement of Puuc in the transitional period allows rather less time than Andrews desires to account for the extensive building projects of the florescent stage but explains this rapid growth in terms of a rapid spurt of prosperity. The regional architectural sequence has always indicated such a placement (Ruz Lhuillier 1945; Foncerrada de Mólina 1962), as does the time at which Puuc influences appear in eastern Yucatán and the Usumacinta (Sabloff and Willey 1967; Thompson 1952, 1957, 1970; Sanders 1960; Ball 1972; Willey and Shimkin 1971). Turning to the Gulf Coast, it would appear that architectural and ceramic resemblances link, in particular, the final, terminal Classic major expansion of Tajín, Tajín Chico, with the Puuc and with both the final expansion of the Great Pyramid and the Cholutecan I period at Cholula, while the Toltex-related Silho fine orange appears only at the very end of the Tajín occupation (Marquina 1951: 118–129; García Payón 1951a: 40–44; 1953; MacNeish, Peterson, and Flannery 1970: 209–210). The presence in Cerro de las Mesas Upper I of Cholutecan *Policroma laca* along with the absence there of Plumbate, metals, and Silho fine orange (which does, however, occur in Isla de Sacrificios I) supports this placement of the Cholula–Gulf–Puuc horizon at the earliest Postclassic, pre-Toltec level (Drucker 1943: 48–50, 82–87; Noguera 1950, 1954: 138; MacNeish, Peterson, and Flannery 1970: 209; Diehl 1971: 43–45). Xochicalco's florescence and strong stylistic ties to both the Puuc and Cholula at this general time are also well known (Marquina 1951: 143–145; Noguera 1945, 1950, 1954; Dumond and Muller 1972; Blanton 1972). Thus, four of the major links on our chain rise to prominence together, and they do so shortly after the demise of Teotihuacán, at the same time as the final Petén Maya collapse (Willey and Shimkin 1971), in the area which was soon to become a route of Toltec expansion and was later the scene of México commercial and military activity. Radiocarbon dates from Lambityeco in Oaxaca (Paddock, Mogor, and Lind 1968) can be extended to both Tajín and the Puuc through the *greca* motif (Sharp 1970, 1972; Seler 1904b; Jiménez Moreno 1966), thereby placing this horizon securely (though somewhat imprecisely) in the late eighth and ninth centuries A.D.

In the Valley of Mexico, we see that the same period is marked by a shift of major activity to such sites as Azcapotzalco and Cerro Portezuelo in the southwest and southeast – both of which contain forms ancestral to later Toltec ceramics, to the Ixtapalapa peninsula in the south, and to the area of the Patlachique range in the northeast, suggesting an orientation to Cholula and Xochicalco to the south and to the region about (emerging) Tula in the north (Tozzer 1921; Noguera 1950; Armillas 1950; Jacobs-Müller 1956–1957; Cook de Leonard 1956–1957; Hicks and Nicolson 1964; J. Parsons 1968; Diehl 1971: 43–46; Blanton 1972). From this period on, it becomes increasingly possible to relate changing population distributions to the boundaries and political histories of specific protohistoric states; states, moreover, whose leaders were much concerned with maximizing their wealth, whether from trade or from development of public works that would increase primary production (J. Parsons 1968; Blanton 1972; Cobean 1972; Wolf and Palerm 1955; Armillas 1971). These desires surely underlie the considerable increase in military competition characteristic of the Postclassic. Indeed, although this horizon precedes the full Toltec period (Dumond and Muller 1972; Diehl 1971: 43–45; D. Healan, personal communication), the relative absence of religious architecture at Azcapotzalco, Cerro Portezuelo, and Tajín Chico, the symbols of sacrifice and death at Tajín and among the western Maya, the defensible nature of Xochicalco, and the legendary history of Cholutecan imperialism and tyranny all indicate that this period was the time when, at last, secular, "true" state controls rapidly became fully established (García Payón 1951a: 28–33, 42–43; 1957; Nicholson 1960; Coe 1963; Piña Chan 1964; Jiménez Moreno 1966; Paddock 1966: 174, 200–211, 233–234; Thompson 1970).

The desirability of granting the societies of this period a distinctive temporal designation has long been recognized by the use of the term "Epiclassic" by such scholars as Jiménez Moreno (1966; see also Paddock 1966: 232–234; Sharp 1970). This seems particularly apt. It has become increasingly clear that these societies were among the most vital and expansive in all of Mesoamerican history. Through the Mixteca–Puebla complex, they – or, at least, some of them – were one of the two principal sources of the cultural tradition that dominated Mesoamerica at the time of the Spanish Conquest, the other tap root of Conquest period culture being the Tula Toltecs, who clearly are later than the former societies and who must themselves have been strongly affected by interaction with them (Noguera 1950; Nicholson 1967; Dumond and Muller 1972; Diehl 1971: 43–44). Thus, the later Classic in a very real sense belongs as much with the Postclassic as with the Classic, because it was during that period that the distinctive Postclassic state pattern was effectively achieved throughout Meso-america as a whole. While this pattern must surely have first taken shape at Teotihuacán itself, it is clear that this center did, in fact, fail as a polity – not only replaced but, indeed, perhaps actually destroyed by the emerging terminal Classic interaction system (Armillas 1964).

Relations between these Epiclassic and Postclassic groups do indeed appear to have been no trivial matter, since the rise and florescence of some evidently implied the collapse or at least con-traction of the influence of others. It really seems as if there were not enough vital, state-sustaining resources to go around, so that the prosperity or even existence of a polity depended on its relative success in competing for such resources, in denying them to its rivals. The expansion of the western Maya to Oaxaca and Xochicalco did not take place until after the seventh-century retraction of Teoti-huacán influence in the south (Brockington 1972), while the period of maximum florescence of the presumed Puuc-Tajín-Cholula network saw the final collapse of Teotihuacán and the end of the Petén Maya (Willey and Shimkin 1971). In the same way, we see that Tula's achievement of hegemony in the highlands was followed by the collapse of the Tajín–Puuc network (although not of Cholula proper), while Tula's decline was marked in Yucatán by the replacement of Toltec Chichén Itzá with the "Maya resurgence" at Mayapán, which fell in turn when the Culhua México (Aztec) again gathered all political and commercial threads into one highland-based imperial order (Wauchope 1964). This continuous alternation strongly suggests that, throughout the Postclassic, the highlands and the Gulf Coast, especially the Maya zone, formed one politico-economic system (Roys 1966).

However, ability to participate successfully in this system clearly was not equally distributed throughout Mesoamerica. Those societies which maintained or even increased their prosperity and influence were precisely those in which the transition to state-level controls could most easily and completely take place. These were located in the highland basins of central Mexico, whose rich but circumscribed store of agricultural and other resources had begun to generate primary states even in the Classic Period, in the Gulf Coast and Yucatán, where control of key trade routes or products encouraged the growth of secondary states, and in the Guatemalan highlands, an area marked by moderate resource circumscription and also by considerable availability of trade goods (Palerm and Wolf 1957). Teotihuacán's replacement by neighbors who apparently had a less intense development of the Classic theocratic system suggests (very reasonably) that a precocious achievement of state patterns was followed by a rigidity which prevented the timely adoption of later, more adaptive developments (Jiménez Moreno 1966; Armillas 1964). In the same way, the sudden and total collapse of the Petén Maya in the terminal Classic reflects their delayed and imperfect achievement of stable state controls, itself the consequence of an environment that was relatively both homogeneous and lacking in critical trade resources. That their maximum florescence took place during the later Classic meant only that these greatest of chiefdoms or most incipient of states must have been in an unusually precarious condition when they began to receive serious pressure from the highly aggressive Epiclassic societies to the north. Since any attempt to compete would only increase social stress, a rapid collapse would be inevitable. Recovery would then largely be inhibited because of the total lack in the Petén of resources useful to the Postclassic societies (Willey and Shimkin 1971; Webb 1973).

A unitary explanation for these phenomena would be economical; one that seems ideal involves the gradual rise and expansion of a Bronze Age trade network, for the control of which a continuous struggle then ensued. As we have seen, at the time of the Conquest, and probably earlier, rivalry over trade was a major cause of war among the Mesoamerican states. This was strongly evident not only in the case of the Aztec expansion to the south and east (Kelly and Palerm 1952: 14–24), but also in the rivalries of the Yucatán Maya (Roys 1957, 1966). Similar motivations appear to have been present among the Mixtec peoples and in highland Guatemala, although in these cases a larger proportion of goods perhaps moved through internal tribute relations (Spores 1967: 4–16, 157–162; Carmack 1967,

1970: 60, 71–72, 76–78; Miles 1957; Thompson 1964). Moreover, this concern with trade was perfectly reasonable. Readers of Acosta Saignes (1945), Chapman (1957), Cardos de Méndez (1959), Miles (1957), Roys (1934, 1957) and, of course, de Landa (Tozzer 1941: 94–98, 107) will be aware of the vital role that long-distance trade wealth played in the maintenance of the social order among both the México and the Maya of the later Postclassic. On the Gulf Coast, particularly among the Maya of Yucatán and Tabasco, for peoples with extraordinarily rich resources of salt, cacao, and honey, long-distance trade was so extensive as to be a mainstay of the total economy. It was therefore carried on by the local ruling lords themselves, for whom it was the major social function and, I would say, a vital source of power. Current fieldwork at the Postclassic Yucatán commercial center of Cozumel Island suggests that, from the end of the Classic, changes in the internal organization, external orientation, and, even, existence of key archaeological sites did, indeed, correlate well with shifts between native and extrapeninsular domination of trade routes (Sabloff and Rathje 1972; Sabloff, Rathje, Freidel, Connor, and Sabloff 1972).

Turning to the densely populated highlands, it would appear that the acquisition of foreign trade products was a major motivation for imperial expansion there, precisely because the availability of such goods on favorable terms was absolutely necessary to maintain a balanced economy (Barlow 1949; Cook 1946; de Zorita 1963: 152–157, 193; Molíns Fábrega 1954–1955; Wolf 1959: 131–142). It was for this reason that the governing elite in Mexico-Tenochtitlán both protected and dominated the wealthy merchant class or caste, the Pochteca, who played a critical role both in the early prosperity and the imperial expansion of that city (de Zorita 1963: 181–188, 279–284; Brundage 1972: 26–32, 43–47, 210–217). Legends and ritual paraphernalia strongly imply that, in fact, the Pochteca originally entered central Mexico from the Gulf in pre-Aztec times by way of Cholula (Acosta Saignes 1945). It would appear that representations of the merchant god are relatively common in various of the surviving late Mixtec codices (Thompson 1966b; León-Portilla 1968: Figure 39), one of which (Borgia) may have been made at Cholula, while another (Fejervary-Mayer) can be located in or near Veracruz (Nicholson 1962, 1966). In later Postclassic times, Cholula came to be the great sanctuary of Quetzalcoatl, who as Ehecatl, god of the wind, guided travellers and was therefore invoked as the merchant god, Yacatecuhtli, Lord of the Nose (León-Portilla 1968: 10, 35). There is, also, a strong Central Gulf element in the background of the Mixteca–Puebla polychromes themselves, the largely undescribed site of Cerro Montoso providing the link (Noguera 1950, 1954; Medillin Zenil 1960;

Strebel 1885–1889). The close resemblances which I feel exist between Plumbate and the Gulf Coast *Cerámica metálica* (Shepard 1948; Medellin Zenil 1955: 44–49; 1960: 124–130, 192, 198; 1965) and the role which the Gulf zone must have played in the transmission of fine-paste ceramic traditions between south and north at the end of the Classic (Medellin Zenil 1965) also would support the conclusion that the protohistoric commercial patterns are the natural end result and, indeed, ultimate expression in the historic record of the Epiclassic interaction system.

Additional data that point somewhat less clearly to the same conclusion might, perhaps, be found in such areas as the rather diffuse connections between Maya vase painting (especially that of western Yucatán and Tabasco) and the Isla de Sacrificios and Mixteca-Puebla styles. It would not, however, be profitable to pursue the question into what is at present rather vague and uncertain territory. From the evidence that is now available, it would appear that both the rhythm of interregional contact and the content of the interacting cultural traditions support the view that, from the end of the Classic Period until the Spanish Conquest, long-distance commerce and commercial wars determined in large measure not only the specific histories of individual Mesoamerican societies, but also the overall social development of the region as a whole. This commercially inspired militarism was the social dynamic, in a sense the material reality, that lay behind the Mixteca-Puebla stylistic complex and its off-spring (Nicholson 1960). It was this increasing orientation to and reliance upon interregional trade, characteristic of fully evolved states, that, during the Postclassic, linked all of Mesoamerica into the firmest cultural and political ecumenical group seen since "Olmec" times. These earlier societies, of course, had themselves, as chiefdoms, also been very dependent upon trade, although, expectably, the ceremonial, nonutilitarian aspect had been greater. This reliance is, indeed, the reason that both the earlier and the later period form horizon styles, in contrast to the intervening Classic, during which trade, while certainly very much present, occupied a smaller and less critical role in the social system. In other words, despite its unique and always strongly theocratic character, Mesoamerican civilization was shaped, kept in motion, and, at critical points, integrated by evolving patterns of trade, a process known to operate in all parts of the world among peoples of generally similar cultural level.

REFERENCES

ACOSTA, JORGE R.
1956–1957   Interpretación de algunas de los datos obtenidos en Tula rela-
tivo a la época tolteca. *Revista Mexicana de Estudios Antropológicos* 14(2): 75–110.

ACOSTA SAIGNES, MIGUEL
1945   Los pochteca. *Acta Antropológica*, época 1; 1(1). Mexico City:
Escuela Nacional de Antropología e Historia.

ADAMS, RICHARD E. W.
1972   Maya highland prehistory: new data and implications. *Contributions
of the University of California Archaeological Research Facility* 16:
1–21.

ANDREWS, E. WYLLYS, IV
1960   Excavations at Dzibilchaltun, Northwestern Yucatán, Mexico.
Proceedings of the American Philosophical Society 104: 254–265.
1962   Excavations at Dzibilchaltun, Yucatán, 1955–1965. *Estudios de
Cultura Maya* 2: 3–35.

ANDREWS, E. WYLLYS, V
1969   "Excavations at Quelepa, El Salvador." Paper read at Annual
Meeting of the American Anthropological Association, December
1969, New Orleans, Louisiana.

ARMILLAS, PEDRO
1950   Teotihuacán, Tula y los Toltecas. *Runa* 3: 37–70.
1964   "Northern Mesoamerica," in *Prehistoric man in the New World*.
Edited by Jesse D. Jennings and Edward Norbeck, 291–329. Chicago: University of Chicago Press for Rice University.
1971   Gardens on swamps. *Science* 174: 653–661.

BALL, JOSEPH W.
1972   "A regional ceramic sequence for the Río Bec area." Paper presented at the Thirty-seventh Annual Meeting of the Society for
American Archaeology, April 1972, Miami Beach, Florida. Mimeographed manuscript.

BARLOW, ROBERT H.
1949   *The extent of the empire of the Culhua México*. Ibero-Americana 28.
Berkeley: The University of California Press.

BARTHEL, THOMAS S.
1964   Comentarios a las inscripciónes clásicas tardía de Chichén Itzá.
Estudios de Cultura Maya 4: 223–244.

BERLIN, HEINRICH
1953   *Archaeological reconnaissance in Tabasco*. Carnegie Institution,
Department of Archaeology, Current Report 7. Washington, D.C.
1956   *Late pottery horizons of Tabasco, Mexico*. Contributions to
American Archaeology 59. Washington, D.C.: Carnegie Institution.

BLANTON, R. E.
1972   Prehispanic adaptation in the Ixtapalapa region, Mexico. *Science* 175:
1317–1326.

BRAINERD, GEORGE W.
1954   *The Maya civilization*. Los Angeles: Southwest Museum.
1958   *The archaeological ceramics of Yucatán*. Anthropological Records
19. Berkeley and Los Angeles: University of California Press.

BROCKINGTON, DONALD L.
  1970   "Cultural sequences on the coast of Oaxaca, Mexico." Paper presented at the Thirty-fifth Annual Meeting of the Society for American Archaeology, April 1970, Mexico City.
  1972   "The end of the Classic on the Oaxaca coast." Paper presented at the Seventy-first Annual Meeting of the American Anthropological Association, December 1972, Toronto.
BRUNDAGE, BURR C.
  1972   A rain of darts: the México Aztecs. Austin: University of Texas Press.
BUTLER, MARY
  1935   A study of Maya mold-made figurines. American Anthropologist 37: 636–672.
CARDOS DE MÉNDEZ, AMALIA
  1959   El comercio de los mayas antiguos. Acta Antropológica, época 2; 2(1). Mexico City: Escuela Nacional de Antropología e Historia.
CARMACK, ROBERT M.
  1967   Análisis historico-sociologico de un antiguo titulo Quiche. Antropología e Historia de Guatemala 19(1): 3–13.
  1970   "Toltec influence on the postclassic culture history of highland Guatemala," in Archaeological studies in Middle America. Edited by Margaret A. L. Harrison and Robert Wauchope, 49–92. Middle American Research Institute, Tulane University, Publication 26. New Orleans.
CARNEIRO, ROBERT L.
  1961   "Slash and burn cultivation among the Kuikuru and its implications for cultural development in the Amazon basin," in The evolution of horticultural systems in native South America: causes and consequences. Edited by J. Wilbert, 47–68. Caracas: Sociedad Ciencias Naturales La Salle.
  1970   A theory of the origin of the state. Science 169: 733–738.
CHAPMAN, ANNE
  1957   "Port of trade enclaves in Aztec and Maya civilizations," in Trade and market in the early empires. Edited by K. Polanyi, C. Arensberg, and H. Pearson, 114–153. Glencoe: The Free Press.
COBEAN, R.
  1972   "Long-distance trade in the Mesoamerican Post-Classic." Paper presented at the Eighth Annual Meeting of the Southern Anthropological Society, February 24–26, 1972, Columbia, Missouri. Mimeographed manuscript.
COE, MICHAEL D.
  1957   Pre-classic cultures in Mesoamerica: a comparative survey. Kroeber Anthropological Society Papers 17: 7–37.
  1962a Mexico. New York: Frederick A. Praeger.
  1962b Costa Rican archaeology and Mesoamerica. Southwestern Journal of Anthropology 18: 170–183.
  1963   "Cultural development in southeastern Mesoamerica," in Aboriginal cultural development in Latin America: an interpretive review. Edited by Betty J. Meggers and Clifford Evans, 27–44. Smithsonian Miscellaneous Collections 146(1). Washington, D.C.: Smithsonian Institution.
  1966   The Maya. New York: Frederick A. Praeger.

1968   *America's first civilization*. New York: American Heritage in association with the Smithsonian Institution.

COOK, S. F.
1946   Human sacrifice and warfare as factors in the demography of precolonial Mexico. *Human Biology* 18: 81–102.

COOK DE LEONARD, CARMEN
1956–1957   Algunas antecedentes de la cerámica tolteca. *Revista Mexicana de Estudios Antropológicos* 14(2): 37–43.

COVARRUBIAS, MIGUEL
1957   *Indian art of Mexico and Central America*. New York: Alfred A. Knopf.

CULBERT, T. PATRICK, *editor*
1973   *The classic Maya collapse*. Albuquerque: University of New Mexico Press for the School of American Research.

DE ZORITA, ALONSO
1963   *Life and labor in ancient Mexico: the brief and summary relation of the lords of New Spain*. Translation and introduction by Benjamin Keen. New Brunswick: Rutgers University Press.

DIEHL, RICHARD A.
1971   "Preliminary report, University of Missouri archaeological project at Tula, Hidalgo, Mexico, 1970–71 field seasons." Mimeographed manuscript, University of Missouri.

DRUCKER, PHILIP
1943   *Ceramic stratigraphy at Cerro de las Mesas, Veracruz, Mexico*. Bureau of American Ethnology, Bulletin 143. Washington, D.C.: Smithsonian Institution.

DUMOND, DON E.
1965   Population growth and cultural change. *Southwestern Journal of Anthropology* 21: 302–324.

DUMOND, DON E., FLORENCIA MULLER
1972   Classic to Postclassic in highland central Mexico. *Science* 175: 1208–1215.

DU SOLIER, WILFRIDO
1945   La cerámica arqueológica de El Tajín. *Anales de Museo Nacional de Antropología, Historia y Etnografía* 3(3): 147–192.

ENGELS, FRIEDRICH
1942   *The origin of the family, private property and the state*. New York: International Publishers.

FLANNERY, KENT V.
1968   "The Olmec and the Valley of Oaxaca: a model for interregional interaction in formative times," in *Dumbarton Oaks Conference on the Olmec, October 28th and 29th, 1967*. Edited by Elizabeth P. Benson, 79–110. Washington: Dumbarton Oaks Research Library and Collection.

FLANNERY, KENT V., MICHAEL D. COE
1968   "Social and economic systems in formative Mesoamerica," in *New perspectives in archaeology*. Edited by S. R. Binford and L. R. Binford, 267–283. Chicago: Aldine.

FLANNERY, KENT, ANNE KIRKBY, MICHAEL KIRKBY, AUBREY WILLIAMS, JR.
1967   Farming systems and political growth in ancient Oaxaca, Mexico. *Science* 158: 445–454.

FONCERRADA DE MÓLINA, MARTA
1962   La arquitectura Puuc dentro de los estilos de Yucatán. *Estudios de Cultura Maya* 2: 225–238.

FRIED, MORTON H.
1960   "On the evolution of social stratification and the state," in *Culture in history: essays in honor of Paul Radin.* Edited by S. Diamond, 713–730. New York: Columbia University Press for Brandeis University.
1967   *The evolution of political society.* New York: Random House.
1972   *The study of anthropology.* New York: Thomas Y. Crowell.

GARCÍA PAYÓN, JOSÉ
1943   *Interpretación cultural de la zona arqueológica de El Tajín: seguida de uno ensayo de una bibliografía antropológica del Totonacapán y la región sur del estado de Veracruz.* Mexico City: Imprinta Universitaria.
1950   Exploraciónes en Xiuhtetilco, Puebla. *Uni-Ver* 2(22, 23): 397–476.
1951a   *La ciudad arqueológica de Tajín.* Jalapa: Universidad Veracruzana.
1951b   *Breves apuntes sobre la arqueología de Chacalacas, Veracruz.* Jalapa: Universidad Veracruzana.
1953   Que es lo Totonaco. *Revista Mexicana de Estudios Antropológicos* 13(2, 3): 379–388.
1957   *El Tajín, guía oficial.* Mexico City: Instituto Nacional de Antropología e Historia.

GIFFORD, JAMES C.
1968   "The earliest and other intrusive population elements at Barton Ramie may have come from Central America." Paper presented at the Sixty-seventh Annual Meeting of the American Anthropological Association, December 1968, Seattle, Washington.

HARNER, M. J.
1970   Population pressure and the social evolution of agriculturalists. *Southwestern Journal of Anthropology* 26: 67–85.

HICKS, F., H. B. NICHOLSON
1964   "The transition from classic to postclassic at Cerro Portezuelo, Valley of Mexico," in *Actas y Memorias del 35° Congresso Internacional de Americanistas, México* 1: 493–505.

JACOBS-MÜLLER, E. F.
1956–1957   Azcapotzalco: estudio tipológico de la cerámica. *Revista Mexicana de Estudios Antropológicos* 14(2): 125–137.

JIMÉNEZ MORENO, WIGBERTO
1954–1955   Síntesis de la historia precolonial del valle de Mexico. *Revista Mexicana de Estudios Antropológicos* 14(1): 219–236.
1966   "Mesoamerica before the Toltecs," in *Ancient Oaxaca.* Edited by John Paddock, 1–82. Stanford: Stanford University Press.

JOHNSON, FREDERICK, RICHARD S. MAC NEISH
1972   "Chronometric dating," in *The prehistory of the Tehuacán Valley, volume four: Chronology and irrigation.* Edited by Frederick Johnson, 3–55. Austin: The University of Texas Press for the Robert S. Peabody Foundation.

KELLY, ISABEL, ANGEL PALERM
1952   *The Tajín Totonac, part one: History, subsistence, shelter and technology.* Institute of Social Anthropology Monograph 13. Washington, D.C.: Smithsonian Institution.

KLUCKHOHN, CLYDE
1949 *Mirror for man.* New York: McGraw-Hill.
KROEBER, ALFRED L.
1948 *Anthropology.* New York: Harcourt, Brace, Jovanovich.
KUBLER, GEORGE
1962 *The art and architecture of ancient America.* Harmondsworth: Penguin.
LEÓN-PORTILLA
1968 *Quetzalcoatl.* Mexico City: Fondo de Cultura Económica.
MAC NEISH, RICHARD S., FREDERICK A. PETERSON, KENT V. FLANNERY
1970 *The prehistory of the Tehuacán Valley,* volume three: *Ceramics.* Austin: University of Texas Press for the Robert S. Peabody Foundation.
MC VICKER, DONALD
1967 "Prehispanic trade in central Chiapas, Mexico." Paper presented at the Sixty-sixth Annual Meeting of the American Anthropological Association, December 1967, Washington, D.C.
MARQUINA, IGNACIO
1951 *Arquitectura prehispánica.* Mexico City: Instituto Nacional de Antropología e Historia.
1968 Exploraciónes en la pirámide de Cholula. *Boletín INAH* 32: 12–19.
1970 *Proyecto Cholula.* Instituto Nacional de Antropología e Historia, Serie Investigaciónes 19.
MEDELLIN ZENIL, ALFONSO
1955 *Exploraciónes en la Isla de Sacrificios.* Jalapa: Gobierno del Estado de Veracruz, Dirección General de Educación, Departamento de Antropología.
1960 *Cerámicas del Totonacapán.* Xalapa: Universidad Veracruzana.
1965 "Culturas del Golfo de Mexico." Lecture presented at the Museo Nacional de Antropología, March 24, 1965, Mexico City.
MILES, SUZANNE W.
1957 The sixteenth century Pokam-Maya. *Transactions of the American Philosophical Society* 47(4). Philadelphia: American Philosophical Society.
MOLÍNS FÁBREGA, N.
1954–1955 El códice mendocino y la economía de Tenochtitlán. *Revista Mexicana de Estudios Antropológicos* 14(1): 303–335.
MORLEY, SYLVANUS G.
1935 *Guidebook to the ruins of Quirigua.* Washington, D.C.: Carnegie Institution.
NICHOLSON, H. B.
1960 "The Mixteca-Puebla concept in Mesoamerican archaeology: a re-examination," in *Men and Cultures: selected papers of the Fifth International Congress of Anthropological and Ethnological Sciences, Philadelphia, 1956.* Edited by Anthony F. C. Wallace, 612–617. Philadelphia: University of Pennsylvania Press.
1962 The Mesoamerican pictorial manuscripts: research, past and present. *Akten des 34. Internationalen Amerikanistenkongresses, Wien* 1: 199–215.
1966 "The problem of the provenience of the members of the 'Codex Borgia Group,' a summary," in *Suma antropológica en homenaje a Roberto J. Weitlaner.* Edited by A. Pompa y Pompa, 145–158. Mexico City: Instituto Nacional de Antropología e Historia.

1967 A "royal headband" of the Tlaxcalteca. *Revista Mexicana de Estudios Antropológicos* 21: 71–106.

NOGUERA, EDUARDO

1945 Exploraciónes en Xochicalco. *Cuadernos Americanos* 4(1): 1–39.

1950 *Enciclopedia mexicana de arte,* volume four: *El horizonte tolteca-chichimeca.* Mexico City: Ediciónes Mexicanas.

1954 *La cerámica arqueológica de Cholula.* Mexico City: Editorial Guarania.

PADDOCK, JOHN

1966 "Oaxaca in ancient Mesoamerica," in *Ancient Oaxaca.* Edited by John Paddock, 83–242. Stanford: Stanford University Press.

PADDOCK, JOHN, JOSEPH R. MOGOR, MICHAEL D. LIND

1968 Lambityeco Tomb 2: a preliminary report. *Boletín de Estudios Oaxaqueños* 25.

PALERM, ANGEL, ERIC R. WOLF

1957 "Ecological potential and cultural development in Mesoamerica," in *Studies in human ecology.* Edited by L. Krader and A. Palerm, 1–38. Washington, D.C.: The Anthropological Society of Washington.

PARSONS, JEFFREY R.

1968 Teotihuacán, Mexico, and its impact on regional demography. *Science* 162: 872–877.

PARSONS, LEE A.

1966 Premier informe sobre las investigaciónes hechas on "Las ilusiónes" (Bilbao), Sta. Lucia, Cotz, Guatemala. *Antropología e Historia de Guatemala* 18(2): 3–8.

1967 An early Maya stela on the Pacific Coast of Guatemala. *Estudios de Cultura Maya* 6: 171–198.

PENDERGAST, DAVID M.

1967a Altun Ha, Honduras Británica: temporadas 1964 y 1965. *Estudios de Cultura Maya* 6: 149–169.

1967b Occupación post-clásica en Altun Ha, Honduras Británica. *Revista Méxicana de Estudios Antropológicos* 21: 213–224.

1969 An inscribed jade plaque from Altun Ha. *Archaeology* 22: 85–92.

PIÑA CHAN, ROMAN

1964 Algunas consideraciónes sobre las pinturas de Mul-Chic, Yucatán. *Estudios de Cultura Maya* 4: 63–78.

POLLOCK, H. E. D.

1967 Brainerd y Ruppert en Xpuhil en 1949. *Estudios de Cultura Maya* 6: 67–80.

1970 "Architectural notes on some Chenes ruins," in *Monographs and papers in Maya archaeology.* Edited by William R. Bullard, 1–87. Peabody Museum of Archaeology and Ethnology, Harvard University Paper 61.

PROSKOURIAKOFF, TATIANA

1951 "Some non-classic traits in the sculpture of Yucatán," in *The civilizations of ancient America; selected papers of the Twenty-ninth International Congress of Americanists.* Edited by Sol Tax, 108–118. Chicago: University of Chicago Press.

1953 Scroll patterns (entrelaces) of Veracruz. *Revista Mexicana de Estudios Antropológicos* 13(2, 3): 389–401.

1963 *An album of Maya architecture.* Norman: University of Oklahoma Press.

RANDS, R.
1967a Cerámica de la región de Palenque, México. *Estudios de Cultura Maya* 6: 111–147.
1967b "Ceramic technology and trade in the Palenque region, Mexico," in *American historical anthropology: essays in honor of Leslie Spier.* Edited by C. L. Riley and W. W. Taylor, 137–151. Carbondale: Southern Illinois University Press.

RATHJE, WILLIAM L.
1971 The origin and development of lowland classic Maya civilization. *American Antiquity* 36: 275–285.

RATHJE, WILLIAM L., JEREMY SABLOFF
1972 "A research design for Cozumel, Quintama Roo, Mexico." Paper presented at the Seventy-first Annual Meeting of the American Anthropological Association, November 29 to December 3, 1972, Toronto.

ROBERTSON, DONALD
1963 *Pre-Columbian architecture.* New York: George Braziller.

ROYS, RALPH L.
1934 *The Indian background of colonial Yucatán.* Washington, D.C.: Carnegie Institution.
1957 *The political geography of the Yucatán Maya.* Washington, D.C.: Carnegie Institution.
1966 Native empires in Yucatán. *Revista Mexicana de Estudios Antropológicos* 20: 153–177.

RUZ LHUILLIER, ALBERTO
1945 Campeche en la arqueología Maya. *Acta Antropológica,* época 1; 1(2, 3). Mexico City: Escuela Nacional de Antropología e Historia.

SABLOFF, JEREMY A., WILLIAM L. RATHJE
1972 "A study of changing Pre-Columbian commercial patterns on the Island of Cozumel, Mexico." Paper presented at the Fortieth International Congress of Americanists, September 1972, Rome. Mimeographed manuscript.

SABLOFF, JEREMY A., WILLIAM L. RATHJE, DAVID A. FREIDEL, JUDITH G. CONNOR, PAULA L. W. SABLOFF
1972 "Trade and power in postclassic Yucatán: initial observations." Paper presented at the Conference on Recent Research in Mesoamerican Archaeology, August 1972, Cambridge, England. Mimeographed manuscript.

SABLOFF, JEREMY, GORDON R. WILLEY
1967 The collapse of Maya civilization in the southern lowlands: a consideration of history and process. *Southwestern Journal of Anthropology* 23: 311–336.

SÁENZ, CESAR A.
1963 Exploraciónes en la pirámide de las serpientes emplumadas, Xochicalco, Morelos. *Revista Mexicana de Estudios Antropológicos* 19: 7–25.
1968 Exploraciónes y restoraciónes en Yucatán. *Boletín INAH* 31: 17–23.

SAHLINS, MARSHALL D.
1958 *Social stratification in Polynesia.* Seattle: University of Washington Press.

SANDERS, WILLIAM T.
1957 "Tierra y agua ('soil and water'): a study of the ecological factors

in the development of Mesoamerican civilizations." Unpublished doctoral dissertation, Harvard University.

1960   *Prehistoric ceramics and settlement patterns in Quintana Roo, Mexico.* Contributions to American Archaeology and History 60. Washington, D.C.: Carnegie Institution.

SANDERS, WILLIAM T., BARBARA J. PRICE

1968   *Mesoamerica, the evolution of a civilization.* New York: Random House.

SELER, EDUARD

1904a   "Antiquities of Guatemala," in *Mexican and Central American antiquities, calendar systems and history.* Edited by C. P. Bowditch, 75–122. Bureau of American Ethnology Bulletin 28. Washington, D.C.: Smithsonian Institution.

1904b   "Wall paintings of Mitla, a Mexican picture writing in fresco," in *Mexican and Central American antiquities, calendar systems and history.* Edited by C. P. Bowditch, 243–324. Bureau of American Ethnology Bulletin 28. Washington, D.C.: Smithsonian Institution.

SERVICE, ELMAN R.

1962   *Primitive social organization: an evolutionary perspective.* New York: Random House.

SHARER, ROBERT J.

1968   "New archaeological research at Chalchuapa, El Salvador." Paper read at the Sixty-seventh Annual Meeting of the American Anthropological Association, December 1968, Seattle, Washington.

1969   "Archaeological excavation at Chalchuapa, El Salvador: the 1969 season." Paper read at the Sixty-eighth Annual Meeting of the American Anthropological Association, December 1969, New Orleans, Louisiana.

SHARER, ROBERT J., JAMES C. GIFFORD

1970   Preclassic ceramics from Chalchuapa, El Salvador, and their relationships with the Maya lowlands. *American Antiquity* 35: 441–462.

SHARP, ROSEMARY

1970   Early architectural grecas in the valley of Oaxaca. *Boletín de Estudios Oaxaqueños* 32.

1972   "Greca, an exploratory study of the relationships between art, society, and personality." Unpublished doctoral dissertation, University of North Carolina, Chapel Hill.

SHEPARD, ANNA O.

1948   *Plumbate, a Mesoamerican trade ware.* Washington, D.C.: Carnegie Institute.

SNOW, DEAN R.

1969   Ceramic sequence and settlement location in pre-Hispanic Tlaxcala. *American Antiquity* 34: 131–145.

SPINDEN, ELLEN S.

1933   The place of Tajín in Totonac archaeology. *American Anthropologist* 35: 225–270.

SPORES, RONALD

1967   *The Mixtec kings and their people.* Norman: University of Oklahoma Press.

STREBEL, HERMANN

1885–1889   *Alt-Mexiko: archäologische Beitrage zur Kulturgeschichte seiner Bewohner.* Hamburg and Leipzig: Leopold Voss.

THOMPSON, J. ERIC S.

1952   *The introduction of Puuc style of dating at Yaxchilan.* Carnegie Institution of Washington, Department of Archaeology, Notes 109.

1957   *Deities portrayed on censers at Mayapán.* Carnegie Institute of Washington, Department of Archaeology. Current Reports 40.

1964   Trade relations between the Maya highlands and lowlands. *Estudios de Cultura Maya* 4: 13–49.

1966a   Maya hieroglyphs of the bat as metaphorgrams. *Man*, n.s. 1: 176–184.

1966b   "Merchant gods of Middle America," in *Suma antropológica en homenaje a Roberto J. Weitlaner.* Edited by A. Pompa y Pompa, 159–172. Mexico City: Instituto Nacional de Antropología e Historia.

1970   *Maya history and religion.* Norman: University of Oklahoma Press.

TOURTELLOT, GAIR, JEREMY A. SABLOFF

1972   Exchange systems among the ancient Maya. *American Antiquity* 37: 126–135.

TOZZER, ALFRED M.

1921   *Excavation of a site at Santiago Ahuizotla, D. F., Mexico.* Bureau of American Ethnology Bulletin 74. Washington, D.C.: Smithsonian Institution.

1941   *Landa's "Relación de las cosas de Yucatán," a translation.* Peabody Museum of American Archaeology and Ethnology Paper 18. Cambridge, Massachusetts: Peabody Museum, Harvard University.

TYLOR, E. B.

1930   *Anthropology,* two volumes. London: C. A. Watts.

VAILLANT, GEORGE C.

1927   "The chronological significance of Maya ceramics." Ph.D. dissertation, Division of Anthropology, Harvard University. Reproduced on microcards as *Archives of Archaeology* 12. Madison: The Society for American Archaeology and the University of Wisconsin Press.

1938   A correlation of archaeological and historical sequences in the valley of Mexico. *American Anthropologist* 40: 535–573.

VON WINNING, HASSO

1965   Relief-decorated pottery from central Veracruz, Mexico. *Ethnos* 30: 105–135.

WAUCHOPE, ROBERT

1964   "Southern Mesoamerica," in *Prehistoric man in the New World.* Edited by Jesse D. Jennings and Edward Norbeck, 331–386. Chicago: University of Chicago Press for Rice University.

WEAVER, MURIEL PORTER

1972   *The Aztec, Maya and their predecessors: archaeology of Mesoamerica.* New York: Seminar Press.

WEBB, MALCOLM C.

1964   "The Post-classic decline of the Petén Maya: an interpretation in the light of a general theory of state society." Unpublished doctoral dissertation, University of Michigan. Ann Arbor: University Microfilms.

1965   The abolition of the taboo system in Hawaii. *Journal of the Polynesian Society* 74(1): 21–39.

1968   Carneiro's hypothesis of limited land resources and the origins of the state: a Latin Americanist's approach to an old problem. *South Eastern Latin Americanist* 12(3): 1–8.

1970 "Evolving systems of trade and the Petén Maya decline." Paper presented at the Sixty-ninth Annual Meeting of the American Anthropological Association, December 1970, San Diego, California. Mimeographed manuscript.

1973 "The Petén Maya decline viewed in the perspective of state formation," in *The Classic Maya collapse*. Edited by T. Patrick Culbert. Albuquerque: University of New Mexico Press for the School of American Research.

WEST, MICHAEL
1965 Transition from Preclassic to Classic at Teotihuacán. *American Antiquity* 31: 193–202.

WILLEY, GORDON R.
1966 *An introduction to American archaeology*, volume one: *North and Middle America*. Englewood Cliffs: Prentice-Hall.

WILLEY, GORDON R., T. PATRICK CULBERT, RICHARD E. W. ADAMS, editors
1967 Maya lowland ceramics: a report from the 1965 Guatemala City conference. *American Antiquity* 32: 289–315.

WILLEY, GORDON R., JAMES C. GIFFORD
1961 "Pottery of the Holmul I style from Barton Ramie, British Honduras," in *Essays in pre-Columbian art and archaeology*. Edited by Samuel K. Lothrop, 152–175. Cambridge, Mass.: Harvard University Press.

WILLEY, GORDON R., DEMITRI B. SHIMKIN
1971 The collapse of the classic Maya civilization in the southern lowlands: a symposium summary statement. *Southwestern Journal of Anthropology* 27: 1–18.

WOLF, ERIC R.
1959 *Sons of the shaking earth*. Chicago: University of Chicago Press.

WOLF, ERIC R., ANGEL PALERM
1955 Irrigation in the old Acolhua domain. *Southwestern Journal of Anthropology* 11: 265–281.

Ports of Trade in Mesoamerica: A Reappraisal

FRANCIS FREI BERDAN

As an outgrowth of Polanyi's project on economic aspects of institutional development, several applications of the concept "ports of trade" of early empires have emerged (Polanyi 1966; Arnold 1957a; Revere 1957; Leeds 1962; Chapman 1957). The fullest theoretical exposition is given in his "Ports of trade in early societies" (Polanyi 1963). Ports of trade are defined as intentionally neutral locales where representatives of political entities meet for the purpose of conducting commercial transactions.

Taken as a whole, these studies point toward a consideration of ports of trade as a predictable socioeconomic structure under specified conditions: notably the presence of powerful neighboring state structures and the operation of non-industrial, non-market economies. Although there are certain features of these trading centers which do define this as a cross-cultural type, many other features serve to highlight the variation among them, and suggest further examination of the concept. It is the purpose of this paper to re-examine the concept "ports of trade" with special emphasis on variation. Late Postclassic Mesoamerica, exhibiting several examples of ports of trade (Chapman 1957), will provide the focus for this study.

ARCHAIC ECONOMIC SYSTEMS

Much of the basic conceptual work on archaic economic systems has been associated with Karl Polanyi and his colleagues. In *Trade and market in the early empires* (1957), Polanyi and others presented a detailed statement of the substantivist position in economic anthropology. For present purposes, this approach will be followed in principle. A brief resumé of the basic tenets of this orientation of economic anthropology follows, insofar as it bears on interpretations Polanyi and others have made regarding archaic economic systems in general and ports of trade in particular.

It is generally agreed that all societies have structured arrangements to provide the material means of individual and community life. It is these structured means that constitute the economic system. There are, indeed, important differences in the ways economic activities are institutionalized in societies, and the substantivist approach is designed to discover these ways. In Polanyi's terms (1957: 248), the economy is viewed as "instituted process"; economic activity as embedded in institutions, such activity involving movements of material elements. This includes both the actual movements of goods and the structural features regulating and controlling these movements.

The importance of this institutionalized process is that it endows the economic process with stability and coherence with reference to the rest of the society. Such stability and coherence may be realized through certain forms of economic integration, and Polanyi has isolated three generalized forms, or patterns, through which economies may be instituted (1957: 250). These are reciprocity, redistribution, and exchange (by which he means market exchange; all three of these forms are means of exchange):

Reciprocity denotes movements between correlative points of symmetrical groupings; redistribution designates appropriational movements toward a center and out of it again; exchange refers to...movements taking place as between "hands" under a market system (Polanyi 1957: 250).

Certain social arrangements are associated with these different modes of transaction: symmetrical groupings, centricity in group organization, or a price-regulated market system. The specific forms of transaction are embedded in these institutional arrangements, and only when these arrangements are present, claims Polanyi, will the particular modes of transaction effectively integrate the economy. For example, specific acts of exchange can produce a large-scale, redistributive transactional sphere only when allocative centers have been established. In the case of archaic economic systems, generally characterized by a redistributive sphere, this necessitates some form of centralization of power regulating the movements of resources through the center. It is important to emphasize that Polanyi does not refer to these different forms of integration as entire economic systems, but rather as modes of transaction, in which two or all may be found in the same economic system. There are, he argues, emphases on particular modes of integration in different societies, but this does not *a priori* exclude the presence of other modes in the same society.

Within this framework, archaic economic systems are considered to form part of the complex organization of state-organized non-industrial societies. The early states are generally considered, economically, to be composed of an internal system of redistribution and a network of external, administered trade. There is also little doubt that patterns of reciprocity operated at a local level. In addition, there is historical evidence that forms of market exchange were also present and important in the circulation of goods in these societies.

It is important to note the social context of these economic networks. Economic arrangements are viewed in terms of a complex political unit: the non-industrial state or empire. It is characterized by centralization of power, and a formal organization of subordinate constituencies. Accordingly, the controlling powers of the center regulate the production and distribution of resources to some degree by imposing tribute and/or tax quotas on their constituencies (whether individuals, regions, or ethnic groups). As such, the center serves as a receiving and allocative center for the unit as a whole. This center is generally considered to be urban in nature, both in terms of spatial-demographic configurations and as a point of concentration of functions and power for the society or region. The structure of this center, or non-industrial city, has been studied cross-culturally by Sjoberg (1960).

The social organization is also characterized by forms of social stratification, exhibiting generally a large social and economic gap between those who produce goods and those to whom goods are distributed. Social stratification can be defined in terms of differential control over strategic resources and is very likely a pre-condition for state organization (Fried 1960). Exclusive control over certain important resources (often as status symbols) is generally restricted to particular statuses in the society. The redistributive system serves to solidify and maintain a specific system of social stratification by controlling the distribution and accessibility of important goods for particular, defined ends (frequently status-related) (Polanyi 1966: 193–194).

Eisenstadt (1963) discusses in depth the nature of social and political organization of the historic "bureaucratic empires " (his terminology for Polanyi's "archaic societies "). According to Eisenstadt, in such empires there is the presence of some relatively non-rigid (i.e. non-ascriptive) status hierarchies, and the presence of special elite positions not necessarily based on ascriptive criteria. The general stratigraphic type he describes is composed of a ruler and the upper echelons of the bureaucracy. Below these were various specialized urban groups and cultural elites, with far less political power at their disposal. The peasantry (and lowest urban classes) comprise the base of this type of society. Eisenstadt notes that many positions potentially and actually drew membership from all societal levels. This is apparent in the case of Mesoamerica. Aztec society, for example, allowed social mobility through non-ascriptive means, and there existed status by achievement (especially in the military realm, and perhaps to a lesser degree through success in commerce and religious activities). Although such channels were available for mobility, it should be emphasized that ascriptive criteria for societal positions still predominated (see also Sjoberg 1960).

Relations with foreign political units are carried on through trading activities administered from the political center. Goods are allocated from the center for such trade, and the persons and groups conducting the transactions enjoy a special status endowed by the controlling political powers. Such professional merchants comprise the groups conducting commercial transactions in ports of trade. Their trade is generally considered to be in the service of the ruling powers and the elite, transactions usually involving status-related luxury goods.

Internally, markets appear to be present, but their exact nature and place in the economic system has not been adequately examined. Evidence points to extensive development of marketplaces and marketplace activity, but rates of exchange appear to be regulated by administrative policy as well as by supply-and-demand factors. There appear to be markets at local, regional, and super-regional levels. The larger markets, at least, involve exchanges among a wide range of goods (both subsistence and luxury) as well as availability of services.[1] Persons conducting the transactions are the producers themselves, as well as professional, full-time merchants.

Features of reciprocity at the state level are evident, and seem to represent alliances of symbolized subjugation. Reciprocity no doubt was extensive in local communities, but the state-level orientation taken here does not lead to a discussion of such exchanges.

Economically, then, archaic societies exhibit forms of redistribution, "foreign" trade,[2] reciprocity, and a variant of market exchange. Each of these can be found with its social correlate: allocative centers, ports of trade, symmetrical political or kinship units, and marketplaces with administrative policies. The relationships among these exchange sub-systems have been little explored. Arnold (1957b) and Polanyi (1966) suggest that market and foreign-trade activities in the port of

[1] In the case of Colonial Mexico (ca. 1560), the Coyoacan market in the Valley of Mexico provided carpenters (AGN ca. 1560). This very likely is a reflection of pre-Conquest patterns (Cortés 1928: 93).

[2] Polanyi (1957: 256) feels that foreign trade in archaic societies is based predominately on the "principle of reciprocity" (see also Sahlins [1965] for a discussion of types of reciprocity). I have used "foreign trade" here as separate from reciprocity because they appear to have very different correlative institutions and functions.

trade of Whydah (West Africa) were separate in both administrative organization and exchange activities. Chapman (1957) and Leeds (1962) follow the same premise for ports of trade in Mesoamerica and India. I have attempted to show elsewhere (Berdan 1973) that these exchange mechanisms may be linked through both actual exchange activities and social organizational features.

PORTS OF TRADE IN EARLY EMPIRES

Ports of trade have been discussed above as they relate to exchange through foreign trade, providing the focal institution for such trade in non-industrial states or empires. The general characteristics of these trading centers have been discussed by Polanyi (1963), Leeds (1962), and Belshaw (1965), and specific applications have been made by Arnold (1957a), Revere (1957), Leeds (1962), and Chapman (1957). These studies have been based primarily on historical materials, as is the present study. Such materials derive primarily from sources *external* to the trading centers. That is, they are predominately reports of foreign travelers or merchants to these locales. Some information is also available from nearby states, indicating their relationship and policies toward ports of trade. Information from the ports themselves, however, is sorely lacking.

The above writers on ports of trade have enumerated a number of characteristics defining the nature of the origin and operation of these localities. Most of these characteristics have been considered to be applicable cross-culturally and through time under the "archaic" conditions discussed above. Variation undeniably exists, as both Polanyi (1963) and Belshaw (1965) agree, but the nature of this variation and its importance in describing this institution have been little explored.

The most frequently mentioned characteristic of ports of trade is that they are deliberately neutral, with guarantees of safety for foreign traders who transact business in that port (which need not be a seaport). According to Polanyi (1966: 100):

Unless the government was both capable and willing to defend its neutrality and to enforce law and impartial justice, foreign merchants had to avoid places occupied by military power.

Beyond neutrality, it is useful to discuss ports of trade in terms of, first, their relationships with nearby powers, and second, in terms of their characteristic internal organization.

It is often observed that ports of trade serve as points of transshipment between distinct ecological regions and, less frequently, that they serve as buffer zones. Politically and militarily, they are placed in positions of peripheral importance to nearby powers. Where powerful states confront one another, yet each controls the production of distinct and important resources, intermediate areas may develop a commercial importance beyond any military or political value. This will, of course, not be the case in each instance.

In terms of the structure of the port itself, it is considered as an autonomous town, city, or state intended to serve as a meeting place for various groups of foreign traders. Its autonomous character is undoubtedly linked to its neutrality, yet some ports seem to have been, at least to some degree, controlled by nearby states. Both eighteenth-century Whydah (West Africa) and Xononochco (Mesoamerica) were overtly controlled by neighboring states. It would appear that the neutrality of the trading center could be seriously jeopardized under such a situation, yet guarantees for the safety of foreign traders apparently could be maintained (Polanyi 1957: 248–249).

Within the locale, there is evidence for a high development of transportation and communication facilities with an abundance of warehouses and other commercially related structures and areas.

Strict administrative control is present in all foreign economic dealings, and prices are frequently fixed by treaty or other admin-istrative arrangement. In addition, the activities of merchants are highly regulated while in the port, although it is often noted that groups of foreign merchants reside in the port itself.

The marketplace is generally considered to be geographically and economically separate from external trade: that is, if a market is present, it is an institution for the benefit of the local inhabitants and not used by foreign merchants. Polanyi, Arnold, Chapman, and others (in Polanyi, et al. 1957) have emphasized the incompatibility of trade (foreign, administered trade) with markets. Arnold's observations on the port of trade of eighteenth-century Whydah emphasize the exclusive nature of market and trade transactional spheres, the former involving exchanges of subsistence, utilitarian goods between local persons, the latter consisting of transactions between representatives of states dealing mainly in luxury goods. Both situations are conceived of as being highly regulated, but through separate administrative channels. It is apparent, at least from the material available on Whydah, that the personnel, goods, and administration of the market and trade networks were institutionally separate and distinct, and served different ends. Similar information has not been adequately collected for other ports of trade. Nonetheless, the Whydah informa-tion has led students of archaic economic systems to consider these modes of transaction as exclusive and even incompatible in ports of trade. Although Chapman follows this premise, arguments for relationships between trade and markets in Mesoamerican ports of trade will be made here.

Two major features of ports of trade involve the range of control of resources by the local inhabitants, and the extent to which local groups engage in external commerce. It appears that the local persons are most commonly responsible for exchanges of goods with foreign traders; that is, they provide the link between the two trading states. For example, the Aztec merchants (*pochteca*) did not conduct commercial transactions directly with the Yucatecan Maya traders (*ppolom*), but rather with the Chontal of the Xicalango area, who traded Maya goods in return. Supposedly the same process held for transactions with the Maya *ppolom*.

Yet some groups appear to be involved in far-flung merchant ventures of their own, notably the Phoenicians (of Sidon and Tyre) and the Chontal of Acalan in Mesoamerica.[3] In a similar vein, these same two groups seem to have developed control over strategic resources, whether through means of production, through secondary manufacture, or through control of regional trade. While some areas are described as basically "empty" or a "no-man's land" (Revere 1957), others exhibit innovative and dynamic characteristics through control of resources: their production, manufacture, and/or distribution. These resources are valuable and strategic not only to the local group, but also to nearby powers. Eventual conquest of these areas by adjacent states appears as an inevitable course.

The historical development of these ports of trade will always be, in some cases, a matter of conjecture. The general view has developed that neutral trading centers grew from the opposition of state societies, each requiring safety and neutrality for exchange of goods, without allowing emissaries of the other state into its territory. A different argument is made for parts of Mesoamerica, whereby it is conjectured that an already-existing trade network (perhaps pre-state-organized) led to the pre-eminence of certain locales which controlled strategic resources. These locales, through control of these resources, became trading centers for long-distance merchants; not necessarily for the original strategic resource (cacao), but for other goods which had been attracted there by the abundance of this crop.

MESOAMERICAN PORTS OF TRADE

Chapman (1957) has discussed at some length certain locales in pre-Conquest Mesoamerica which she considers ports of trade according to the preceding characteristics. Preliminary to that discussion, she

[3] Scholes and Roys (1968) present a particularly well-documented study of this group.

details the role and activities of the Aztec and Maya merchants both in the ports of trade and in their homelands.[4] I do not intend here to duplicate Chapman's efforts in this regard, but would like to emphasize some of the more salient features of merchant organization, especially as it relates to activities in ports of trade.

At the time of the Spanish Conquest, Aztec society had emerged as a state organization, with social stratification, legally sanctioned centralization of power, and complex economic specialization and networks. At that time, and probably for many centuries earlier, the professional merchant groups of Central Mexico (*pochteca* or *oztomeca*) enjoyed special privileges and a special status in relation to the state. The importance of merchants in entering enemy territory and transmitting information to the Aztec ruler is widely documented. In addition, they could declare and undertake wars (Katz 1966: 79) as well as conquer areas and found locales (Acosta Saignes 1971: 438). Their enormous military value to the state was complemented by an economic value: they provided the luxury items so necessary for the nobility. Outward symbols of status were prevalent in Aztec society, and rigidly defined.[5] Each rank in the society, whether ascribed or achieved, was associated with certain exclusive items of dress and ornamentation. Several manufactured items were provided through tribute, notably decorated cloth and warriors' costumes. Luxury raw materials were brought to the Basin of Mexico by the traveling merchants, as well as through tribute levies.

The position of the merchant in Aztec society appears to be one of transition. Statuses traditionally were divided into two categories: nobility and commoner, and attainment of status was primarily by ascription.[6] Earmarks of status were not only access to and control over strategic resources (notably land and commoners to work that land), but also to specific luxury goods as outward displays of rank. The merchants emerge as a group intermediate between the commoners and the nobility. While they paid tribute (in goods only), they were at the same time greatly esteemed by the ruler, allowed to sacrifice slaves, and permitted to wear certain symbols of noble status at special annual festivals (de Sahagun 1950–1969: Book 9). Although it is not clear whether they could own land,[7] this type of endowment

[4] There are a number of these trading centers in Mesoamerica as discussed by Chapman: Xicalango and Cimatan on the Gulf Coast between the Maya and Aztec states, Xoconochco on the Pacific Coast near Guatemala, Nito and Naco on the Gulf of Honduras, and Acalán inland from the Xicalango area. Not only Xicalango, but the "Xicalango area," is considered as a port-of-trade "area," with numerous commercial communities.

[5] See Durán (1967: 211–214) for an enumeration of several laws relating to status.

[6] High status in the society could be achieved primarily through success in warfare, but also through commercial and religious (priestly) activities.

[7] Katz (1972: 217) mentions this, the source apparently being Oviedo.

does not appear as a regular occurrence as with the nobility. Rather than display their wealth (which was considerable in some cases), the merchants were constantly admonished by their elders to appear humble and dress simply (de Sahagun, Book 9: 31). This was not necessarily a choice available to the merchants, as it appears that there were definite social obstacles to luxury consumption on their part (Katz 1972: 214). A possible conflict with the Otomi warriors is alluded to briefly in de Sahagun (Book 9: 32), and may suggest broader social tensions. It should be noted that at the time of the Spanish Conquest strains had been developing in Aztec society in terms of the definition of nobility status. Although there existed both nobility by achievement and nobility by ascription, the latter were placing pressures on the state to restrict the development of the former. In such a social climate, a group like the merchants would only provide additional tensions were they to attempt to also compete with the hereditary nobility. The secrecy of their dealings and concealment of their wealth,[8] then, are not difficult to understand.

Professional merchants are recorded for twelve Basin of Mexico cities,[9] and groups in each city were probably similarly organized. More important, there appears to have been an overall organization of *pochteca* from all these cities, and a system of internal ranking and laws applicable to all. This guild organization is characterized by exclusive residence, internal laws and codes, control over membership, rank in the organization and dispersal and allocation of tasks and rewards.

Most of the historical sources agree that merchants and artisans occupied exclusive sections (*calpultin*, *barrios*) of the cities of Tlatelolco, Tenochtitlán, and Texcoco, and probably of other cities in the Basin of Mexico which contained organized merchant groups.[10] De Zorita, however, mentions that each *barrio* contained its complement of merchants as well as agriculturalists (1963: 112). It is not entirely impossible (though undocumented) that merchants of a different order than those called *pochteca* or *oztomeca* were scattered about in other *barrios* or *calpultin*, and perhaps engaged exclusively in local or regional rather than international trading activities. On the other hand, trade in local markets was carried on by individuals who produced goods themselves, and de Zorita may mean this when he lists "merchants" in this context.

---

[8] As de Sahagun states (Book 9: 31): "And as to their goods, no one could see how much there was; perhaps they carefully hid – covered up – all the boats. Not at one's home did one arrive, [but] perhaps at the house of his uncle or his aunt. . . ."

[9] Tenochtitlán, Tlatelolco, Uitzilopochco, Azcapotzalco, Quaubtitlán, Mixcoac, Texcoco, Uexotla, Coatlichán, Otompán, Xochimilco, and Chalco.

[10] The notion of exclusive merchant *barrios* is emphasized by de Sahagun, and supported by Ixtlilxochitl.

The system of exclusive residence has been investigated in detail by Acosta-Saignes (1971),[11] who suggests that the merchants occupied certain *barrios* in Tlatelolco, Tenochtitlán, and adjacent areas: Acxotlán, Atlauhco, Auachtlán, Itzolco, Pochtlán, Tepetitlán, and Tzonmolco.[12] Van Zantwijk (1970: 5–6) offers the suggestion that Acxotlán and Pochtlán were dominant *barrios*, each with two lesser merchant *barrios*, while Tzonmolco was the major religious and educational center of the Tlatelolco–Tenochtitlán merchant guild as a whole. This hypothesis is consistent with other aspects of Aztec social organization, as *calpulli* (*barrio*) ranking was apparently the rule (Acosta-Saignes 1971: 448). In any event, if the organized merchants did indeed occupy exclusive *calpultin*, and given the tendency toward *calpulli* endogamy (Carrasco 1971), this would tend to isolate them socially from the remainder of the urban population.

The strongest representation of merchants was found at Tlatelolco, which had undergone an extraordinary development of merchant activity. When Tlatelolco was conquered by Tenochtitlán in 1473, these merchants became closely related to the state organization at Tenochtitlán. It is a significant fact, and certainly no coincidence, that the great market of Tlatelolco was located at this center of *pochteca* activity and control.

The merchants, of all groups in Aztec society, were the ones allowed to create and enforce their own laws and codes, and to redistribute private goods through the enactment of lavish feasts. Furthermore, merchants could extend their power to the marketplace, where they sat in judgment daily over the proceedings of the market of Tlatelolco, enforcing fair prices and proper conduct.

Little data exists on the extent to which the merchant guilds exercised control over membership.[13] Most secondary sources, however, agree that entry into commercial activities was through an hereditary path (Sanders and Price 1968: 152; Soustelle 1961: 61; Chapman 1957: 122). Membership of these guilds may indeed have been exclusive, based on kinship relations, and probably membership of a merchant *calpulli* was a prerequisite.

The manner in which the merchants obtained state goods for trade outside the empire is illustrative of their internal relations. According to de Sahagun (Book 9: 7–8), merchants from Tenochtitlán were given 1,600 *quachtli*[14] which belonged to the Aztec ruler. They carried these *quachtli* to Tlatelolco where the merchants of the two cities exchanged

---

[11] Originally 1945.
[12] From de Sahagun (Book 9: 12).
[13] The hereditary nature of merchant guilds is suggested both by de Zorita (1963) and de Sahagun (Book 9: *passim*).
[14] *Quachtli*: large white cotton mantas, or pieces of cloth generally worn like capes. There is frequent mention of these *quachtli* in the sources as a form of money.

gifts and then divided the *quachtli* equally between them. With these, they purchased the goods (undoubtedly in the market of Tlatelolco) which they were to trade with the rulers in the ports of trade. The division of the *quachtli* is mystifying, although it may indicate some degree of equality in transactions involving state goods. The merchants of Tlatelolco and Tenochtitlán, along with those of Uitzilopochco, Azcapotzalco, and Quauhtitlán, were permitted to trade outside the empire, while those of seven other Basin of Mexico cities were required to remain within the empire for their commercial activities.[15]

Among state goods exported were (de Sahagun 1950–1969: Book 9: 8, 17):

rulers' mantas, feathered in cup-shaped designs
mantas of eagle face designs, and striped on the border
   with feathers
rulers' breech clouts with long ends
embroidered skirts and shifts . . .

Of the actual transactions in these ports of trade, information is scanty. De Sahagun (Book 9: 17) does state that the property of the Aztec ruler was traded with the rulers of Anahuac[16] (in this case, Xicalango, Cimitan, and Coatzacualco on the Gulf Coast) for quetzal feathers, green feathers, blue cotinga feathers, and trogonorus feathers. Elsewhere (Book 9: 18–19), the same author adds other goods: jade (some cut), turquoise mosaic shields, shells of many kinds, tortoise-shell cups, feathers of the red spoonbill, of the troupial, the blue honeycreeper, and the yellow parrot, and skins of wild animals. De Sahagun emphasizes that these goods, through all transactions, remained the property of the Aztec ruler.

Van Zantwijk (1970) presents a detailed outline of the complex hierarchy of ranks within the merchant organization. A series of "rites of passage" were necessary for an individual to become an esteemed or powerful member of the merchant guild. These rites included not only success in distant trading ventures, but also the accumulation of sufficient wealth to enter into a series of feasts. One of these feasts is described in detail by de Sahagun (Book 9: Chapters 10–14). Briefly, such a ceremony involved the dispersal of goods "allowing one to become eligible" to sacrifice a slave at an annual festival. If he survived the feasts and exhibited the ability to supply sufficient goods (especially great quantities of food, drink, and mantas), the merchant

---

[15] Mixcoac, Texcoco, Uexotla, Coatlichán, Otompán, Xochimilco, and Chalco. That these merchants were prohibited from trading outside the empire is a sound indication that professional merchants traded within the empire.
[16] Anahuac is the term used by de Sahagun to refer to the two coastal trading areas on the Gulf and Pacific coasts.

was permitted to sacrifice the slave and enter into a higher category within the merchant organization. Merchants from other cities, as well as members of the hereditary nobility, were invited to these feasts. Apparently each rise in the ladder required similar outlays of goods, each probably more expensive than the last. It is clear that de Sahagun is discussing the merchants of Tlatelolco, and possibly also of Tenochtitlán, but Acosta-Saignes (1971: 447) feels that these ranks also applied to other towns with merchant populations.

As considerable personal wealth was involved in the performance of these feasts, the ability of the merchant to amass such wealth is an important consideration. While it is true that the merchants acted as emissaries for the state in carrying state goods to extra-empire trading centers,[17] it is clear from de Sahagun that they also carried their own personal goods to these same areas.[18] The private property of the merchants on such expeditions was as follows (de Sahagun, Book 9: 8, 17–18):

golden mountain-shaped mitres
golden forehead rosettes
golden necklaces of many kinds
golden ear plugs
golden covers used by the women of Anahuac
finger rings
rock crystal ear plugs. . .

Additional private merchant goods are listed by de Sahagun (Book 9: 8, 18) as items for the commoners of these locales:

obsidian ear plugs
copper ear plugs
obsidian razors with leather handles
pointed obsidian blades
rabbit fur
sewing needles
shells
cochineal
alum
herbs of different kinds. . .[19]

Principal merchants and slave dealers also traded in these areas selling men, women, and children slaves.

In return for trading state goods in extra-empire ports of trade, the merchants received specified rewards from the ruler: a bundle of rabbit-fur capes, and a boat load each of dried maize, beans, and chia.

---

[17] De Sahagun documents trips to Xicalango and Xoconochco, the Xicalango trip in greater detail.
[18] De Sahagun clearly makes this distinction, although Chapman does not.
[19] These first three items mentioned were presented as gifts to distinguished warriors and nobles.

They also received decorated mantas and breech clouts of different designs (de Sahagun, Book 9: 5–6).

This list of goods should be compared, however, with that of the goods required by a merchant for the performance of a feast (de Sahagun, Book 9: 47–48):

800 or 1200 mantas
400 breech clouts of different types
women's skirts and shifts of different designs
dried maize
beans
chia (wrinkled and small varieties)
atole with squash seeds
chile
40 or 60 jars of salt
tomatoes (worth 20 small mantas)
80 or 100 turkeys
20 or 40 dogs
20 sacks of cacao beans
2000 or 4000 chocolate beaters
sauce dishes
large baskets
earthen cups
merchants' plates
wood and charcoal
3 or 4 boats (loads) of water....[20]

It is clear that the merchants could not have amassed sufficient wealth for feasts simply through gifts from the state. Therefore, the role of the merchant as entrepreneur must be considered as a source of this wealth.

There are numerous indications[21] that these merchants traded in markets within the empire, notwithstanding the hypothesis by Acosta-Saignes and Chapman that trade preceded tribute, and that once an area was conquered by the Aztecs, trade by professional merchants ceased there. It is not clear to what degree the professional merchants possessed a monopoly on such regional trade.

It has already been mentioned that the professional merchants traded both state and private goods. Although de Sahagun describes transactions of state goods, he regrettably fails to mention the nature of transactions involving the personal goods of the merchants. However, an unpublished document in the Archivo General de las Indias (AGI 1541) observes that Mexican Indian merchants in 1541 were trading in markets (*tianguiz*) in these areas "as was their custom" (AGI 1541: Justicia 195). In addition, contentions are made that these merchants regularly took advantage of local inhabitants in their

[20] Goods required at other ceremonies and feasts are listed in de Sahagun (Book 9: 27, 28, 33).
[21] See especially Durán (1967: vol. 2, 185, 272, 327) and note 15 above.

dealings, a situation also noted by Durán (1967: vol. 2, 357–358). The suggestion is that this trade was a pre-Conquest pattern, and that the locations for transactions involving the personal goods of the merchants were the markets in these port-of-trade areas. Local persons involved in such trade apparently were of both nobility and commoner status, given the types of goods carried by the merchants. The only commodity mentioned in trade is cacao, which the Mexican merchants obtained in these markets. This is consistent with the fact that the merchants are recorded in de Sahagun (Book 9: 27, 30)[22] as possessing cacao in their personal inventory after returning from trading ventures. Yet this valuable item is not mentioned specifically in trade with state goods. It is possible that cacao obtained in tribute was sufficient for the needs of the state, and that the Aztec merchants traded in these cacao-rich lands for other goods attracted there by the cacao.

Admittedly, there exists limited direct evidence for the trading of merchants' private goods in extra-empire centers. However, this evidence is substantiated by the indirect evidence of the great wealth of the merchants, and the suggestion that this wealth must have been accumulated primarily through success in personal trading activities. These factors constitute a reasonable argument that merchants were engaged in activities from which the port-of-trade model normally excludes them.

Goods which the Aztec merchants found in the ports of trade would have been supplied locally or by the Maya merchants, especially from Yucatán, but also perhaps from Guatemala. Although there is little information on the activities of Maya merchants (*ppolom*), some conclusions can be drawn regarding the types of goods in which they dealt.

The merchant of Yucatán apparently operated more as an individual, in contrast to the Aztec merchant, who could only trade as a member of a guild. Again in contrast to the Aztec *pochteca*, the Maya *ppolom* could be, and perhaps was required to be, of noble status. According to Roys (1943: 51):

Merchants ranged from the wealthy and noble wholesalers, who had their own factors, trading canoes, and slave carriers, to the petty itinerant who carried his own pack.

In an oft-mentioned statement, the son of the ruler of Cocom is noted as engaging in trading activities in Honduras (de Landa 1941: 39).

[22] The statements in de Sahagun are not clear, and the possibility exists that the merchants could have obtained the cacao after their return to Tenochtitlán-Tlatelolco, or as disguised merchants.

Details of such commercial relations are provided by de Landa (1941: 94–96):

The occupation to which they had the greatest inclination was trade, carrying salt and cloth and slaves to the lands of Ulua and Tabasco, exchanging all they had for cacao and stone beads, which were their money; and with this they were accustomed to buy slaves, or other beads, because they were fine and good, which their chiefs wore as jewels in their feasts. . . .

Other sources, notably the "Relaciónes de Yucatán," indicate trading activities in 1579–1580, generally suggesting pre-Conquest antecedents. In most cases, the merchants of Yucatán travel to Tabasco or Honduras for cacao, trading cotton mantas, salt, beeswax, and honey (RY 1898–1900: vol. 1, p. 71, 369, 370). De Torquemada clearly notes that trade from Yucatán to Honduras was by canoe and, once again, for purposes of obtaining cacao (p. 335). References to Yucatec trade with "Mexico" are made in these same "Relaciónes,"[23] but may refer to the Nahuatl speakers in Tabasco and perhaps Nito in Honduras.

In terms of movements of goods to and from these ports of trade, cacao played a dominant role for Yucatec merchants, while feathers, jade, and salt[24] occupied a similar position among the Aztec merchants. Slaves were traded in ports of trade by both Aztec and Maya merchants and present a curious situation. Roys (1943: 68) suggests that the warfare common among the eighteen Yucatec provinces generated large quantities of slaves who were sold; and slaves from more distant areas were purchased for service in these provinces. Other slaves may have been required for work on cacao fields in the actual port-of-trade areas, as well as for laborers in the widespread commerce of the area (Scholes and Roys 1968: 29). It is suggested by Roys (1943: 54) that central Mexican goods of copper and rabbit fur were traded to Yucatec traders (probably through the Gulf Coast centers). These goods, brought to Xicalango by Aztec merchants (de Sahagun, Book 9: 8, 18), may have originated in Oaxaca and were common commercial items in central Mexico. On the whole, it appears that the Aztec merchants traveled to these coastal areas primarily for goods available from more distant regions (Yucatán, Guatemala), while the Yucatec merchants traded mainly for goods actually produced in these port-of-trade areas (especially cacao) (see also Scholes and Roys 1968: 29).

Several of the Gulf Coastal towns are recorded with populations of Nahuatl-speakers, many of whom were probably merchants (Scholes and Roys 1968: 27). It was apparently not unusual for foreign

[23] See Millon (1955: 153) for a listing of these "Relaciónes."
[24] Roys (1943: 53) observes that all the salt found in Tabasco was brought from Yucatán.

merchants to reside in such towns, and in a similar type of locale in Honduras (Nito), Cortés (1928: 307) noted that an entire section of the town was occupied by merchants from Acalán.

Aspects of neutrality appear to pose problems in the port-of-trade model, as it is clear from de Landa (1941: 32) that a garrison of Mexican soldiers was stationed at Xicalango and Tabasco. Although Tozzer (1957) observes that the event took place around A.D. 1200, this pattern no doubt continued through Aztec times. The "Relación de la villa de Santa María de la Victoria" indicates a fortress at Xicalango in Montezuma's time (RY 1898–1900: vol. 1, p. 364). Díaz del Castillo (1964: 396) observes fortifications at one of these coastal communities, and Scholes and Roys (1968: 34–36) infer that Aztec control was extensive in Xicalango, suggesting that a relative of Montezuma was the leader of the resident Aztec merchants. These features would seem to indicate more control than usually considered appropriate for a neutral port-of-trade area.

The issue of neutrality again arises with Xoconochco. This province is described as a port of trade by Chapman, yet this was a province conquered by the Aztecs,[25] rendering semi-annual tribute primarily in luxury raw materials.[26] Although it is reported that Aztec merchants traded there, little information exists on merchants from other areas trading at Xoconochco. A reference is made regarding merchants trading *huipiles* [blouses] from Teotitlán del Camino (allied to the Aztec Empire) for cacao in Xoconochco, Guatemala, Chiapas and Suchitepeque, although the origin of these merchants is not made clear (RTC 1905–1906: 215, 223). Mention is also made of cacao passing through this province from the Suchitepeques to New Spain in 1574, but it is inconclusive regarding actual exchanges in Xoconochco in pre-Conquest times (Ponce de León 1961: 140).

Acalán poses quite a different problem. At the time of the Spanish Conquest, it was an independent state, and very likely neutral. Yet there is no direct information that Aztec merchants traded there, or were even allowed to do so. If this were the case, it would be difficult to include it among ports of trade.

Yet Acalán, with its capital of Itzamkanac, was a merchant center in itself, and provided traveling merchants not only for the Gulf Coast region, but for Honduras and probably beyond as well. Speaking of this Chontal Maya province, Cortés states:

Many traders and natives carry their merchandise to every part, and they are

[25] De Sahagun (Book 9: 3–6) states that it was the merchants who conquered this province, an interesting possibility given their activities there as merchants in later times (de Sahagun, Book 9: *passim*).
[26] According to the *Matrícula de tributos*, Xoconochco gave feathers, birds, cacao, jaguar skins, amber, lip plugs, and pottery.

rich in slaves and such articles as are commonly sold in the country...from here they carry on a great trade by means of canoes with those of Xicalango and Tabasco...(1928: 307).

It is noteworthy that while merchants from other areas traveled to trading centers of Xicalango, Xoconochco, Nito, and perhaps Naco, there is no record of their entering the lands of Acalán. On the contrary, merchants from Acalán traveled to other areas, at times establishing themselves in sections of towns, as at Nito in Honduras:

> There was one quarter of the town peopled by his [the ruler of Acalán] agents, among whom was his own brother, who sold such goods of his as are most common in these parts...cocoa, cotton cloths, colours for dyeing, another sort of paint which they use to protect their bodies against the heat and the cold, candlewood for lighting, pine resin for burning before their idols, slaves, and strings of coloured shells... (Cortés 1928: 307).

In addition to controlling extensive commercial networks, these same Chontal Maya of Acalán controlled the production of vast amounts of cacao, a strategic resource for the Aztec and Maya as well. These two latter areas controlled little of this crop, and obtained most of their supply from the coastal areas and Acalán.

From this brief overview, it is suggested that some Mesoamerican areas generally considered ports of trade tend to deviate from the characteristic model. Investigation has centered on the place of markets in these trading centers, the nature of neutrality, and the passive/dynamic nature of local involvement.

The first point of investigation would lead toward a broader definition of the role of professional merchants in ports of trade. It is entirely possible that their contacts in such locales were not limited strictly to administrative officials.

As the most diagnostic feature of ports of trade, neutrality stands out as a determining characteristic. That is, for example, Xoconochco was unquestionably integrated into the Aztec empire and its port-of-trade status should be reconsidered. Xicalango and other Gulf Coastal towns also exhibited features of Aztec control, as well as elements of defense. Although, as Polanyi has suggested, the safety of foreign merchants could be guaranteed under such conditions, further investigation is warranted in this area.

The last point considers the extent to which the locality is an innovative center on its own right, whether controlling resources in terms of production, distribution, or manufacturing. While Whydah, east coast India (Leeds 1962) and Al Mina/Ugarit (Revere 1957) appear to have been relatively passive points of transshipment of goods, the Phoenician cities and Mesoamerican Gulf towns either controlled the actual production of resources or were involved in the manufacture of highly desirable goods. In both cases, distribution was carried on by the local commercial group. Both Phoenicia and the Mesoamerican locales actively participated in interactions involving their own commercial groups. In these places, the strong economic-commercial organization seems to have had some impact on the structure of political power. In Mesoamerica this may have influenced the neutrality of these centers.

Although the port-of-trade model has served to define a particular structural type, important regular variations do exist among members of this type. In the case of Mesoamerica, the passive/dynamic role of local groups is especially noteworthy. Variations of this order should be recognized and incorporated into the port-of-trade model as alternative patterns of this general type.

REFERENCES

ACOSTA SAIGNES, MIGUEL
  1971   "Los pochteca," in De Teotihuacán a los Aztecas. Edited by Miguel Leon-Portilla, 436–448. Mexico City: UNAM.
AGI (ARCHIVO GENERAL DE LAS INDIAS)
  1541   "Son los de el Fiscal contra Alonso Lopez, vecino de la villa de Santa María de la Victoria, sobre haverse titulado visitador, y exigido a los indios de la Provincia de Tabasco diferentes contribuciónes." Justícía legato. 195. Seville.
AGN (ARCHIVO GENERAL DE LA NACIÓN)
  ca. 1560   "Juan Hidalgo Cortés Moctezuma y Guzmán, principal de esa villa, contra María, Petronila y Teresa Guzmán, por posesión del cacicazgo que disfrutó Juan de Guzmán Ixtolinque. Tierras volúmen 1735 exp. 2. Mexico City.
ARNOLD, ROSEMARY
  1957a   "A port of trade: Whydah on the Guinea Coast," in Trade and market in the early empires. Edited by Karl Polanyi, C. Arensberg, and H. W. Pearson, 154–176. New York: The Free Press.
  1957b   "Separation of trade and market: great market of Whydah," in Trade and market in the early empires. Edited by Karl Polanyi, C. Arensberg, and H. W. Pearson, 177–187. New York: The Free Press.
BELSHAW, CYRIL S.
  1965   Traditional exchange and modern markets. Englewood Cliffs, N.J.: Prentice-Hall.
BERDAN, F. F.
  1973   "Interrelations among economic exchange spheres in the Aztec empire." Paper presented at the 1973 Annual Meeting of the Southwestern Anthropological Association. San Francisco.
CARRASCO, PEDRO
  1971   "Social organization of ancient Mexico," in Handbook of Middle American Indians, volume ten, 349–375. Austin: University of Texas Press.
CHAPMAN, ANNE C.
  1957   "Port of trade enclaves in Aztec and Maya civilizations," in Trade

and market in the early empires. Edited by Karl Polanyi,
C. Arensberg, and H. W. Pearson, 114–153. New York: The Free
Press.

CORTÉS, HERNÁN
1928 *Five letters of Cortés to the emperor.* Translated by J. B. Morris. New
York: W. W. Norton.

DE LANDA, DIEGO
1941 *Relación de las cosas de Yucatán.* Edited by A. M. Tozzer. Cambridge, Mass.: Peabody Museum of American Archaeology and
Ethnology.

DE SAHAGUN, BERNARDINO
1950–1969 *Florentine codex.* Translated by J. O. Anderson and C. E.
Dibble. Norman: University of Oklahoma Press.

DE TORQUEMADA, JUAN
1723 *Los veinte i un libros rituales i monarchía indiana,* three
volumes.

DE ZORITA, ALONSO
1963 *Breve y sumaria relación de los señores de la Nueva España.* Mexico
City: UNAM.

DÍAZ DEL CASTILLO, BERNAL
1964 *Historia de la conquista de la Nueva España* (third edition). Mexico
City: Porrua.

DURÁN, DIEGO
1967 *Historia de las Indias de Nueva España e islas de la tierra firme 2.*
Mexico City: Porrua.

EISENSTADT, S. N.
1963 *The political systems of empires.* New York: The Free Press.

FRIED, MORTON
1960 "On the evolution of social stratification and the state," in *Culture
in history.* Edited by S. Diamond, 713–731. New York: Columbia
University Press.

KATZ, FRIEDRICH
1966 *Situación social y económica de los Aztecas durante los siglos XV
y XVI.* Mexico City: UNAM.
1972 *The ancient American civilizations.* New York: Praeger.

LEEDS, A.
1962 "The port of trade in pre-European India as an ecological and
evolutionary type." *Proceedings of the 1961 Annual Spring Meeting
of the American Ethnological Society.* Seattle: University of
Washington Press.

"*Matrícula de tributos*"
n.d. Manuscript in the Museo Nacional de Antropología, Mexico City.

MILLON, R. F.
1955 *When money grew on trees: a study of cacao in Mesoamerica.* Ann
Arbor: University Microfilms.

POLANYI, KARL
1957 "The economy as instituted process," in *Trade and market in the
early empires.* Edited by Karl Polanyi, C. Arensberg, and H. W.
Pearson, 243–269. New York: The Free Press.
1963 *Ports and trade in early societies. Journal of Economic History*
23(1): 30–45.
1966 *Dahomey and the slave trade.* Seattle: University of Washington
Press.

POLANYI, KARL, C. ARENSBERG, H. W. PEARSON, editors
1957   Trade and market in the early empires. New York: The Free Press.
PONCE DE LEÓN, LUIS
1961   "Relación de la provincia de Soconusco," in La Victoria. Edited by Michael Coe, 139–140. Cambridge, Mass.: Peabody Museum of Archaeology and Ethnology.
REVERE, ROBERT B.
1957   "No man's coast: ports of trade in the eastern Mediterranean," in Trade and market in the early empires. Edited by Karl Polanyi, C. Arensberg, and H. W. Pearson, 38–63. New York: The Free Press.
ROYS, RALPH
1943   The Indian background of colonial Yucatán. Washington: Carnegie Institution of Washington.
1905–1906   "Relación de Teutitlán del Camino, 1581," in Papeles de Nueva España. Edited by Paso y Troncoso, volume four, 213–231.
1898–1900   "Relaciones de Yucatán," in Colección de documentos inéditos relativos al descubrimiento, conquista y organización de las antiguas posesiones españoles de ultramar, second series. Madrid: Real Academia de la Historia.
RTC (RELACIÓN DE TEUTITLAN DEL CAMINO, 1581)
1905–1906   In Papeles de Nueva España. Edited by Paso y Troncoso, volume four, 213–231.
RY (RELACIÓNES DE YUCATAN)
1898–1900   In Colección de documentos inéditos relativos aldescrubrimiento, conquista y organización de las antiguas posesiónes españoles de ultramar, second series, volumes 11 and 13. Madrid. Real Academia de la Historia.
SAHLINS, MARSHALL
1965   "On the sociology of primitive exchange," in The relevance of models for social anthropology. Edited by M. Banton, 139–186. New York: Praeger.
SANDERS, W. T., B. PRICE
1968   Mesoamerica: the evolution of a civilization. New York: Random House.
SCHOLES, F. V., R. L. ROYS
1968   The Maya Chontal Indians of Acalán-Tixchel. Norman: University of Oklahoma Press.
SJOBERG, GIDEON
1960   The preindustrial city: past and present. New York: The Free Press.
SOUSTELLE, JACQUES
1961   The daily life of the Aztecs on the eve of the Spanish Conquest. Stanford: Stanford University Press.
TOZZER, A. M.
1957   Chichén Itzá and its cenote of sacrifice: a comparative study of contemporaneous Maya and Toltec. Peabody Museum Memoirs 11–12. Cambridge, Mass.: Harvard University.
VAN ZANTWIJK, RUDOLF
1970   Las organizaciónes social-económicas y religiosas de los mercaderos gremiales Aztecas. Boletín de Estudios Latino-Americanos 10: 1–20.

PART THREE

*Ethnographic Contributions to
Prehistory*

Introduction

Archaeologists are making increasing use of ethnographic analogy to generate models and hypotheses to be tested in the reconstruction of political, economic, and religious subsystems for archaeological cultures. Present information suggests a great deal of cultural continuity between archaeological, extinct cultures, and current ethnographic studies, forming the basic theme of this volume.

For Gifford, in his two papers in this section, there are a number of very important parallels to be drawn between studies of the modern Zinacantecos and the ancient Mayans. Running through both posthumous papers is the concept of hierarchy in world view, a hierarchy most clearly exhibited in a bipart division of the ceremonial world. The basic unit of the belief system was the local level, where both contemporary and archaeological groups were concerned with the maintenance, proper functioning, and believability of the local cargo systems.The second level of belief system was an empire system, a system predicated, in Gifford's view, upon a belief in the future in a world-view sense, a belief that the state itself is necessary or vital to proper functioning of the belief system and to the future of the system. This prehistoric Mayan preoccupation with time is seen in part as a concern with establishing a future for the empire level of the belief system.

There is thus a two-level model, cross-cutting several cultural subsystems. The first level is the relationship of the local-level rural populations to archaeologically known "minor" ceremonial centers. These minor centers were serviced by a rotating cargo system of religious specialists; they are perceived as centers with homeland or subregional orientation, specifically dedicated to the satisfaction of strictly local commitments. The second level of the system is that of the "major" ceremonial centers. These major centers had small, permanent populations of religious specialists, whose preoccupation was empire-oriented, devoted to the maintenance and future of the empire. Labor contributions to these centers were not in terms of local needs but rather were visualized more in terms of a need felt to insure the future of the civilization. Recruitment, service, and function of the major centers thus differed markedly from the more pragmatically oriented minor ceremonial centers.

At the current time, Zinacantecos and other lowland groups are seen to be functioning at only the lower of the two levels of the system, in contrast to the earlier Mayan state which functioned at both levels. Gifford proposes a new factor to be added to those previously proposed for the collapse of the Mayan empire (Culbert 1973). Specifically, he proposes that the empire, or second level of the belief system, turns on the notion that this level is needed to provide for the future of the people. In the case of the Mayan collapse, Gifford proposes that this belief turned to disbelief, accelerated by the increasing conflict and disarticulation of various Mayan ethnic groups; and that the full-time specialists at the major ceremonial centers simply packed up and returned home to their kin, bringing about the dissolution of the empire.

Howry sees the use of ethnographic analogy as being relevant for the reconstruction of Mayan ceramic precepts, as well as for religious concepts. Archaeologists have turned to studies in the cultural ecology of ceramics and the sociology of ceramics in order to extract the fullest possible information contained in these fossilized pieces of social behavior, no longer being satisfied with only ceramic typologies and ceramic chronologies. Crucial to many arguments are ideas surrounding fabrication and longevity of ceramics, such as discussed by Thompson (1958), Foster (1965), Weigand (1969) and Howry for the Mesoamerican area. As part of his argument, Howry has investigated the utility of the type-variety method of ceramic analysis (Gifford 1960; Smith, Willey, and Gifford 1960) as applied to Mesoamerican ceramics in the light of contemporary ceramic technology of the Chamula potters. Howry's research appears to verify the importance of ceramic paste as a critical factor for the reconstruction of ceramic-producing centers and their exchange boundaries.

Fruitful here also is the discussion of the ceramic distribution, not only through the more frequently mentioned marketing system, but also through a system which Howry terms "invisible exchange" through which special ceramics are prepared for cargos or religious prestige offices. Cargos are important, not so much because of the quantity of vessels involved, which generally is small, but since they are the organizing foci of the entire community's religious celebration.

In Chamula, the temper, paste and form are exactly the same for cargo vessels as utilitarian ware, the only distinguishing criterion being a larger size; hence the archaeologist might not recognize their importance unless keyed into it through such ethnographic studies. Fragility of ceramics effectively limits distribution distances; Howry suggests a limit of three hours' walking time as the effective distance for one locale for ceramic sales. In terms of archaeological locational analysis, one might say the site catchment of ceramic sales has a three-hour radius.

Hobgood and Riley utilize ethnohistoric data in another fashion, to investigate the interactions of the Tlaxcaltecan settlements on the northern frontiers of New Spain. Their work indicates that the Spanish maintained a practice that had long standing in both the high civilizations of Mexico and Peru prior to the Spanish Conquest – that of introducing colonies of different ethnic groups into diverse areas for both economic and political reasons. Thus the Tlaxcaltecans were moved into a frontier area to serve on one hand as a teaching group, introducing agricultural ways and settled lifeways into an area where the extant Indian groups utilized nonagricultural nomadic techniques to exploit the local ecology. But the Tlaxcaltecans were also moved in for garrison or military purposes. They were to be used as mercenaries to keep the local Indians honest and peaceful; and we should note that the reverse was equally as important – the use by the Spanish of the local Indians to keep the Tlaxcaltecans in line. Special privileges were accorded the Tlaxcaltecan colonists in return for their teaching and garrison obligations, similar to those privileges we find granted by Aztec and other imperial American states in pre-Hispanic times. In the case of the Tlaxcaltecans, because they were moved into an area of relative political instability, an area inhabited by the Lipan or Apache, the special privileges granted to the Tlaxcaltecans persisted for an unusually long period of time, from the 1590's until the 1790's, when the local Apache finally became sedenterized, marking the death knell of the special privileges for the Tlaxcaltecans. Because of this unusually long period of time as a group with special privileges, Riley and Hobgood argue that the Tlaxcaltecans were particularly important as cultural brokers interacting between the nomadic Indians to the north such as the Apache and the Spanish and Ladinos to the south.

REFERENCES

CULBERT, T. P., *editor*
   1973   *The Classic Maya collapse.* Albuquerque: University of New Mexico Press.

FOSTER, G. M.
1965 "The sociology of pottery," in *Ceramics and man.* Edited by F. R. Matson, 43–61. Viking Fund Publications in Anthropology 41. New York.

GIFFORD, J. C.
1960 The type-variety method of ceramic classification as an indicator of cultural phenomena. *American Antiquity* 25(3): 341–346. Salt Lake City.

SMITH, R. E., G. R. WILLEY, J. C. GIFFORD
1960 The type-variety concept as a basis for analysis of Maya pottery. *American Antiquity* 25(3): 330–340. Salt Lake City.

THOMPSON, R. H.
1958 *Modern Yucatecan Pottery making.* Memoir of the Society of American Archaeology 15. Salt Lake City.

WEIGAND, P. C.
1969 *Modern Huichol ceramics.* Mesoamerican Studies 3. Carbondale: Southern Illinois University Press.

The Ancient Maya in Light of Their Ethnographic Present

JAMES C. GIFFORD

> Every society has a logic to its thinking – so too, there was
> an Old Empire Maya logic. In the elaboration of their art
> style, I feel the Maya ceremonial center populations were
> literally trying to talk to their gods, attempting to compel the
> gods through the sheer power of Maya beauty and perfection
> to be kind to the real Maya world, soften the burdens of life,
> and bestow favor upon the Maya people.
>
> JAMES C. GIFFORD, 15 February 1972

"Today archaeology has become a part of anthropology, and we are
ambitious enough to believe we may find the answers to the old and
ever-fascinating questions of how and why man behaved as he did "
(Willey 1968: 225). With this thought uppermost, we can address
ourselves to a comprehension of the ancient Maya by examining
certain dimensions of the Zinacanteco way of life based on information provided by Vogt (1969) and his associates.

THE MAYA BELIEF SYSTEM

...the Mayan culture complex revealed in the contemporary behavior of
the Zinacantecos goes far beyond limited survivals in costume. Living
arrangements, subsistence, social relations, the hierarchical ceremonial structure, and particularly the elaborate conceptual ordering of the universe and
other relations between man and the supernatural all exhibit a basic Mayan
character. The Spanish-Catholic elements, particularly in the form of religious

At the time of Dr. Gifford's death in January 1973, he was engaged in reviewing and
rewriting sections of this manuscript, which was initially prepared in 1971. The paper
presented here represents an edited first draft with the inclusion of additional notes
written by him during 1972. I would like to acknowledge the assistance of R. E. W.
Adams, who read the paper and answered certain questions, and Mrs. Jean Adelman
(University Museum Librarian, Philadelphia), who kindly supplied several references.

Carol A. Gifford

figures, religious fiesta days, some priestly functions and ceremonial observances, and in terminology, have synthesized so smoothly with the Mayan complex that the result is a unique, very elaborate and highly integrated cultural system.

Every step in life for the Zinacantecos is ceremonial: being pregnant, giving birth, courting, borrowing and repaying money, taking religious office, being cured of illness, and being buried. . . . The Zinacantecos have. . . created a collective representation of reality that governs the behavior of individuals in every facet of life and that is replicated at all levels of the social structure. The Zinacantecos have gone further in their elaboration of a belief system materially represented in ceremonies, ritual behavior, and daily life than have many other distinctive human communities. This belief system serves as a philosophy, cosmology, theology, code of values, and as a science. It defines, explains, and defends everything about the world. So long as the individual remains within this belief system and so long as the externally imposed conditions of existence do not change too drastically, nothing else need be "known" (Spindler and Spindler 1970: viii).

Consider this passage concerning

. . . the ceremonial movement that must occur in a major curing ceremony from the sitio of the patient to the ceremonial center. The curing group consists of the patient, the h-'ilol (curer), and a group of assistants, the number depending upon the type of ceremony. The group visits, in fixed order, four sacred mountains located around the ceremonial center. At the first three mountains, prayers are said and offerings are left at crosses located at the foot and/or on the summit of each of the mountains. The fourth mountain is kalvaryo, where the ancestral gods are believed to conduct their council meetings. Special rituals, including the sacrifice of a black chicken, take place here, and the curing group then returns to the sitio of the patient to continue with the ceremony. The important point here is that no other mountain close to one's paraje can be visited for this ceremony. Regardless of how far one lives from the ceremonial center, this ceremonial pilgrimage must ordinarily be made to the proper mountains, which are all located around the central ceremonial center (Vogt 1968: 161).

So completely does the Zinacanteco belief system seem to recapitulate that which the archaeological evidence suggests was the lifeway of the Maya Old Empire that we can modify this description and say that the group visits, in fixed order, four sacred temples located in the principal ceremonial center. At the first three temples, prayers are said and offerings are left at stelae located at the foot and/or on the summit of each of the temple structures. The fourth temple is the most important and is where Old Empire priesthood representatives conduct their special council meetings. These statements do not seem disharmonious, even though as much as 1,200 to 1,500 years intervene and the degree of social complexity differs (high civilization in contrast to the municipio of Zinacantán). Vogt (1968: 167) indicated his own view by stating that

. . . there is probably an important historical and structural relationship between. . . the ritual performed at cross shrines at the foot and on top of sacred mountains in Zinacantán and the ritual performed at the round altars in front of stelae at the foot of the Classic Maya pyramids and in the temples atop the pyramids.

The heart of the contemporary matter is that the ancestral gods do in fact live inside these mountains:

These ancestral gods are the most important Zinacanteco deities, judging from the frequency with which the people think about them, pray to them, and perform rituals for them. They are remote ancestors of the living Zinacantecos (no one can now trace direct genealogical connections with them), and they were ordered to take up residence inside the mountains by the Four-Corner Gods in the mythological past. They are pictured as looking and behaving as elderly Zinacantecos living eternally in their mountain homes, where they convene and deliberate, survey the affairs of their living descendants, and wait for the offerings of black chickens, candles, incense, and rum liquor which sustain them.

In the Zinacanteco view, these ancestors provide the ideal for human life – they know best how to grow corn, build houses, weave clothing, herd sheep, court and marry, cope with kinsmen, and perform ceremonies with all the necessary rituals. When living Zinacantecos perform ceremonies, they model their behavior upon what the ancestors are believed to be doing inside the mountains.

But the ancestors are not only repositories of the important social rules and cultural beliefs that compose the Zinacanteco way of life, they are the active and jealous guardians of the culture. Deviations are instantly noted, and guilty Zinacantecos are punished. . . . (Vogt 1970: 6).

THE NATURE OF ANCIENT MAYA SOCIAL STRATIFICATION

Vogt's studies indicate, I believe, that Zinacanteco predecessors participated in the ancient Maya configuration. On the basis of what is known archaeologically, I also believe that Lowland Maya civilization (the Old Empire), the Tzakol-Tepeu peoples of A.D. 200–900 in the Petén (Gifford 1970a), was composed not only of representatives of the present Zinacanteco population unit (and other Tzotzil speakers), but also of several other population units such as the Lacandon Indians. I believe these components were arranged hierarchically within ancient Maya society of the Old Empire and that each was associated with a role within the ancient social stratification:

By Vogt's account the Zinacanteco are lineage oriented. It is possible that the ancient Zinacantecos had specific defined functions in the Old Empire ceremonial center world because considering the entire tribal whole of the Old Empire, the Zinacanteco would have had certain lineages. Unlike the present, the situation then might well have involved severe *lineage* stratification, which included job specialization (Gifford 1974: 92).

The Lacandones perhaps occupied the echelon and role corresponding to the Old Empire Maya priesthood. Because Zinacanteco participation may have been near the middle or upper middle of the hierarchical arrangement of echelons, I think that their capacity to appreciate the entirety of the ancient Maya Old Empire was as great as, or greater than, others stratified below them. In a sense, they may have been the solid backbone of that society and so were in a favorable position (not overly specialized) to retain symbolically in their *present* belief pattern an intense resemblance to the *ancient* configuration. But because the empire was composed of many population units, some serving highly specialized roles that to varying degrees may have involved social isolation, no single population on its own could recapitulate the ancient civilization in terms of overt behavior and physical monumentality even on a modest scale. Accordingly, I believe that the Zinacantecos of today show us only a part of ancient Maya society in their overt behavior and in the empirical (artifactual) world with which they surround themselves; but at the same time I feel that in their myths, in their belief system, in their values, and in their realm of the spiritual and the symbolic, the Zinacantecos have retained a world view identical to the ancient one. What now is projected as the Zinacanteco way of life was, during the Classic Period, of far greater elaboration and complexity for those residing in the ceremonial centers, involving homeland Zinacantecos, various Tzotzil speakers, Lacandones, and other population units arranged within a highly stratified social setting.

Interred in tombs of the major ceremonial centers such as Burial 116 beneath Temple I at Tikal (W. R. Coe 1967: 32–33) or the Funerary Crypt in the Temple of the Inscriptions at Palenque (M. D. Coe 1966: Plate 50) are the ancient "Great Ones." They may be representative of one or more of these other population units, as yet unidentified, small in number, highly specialized for occupancy of the pinnacle position and role in ancient times but with whom all societal components identified, especially the Zinacantecos. Now they are ancestral gods living in "mountains (including smaller prominences that we would call hills) located near Zinacanteco settlements" (Vogt 1970: 4); then they were living ecclesiastical rulers. Even the location of buildings in and around a Classic Maya ceremonial center may have been determined, when possible, on this basis.

While describing the peripheries about Seibal, Tourtellot (1970: 409) observes:

The great majority of structures surveyed share the same siting characteristics of location on topographic highs, with the grandest ruins on the most elevated ridges, and commonly an orientation toward the magnetic cardinal points. While drainage is certainly a consideration in the choice of site, the possible symbolic value of relative height for a hierarchical social communication system should not be overlooked.

Archaeologists who have excavated sites and materials related to the Lowland Maya civilization, the Classic Maya or Maya Old Empire, generally feel (sometimes rather strongly) that they have dealt with the remains of a stratified society and that the severity of that stratification increases as time advances during the Late Classic interval. Thompson's synthesis (1966), Morley's older work as revised by Brainerd (1956), Proskouriakoff's more particular studies of portraits of women (1961), among a number of others, tend to emphasize this idea. I personally feel the pictorial representations with which the Classic Period Maya illustrated themselves in stone (Easby and Scott 1970: Figures 171–176, 184–186; Graham 1967; Greene 1967), in wood (W. R. Coe 1967: 14, 76), in pottery (W. R. Coe 1965: 42; Adams 1963: 90–92; León-Portilla 1964; Figure 339), and in jade (Digby 1964; Lothrop 1964: 116; Dockstader 1964: Plate 58; Kidder and Chinchilla 1959: Figure 90), for instance, seem to indicate this. Architecture (Proskouriakoff 1963), the arrangement of buildings (Bullard 1960; Tourtellot 1970), and special constructions such as ball courts (Pollock, 1965: Figure 32) with associated markers (Graham 1971: 34–35; Anton 1970: Plates 30, 31; Keleman 1956: Plate 82a; Kidder and Chinchilla 1959: 72; Piggott 1961: 364–365; Cottrell 1962: 388–389) also reflect the societal nature of the configuration.

Lesser ceremonial centers, in special ways, fortify these thoughts. Three spectacular examples occur: in a vault beneath a small temple at Tonina, where the Squier Jades were "carefully placed in the largest and most elaborate urn... [of] a series of sepulchral vases containing the ashes of the dead" (Easby 1961); in "a typical Maya structure of ceremonial type with three rooms, each with its own doorway, arranged in a line" where the Bonampak Murals completely covered the interior walls and vaults (Ruppert, et al. 1955); and in a relatively simple temple structure at Altun Ha where the complex burial called "the Sun God's Tomb" with associated materials of an astonishing sort included "the giant jade head of the Maya Sun God, *Kinich Ahau*" (Pendergast 1969: 34–38). These are indications of upper-echelon representation in *local* contexts rather than of individual lower-level mobility penetrating higher levels of the prevailing social stratification.

It is important to realize that these aspects of culture highlight other Classic Maya preoccupations as well. They visually impress, even stun, the viewer and were in part designed for that purpose; they connote pageantry and ceremonialism of an impressive kind and they display craft specialization and craft expertise of high attainment, always rendered completely within a religiously oriented value structure. The "Maya art style" is recognizably distinct and definable as such on that account; it "was closely allied with ritual activities and was predominantly monumental" (Proskouriakoff 1965: 469). Archaeological research has brought us to a point where we are 'beginning to understand something of the nature of the upper class which presumably exercised political, social and religious control during the Maya Classic Period" within a southern Maya Lowland social organization that "has traditionally been described as stratified." This comprehension now derives "from the material itself" rather than from interpretations "imposed upon it from European models" (Adams 1970: 489).

The middle register of ancient Maya society probably included many persons who may be considered either part-time or full-time specialists in the production of goods or the rendering of services. I suspect that the celebrated "Jaina figurines" (Groth-Kimball 1961; Von Winning and Stendahl 1968: Frontispiece, Figures 439–461; Lothrop 1964: 108–109; Lothrop, et al. 1957: Plates LXIX–LXXVIII; Gifford 1970b) were not only made by some of these people but are, together with Jaina Island burials (Ayeleyra Arroyo de Anda and Ekholm 1966; Piña Chan 1968), telling us about them. These individuals produced a wide spectrum of items, from intricately carved stelae and lintels (Bernal and Groth 1968: Plate 29) to the codices and the ingredients that went into them (Anton and Dockstader 1968: 148–150), and they consummated a wide variety of activities from calendrics (Satterthwaite 1965) to preparing fancy textiles and garments (Mahler 1965) to making music (Leonard 1967: 109–110, 117). Adams perceptively reviews occupational specialization as it may well have prevailed in the Old Empire. He concludes by saying:

It has been suggested that Maya society was much more complex in nature than heretofore defined. The hierarchical class was at the top and perhaps of semi-divine status. It seems likely that associated with this class were occupations largely connected with political administration, religious activities, warfare, trading and planning and directing public works types of architectural construction. The status of lower occupational classes would largely depend on the degree to which specific occupations brought members of these classes into contact with the topmost class in terms of hierarchical skills and knowledge. Thus, it is suggested that, if there were a class of scribes and accountants, their status was higher than that of stone-tool makers. Likewise, the occupational specialization of sculptor would be that of relatively high status. Below these would fall the artisan specialities in such lines as elaborate ceramics, weaving, costume-making, music, and perhaps, certain types of personal service (Adams 1970: 497).

So the stratified nature of Lowland Maya civilization is well described. We can think that in all probability it was composed of upper echelons, a middle register, and a lower food-producing population such as that revealed by the evidence at Barton Ramie (Willey, et al. 1965). In all likelihood, the Zinacantecos of today, other Tzotzil speakers, the Lacandones, and still other population units articulated in some way so as to have affected Lowland Maya civilization from shortly after the time of Christ to about A.D. 900. I view my recapitulation of these social processes not so much in terms of whether Lowland Maya civilization was a civilization, was stratified or to what extent, and so on, but rather in terms of *how* the various components articulated during the Classic period and *how* the entirety that was the Old Empire fragmented into tribal pieces such as the present-day Zinacanteco population unit.

SETTLEMENT PATTERN AND THE CARGO SYSTEM

Building on our discussion and accepting these premises, we want to know how the specific Old Empire relatives of the Zinacantecos meshed with their civilization. In seeking a possible explanation that is compatible with the descriptions just expressed, a model composed of two hitherto allegedly conflicting views is of interest. The interpretation stressed above, augmented by positions strongly taken by Haviland (1966, 1967), seems to me entirely in keeping with evidences we can attribute to the upper echelons of ancient Maya society and to the impressive ceremonial centers such as Tikal, Copan and Palenque. On the other hand, Vogt and Cancian (1970: 101) say:

In our discussions we have pointed out the similarity of modern Zinacanteco and ancient Maya settlement patterns. Both have ceremonial centers with outlying hamlets and house compounds which appear to be dwelling areas for domestic groups composed of patrilocally extended families, which are in turn parts of localized patrilineages. We have also suggested that the ritual and political officials in the Classic Maya ceremonial centers were at least in part drawn from the outlying hamlets by some kind of system of rotation that is so characteristic of the contemporary cargo systems. . . .

This view is immediately reminiscent of Barton Ramie (Willey, et al. 1965), and the interpretation these scholars stress is much in keeping with the Barton Ramie data. The two views, the two worlds of the ancient Lowland Maya civilization, meet in the middle register of Maya society and at such sites as Altun Ha (Pendergast 1969) and Baking Pot (Bullard 1965b).

Proceeding from contexts like Barton Ramie (where the Vogt model seems most nearly fulfilled), when we reach the level of Altun Ha, Baking Pot, or Bonampak, another set of circumstances begins to prevail – almost a different world starts to appear, a world devoted to the richest sort of professional socioreligious pageantry, ceremonialism, and ritual. The closer one comes to the major ceremonial centers, the more the persons therein engaged were in fact full-time specialists, each with special activities to consummate, a special role to occupy, and a special (comparatively exalted) status that the individual maintained during the major portion, if not the duration, of his lifetime. It resembled a sliding social progression – cultural elaboration, complexity, intensity of stratification and specialization increasing toward the major ceremonial centers – until in such a context the Haviland model seems most nearly fulfilled. The progression also occurred through time from the late Preclassic or the Proto-classic intervals to the late portion of the Late Classic. At all times, the progression as basic value orientation, now visible in the Zinacan-teco belief system, extended from lowest elements to highest echelons. The more removed and distant the highest echelons became from the fundamentals of that value orientation, the more likely the Old Empire was to collapse.

Interpretive thinking along these lines has led me to postulate that the southern

. . . Lowland Empire was essentially the composite, intertwined outcome of two basic pictures superimposed upon each other and fabricated into the montage we recognize archaeologically as Lowland Maya civilization. One of these pictures is that of, the relates to, the tribal "homelands," individually or collectively during the Classic Interval. In the other picture we can recognize the portrayal of a highly-structured hierarchy, intensely theological in its orientation but at the same time made up of a series of stratified echelons that included numerous special roles, each with its own special prestige and status associations and its own responsibilities with regard to special activities that had to be carried out on a permanent, full-time basis. The two together constitute the Civilization that was the Lowland Maya Empire (Gifford 1970a).

In constructing the Gifford model, one approach is through settlement-pattern data.

The twin-engine plane leaves the airport at 8 o'clock in the morning and climbs to 10,000 feet to clear the mountains that ring the broad valley in which the city of Guatemala lies. The mountains become more rugged as the plane flies north over coffee plantations and scattered cornfields. Suddenly, the mountains drop away as the plane reaches the jungles of El Petén, one of the great rain forests of the world, its dense foliage often obscured by the morning mist. Where the clouds part, we see muddy, serpentine rivers and, here and there, solitary farms hacked laboriously from the forest. Soon, the jungles are broken further by great tracts of almost treeless grasslands, or savannas. . . . It is now almost 10 o'clock. The sun has cleared the mists from the jungle and soon the limestone-crested summits of the Temples of Tikal appear. For more than a thousand years these gigantic temples have humbled the forest and now mark the site of the vanished Mayan civilization (W. R. Coe 1968: 161–162).

This is the kind of terrain on which the ancient Maya constructed their settlements.

The Maya built for themselves massive ceremonial centers. Willey and Bullard (1965: 374) estimate that a 100-square-kilometer sustaining area for a major ceremonial center could have contained thirteen to twenty-six zones or possibly as many as 130,000 persons in ancient times. There are, of course, other estimates and there were a number of major ceremonial centers.

The population estimate for Tikal is 10,000–11,000, and this is regarded as conservative. It may turn out that the major "palaces" at Tikal, which are not considered in this estimate, were houses of the elite, in which case the figure would have to be raised. The estimate of population density at Tikal runs from 448 to 2128 persons per square kilometer, depending on the sample area chosen (Haviland 1966: 35).

. . . we still do not have enough settlement samplings for large-scale population reckonings. Some centers, such as Seibal, appear to have been supported by sustaining area populations of 5,000 persons – or certainly fewer than 10,000. In contrast to this, the great center of Tikal is estimated to have drawn upon the services of 50,000 (Willey and Shimkin 1973).

The Belize Valley. . . from Cocos Bank westward and southward to Benque Viejo and beyond into Guatemala, had at its peak of aboriginal occupation about 24,000 inhabitants. These valley groups lived mostly in the river bottom strip (Willey, et al. 1965: 577).

[In] the Great Plaza, the ceremonial heart of Tikal. . . masses of people once gathered to watch their priest-rulers, and most elite clothed in many pounds of jade, rich fabrics, jaguar skins, and the emerald plumes of the sacred quetzal bird, as they climbed the temple steps to the sounds of drums, flageolets, and wood trumpets and the moan of conch shells.
  The Great Plaza was only part of a complex that covered about four and one-half acres, but the great city – if it was a city – was at least six square miles in area. In addition, remains of buildings have been found in all directions from the city. . . . The detailed contour map of central Tikal now shows nearly 3,000 surface constructions – plazas, causeways, temples, shrines, palaces, ball courts, and small- to medium-size residences (W. R. Coe 1968: 162–164).

We now know that there was a fairly dense and permanent population at Tikal during Late Classic times. Great differences in houses, burials, and other features found in. . . low level. . . mounds suggests extensive functional and social diversity throughout a population that must have numbered at least 10,000 within the central six square miles of Tikal. Small residences formed distinct clusters, usually quadrangular in layout and well separated from neighboring groups, perhaps by back-yard gardens. Many such groups fit a pattern in which the west-facing structure contains a large number of burials and signs of ceremonies once performed there. These facts combine to suggest its use as a shrine. The most reasonable conclusion is that these patterned groups of structures were once residential compounds, each perhaps populated by an extended family incorporating married sons with their own families. The economic basis for such living is still not known though signs of manufacturing specialities have been found in the excavations.
  The cornfields on which the economy of Tikal was based required large

tracts of land chopped and burned from the forest. They must have been located far beyond the center of Tikal. How far out, it is almost impossible to calculate. Exploration of the outlying portions of Tikal has shown that there are about as many structures two to three miles out from the Great Plaza as there are in the city's center (W. R. Coe 1968: 172–173).

In contrast to the cultural picture just presented, the site of Barton Ramie along the Belize River in what is now British Honduras is thought to be representative of the more rural agricultural segment of the population. Like the present-day Zinacanteco who, "in a very important sense...lives in a milpa and looks out at the world from between the stalks of corn" (Vogt 1968: 159), perhaps the ancient Maya farmer lived similarly at Barton Ramie. Over the territorial extent of the Old Empire, ecological diversity was not great. The people in different subregions seemed to have exploited (in a cultural sense) different resources (Rathje 1969) for different cultural purposes (Silva-Galdames 1971) within the empire and so maintained and reinforced certain cultural (participant population unit) distinctions on a subregional basis. Such essential resources (some being more essential than others) as salt, certain kinds of rock for grinding implements, obsidian, or cacao lands were not evenly distributed over Old Empire territory (Rathje 1972), but basic ecological uniformity is descriptively appropriate when referring to the empire's natural setting as a whole. Bullard's review (1965a) of the Barton Ramie setting resembles what has been said for El Petén. The one primary difference between the perimeters (both eastern and western) of the empire and its central domain is the presence of rivers toward its edges.

The work of Willey and his associates in the Belize Valley was a milestone, for it was the first full-scale research project concerned specifically with the living patterns of the Classic Maya as opposed to investigation of large and presumably functionally specialized buildings (Haviland 1966: 28).

Willey (Willey, et al. 1965: 561–581) has provided us with a fine summary of Belize Valley settlement during ancient times. A most important observation, however, is necessary, Willey is talking only about the Belize Valley here, so that when he uses the term "major ceremonial center" he means by this a major ceremonial center within the Belize Valley, such as Benque Viejo. Bullard (1960) uses the same term, "major ceremonial center," in his review of ancient Maya settlement in the Petén and in that context is talking about the Old Empire as a whole. When he speaks of a major ceremonial center, he is talking about ruins such as Holmul (a small major ceremonial center) and Tikal (a very large major ceremonial center). This is of considerable importance because it would seem to me that what Willey calls a major ceremonial center is, in Bullard's synthesis for the empire, simply a large "minor ceremonial center." While this perhaps appears to be a lesser matter, I think it is far more important than at first might seem to be the case. Bullard's major ceremonial centers from Holmul to Tikal occupied an *empire-oriented* role within the Old Empire as opposed to the *homeland* or local subregional orientation of minor ceremonial centers like Benque Viejo and the Barton Ramie Mound 180–182 (168) complex. If my observation is valid, Vogt's (1968: 166) *cabecera* (of the *municipio*) would equate *not* with Bullard's major ceremonial center but with his large minor ceremonial center – a matter of serious interpretative significance. Furthermore, a Bullard "district" would not equate with a Willey "district" within the Belize Valley.

I would like to attempt a revaluation in terms of Vogt's outline. Vogt's *sitio* [patrilocal extended family] equals a Barton Ramie (Belize Valley) house-mound group or Bullard's house-ruin group. Vogt's *sna* equals a Barton Ramie (Belize Valley) small *plazuela* group or Bullard's small cluster group. Vogt's waterhole group equals a Barton Ramie (Belize Valley) large *plazuela* group or Bullard's large-cluster group. Vogt's *paraje* equals a Barton Ramie (Belize Valley) minor ceremonial center, such as the Barton Ramie Mound 180–182 (168) complex, or Bullard's small minor ceremonial center. Vogt's *cabecera* (of the *municipio*) equal a Belize Valley major ceremonial center, such as Benque Viejo, or Bullard's large minor ceremonial center. Here Vogt ends his consideration of the Zinacanteco *municipio* and Willey ends his consideration of the Belize Valley in ancient times. Bullard and the Old Empire, however, go on. Holmul and Altun Ha, among others, are small major ceremonial centers; Copan and Palenque are examples of larger major ceremonial centers; and Tikal is a very large major ceremonial center. A Willey Belize Valley district such as the Baking Pot district ("population estimate of 6000 inhabitants as of the Spanish Lookout Phase" [Willey, et al. 1965; 577]) and a Vogt *municipio* are large zones in the Bullard sense, including in their domain 1,000 or more houses.[1]

---

[1] During "the Early Classic Period of Maya culture history, the Belize Valley was closely linked to other districts of Maya population, such as those of the Petén" (Willey, et al. 1965). If we were to revise our wording to say – other Large Zones of the Petén – we could then use the term district in a broader interpretive sense concerning cultural and territorial designations with respect to the empire. I favor this wording shift because it could give rise to designations such as the Belize Valley district, the Chama or Alta Verapaz district, and in Yucatán the Río Bec district, the Chenes district, the Puuc district, and so on. These would seem to accord rather well with Pollock's observations (1965) on architecture and would mesh better with Bullard's overall "district" intent (1960). Other than the last three in Yucatán, these districts would be within what Rands and Smith (1965: 96) and others following them (see Smith and Gifford 1965; Figure 1) seem consistently to refer to as the southern Lowland Maya subregion within the Lowland Maya region. This range of territorial designation from house-mound groups of various kinds, to zones of differing size, to districts within a subregion, to the Lowland Maya region as a whole seems to me to fit Maya cultural

Small and intermediate major ceremonial centers can be related in the Bullard sense to "districts" within the Old Empire. In this view, then, we can think of the Belize Valley (the entire subject of Willey's remarks) as one of these districts within the empire; its particular economic contribution to the empire was probably cacao. This district and others like it were the tribal components of the Old Empire. During the Early Classic there was a single integrated structure – one totality, one model. During the Late Classic the districts were all very much alike but controlled different resources. The structure of the model was replicated in each district: the districts were distinct entities in themselves, but all worked together to form the old Empire.

Any major ceremonial center served a special role to the *empire*, while the essential role of any minor ceremonial center was toward *local* communities, even though empire representation was surely present at a minor ceremonial center. In this light Zinacantán and Benque Viejo (or Cahal Pech or Baking Pot) are on the same level of social integration. A higher level of sociopolitical integration occurs forcefully for the Zinacantecos in San Cristóbal – the world of the Ladino and the Catholic Church. Zinacantecos come to San Cristóbal, as do Chamula and Lacandones and many others. A higher level of socioreligious integration in ancient times occurred after Benque Viejo, that is, as Holmul and on up to Tikal – the world of the upper echelons and the aristocratic Old Empire ecclesiastical rulers. Accordingly, I can believe that San Cristóbal and such ancient places as Altun Ha and Holmul have something in common with regard to societal role. What one offers the other in goods and *services* differs when one moves from a minor ceremonial center to a major ceremonial center, possibly in some way analogous to what Rathje (1972) postulates.

Scholars of the Old Empire Maya Classic Period such as Thompson (1966: 91–92) have expressed doubt about the validity of Vogt's Zinacanteco model with reference to the occupancy and use of the ancient major ceremonial centers. Both postulates are compatible, however, if, somewhat along the lines drawn above, we see two worlds for the ancient Maya: one, that of the homelands (the Belize Valley is an example of a homeland setting), and the other, that of the ecclesiastical rulers (Tikal is an example of a setting where Great Ones lived and ruled the empire). Thompson tends to view the Maya from Tikal, while Vogt tends to view them from a homeland setting. In ancient times these two real worlds joined at communities such as Benque Viejo and Holmul – at places like these the local homeland world joined hands with the empire.

ecology as it develops through time inside the general ecology which prevails over the territorial extent of the Lowland Maya region.

Many authorities are willing to concede that on a local level during the Classic interval something resembling the operative framework of the Zinacantecos might have existed. With the higher levels of the middle register and with upper-echelon Maya society, it is not possible to reconcile the Zinacanteco cargo system (Cancian 1965) with the archaeological evidences. On levels of ancient Maya society above Benque Viejo or Holmul the cargo system is not in tune with the ancient remains. Below these levels of society, however, in the context of what I would like to see called large and small zones, an ancient form of the Vogt model from the Zinacanteco is quite believable interpretively.

However, the present cargo system would seem to resemble the present Zinacanteco male headdress in that it relates to the ancient largely in symbolic ways. Headdress modifications have been imposed or made necessary by conquerors of the recent past. So I would believe that the present cargo system owes many of its empirical specifics to the most recent conquerors and that the ancient pattern persists within the guise of a symbolic dimension. I feel this is also true of San Cristóbal, which in the abstract now occupies the position occupied in ancient times by the major ceremonial center. Today it is the world of another religion, another kind of administration, another kind of economic outlook, and so on. People come here from all around – from Zinacantán, Chamula, Huistan, and many other places – to avail themselves of certain goods and services not obtainable or not sufficiently rendered in their local settings. The analogue of San Cristóbal in ancient times was the seat of upper echelon Maya religion, administration, pageantry, and predictive learning. In ancient times, however, the upper-echelon world derived from a fundamental Maya configuration primarily by processes of cultural *development* rather than from cultural *overlay* which is responsible for the differences of today. The present Zinacanteco belief system justifies and integrates the foreign overlay; in ancient times it justified and integrated that which had largely developed from the Maya totality itself over something in excess of a thousand years.

MAYA ORIGINS AND EMPIRE DISSOLUTION

Archaeological probing has thus far not recovered evidences of population units in the southern Maya Lowlands prior to about 1000 B.C. (Willey, Culbert, and Adams 1967). Consequently, cultural configurations had to develop elsewhere before being introduced into the lowlands.

We begin our story with the first human occupants of the Barton Ramie site zone, those of the Jenny Creek Phase. These early settlers – and one thinks of them as pioneer settlers in the full meaning of the term – may have been of Maya speech. . . . They appear to have entered the Belize Valley when it was in primeval forest and were probably the ones to make the first clearings in that forest. . . . The 18 Jenny Creek house locations are dotted rather widely over the Barton Ramie zone although there is a hint that settlement was in small clusters of two, three, or more houses. Houses in these clusters were usually about 50 m. apart, a spacing which continues to be an approximate standard throughout the Maya occupation of Barton Ramie. Another suggested pattern of the occupation is that of preference for the edges of old river channels (Willey, et al. 1965: 562).

I have called this interval of the Maya commencement Lowland Proto-Maya IA and refer to the population units as the Xe peoples (1000–700 B.C.). In addition to Barton Ramie, they are represented at Seibal and at Altar de Sacrificios:

. . . the pottery of the Real Xe phase represents the debris of the earliest inhabitants of Seibal. . . . These Real Xe inhabitants lived in a village community, and judging from the depth and compact nature of their refuse, they had lived in this community for quite a long time. Although a place of sedentary residence, the village does not appear to have been a ceremonial center. . . . In brief, everything that we know about the Real Xe occupation at Seibal adds up to a pattern of rather simple village farming life carried on in a jungle environment. This accords with the evidence of the Xe phase at Altar de Sacrificios. . . . The time period. . . is the Middle Preclassic –, probably the earlier part of that period. Estimated dates would be about 1000 to 600 B.C. (Willey 1970: 321, 355).

Speaking of Xe (including Barton Ramie, Jenny Creek, Early Facet, and other Jocote-like pottery makers) as well as of immediately subsequent population units, Sharer and Gifford (1970) and Gifford (1970c) have suggested that population units, from Central America to the southeast and from Mexico to the west, entered the unique ecological setting wherein the southern Lowland Maya cultural continuum developed. These entries seem to have taken place during a 500- to 600-year interval starting about 1000 B.C. Possibly those peoples from the general area of El Salvador arrived first. Some time later, at about the time of Christ, still another new population increment from Central America joined those already established. Soon thereafter "high civilization" is discernible and the Maya Old Empire commences.

I visualize the Chicanel peoples (Lowland Proto-Maya IIA) as hinging on powerful chiefdoms (Gifford 1970c); in amount of societal complexity and elaboration achieved they resembled Temple Mound or Mississippian configurations of North America (Willey 1966). One of the characteristics of Lowland Proto-Maya IIA, however, was developmental suffocation from 400 to 100 B.C. From 100 B.C. through

A.D. 200 new influences arrived in the Maya Lowlands from elsewhere. I have called this the Lowland Proto-Maya IIB and referred to the Floral Park peoples and the Holmul I style (Willey and Gifford 1961). In the Maya Lowlands the Holmul I style marked the appearance of intrusive elements, which in turn figured importantly (possibly as catalytic agents when mixed with Chicanel) in the development of Maya civilization and of the Maya Classic interval.

One of the elements introduced at this time was recognizably distinct social stratification and comparatively intense full-time specialization. Subsequently, from A.D. 200 to 900, we see the development of the Lowland Maya civilization, the Old Empire, shown to us in part through the murals at Bonampak (Tejeda 1955). Then the collapse, the disintegration, the decapitation of the empire occurred. The Maya people did not disappear, but societal stratification vanished abruptly from the southern lowlands. I see it as a disarticulation of the component population units. The specialists returned to their homelands; they followed their lineages back down to the *milpa*. Population units of today such as the Zinacantecos, the Lacandon, and others, are remnants of the empire disarticulated. What was once the empire itself is dramatically shown in all its splendor, pomposity, and sumptuous power in a series of incredible plates by Soustelle (1967: 88–123).

Slash-and-burn agriculture figured importantly in the ability of human populations to productively establish themselves in the Lowland Maya terrain. This agricultural technique may originally have been sociopolitically perfected by the Olmec. The Olmec were represented in El Salvador, and the first population units to penetrate the Maya Lowlands may have come from this general area. Secondary population units may have come from the areas of Mexico to the west or northwest, perhaps initially deriving from Veracruz territories. The religious orientation of the Old Empire contained many elements that remind one of the Olmec (M. D. Coe 1968), and what Willey and Shimkin (1973) have said bears repeating: "Maya Classic society, let us remember, was the old kind of Mesoamerican society, the kind that was born with the Olmec."

Despite the fact that I believe Olmec influences weighed in upon the Maya for a lengthy portion of their early continuum, I do not believe any of the Maya people were, strictly speaking, Olmec people. The Olmec phenomenon (M.D. Coe 1968), in my thinking, is a separate one, centering in other places. On the other hand, Olmec influences from possibly before 1500 B.C. up to near the time of Christ, may have been enormous. Regarding Middle America as a whole, no people may have been more fundamentally influential than the Olmec. They possessed certain specialized skills and knowledge concerning elements leading to power control that were unparalleled in their effectiveness and survival value. They also traveled widely. We do not know exactly how all that was Olmec articulated, but I believe that they were more a rulership and that their people were a wide variety of population units, some far more under direct Olmec influence than others. And because of their obvious success and extended travel, parts of their configuration may well have been emulated in different places and in different ways, thus leading to different Olmec-inspired developmental trends that eventually crosscut and cross-fertilized one another through southern and central Middle America well after Olmec proper had terminated (Gifford 1974: 80).

Unlike the Maya collapse, I visualize the Olmec disintegration as a fragmentation of the *leadership*, a coming unstuck of the components of the Olmec leadership structure. The core Olmec *religious* leadership somehow went to the Maya with jade, cranial deformation, calendrics, numerology, and the concept of the ceremonial center, but because it never did have a ceramic component, it is not seen in Maya Preclassic pottery. Other aspects of Olmec leadership went off in their own way, as sprouts severed from their main roots, each continuing to live but growing separately. *Izapa* is one of these, but in my view it, and the others, had nothing to do directly with the Maya. Other Olmec aspects of leadership were more externally oriented and after severance each simply capitalized on its own facet of the external picture to live on in accord with the orientation of its particular facet of the true Olmec phenomenon.

Perhaps the Xe peoples from Central America brought slash-and-burn agricultural techniques to certain southern Maya Lowland riverine districts, having learned or developed this technique from Olmec-influenced parent population units in Central America (Stone 1972: Green and Lowe 1967: 71). It is a further possibility in my mind that Chiapas-Olmec could have had direct relationships of some kind with the introduction to the southern Maya Lowlands of what we there recognize as the Chicanel Horizon and the Chicanel ceramic sphere (Willey, Culbert, and Adams 1967). As it develops through time in the southern Maya Lowlands, though, the powerful chiefdom conceptual lattice suggested by Chicanel-like manifestations builds up highly conservative reservoirs of vested interests that inhibit social trans-position to the higher levels of cultural complexity and elaboration generally associated with civilization. Service (1971) even seems to feel that such vested interests eventually may have been self-destructive. The injection of strains of sociopolitical mobility and flexibility was necessary in the Maya Chicanel Horizon in order to effect the development of civilization from the stolid setting of the Late Preclassic. We feel the Holmul I style (Willey and Gifford 1961) reflects such an injection. Because of the character of the elements in the Holmul-I-like Protoclassic Floral Park ceramic complex:

Chalchuapa, and other sites in the southeastern Highlands can be suggested as points of origin for this intrusive complex at Barton Ramie.... The ceramic evidence from Chalchuapa and our suggestion of its significance as a contributor to Protoclassic ceramics in the Lowlands adds weight to hypotheses of Central American Protoclassic origins made previously (Vaillant 1940; Smith and Gifford 1965; Adams 1966).... The advent of what are essentially terminal facet elements of the Chalchuapa-Chul-Caynac sphere into the eastern Lowlands may have become one of several ingredients in the catalyst that went on to 'break the mold" of the very conservative and homogeneous Chicanel ceramic sphere, whereupon a new Classic Period ceramic unity was produced over most of the Maya area (Sharer and Gifford 1970: 456, 460).

With the addition of the Protoclassic materials and the influences they represent, shifts occurred in the southern Lowland Maya configuration that altered tribal constructs into ranked echelons of social stratification (Willey and Shimkin 1973). Areas of specialized knowledge and of craft artistry were cultivated to the extent that I would agree with Rathje's comments (1972) which emphasize what Morley originally observed – a cult, developing out of the Protoclassic and hinged to the ceremonial significance of stela ritual and the symbolically predictive essences of hieroglyphic writing, mathematics, and astronomy. Such special knowledge was in the hands of a Lacandon-like full-time priesthood who developed special skills in writing, arithmetic, and the "control of time" (seemingly to the Classic Maya a divine dimension in its own right). The Protoclassic-Early Classic transformation reveals the effects of this knowledge combined with incipient Great Ones cared for by Zinacanteco-like attendants who ministered to their ceremonial needs and helped to stage the impressive religious pageants.

Today the Empire world is gone: it disappeared with the collapse and attendant societal decapitation associated with the abrupt termination of the Empire by approximately A.D. 900. But the homeland world persists and the Zinacantecos maintain the spiritual essence of the Empire in their religion and ritual, and in the depths of the belief system they still tenaciously retain.... Sabloff and Willey (1967: 311–336) and Willey and Shimkin (1971: 1–18) assess the collapse of Classic Maya civilization in the southern Lowlands. They deal with its many possible and probable causalities and evaluate the empirical evidence.... [To their observations] I would add the idea of the disarticulation of the Old Empire tribal units in such ways as to disconnect the two real worlds of the Old Empire from one another, resulting in a disintegration of the civilization... So many specific ills in so many aspects of the Empire, including astronomical miscalculations or omissions, led them to feel the vital communication system with the gods had failed and was no longer operative .... The vast middle echelon of persons living in the ceremonial centers held lineage relationships that in some way tied them to a village context in their tribal homeland part of the Empire, and so they returned to their kin (Gifford 1974: 93–95).

In their upper echelons the Classsic Maya were obsessed with "time" – the interminable, ongoing, unending nature of time – not with war or human sacrifice or trade or any other institution as an end in itself, simply with the monumentality of time and its careful and accurate calculation. Maya timekeeping may have been recorded continuously for more than 800 years, so when Willey and Shimkin (1973) note that following approximately A.D. 790 "there are losses of lunar information and full calendrical terminology," we may be recognizing a factor in the collapse of far greater significance than we can properly assess.

In any event, once begun from Preclassic roots, southern Lowland Maya culture is relatively long-lived, stable, and conservative in its own intrinsic cultural integrity. Eventually it disintegrates and becomes disarticulated to the extent that recapitulation of the Old Empire is not possible. The two settlement dimensions of the Old Empire may have grown apart from one another – the homeland rural setting, where the village and slash-and-burn or *milpa* agriculture were the basic elements of focus, and the ceremonial center, where pageantry and full-time specialization of human effort synchronous with an all-powerful religious overview were the basic elements of focus. Corn to one, jade to the other – symbols of that which pleases and brings comfort.

The bonds that had kept Tikal together so long came apart rapidly. From around A.D. 900, convincing evidence of a continuing, creative rulership disappears from our records. Buildings fall into disrepair, their roofs and vaults crashing into the rooms below as the weeds and trees take over. Monuments and new buildings cease to be commissioned. The near-magicians who had so long manipulated their timebound gods simply disappear (W. R. Coe 1968: 175).

If you look archaeologically at the great ceremonial centers, you see that they did not stop all of them at once, but seem to have quietly shut down one after another over the time space of a generation or so, as for each in its turn the last Great One . . . died forever with no thought to a successor (Gifford 1974: 96).

The Maya's faith and trust in their gods did not perish, however, and the Great Ones were relegated to a spiritual context deep within mountains and to an abstract belief system saturated with predictive omens and personal ritual.

REFERENCES

ADAMS, R. E. W.
  1963   A polychrome vessel from Altar de Sacrificios. *Archaeology* 16: 90–92.
  1966   "The ceramic chronology of the southern Maya: second preliminary report, 1966." Mimeographed manuscript, University of Minnesota.

1970 "Suggested Classic Period occupational specialization in the southern Maya Lowlands," in *Monographs and papers in Maya archaeology*. Edited by W. R. Bullard, Jr., 487–502. Cambridge, Mass.: Peabody Museum.

ANTON, F.
1970 *Art of the Maya*. New York: Putnam.

ANTON, F., F. J. DOCKSTADER
1968 *Pre-Columbian art and later Indian tribal arts*. New York: Abrams.

AYELEYRA ARROYO DE ANDA, L., G. F. EKHOLM
1966 Clay sculpture from Jaina. *Natural History*, 75: 40–47.

BERNAL, I., I. GROTH
1968 *Ancient Mexico*. New York: McGraw-Hill.

BRAINERD, G.
1956 Changing living patterns of the Yucatán Maya. *American Antiquity* 22: 162–164.

BULLARD, W. R., JR
1960 Maya settlement pattern in northeastern Petén, Guatemala. *American Antiquity* 25: 355–372.
1965a "The natural setting of the Belize Valley," in *Prehistoric Maya settlements in the Belize Valley*, by G. R. Willey, et al. Peabody Museum Papers 54: 21–24. Cambridge, Mass.: Peabody Museum.
1965b *Late Classic finds at Baking Pot, British Honduras*. Art and Archaeology Occasional Paper 8. Toronto: Royal Ontario Museum.

CANCIAN, F.
1965 *Economics and prestige in a Maya community: a study of the religious cargo system in Zinacantán, Chiapas, Mexico*. Stanford, Calif.: Stanford University Press.

COE, M. D.
1966 *The Maya*. New York: Praeger.
1968 *America's first civilization: discovering the Olmec*. New York: American Heritage.

COE, W. R.
1961 "A summary of excavation and research at Tikal, Guatemala: 1956–1961." Mimeographed manuscript, University Museum, University of Pennsylvania, Philadelphia.
1965 Tikal: ten years of study of a Maya ruin in the lowlands of Guatemala. *Expedition* 8: 5–56.
1967 *Tikal: a handbook of the ancient Maya ruins*. Philadelphia: University Museum.
1968 *Tikal: in search of the Mayan past*. Chicago: Field Enterprises Education.

COTTRELL, L.
1962 "The riddle of the Maya," in *Lost worlds*. New York: American Heritage.

DIGBY, A.
1964 *Maya jades*. London: British Museum.

DOCKSTADER, F. J.
1964 *Indian art in Middle America*. Greenwich: New York Graphic Society.

EASBY, E. K.
1961 "The Squier Jades from Toniná, Chiapas," in *Essays in Pre-Columbian art and archaeology*, by S. K. Lothrop, et al., 60–80. Cambridge, Mass.: Harvard University Press.

EASBY, E. K., J. F. SCOTT
1970 *Before Cortés, sculpture of Middle America*. New York: Metropolitan Museum of Art.

GIFFORD, JAMES C.
1970a Residual social consequences of societal stratification in ancient Maya society. *Cerámica de Cultura Maya* 6: 11–20. Philadelphia: Laboratory of Anthropology, Temple University.
1970b Jaina study number one. *Cerámica de Cultura Maya* 6: 67–83. Philadelphia: Laboratory of Anthropology, Temple University.
1970c The earliest and other intrusive population elements at Barton Ramie may have come from Central America. *Cerámica de Cultura Maya* 6: 1–10. Philadelphia: Laboratory of Anthropology. Temple University.
1974 "Recent thought concerning the interpretation of Maya prehistory," in *New approaches in Mesoamerican archaeology*. Edited by Norman Hammond, 77–98. Austin: University of Texas Press.

GRAHAM, I.
1967 *Archaeological explorations in El Petén, Guatemala*. Middle American Research Institute Publication 33. New Orleans: Tulane University.
1971 *The art of Maya hieroglyphic writing*. Cambridge, Mass.: Harvard University Press.

GREEN, D. F., G. W. LOWE
1967 *Altamira and Padre Piedra, early Classic sites in Chiapas, Mexico*. New World Archaeological Foundation Papers 20.

GREENE, M.
1967 *Ancient Maya relief sculpture*. New York: Museum of Primitive Art.

GROTH-KIMBALL, I.
1961 *Mayan terracottas*. New York: Praeger.

HAVILAND, W. A.
1965 Prehistoric settlement of Tikal, Guatemala. *Expedition* 7: 14–23.
1966 *Maya settlement patterns: a critical review*. Middle American Research Institute Publication 26: 21–47. New Orleans: Tulane University.
1967 Stature at Tikal, Guatemala: implications for ancient Maya demography and social organization. *American Antiquity* 32: 316–325.

KELEMAN, P.
1956 *Medieval American art*. New York: Macmillan.

KIDDER, A., C. S. CHINCHILLA
1959 *The art of the ancient Maya*. New York: Thomas Y. Crowell.

LEONARD, J. N.
1967 *Ancient America*. New York: Time.

LEÓN-PORTILLA, M.
1964 *El reverso de la conquista: relaciónes aztecas, mayas, y incas*. Mexico City: J. Martiz.

LOTHROP, S. K.
1964 *Treasures of ancient America: the arts of the pre-Columbian civilizations from Mexico to Peru*. Cleveland: World Publishing Company.

LOTHROP, S. K., W. F. FOSHAG, J. MAHLER
1957 *Pre-Columbian art: Robert Woods Bliss Collection*. London: Phaidon Press.

MAHLER, J.
1965 "Garments and textiles of the Maya Lowlands," in *Archaeology of Southern Mesoamerica*. Edited by G. R. Willey, 581–593. *Handbook of Middle American Indians*, volume three. Edited by R. Wauchope. Austin: University of Texas Press.

PENDERGAST, D.
1969 *Altun Ha, British Honduras (Belize). The Sun God's tomb*. Art and Archaeology Occasional Paper 19. Toronto: Royal Ontario Museum.

PIGGOTT, S.
1961 *The dawn of civilization*. London: Thames and Hudson.

PIÑA CHAN, R.
1968 *Jaina*. Mexico City: Instituto Nacional de Antropología e Historia.

POLLOCK, H. E. D.
1965 "Architecture of the Maya Lowlands," in *Archaeology of Southern Mesoamerica*. Edited by G. R. Willey, 378–440. *Handbook of Middle American Indians*, volume two. Edited by R. Wauchope. Austin: University of Texas Press.

PROSKOURIAKOFF, T.
1961 "Portraits of women in Maya art," in *Essays in Pre-Columbian art and archaeology*, by S. K. Lothrop, et al., 81–99. Cambridge, Mass.: Harvard University Press.
1963 Historical data in the inscriptions of Yaxchilan. *Estudios de Cultura Maya* 3: 149–167.
1965 "Sculpture and major arts of the Maya Lowlands," in *Archaeology of Southern Mesoamerica*. Edited by G. R. Willey, 469–497. *Handbook of Middle American Indians*, volume two. Edited by R. Wauchope. Austin: University of Texas Press.

RANDS, R. L., R. E. SMITH
1965 "Pottery of the Guatemalan Highlands," in *Archaeology of Southern Mesoamerica*. Edited by G. R. Willey, 95–145. *Handbook of Middle American Indians*, volume two. Edited by R. Wauchope. Austin: University of Texas Press.

RATHJE, W. L.
1969 "The daily grind." Mimeographed manuscript, University of Arizona, Tucson.
1972 "Praise the gods and pass the metates: a hypothesis of the development of lowland rainforest civilizations in Mesoamerica," in *Contemporary archaeology*. Edited by M. Leone, 365–392. Carbondale: Southern Illinois University Press.

RUPPERT, K., J. E. S. THOMPSON, T. PROSKOURIAKOFF
1955 *Bonampak, Chiapas, Mexico*. Carnegie Institution of Washington Publication 602.

SABLOFF, J. A., G. R. WILLEY
1967 The collapse of Maya civilization in the southern lowlands: a consideration of history and process. *Southwestern Journal of Anthropology* 23: 311–336.

SATTERTHWAITE, L.
1965 "Calendrics of the Maya Lowlands," in *Archaeology of Southern Mesoamerica*. Edited by G. R. Willey, 603–631. *Handbook of Middle American Indians*, volume three. Edited by R. Wauchope. Austin: University of Texas Press.

SERVICE, R. R.
1971 *Cultural evolutionism*, New York: Holt, Rinehart and Winston.

SHARER, R. J., J. C. GIFFORD
1970   Preclassic ceramics from Chalchuapa. El Salvador, and their relationships with the Maya Lowlands. *American Antiquity* 35: 441–462.

SILVA-GALDAMES, O.
1971   Trade and concepts of nuclear and marginal culture areas in Mesoamerica. *Cerámica de Cultura Maya* (supplement) 1: 1–74. Philadelphia: Laboratory of Anthropology, Temple University.

SMITH, R. E., J. C. GIFFORD
1965   "Pottery of the Maya Lowlands," in *Archaeology of Southern Mesoamerica*. Edited by G. R. Willey, 498–534. *Handbook of Middle American Indians*, volume two. Edited by R. Wauchope. Austin: University of Texas Press.

SOUSTELLE, J.
1967   *Mexico*. Archaeologia Mundi. Cleveland: World Publishing Company.

SPINDLER, G., L. SPINDLER
1970   "Foreword," in *The Zinacantecos of Mexico*, by E. Z. Vogt, vii–viii. New York: Holt, Rinehart and Winston.

STONE, D.
1972   *Pre-Columbian man finds Central America, the archaeological bridge*. Cambridge, Mass.: Peabody Museum Press.

TEJEDA, A.
1955   *Ancient Maya paintings of Bonampak, Mexico*. Carnegie Institution of Washington Supplementary Publication 46.

THOMPSON, J. E. S.
1966   *The rise and fall of Maya civilization* (second edition). Norman: University of Oklahoma Press.

TOURTELLOT, G.
1970   The peripheries of Seibal, an interim report. *Peabody Museum Papers* 61: 407–420. Cambridge, Mass.: Peabody Museum.

VAILLANT, G. C.
1940   "Patterns in Middle American archaeology," in *The Maya and their neighbors*. Edited by Clarence L. Hay, et al., 295–305. New York: Cooper Square.

VOGT, E. Z.
1968   "Some aspects of Zinacantán settlement patterns and ceremonial organization," in *Settlement archaeology*. Edited by K. C. Chang, 154–173. Palo Alto, Calif.: National Press.
1969   *Zinacantán: a Maya community in the highlands of Chiapas*. Cambridge, Mass.: Harvard University Press.
1970   *The Zinacantecos of Mexico, a modern Maya way of life*. New York: Holt, Rinehart and Winston.

VOGT, E. Z., F. CANCIAN
1970   Social integration and the Classic Maya: some problems in Haviland's argument. *American Antiquity* 35: 101–102.

VON WINNING, H., A. STENDAHL
1968   *Pre-Columbian art of Mexico and Central Ameria*. New York: Harry N. Abrams.

WILLEY, G. R.
1966   *An introduction to American archaeology*, volume one: *North and Middle America*. Englewood Cliffs, N.J.: Prentice-Hall.
1968   "Settlement archaeology: an appraisal," in *Settlement archaeology*.

Edited by K. C. Chang, 208–226. Palo Alto, Calif.: National Press. Press.

1970   Type descriptions of the ceramics of the Real Xe complex, Seibal, Petén, Guatemala. *Peabody Museum Papers* 61:315–355. Cambridge, Mass.: Peabody Museum.

WILLEY, G. R., W. R. BULLARD, JR.

1965   "Prehistoric settlement patterns in the Maya Lowlands," in *Archaeology of Southern Mesoamerica.* Edited by G. R. Willey, 360–377. *Handbook of Middle American Indians*, volume two. Edited by R. Wauchope. Austin: University of Texas Press.

WILLEY, G. R., W. R. BULLARD, JR., J. B. BLASS, J. C. GIFFORD

1965   Prehistoric Maya settlements in the Belize Valley. *Peabody Museum Papers* 54. Cambridge, Mass.: Peabody Museum.

WILLEY, G. R., T. P. CULBERT, R. E. W. ADAMS

1967   Maya Lowland ceramics: a report from the 1965 Guatemala City Conference. *American Antiquity* 32: 289–315.

WILLEY, G. R., J. C. GIFFORD

1961   "Pottery of the Holmul I style from Barton Ramie British Honduras," in *Essays in Pre-Columbian art and archaeology.* Edited by S. K. Lothrop, et al., 152–170. Cambridge, Mass.: Harvard University Press.

WILLEY, G. R., D. B. SHIMKIN

1971   The collapse of Classic Maya civilization in the southern lowlands: a symposium summary statement. *Southwestern Journal of Anthropology* 21: 1–18.

1973   "The Maya collapse: a summary view," in *The Classic Maya collapse.* Edited by T. P. Culbert. Albuquerque: University of New Mexico Press.

Ideas Concerning Maya Concepts of the Future

JAMES C. GIFFORD

The unique kind of high civilization embraced by the Old Empire Maya, to whom we can unquestionably relate the Zinacantecos of present-day Mexico, was indicative of a cultural configuration which had become elaborated to an unusual degree, especially in the direction of ecclesiastical and ritual development. As one dimension of this elaboration, so spectacular in its religious aspect, we can think of the southern lowland Maya Old Empire as being not only socially stratified but as relying on the existence of two different worlds – the village homeland and the major ceremonial center. As this high civilization unfolded through time, these two patterns of living became more and more remote from one another, and full-time specialization became increasingly accentuated as well as characteristic of the ceremonial center lifeway. As they gradually became differentiated from one another, two lifeway patterns arose which, though recognizably distinct, combined with one another to form, in their cumulative articulation, the high civilization. The Old Empire Maya participated in their kind of high civilization with full knowledge of these two very different worlds. A crucial societal difference between the two worlds, evidently not at all so obvious to every participant in this ancient configuration, lay in the fact that the major ceremonial center was dependent on the village homeland, while the homeland was self-sufficient. Despite its unparalleled theological opulence, its ritualistic splendor, and its hierarchic superposition over homeland population units, the world of the major ceremonial center could not exist without its articulation in the setting of the village. When that articu-

In developing my interpretation of the Maya cultural continuum, I have relied heavily on the written works of Evon Z. Vogt, Gordon R. Willey, Eric S. Thompson, and Sylvanus G. Morley.

lation ceased, the world of the ceremonial centers vanished and so did this kind of high civilization.

Within the Zinacanteco setting, the village homeland world survives in much of its absolute reality; but the highly specialized ceremonial center world, so much the outward symbol of the Old Empire, survives only as a glimmer and a shadow appearing sporadically in the overt behavioral manifestations of the Zinacanteco people. Evidence of the ancient empire pattern, diffused and altered, appears most clearly in the components of Zinacanteco belief and thought patterns. The Zinacantecos hold on to the essence of what was once a second world in their ancient high civilization by means of intangible images and symbols which now reside deep beneath more tangible expressions of their ritualistic and philosophic rationale. Many seem at first to be so obscure and unrelated that their derivation might easily have remained unrecognized but for our knowledge of Maya prehistory. But these dimensions of the second world of the major ceremonial center, today faded among the Zinacantecos and other population remnants, were all-pervasive for over 800 years after Christ in the natural biome of the Petén lowlands, with its infinitely more productive agricultural system, far greater societal wealth, and the resources of the empire.

As a consequence of the empire's cultural mechanisms, there existed throughout the lowland jungles a vast expanse of contiguous tribal homelands, constantly interacting and possessing numerous ceremonial centers of varying sizes. In this extensive cultural milieu, which increased in complexity through time, each tribal unit provided different cultural essentials for the others. Today as well, the Zinacantecos rely on their Chamula neighbors for *metates*, sandals, and other items: they use Ladino musicians on certain occasions rather than providing this service for themselves, etc. Many more examples could be given. In the ancient village setting and homeland world, population units relied on one another for goods and services and for the fulfillment of certain roles. This was an internal reliance within the empire. The population units provided the empire with its food base – maize. Their system of maize production was efficient and, among other things, resulted in a labor surplus which could be a potential source of power under the direction of full-time specialists of comparatively exalted rank.

Within the ancient empire's structure, the other world – the world of the full-time specialist and the major ceremonial center, the second world which perished with the disintegration of the empire – vigorously tapped this surplus labor through the ancient version of the Zinacanteco "cargo" system. The cargo of a villager was in significant measure the *labor* he owed the empire. With that labor, the "Great Ones" of the empire, supported by the religious, ritualistic, administrative, and other full-time specialists surrounding them in a hierarchical system dedicated to the most intense ecclesiastical devotions, created a physical setting for a cultural environment of massive proportions in which the empire's second world existed. Although the ancient cargo system may have strongly resembled what we see among the Zinacantecos today, the participant provided his society with something above and beyond what was required of him for the satisfaction of strictly homeland commitments. In the ancient system, men went to their ceremonial center part-time to help build the monumental structures believed to be essential for the perpetuation of their civilization. The future existence of the ceremonial centers came to depend on labor contributed as a ceremonial aspect of the cargo system; this no longer exists because ceremonial centers of that kind no longer exist. A comparable concept of the future was not, however, necessary in the homeland setting. A world view involving a pre-occupation with the future was necessary only for the maintenance of the *empire* and so was vital only to the permanent denizens of its second world, the world of ceremonial centers and the elaborate religious dimension. The Zinacantecos today need no preoccupation with the future on this level of abstraction and do not seem to have one. On an operative level, their cargo system has now reverted strictly to the village setting where it is used by them to maintain local ritual and ceremonial essentials. In the beginning of the Maya Classic interval, however, the rituals and ceremonialism were necessary to the life of a high civilization and as such eventually came to justify the *empire*. They remain necessary but now they simply justify *life*; and since that justification is complete and total to the Zinacantecos, they take their cultural future for granted. No overt concern for the future is needed if from a practical standpoint the responsibility for the future rests entirely with the ancestors.

One's view of the future more or less relates to the fulfillment of a good life and does not go far beyond day-to-day goals. For a Zinacanteco, a major concern with the future relates to *his* specific cargos. According to Vogt (1970: 73–74):

Following his wedding, a young Zinacanteco ordinarily has to work diligently for a few years not only to provide for his new family, but to pay off the debts incurred by his marriage. He and his wife also look forward to having a house of their own, and this stage is usually achieved by the time he is about twenty-five. Between about twenty-five and thirty he can begin to think about serving in the cargo system. . . . When a Zinacanteco calculates that he will be ready for his first cargo some years in the future, he takes a bottle of liquor to present to the *moletik* (elders) on August 8th. On this date each year the *moletik* sit outside the wall of the church of San Lorenzo and receive requests for cargos. The "waiting lists" are kept by the Scribes in hardcover notebooks which have a page or two devoted to each year in the future for which there is a cargo requested. . . . A man might. . . request in 1966 the cargo of Senior Mayordome Rey for 1980, only to be told that 1980 is already taken and that he may have the position in 1986. . . . Once his name is recorded in the sacred book, he must reappear each August 8th, present another bottle of liquor, and reaffirm his intention to serve.

This was not so under the empire. The lifeway of those who occupied the ceremonial centers was dependent on the perpetuation of their world view. Without this kind of orientation towards the future, there would have been no reality for the second ceremonial center world of the empire even though the functional role of the ceremonial center may well have included important commercial and other dimensions. Consequently, as an empirically believable concept of the future became increasingly difficult to maintain and as philosophical and conceptual involvement became more abstract and removed from the homeland settings, difficulties mounted with respect to the balanced effectiveness of the empire.

The empire itself had been built up based upon an internal reliance on homeland belief in the validity of an overall view of the future propounded by the occupants of the ceremonial center. Toward the end of the empire there is evidence that the societal lifeline between homelands and ceremonial centers may have been pulled very taut by the demands of the major ceremonial center (Willey, et al. 1965). These connectors may also have become badly frayed by a deepening sense of incredulity concerning the effectiveness of ceremonial center activities and a changing view of the future. These and other factors, heightened by a wide variety of circumstances (Willey and Shimkin 1971), including a threat of invasion (Sabloff and Willey 1967), may have caused the homeland world to sever irreversibly its ties with the now-remote ceremonial center world.

To the Zinacantecos, their system of beliefs – its maintenance, proper functioning, and credibility – is life itself. If those beliefs could no longer be held supraordinate with regard to the empire's second world, the empire itself would vanish with astonishig rapidity – its inner soul fragmented, its parts disarticulated, it would quickly die. The remnants of this inner soul have survived in the Chamula, the Zinacantecos and other population units who for the most part embrace only the village life aspect of what was once the empire.

The great ceremonial centers are gone, the stupendous architecture is gone, the real Great Ones are gone, but it is all ritually remembered and Zinacanteco ancestors live today within pyramid-shaped moun-tains, where they preside over Zinacanteco societal life, care for inner souls, and know and control the future. As long as close touch is maintained with the ancestors, there is no need for concern with the future – the ancestors control the future. The role of the cargo system is still the same – it links the people with their rulers. Yesterday the rulers lived in the ceremonial centers and the cargo system helped to build and maintain their special lifeway within an empire. Today the people live in villages and the cargo system maintains their lifeway by providing a means of communication with the ancestors. The cargo system does not accomplish this among the Zinacanteco by itself; the shamans, too, are always needed. These shamans are the closest remaining approximation of the full-time specialist residents of the imperial ceremonial center. The empire needed both of its worlds; the Zinacantecos need *people* who fulfill the same functions. The three-year renewal ceremonies among the Zinacantecos provide an insight into this matter. According to Vogt (1970: 99): "The ceremony has deep structural significance for Zinacantán since it links together the two peaks of sacred terrestrial power – the top-ranking cargoholders and the top-ranking shamans – and relates them both to the all-important Ancestral Gods in the supernatural world."

The village homeland setting has three essential aspects: the production of food, a dependence on other population units for certain special goods and services, and a reliance on certain individuals to fulfill special roles. Among the Zinacantecos, all of these, but particularly the last, are achieved on a purely part-time basis. Structurally speaking it was profoundly different within the empire, where tribal population units were the maize producers and part-time builders of the empire's second ceremonial center world, furnishing full-time specialists who became residents of the large ceremonial centers.

The point that requires emphasis here is that the homeland settings contributed some individuals on a permanent basis for the performance of full-time roles in the ceremonial centers themselves. Thus as a societal unit the Zinacantecos had a role to which they contributed some of their people from generation to generation. And these people acted out a particular Zinacanteco role in the second ceremonial center world on a continuing (perhaps lifelong) basis as full-time specialists. This, then, was a third and vital contribution to the empire and its existence, made by each of its population units. Although each population unit made this contribution in its own way, it was largely determined along lines which paralleled homeland tribal interdependence for the exchange of goods and services on local levels, and perhaps also by factors more internal to the population unit itself. For example, among the Zinacantecos "a younger brother spends his life in a struggle for status in a system that has led his older brother to resent him" (Vogt 1970: 68). This setting favors the older brother within the homeland context. If an alternative lifeway were available, however the same kind of system might encourage a younger brother to travel from the homeland setting to the second world of the ceremonial center. In staying there on a full-time basis in a capacity or position that was traditionally occupied by Zinacanteco tribesmen, he could move unimpeded toward a level of achievement and prestige comparable to or exceeding that accorded an older brother remaining in his homeland.

Within the ancient configuration special roles no longer extant were primarily concerned with the future of the empire. Old Empire Maya astronomy, mathematics, numerology, hieroglyphic writing – these and many other arts concerned with prediction – were necessary because the Great Ones relied on the practitioners of these extremely specialized fields in order to comprehend the Maya future and rule their empire. Conversely, without the imperial structure, tribal units need only to govern themselves; there is consequently no need for a long-range view of the future as long as total confidence in the ancestors is maintained and communication with them is uninterrupted.

Accordingly, one has the impression that the Zinacantecos of today are preoccupied with what the ancestors accomplished in the past, with pleasing the ancestors who now reside in the spirit world (mostly inside mountains), and with day-to-day Zinacanteco activities which will not change in the future because they have been determined and set by the ancestors. Since the Zinacanteco world was fixed in all its dimensions by the ancestors, and since the present Zinacanteco system of beliefs is inviolable with respect to the ways of the ancestors, there is no need for concern with the future because the world will always be as it is today. As far as is known, there is no great myth among the Maya relating to the return of a Great One (such as the myth of Quetzalcoatl in Mexico) or to the return of the ancestors, so that there is not even an abstract, philosophical expression of future "deliverance" from that which now prevails. The future will be as it is now for Zinacantecos because the ancestors control the future. If change does come it will be because the ancestors have so determined it. If communication with the ancestors has been kept in good order, Zinacantecos will know what to do.

Homeland settings of the Old Empire may well have held a similar absolute view, and the absoluteness of this view, so complete and so obvious to this day, may have been a major factor in the building and perpetuation of the empire. The most far-reaching difference is that the ancestors of the Zinacantecos are fixed abstractions; their counterparts in the empire were alive as the Great Ones and their advisors. These Maya peoples, the Great Ones and their advisors, evidently concerned themselves very much with the ideas of the future. This is apparent even though our evidence comes entirely from the prehistoric record. What is known about the lifeway of the Old Empire

Maya second ceremonial center world has been inferred from data amassed by archaeologists rather than ethnologists.

The data strongly suggest that this second ceremonial center world was committed to a world view which was deeply concerned with the future. There are indications of a philosophial dimension to certain activities and certain highly specialized roles. In the archaeological record, some of these are more obvious than others. There is considerable evidence, for instance, that some individuals were totally involved with astronomy and the making of permanent records relating to astronomical observations which were not only incredibly accurate but which required extremely long periods of uninterrupted observation. These records were accumulated in book form and transcribed by means of a hieroglyphic writing peculiar to the Maya Old Empire. "Actually, as the Maya priests reckoned hundreds of millions of years into the past, it is probable that they grasped the concept of time, and therefore perhaps a world, without beginning" (Thompson 1966: 261).

In discussing the first public showing of a newly discovered, eleven-page fragment of a manuscript executed on bark cloth coated with stucco and folded like a screen, M. D. Coe perceptively touched on the extent to which certain activity patterns must have been emphasized in the ancient configuration.

The eleven-page fragment. . . is part of a larger book that originally must have been twenty pages in length. It deals exclusively with cycles of the planet Venus as seen from the earth (M. D. Coe, unpublished data).

Each cycle was measured by Maya priests as 584 days. . . . Modern astronomers have calculated this cycle to average 583.92 days. So you see, the figure is extraordinarily accurate. The complete codex would have given 65 Venus cycles, so that the whole table would cover slightly less than 104 solar years . . . the Maya were the greatest thinkers of the entire New World! (Gent 1971).

No other people in history has taken such an absorbing interest in time as did the Maya, and no other culture has ever developed a philosophy embracing such an unusual subject. . . For the Maya time was an all-consuming interest. . . . The Maya wished to know which gods would be marching together on any given day because with that information they could gauge the combined influence of all the marchers, offsetting the bad ones with the good in an involved computation of the fates and astrological factors. On a successful solution depended the fate of mankind. . . . Each lunar month in the series and each division of each revolution of the planet Venus had its divine patron, and the influences of all those gods had to be taken into consideration. The Maya priest-astronomer was anxious to find the lowest common multiple of two or more of these cycles, or, to state it in the Maya pattern of thought, how long would be the journey on the road of time before two or more of the divine carriers reached the same resting place together. . . . So far as we know no other people in Middle America used tables comparable in accuracy to those the Maya developed to predict possible solar eclipses and to compute the synodical revolutions of Venus, nor, so far as we know, did any other people in Middle America measure the length of the tropical year with the skill the Maya attained (Thompson 1966: 162–183).

It is clear from an abundance of archaeological data that a deep feeling for the future and correlative prediction in itself became a vested interest of the Great Ones and for associated specialists, and that this vested interest was vital to the world of the second ceremonial center for the maintenance of its highly specialized lifeway.

GENERAL CONSIDERATIONS

An inordinate interest in the future and in ways and means of influencing it may have become an obsession with the leaders in Maya prehistoric society. In the name of this obsession they may have made demands on their society which exceeded the society's capacity to meet them. The consequences may have been severe societal dislocation which, combined with other difficulties (such as threats of invasion), resulted in the sudden disintegration of the belief system of the empire. Without the binding mechanism of this system of beliefs, the physical disarticulation of population units and the abandonment of the ceremonial centers may have occurred swiftly, causing the disappearance of the second ceremonial center lifeway.

One wonders if it could be said that vested interests, when transformed into rulership obsessions, have lethal potentialities for their societal hosts. Certainly it is possible to think that the Maya and Sumerian kinds of high civilization were actually victims of this process. Perhaps the same could also be said of the Aztec and Assyrian high civilizations. The obsession and its specifics, of course, differ from one civilization to another. Also interesting and potentially suggestive is the dynamics of change in the culture's view of the future. It is possible to observe the debilitating nature of a general over-concern with the future which can lead to population-wide obsession. In the past, however, leadership obsession has been a more common behavioral pattern because education and communication have been limited. Despite the universal presence of cultural change, systems are developed for introducing and maintaining societal order and efficiency within a cultural configuration. This is often profitable to those in power, so the systems are maintained, strengthened, and elaborated in order to inhibit or prevent additional change and perpetuate the status quo, thereby protecting vested interests.

As a line of evolution, our chances for survival and success were enhanced by a certain mobility factor. This kept our population units in contact with each other, thus favoring the exchange of genetic information on a wide front and implementing the perpetuation of a broad genetic base rather than one or a series of separate narrow ones. The former situation is genetically advantageous in the face of change, especially rapid change. This process not only continues today but has accelerated dramatically. As the genetic base for *sapiens* becomes even more broadly based, to the point that it becomes almost homogeneous the world over, it will be necessary to foster cultural diversity, especially with reference to beliefs or ideological outlook, beneath a configuration of negative imperatives (Gifford 1971). This will be needed to prevent a single mental outlook from prescribing the boundaries of the future biological development of the worldwide *sapiens* population. The genetic resource of the Maya was certainly bound by the confines of their ideological outlook, total value orientation and system of beliefs; this was the case, too, with the Sumerians and the ancient Egyptian high civilization. The priesthood of ancient Egypt managed a "comeback " time and time again, thereby fixing its image and perpetuating perhaps the most lengthy among the various high civilization continua (Riley 1969).

In the future *sapiens* genetic pool of the world, and with respect to its development, we cannot afford a narrow adherence to a single ideological outlook. Diversity in mental propensity may hold distinct advantages for the *sapiens* genetic base of the future, especially in a societal context where imaginative or creative thought may be a paramount asset to a constructive cultural continuity.

A further advantage may rest with a capacity, in this *sapiens* "mental pool," to react favorably to sharp changes in outlook. The potential to react successfully to a rapid rate of ideological change could confer a decided advantage. This would be true even though one will recognize that the limitation of the mind may lie not so much in degree of complexity as in the number of variables it can successfully handle at any one time; there may be a limit to the rapidity of cultural change with which it can cope in such ways as to achieve psychic comfort.

In a more immediate circumstance than that of the ancient Maya, involving a potential contemporary obsession, it may not be that technology *per se* is the villain – rather, technology may simply be the most obvious, tangible indicator of too rapid cultural change which is causing psychic distress to associated population units. These observations may have suggested more questions than they answer. It is my firm view as an anthropologist that, in order to gain insight into contemporary human nature and that which will evolve in the future, one must achieve a basic comprehension of the prehistoric derivation of the *sapiens* populations that exist today.

REFERENCES

GENT, GEORGE
1971   "Manuscript part may alter theories on Maya religion." *New York Times*, April 21.
GIFFORD, JAMES C.
1971   "The prehistory of *sapiens:* touchstone to his future," in *Human futuristics.* Edited by Magoroh Maruyama and James A. Dator. Honolulu: University of Hawaii Social Science Research Institute.
RILEY, CARROLL L.
1969   *The origins of civilization.* Carbondale: Southern Illinois University Press.
SABLOFF, J. A., G. R. WILLEY
1967   The collapse of Maya civilization in the southern lowlands: a consideration of history and process. *Southwestern Journal of Anthropology* 23: 311–336.
THOMPSON, J. ERIC S.
1966   *The rise and fall of Maya civilization* (second edition). Norman: University of Oklahoma Press.
VOGT, EVON Z.
1970   *The Zinacantecos of Mexico.* New York: Holt, Rinehart and Winston.
WILLEY, G. R., W. R. BULLARD, JR., J. B. GLASS, J. C. GIFFORD
1965   *Prehistoric Maya settlements in the Belize Valley.* Papers of the Peabody Museum, Harvard University 54. Cambridge, Mass.
WILLEY, G. R., D. B. SHIMKIN
1971   The collapse of Classic Maya civilization in the southern lowlands: a symposium summary statement. *Southwestern Journal of Anthropology,* 27: 1–18.

Ethnographic Realities of Mayan Prehistory

JEFFREY C. HOWRY

Much of the cultural history of societies throughout the world depends upon reconstruction by means of the nonperishable evidence. Detailed consideration of particular categories of material is essential in order to comprehend more fully the significance of the general evidence. Perhaps the single most important category of evidence pertaining to everyday life is that of ceramics. This paper reports on recent field research whose specific goal was to obtain information on the nature and significance of an ongoing ceramic tradition in its many cultural contexts. This paper also discusses the implications for existing prehistoric research and future work.

The focus of study was in the northernmost extent of the highland Mayan culture area, the central highland plateau of the state of Chiapas, Mexico (see Map 1). Although politically part of Mexico, culturally it is of the Mayan tradition which stretches south through Guatemala. Until the coming of the Pan-American Highway in the 1940's, it was among the more isolated and more densely populated regions in Mexico. The unique nature and exceptional value for study of the highlands lie in the fact that many of the communities retain a dispersed settlement pattern probably characteristic of the same population since before the intrusion of European influences in the sixteenth century (Vogt 1961).

My particular study dealt with the municipality of Chamula, which

The research reported here was conducted under an NIMH Traineeship in Anthropology from late 1971 until early 1973. Earlier summer projects of the Harvard Chiapas Project (Russ 1967; Miyamoto 1967) encouraged me to conduct a long-term project for a doctoral thesis. This paper is a preliminary report of some findings. I wish to thank Jeremy Sabloff and David Freidel for helping me clarify my thoughts on archaeological matters. Also my special thanks to Evon Z. Vogt for his encouragement and support through my research.

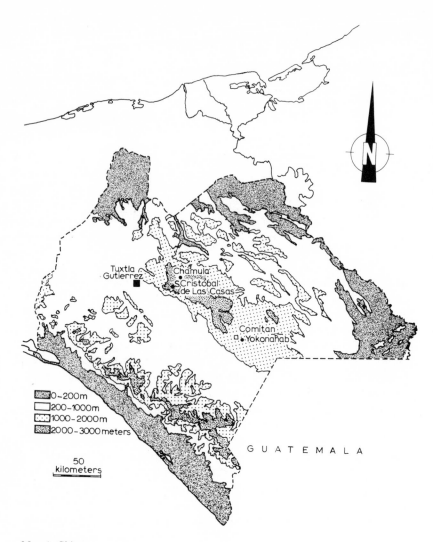

Map 1. Chiapas

occupies the highest region of the mountainous plateau from 2,200 to 3,000 meters (7,000 to 9,000 feet). Chamula today retains a dispersed settlement of houses over an uneven terrain where hamlets are the smallest political unit. Next in importance for ritual matters are hamlet alliances with one or more of three *barrios* which are united together by a ceremonial center minimally occupied except during times of fiestas. The center has resident civil authorities who are the liaison with the larger Mexican society. This social structure, with variations, exists in other parts of the highlands. A single municipality may encompass several ceremonial centers, or the population of an entire

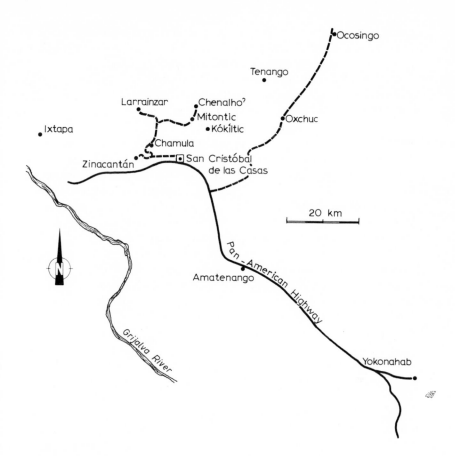

Map 2. Chiapas highland

municipality may live in a densely populated center. The latter cases are examples of stronger Spanish influence.

Native accounts and colonial remains indicate that the Chamula ceremonial center was relocated by missionaries several centuries ago to a small valley. The majority of the widely scattered population has probably remained *in situ*, gradually increasing in numbers. Relocation of the Chamula center was undoubtedly a response to Chamula hostility towards the Spanish, who claimed a large highland valley adjacent to Indian-dominated mountaintops. This ethnographer would also add that the centuries of European contact have in some cases only slightly diminished the strong Chamula hostility toward outsiders.

Ceramic traditions exist in several communities throughout the highlands (see Map 2), but Chamula continues to be the only major one which also has a dispersed settlement pattern. Others exist in either re-settled centers containing a majority of a group's members (e.g. Amatenango, Tenango) or in isolated hamlets with a limited inventory of ceramic types (e.g. Chenalhoʔ, Oxchuc).

Within Chamula there are five or six major ceramic-producing hamlets, all located within approximately an hour's walk from either the major or secondary sources of clays. The hamlet where I intensively worked was located about three kilometers north of the major source area but was near to the secondary source as well. The *paraje*, the regional term for a hamlet, was called /Zahalte'tik/ ["red trees" after a particular species of oak][1] and was the most concentrated ceramic-production locale in Chamula. A number of people used both clay sources, but the major source located near the ceremonial center contained certain clay minerals in sufficient abundance to make collecting there worthwhile for nearly all potters.[2]

The most important factor relating to the distribution of ceramic producing *parajes* was not the access to clay. More critical was the access to the necessary quantities of wood required for firing the ceramics. Gathering from the earliest reliable reports (Pozas 1959) and from my conversations with earlier visitors of twenty years ago, the former center of production was probably the *paraje* nearest the major clay source, /Kučulumtik/ [carry the earth]. Visitors have commented on the great deforestation which has occurred during the past decades in the immediate area around the ceremonial center and for a radius of several kilometers. This results from overgrazing of sheep and greater population demands for ordinary firewood. The radius of this circle would encompass the *paraje* of the clay pits as well. Today the *paraje* of /Zahalte'tik/ is located on the fringe area of deforestation. My friends there complain of the growing shortage of wood and are uncertain as to what land they can purchase for more wood. The shift of ceramic production within Chamula to the north and to less densely populated lands clearly emphasizes that the critical resource is wood, not clay.

The particular status of the potter further illustrates the importance of wood as the critical resource. In Chamula, men as well as women are potters. Men are in fewer numbers, however, and limit themselves to producing primarily special vessels utilized by other men in fulfilling the obligations of religious and civil offices in the ceremonial center. I have never met any potter who was well-off financially by Indian

---

[1] Throughout the text the following orthographic conventions are used: square brackets [] indicate an English gloss; italicized words indicate a Spanish word; words in Tzotzil, the Maya language of Chamula, are indicated by slashes (//) and use these phonetic abbreviations – /x/ for 'sh', /c/ for 'ch', /'/ for a glottalized consonant or vowel, /ʔ/ for a glottal stop. Place names have Spanish spellings.

[2] It would be rare, if possible at all, that more than one closely related community of potters shared a single (or geologically related) group of clay resources.

standards. In fact, the women and men potters tend to be from households which possess very limited agricultural land. Women often make pots to gain extra income to purchase food or raw materials for making their clothing (wool, cotton yarn, thread, etc.). A few very elderly women who have inherited a house and some land gain enough cash from the sale of pots to barely support themselves. The men who make ceramics typically have little land in proportion to their household size and subsist through cash purchase of staples of corn and beans. Woodlands are much less expensive than agricultural land because of their limited fertility on remote and steep terrain. Investment in such land for a potter would probably bring greater return, in terms of the ceramics he could fire, than equivalently priced farmland.

A pattern appears which indicates that potters are people who are "land poor" or who live in areas of poor agricultural land. The heaviest concentration of potters is found in those areas where, due to mountainous conditions good agricultural land is scarce but wood is relatively abundant. When the wood supply becomes short, the industry gradually phases out and shifts to less populated, more heavily wooded areas.

The access to resources and economic alternatives in Chamula are similar to those among other highland Maya. Pokomom communities in Guatemala, who have access to clay minerals but reside in areas of low soil fertility, have chosen to develop local ceramic industries (Arnold 1971). Those Pokomom communities where soil fertility is high lack any ceramic industries whatsoever. The fertility zones are not as clear-cut in Chamula, but lack of sufficient agricultural land has clearly been a determining motive for people to seek other means of income, including ceramic production.

CHAMULA CERAMIC TECHNOLOGY

For Chamula potters the same major clay source is available to all. Any new potters may avail themselves of the clay sources since the actual owner no longer collects any taxes from users. The owner's land is so infertile that he has left the Indian municipality entirely and has joined a colony of similarly impoverished persons some distance away where inexpensive government lands were made available.

The potters mine the clays they desire from the banks of a seasonal stream bed. The better potters distinguish three major types of clay: /but'/, /c'ix/, and /cablum/.[3] Good potters combine all three of these

[3] John D. Sims of the Geological Survey, Menlo Park, California, analyzed samples of the clays used in Chamula by X-ray diffraction techniques. Future work will include

clay compounds. At this stage of analysis it does not appear that the clay proportions significantly vary with the size or function of the vessel. The exception is a /semet/ – a *comal* or tortilla griddle – which is exposed to exceptionally high heat and to which a special /cablum/ with greater sand is added. Some of the less proficient potters do not blend the three clays; some, in fact, fail to sort out large nodules of impurities and consequently produce vessels that have very uneven surfaces, often with considerable cracking.

Clay retrieved from the pits is frequently stored in underground cavities, a few feet below the surface. These pits may be formed by partially submerging the top of a large broken pot. Many potters who make vessels of considerable size gradually accumulate large vessels which have cracked slightly during firing and are therefore unfit for sale. These make excellent storage containers. A potter will attempt to keep several weeks' supply of clay ready and not put himself in the position of using fresh, raw clay. Aging varies from a few weeks to several months. Clays like /cablum/ are carefully kept moist, since natural drying will result in an exceptionally hard compound. The /c'ix/ may be kept for as long as a year before its use. Extended storage of these two clays is partially the result of their use in smaller quantities than the /but'/, hence these clays remain longer in the potter's household before blending as a working compound. Storage for future work is planned, since the digging for /cablum/ and /c'ix/ is an arduous task.

Some women potters apparently use the clay raw. Very frequently I would observe women returning to the *paraje* on a Monday or Tuesday with a load of clay that would eventually end up as pots in the following Sunday market. The short scheme of production is probably the result of strong pressures for cash income, rather than a desire to make a good pot. Such a scheme requires very rapid drying which can easily produce cracking, the potter's greatest threat.

The three clays are mixed by hand on a flat stone; at this time large nodules of impurities are removed. The most difficult task involves grinding the mixture with a wooden *mano* on a limestone *metate* until a smooth consistency is achieved.

Once blended, the clay is kneaded on a short board with slight amounts of water added until the clay has the right consistency.

analysis of extensive sampling done in the clay pits and of the ceramics from those clays.

Total clay of sample	(%)	Mont- morillonite	Percent of total clay Kaolinite	Other (mixed)
/but'/	89	28	69	3
/c'ix/	100	64	32	4
/cablum/	80	45	10	45

Grinding involves a quantity of clay of perhaps a kilogram (2.2 pounds) or more. Only the amount of clay that will be used on the particular day is ground. The actual kneading of clay to a working consistency is performed on the portion to be used immediately. The remainder of the ground clay is put aside in the shade, wrapped in leaves or the newly available plastic. The final step leading to the actual forming processes is the rotation in the hands to form a short, solid cylinder.

The actual working base for the formation of all vessel or *olla* forms takes place on either the circular broken base of a large vessel or a specially made piece called a /tilebal/. The latter is simply a flat dish twenty-five to thirty centimeters (approximately one foot) in diameter whose edges are slightly angled upward. Upon this dishlike base is placed the cylinder of clay. Through a process of stretching this cylinder outward, the base of the pot is formed and the walls are raised. Small cooking pots can actually be made from a single cylinder of clay. Most vessels are larger and a simple modification enables them to be made from the same base form. The desired diameter of a pot is determined by the angle of the walls extending up from the base. This angle is easily adjusted by stretching the wall further outward. However, it is here that the potter's acute knowledge of his clay is critical. The larger pots require narrower angles relative to the horizontal base. If the clay is too wet or does not have the right consistency to support itself, the walls will collapse.

When the vessel base has dried sufficiently, more clay is prepared by kneading and rolling into a thick coil. The coil is then affixed to the edge of the base wall by a series of squeezing motions. Once attached, the coil is stroked upward with the forefinger while the other hand provides a support to the other side of the wall. By this process the wall is extended higher with each successive coil. Depending on the intended use of the vessel, a slightly outward-curving rim is the finishing touch for both wide- and constricted-mouth vessels.

The ability to make vessels more than sixty centimeters in diameter and one meter in height is possessed by less than half-dozen men in Chamula (whose total population exceeds 30,000). It is likely that some women could make vessels this large, but the reason they do not is probably cultural, rather than lack of ability. The largest vessels are used exclusively by men in fulfilling certain prestigious religious positions. Since there is considerable ritual associated with the petitioning of the potter to make these vessels, it would be incongruous within the male-dominant values of Chamula culture for a man to ritually petition a woman to make someting for him (this is typically an informal act between a husband and wife). I suspect that during the past decades, as the religious positions have required greater quantities of food to be prepared, the demand exceeded the efficient use of the smaller pots regularly produced and purchasable in the Chamula market. Men filled the role, which the general social system had created or made a necessity, of potters of special ware, thereby preserving the appropriate social relations between men and women. There is a counterpart to this male producer-user relationship. Women are the exclusive producers of the *comal*, or the tortilla griddle. This large ceramic surface, sometimes a meter in diameter, is only used by women since only they prepare and cook tortillas. The producer-user relationship with regard to the *comal* reflects one of the most basic Chamula values: the sexual division of possession is equivalent to the sexual division of labor.

It is evident, from their own accounts, that almost all male potters learned from women, with a few exceptions, in which a female potter lies behind a second generation of teachers. Potter friends claim that thirty or forty years ago all Chamula potters were women. It is interesting to note that within the last generation or two, the land squeeze within the territorial limits of Chamula has become extremely severe. The men's choice to make ceramics for cash income may be linked to the land shortages and made acceptable in terms of values by focusing the production on the sphere of men's religious activity.

CERAMIC VARIATION AND STYLE

There is difficulty in defining the categories of Chamula ceramics since there are at least two different classifications recognized: that of the manufacturers and that of the users. Both groups recognize the more obvious categories of /k'ib/ [water jug], /semet/ [*comal* or tortilla griddle] and /bocilum/ [small bowl]. The difficulty arises with the larger vessels which are roughly categorized by potters as small and large, /nene/ and /muk'/. There are many gradations between the two categories as exemplified by the prices brought by different size pots in the market. However, a more definitive designation is given by the buyer. For example, a medium-sized vessel with a maximum inside diameter of thirty-five centimeters could be designated at least three different ways: as a /binal ʔik'alum/ [a vessel used for dying woven wool], a /binal maʔil/ [a pot for cooking a large native squash], or a /pokob tan/ [a vessel for mixing lime and water needed in preparing corn.] Use, not manufacture, in many cases determines a pot's final functional category. Only the vessel's relative size, in relation to vessels of similar manufacture, would be a useful attribute in designating categories of cultural behavior associated with its form.

While some *parajes* produce specific ceramics, others produce nearly all varieties of wares. The relevant level of differentiation is the household. The lineal descendants of households will often continue the production of specific wares, such as especially large cooking vessels or ritually used incense burners. It is also at the household level that distinct varieties of wares exist. In learning to make ceramics, the child so rigorously imitates the instructor that the peculiarities of the instructor are passed along. This is particularly true of surface treatment, vessel shape, rim form and, to an extent, the particular clay combination (paste). There is no formal teacher-student relationship; rather, during late adolescence and early teens a novice will begin learning the necessary processes. First, a child accompanies a parent to the clay pits and carries back some clay as part of the family activity along with older children. By copying the parent, the child will make small, unfinished vessels and receive correction most frequently from an adult of the same sex.

When the child decides to fire his ceramics, he will have to collect firewood on the family land. (Collection of firewood is already a part of the daily activity for the child.) There is also an indirect age limitation on ceramic production, since it is not until the early teens that a child can effectively use a machete, the simplest of woodcutting tools. By mid-teens a male can effectively use an axe. A difference in fuel-gathering techniques for men and women may directly affect the absolute firing temperatures each can achieve. In Chamula the axe is strictly a male tool, seldom used by women; the machete is the largest woodcutting tool permitted a woman, though it may be used by men. A machete limits the size of branches and small trees which can be cut. Using an axe, a man can easily split large logs into sixteenths for heavier wood. Even when a husband and wife are potters, the wood they collect for firing is usually separate. Practically, some sharing does exist, but single women and especially *comal* makers definitely use smaller wood and more open fires than men, who use large logs and split wood closely piled together.

The young and old potter alike derive style and technological facility from the household in which they live. The influence from other potters is minimal and takes the form of simple imitation of vessel shape at the most. Through the gossip of the *paraje* and observation in the market, a potter may come to know a number of other potters. It is more likely that a potter will not know a potter living in another *paraje*. Social courtesy inhibits exchanges between strangers; conversation is limited to buying and selling, while nothing related to ceramic production is discussed. The knowledge of ceramic techniques is considered a private matter and is discussed only within the family. Conversation in a market situation, one of the few appropriate contexts for casual exchanges, is confined largely to relatives or close friends (often the same persons). The isolation of a household is not appreciated until one realizes that with a settlement pattern of dispersed housing, the social as well as physical distance between families is enormous. Visiting is done only among close relatives, whereas interaction with unrelated persons, acquaintances, or strangers is structured by formalities that inhibit free exchange.

Imitation of style by Chamula potters whom I have observed consists of slight changes in vessel forms. These included the addition of small handles to cooking pots such as those made in a nearby Mexican town and another Indian community. I also observed the copying of a rim form from a ware made in a distant community. These changes permitted greater ease in lifting the pot from the fire. Both innovations were attempts to make the Chamula ware easier to handle, that is, more functional.

CERAMIC DISTRIBUTION

Throughout the highlands in the last few centuries a market economy has developed in several of the Indian communities. The Mexican town of San Cristóbal de La Casas has become the primary center for the production and sale of many manufactured goods. The market contains ceramics of several Indian communities as well as those of San Cristóbal. To consider the marketing system as the exclusive means of ceramic distribution would be to ignore another system existing in the Indian communities, particularly Chamula, which has a very special importance. This can be characterized as "invisible exchange," since wares do not pass through the open market. The primary items exchanged in this manner are special ceramics required for performing the most prestigious religious offices, called cargos. The "ritual ceramics" involved would include large incense burners, animal images or bulls, with riders, very large vessels of a meter or more in height used for preparing *atole* [cornmeal cooked with sugar and water], and cooking vessels for meat and vegetables. Those needing these items seek out the houses of the few potters who know how to make them. A "cargoholder" petitions a potter to make the desired items, offering him gifts of native liquor and partial prepayment. On an appointed day, the "cargoholder" arrives with helpers, petitions the potter again, offers him more liquor, and makes final payment. He then carries his new pots or other items to his house or the ceremonial center where necessary ritual activities will take place.

Sometimes ordinary persons will seek out a potter if they want an especially large vessel not commonly available in the market. In *parajes* of potters, individuals may often buy among themselves. Potters who make pottery vessels do not make *comales*. They will frequently go to the house of an acquaintance and buy one directly, eliminating the chance of breakage when returning from the market. More important, it may result in a slightly lower price since there is no portage to the market.

For the majority of Indians, "invisible exchange" has little significance. However, the special ceramics involved in religious offices, upon which the whole community in a sense depends, are distributed in an entirely different manner from the ordinary utilitarian varieties. The importance of these cargos cannot be overemphasized, for they are the organizing foci of the religious celebrations for the entire community. A crucial realization for the prehistorian is that they are not distinguished from the utilitarian varieties in terms of paste, body temper, or rim form. The only distinguishing criterion is larger size relative to ordinary varieties.

It must also be mentioned that religious and civil officeholders use larger quantities of utilitarian ceramics for their houses in the ceremonial center. These are purchased in the Sunday market in Chamula center. Here potters come weekly to sell a varity of ceramics, along with vendors of seasonal fruits and vegetables, salt, wool, fish, meat, native liquors, and a variety of small manufactured goods. The quantity of ceramics sold at any market depends on two factors: the season of the year and the proximity to a religious fiesta. During the rainy season from late May through September, the almost daily rains significantly increase the drying times between the various stages of manufacture. Consequently, the greatest amount of ceramics is made in the winter months when rains are less frequent. There is also a greater economic incentive to produce pots in time for sale at the large markets which often precede a fiesta market by a week's time. Many people want extra money for the large fiesta market in order to buy extra or special foods not normally available, as well as new clothes, or materials for making them, to wear at future fiestas.

Chamula's large population with wide economic diversity draws people from neighboring communities to its market. Ceramics are certainly one of the attractions: neighboring Zinacantecos (see Map 2) often come to buy *comales*, sometimes even ordering extra large ones from sellers in the market. They then return on another market day and carry them back to their houses in the Zinacantán center where cargos are also held. More commonly, ceramic sellers carefully pack a large number of pots in a net bag with grass, or several dozen *comales* in a special rack, and carry them to the market in a nearby ceremonial center. Those most frequented by Chamula potters were Larrainzar, Mitontik, and the market in San Cristóbal. The Mitontik market is removed from the center, in a place designated /K'ok'iltik/, far enough away not to compete with the market in Chenalho?. The

/Kok'iltik/ market lies directly across several mountain ranges from the manufacturing *parajes* of Chamula. Only men make this journey, which may take eight to ten hours of walking with a load of as many as three dozen *comales* (Indians count in dozens for some things, a marketing habit they adopted from Mexicans). For the nearer markets of Larrainzar, San Cristóbal, and Chamula, women often go accompanied by their husbands or in groups with other women. Frequently a woman will go alone to the Chamula market with her pots since she feels most safe there.

Actual boundaries for the limits of ceramic sales from a single production locale can be roughly defined. The distance covered in three hours of walking would be the maximum distance that could be covered by women potters or husbands and wives together. The primary limiting factor is that indigenous markets begin at approximately 7 A.M., so that traveling more than three hours would mean a trip mostly in the dark. Aside from the great difficulty of walking barefoot in the dark over narrow, rock-strewn trails, Chamula culture has an assortment of demons who lurk on the dark paths, ready to threaten a passerby. The alternative way to reach farther markets, by traveling the day before and sleeping overnight in the market plaza, is one most often taken by men alone. Occasionally wives will accompany their husbands to distant markets if they occur during a fiesta. In this case the children go along, making it a family affair. It is fair to say in general, however, that distant trade involving at least a day's travel is a male endeavor.

The most recent development in the highlands is the expansion of the road network allowing greater transportation by trucks and some buses. This has altered the wholesaling and retailing network of foodstuffs and manufactured goods. Ceramics have been largely unaffected, since ceramics are easily damaged and hence require the more careful handling that only personal carrying can give. Second, and more important, is the problem of profit margin, which is relatively low for ceramics considering their bulk, The cost of transporting the seller and his ceramics both ways by truck to a market would be greater than the profit. If the Chamula ceramic industry were more centralized and potters collectively transported goods they could more successfully exploit their resources. This appears to be exactly what is done by another highland community, Amatenango, which widely distributes its wares, especially water jugs, by shipping large truckloads to the market in San Cristóbal from the center of production on the western edge of the highlands.

The actual range of Amatenango water jug distribution characterizes the truck economics. Truckloads of water jugs are shipped to San Cristóbal middlemen with storage facilities and permanent stalls for selling. Chamula traders come to these stalls and buy, say, twenty vessels, receiving a discount for buying in quantity. These men, in turn, repack the vessels in net bags and carry them eight to ten hours to the center of Larrainzar the day before the market.

Shipping in quantity from Amatenango to San Cristóbal on a paved road obviously has a sufficiently low risk and high profit to make the truck system worthwhile. However, walking is the practical economic choice for transporting a smaller quantity at lower cost and risk over a shorter distance on a dirt road.

ETHNOGRAPHIC IMPLICATIONS FOR HIGHLAND PREHISTORY

The following discussion is divided into two parts. The first is a consideration of the theoretical framework used for describing Mayan ceramics in light of the evidence from Chamula and the highlands. Second, the context of highland settlement patterns in the centuries before the arrival of the Europeans is re-evaluated.

The single most salient piece of ceramic evidence from the Chamula research is the importance of the paste – the clay constituents – in defining the social unity of any group of potters. The importance of paste for reconstruction of ceramic-producing communities and their boundaries of exchange was well demonstrated by Rands (1967). Upon microscopic examination of many sherds from the Palenque region of Chiapas, he found that: "Inclusions in clay form a more complex distributional pattern than do the temper and textural classes " (Rands 1967: 142). Actual impurities in the clays themselves were the key that enabled the reconstruction of regional exchange between Palenque and outlying centers.

A recent study of the prehistoric ceramics of the Chiapas highlands (Culbert 1965: 49) made a similar analysis:

. . . paste and temper proved to be the best basis for separating types. Pastes and tempers were different enough so that the sherds could be separated by inspection, and the use of these characteristics permitted the inclusion of both rim and body sherds, even when they were small or badly weathered.

A sizable number of the ceramics Culbert dealt with were utilitarian wares, like those described for Chamula. Culbert first tried to sort the ceramics into varieties on the basis of surface treatment, according to the "type-variety" system, the method of analysis most widely used in the study of Mayan ceramics (Smith, Willey, and Gifford 1960: 330):

Surface finish has been given particular emphasis by those who have dealt with pottery from the Maya subareas. Once wares' key to surface finish or allied criteria were established, vessel shape was used for the first level of subdivision.

However, Culbert says, "It soon became evident that surface treatment did not vary enough in the ceramics of the area to be of much use in the separation of varieties" (1965: 49). Surface treatment is an important criterion only when one is dealing with large quantities of finely made, reasonably well-preserved ceramics proceeding from graves or building fill. Considering, however, that most of the Mayan area lies in a tropical or subtropical environment, ceramics recovered from open areas surrounding house settlements are likely to be well weathered. Surface treatment is therefore a minor consideration. The exact methods for analysis depend on the conditions of the specific case. Paste always exists, regardless of surface treatment or sherd size and form. If any uniform system is to be adopted for sorting "varieties" of prehistoric ceramics, I would recommend paste and temper considerations as the starting point of any analysis.

Such an approach is consistent with what is known about the Chamula ceramic industry and the behavioral correlates of "varieties" which reflect ". . . individual and small social group variation" (Gifford 1960: 243). Even if within the larger community of potters there were quantitatively discernible differences in clay mixtures deriving from the same source, such differences might be an asset in making finer distinctions, possibly to the extent of identifying individual potters.

The pottery "type" as a ". . . combination of pottery traits that were acceptable not only to the potter but to most others adhering to the cultural pattern" (Gifford 1960: 343) would probably best define the attributes of a specific vessel form or functional class, such as a bean pot. Chamula potters, as mentioned earlier, make a number of different functional classes of vessels all with the same relative shape but differing in size. If "type" is to be a useful category in predicting Chamula behavior, an investigator must consider similarities of paste, temper, and vessel form plus the relative sizes of vessels with the same form.

Surface treatment considerations are of limited value in analyzing Chamula ceramics at the "type" of "variety" level. The absence of any slip, for example, simply indicates that the vessel is utilitarian ware since most wares are without any slipping or decoration whatsoever. The presence of a red or buff slip may indicate that the vessel belongs to a specific functional category. All water jugs made in Chamula have either a red or buff slip, as do incense burners. Some larger, ritually used ceramics have a buff slip, but may also have a red slip or none at all. Here is where the use of surface treatment as a diagnostic attribute for utilitarian wares becomes an acute problem, since the use of slips on ordinary vessels is arbitrary. Some less experienced potters may use a slip in attempting to cover surface imperfections. Good potters may use slips on their special wares but may feel that the ordinary wares which other potters slip are not worth the additional work. One young woman who specialized in incense burners would always apply a red iron oxide before firing. She might also apply the same slip after firing if discoloration from overheating occurred, if surface imperfections developed, or if she wanted to achieve a redder color. Techniques of surface treatment in Chamula do not have a significant consistency in relation to utilitarian vessel form or function: consistency in slip application only exists for single potters or groups of related potters.

On a higher taxonomic level of analysis, the concept of "ware" as proposed by Sabloff and Smith (1970) is useful in dealing with problems of surface treatment and paste to enable a coherent picture of cultural behavior to emerge. "Ware" is ". . . a conceptual unit which is concerned with paste and surface finish" (Sabloff and Smith 1970: 98). An archaeologist applying this concept of "ware" would also use vessel form as a more inclusive category than decorative technique, equivalent to vessel color (Sabloff and Smith 1970: 98). Carefully used, "ware" may delineate the major categories of ceramics produced community-wide in Chamula.

To proceed with the archaeological framework, it might be useful to point out that Chamula can be rightfully classified as a single "ceramic complex." That is, it represents ". . . the sum total of associated ceramics which has a convenient and easily distinguished geographical and temporal meaning" (Willey, Culbert, and Adams 1967: 304). Two "sub-complexes" can also be described: utilitarian ceramics, and those used in religious activities. The highlands of Chiapas may be considered to be a "sphere" (Willey, Culbert, and Adams 1967: 306) because they include at least four other major "complexes" (Amatenango, Tenango, Yokonahab and Ixtapa) besides Chamula, and several smaller ones (Oxchuc and Chenalho?). The geographical extent of ceramics distributed among these "complexes" or centers overlaps considerably in some cases, but no more than three ever exist in any definable sector of the "sphere." There is within the "sphere" a single "ware" largely consisting of one vessel form, the three-lug water jug, which essentially cross-cuts the four "complexes" that produce it (Chamula, Amatenango, Tenango, and Yokonahab). The analysis of prehistoric ceramics in the highlands reveals that forms cross-cut "types," ". . . and even some of the more characteristic forms were produced in more than a single ceramic . . . . If the forms had been considered merely modes of the ceramic types, the unity of multiple-type forms would not have been apparent" (Culbert 1965: 49–50).

Today there is clearly an attempt among Amatenango and Yokonahab potters to produce an almost identical water jug – not just in vessel form, but even down to a similar flower surface decoration. Their respective vessel forms can sometimes be difficult to distinguish. The best criterion is the primary slip: Yokonahab water jugs are always buff-slipped, whereas Amatenango potters produce a water jug with a slip which is very similar but which is generally red. Tenango and Chamula water jugs are both more elongated in form, the latter having only a red or buff slip with no decoration. This one "ware" is the only one used by all the indigenous communities throughout the highland "sphere" for carrying water.

Imitation of the water jug in different "complexes" is probably due to inherent functional qualities of the ware, which carries a large amount of water and does not spill easily. I came across a current example of vessel-form duplication while doing research in Chamula. Small vessels intended for cooking on an open fire, like bean pots, were being imported from Ixtapa. These vessels had small handles or "ears" on the lip enabling an easier lifting movement when removing them from the fire. Ordinary Chamula vessels have only a small outward-flared rim to grab. A Chamula woman potter recently began making small pots as usual but added two "ears" to the rim. This innovation was self-taught since the vendors of Ixtapa ceramics are middlemen totally without ceramic technological knowledge. To what extent a change in ceramic style may or may not reflect significant cultural changes might be carefully reconsidered in light of this example.

There is another dimension to the analysis of the Chiapas highland "complexes," the prehistoric settlement pattern. During the two or three centuries prior to the Spanish arrival (the late Postclassic in Mesoamerican chronology),[4] there was a population reorganization in the highlands. Communities apparently developed "capitals" in their social organization and located them near valleys (Adams 1961: 357), most frequently on defensible summits or ridges. There is limited data available from the highlands for this period, partially due to the scattered nature of the remains (Culbert 1965: 86). Those which do exist suggest that the highlands were relatively isolated from the adjacent Grijalva lowlands, but had connections with Ixtapa along a valley leading down from the plateau. To the east there was an expansion of trade compared to earlier times. Highland ceramic "types" appeared at a site in the Ocosingo valley during the Post-classic with strong similarities to highland traditions (Culbert 1965).

Directly relevant to the prehistory and present circumstances of the

[4]   The Postclassic spans a period of approximately 500 years with two subdivisions: early Postclassic (A.D. 1000–1250) and late Postclassic (A.D. 1250–1524).

highlands is Culbert's tentative conclusion that "...there were villages specializing in the production of pottery in the Chiapas Highlands from the beginning of the Classic period until the present" (1965: 46). This conclusion was reached because "...the 'feel' for the pottery, established by working with large numbers of sherds from several sites, gave the distinct impression that all the examples of each of a number of varieties were so nearly identical that the best assumption is that they were produced at a single location" (Culbert 1965). Culbert was able to indicate that one particular "type" had two "varieties," both with similar pastes and equivalent regional distribution, and probably originating from the same source. In light of what was discussed about the present state of the highland production centers, such conclusions are more than likely the case.

Today the community organization in highland Chiapas is quite similar to that of the Postclassic "capitals," with the exception that the centers are now in valley bottoms rather than mountain tops. As in the past, centers are distinguished by ceremonial architecture. The church has replaced the platform temple. The centers are special locations and their ceramics should reflect different forms of activity from that of household areas. The refuse of a center would parallel normal house refuse but would also have to include vessels of special use, such as incense burners. Culbert (1965: 55) did not find distinctions in the ceramics excavated from what he calls "ceremonial contexts" and "domestic contexts." This may partially be due to the combining of material within the ceremonial precincts with that of the terraces below. The terraces, often delineated by finished stone, may have been the more permanent location of houses of officials who were involved in the activities of the center (as the present-day analogy would suggest). Most of the refuse from such a context would be very similar to that of any household, with the possible exception of utilitarian vessels of extraordinary size. Culbert does report, however, that a cache of incense burners was found at the foot of a small pyramid (1965: 45). This at least confirms the idea that certain special ceramics were used in the same context prehistorically as they are presently used in many indigenous churches.

Finding representative prehistoric refuse deposits from the Postclassic or earlier will be difficult if the present patterns of disposal are any indication of what was done before. Today most decomposable material from the Maya house is distributed to decay and fertilize the surrounding maize fields. Ceramic refuse is very often carefully removed a considerable distance from any dwelling area which potentially can be planted. This is done, it was explained to me, because in turning over the soil for each season's cultivation a sherd struck by a hoe might damage the tool's digging edge. Although today the hoe head is metal, the threat of damage is seriously considered. In the premetal technology before the Spanish this must have been even of greater concern, since stone and wood are more susceptible to damage. Instead of casual disposal, the pieces of a broken pot are gathered together and carried to nearby land which is used only for timber, not for farming or habitation. In the ceremonial center of Chamula, the wooded disposal areas are more distant. Houses are very much closer than in the *parajes*, with less agricultural land between them. Here there is no choice but to scatter the refuse around the houses. This pattern is the exception and if found archaeologically would be a good clue that the location was of special significance.

One further ethnographic note may well explain why Postclassic household evidence is scarce and scattered in the highlands. Today the traditionally built house of earth walls and grass roof may last twenty years (or slightly more). After this period the walls are usually well eroded by seasonal rains and the roof decomposed, to say nothing of the long accumulation of fleas, mice, and the soot of many years' fires. When a new house is built, the land of the old house is often cleared. This involves disassembling the house for its major beams which may still remain good, or simply burning the house to the ground. Most household items are moved to the new house. The inventory would include the family water storage vessels, water jugs, and whatever household ceramics the family possesses. The leveled house platform is allowed to go fallow and in a few years may be cultivated. When totally abandoned, erosion on sloping terrain will remove most features of the house platform in a few decades. For these reasons the "domestic contexts" for archaeological research in the highlands are relatively scarce in both quantity and quality.

CONCLUSION

This paper has explored various aspects of the ceramic tradition of the highlands of Chiapas in its present situation and its implications for the reconstruction of the area's prehistory. The cultural continuity from the Postclassic to the present seems fairly certain, lending weight, I believe, to the assertions concerning the relationships between the archaeological categories of analysis and the ethnographic realities. While there have been quite a few studies of traditional ceramic industries, only a few have attempted to relate their findings to the prehistory of their particular areas (Thompson 1958 and Fontana, et al. 1962 are two good examples). If models of cultural development used by prehistorians are ever to have definitive meaning, systematic investigations must be conducted to understand the human realities behind the existing evidence.

REFERENCES

ADAMS, R. M.
1961 Changing patterns of territorial organization in the central highlands of Chiapas, Mexico. *American Antiquity* 26: 341–360.

ARNOLD, D. E.
1971 "Intercommunity ceramic differences among the central Pokomom, Guatemala." Revised version of a paper presented at the American Anthropological Association meetings.

CULBERT, T. P.
1965 *The ceramic history of the central highlands of Chiapas, Mexico.* Papers of the New World Archaeological Foundation 19. Provo, Utah.

FONTANA, B. L., W. J. ROBINSON, C. W. CORMACK, E. E. LEAVITT, JR.
1962 *Papago Indian pottery.* Seattle, Wash.: University of Washington Press.

GIFFORD, J. C.
1960 The type-variety method of ceramic classification as an indicator of cultural phenomena. *American Antiquity* 2.5.

MIYAMOTO, J. M.
1967 "Ritual objects: their pre-fiesta logistics." Unpublished research, Harvard Chiapas Project, Cambridge, Mass.

POZAS, R.
1959 *Chamula, un pueblo indio de los altos de Chiapas.* Memorias del Instituto Nacional Indígenisto 8. Mexico City.

RANDS, R. L.
1967 "Ceramic technology and trade in the Palenque region, Mexico," in *American historical anthropology, essays in honor of Leslie Spier.* Edited by C. L. Riley and W. W. Taylor, 137–152. Carbondale: Southern Illinois University Press.

RUSS, J.
1967 Unpublished research, Harvard Chiapas Project. Cambridge, Mass.
1969 "Pottery making in Chamula." A.B. Honors thesis, Harvard College, Cambridge, Mass.

SABLOFF, J. A., R. E. SMITH
1970 Ceramic wares in the Maya area: a clarification of an aspect of the type-variety system and presentation of a formal model for comparative use. *Estudios de Cultura Maya* 8: 97–115.

SMITH, R. E., G. R. WILLEY, J. C. GIFFORD
1960 The type-variety concept as a basis for analysis of Maya pottery. *American Antiquity* 25: 330–340.

THOMPSON, R. H.
1958 *Modern Yucatecan Maya pottery making.* Memoirs of the Society for American Archaeology 15. Salt Lake City: Society for American Archaeology.

VOGT, E. Z.
1961 Some aspects of Zinacantán settlement patterns and ceremonial organization. *Estudios de Cultura Maya* 1: 131–145.

WILLEY, G. R., T. P. CULBERT, R. E. ADAMS
1967 Maya lowland ceramics. *American Antiquity* 32: 289–315.

Mesoamericans as Cultural Brokers in Northern New Spain

JOHN HOBGOOD and CARROLL L. RILEY

During the course of the sixteenth, seventeenth, and eighteenth centuries, as the Spaniards pushed into the silver-rich areas of northern New Spain, the question of security and the development of new sources of food for the mining camps became increasingly important. In order to maintain contact with the mining camps of Zacatecas, Durango, Chihuahua, and Coahuila, and in order to press forward with the conversion of hostile nomadic Indians ranging throughout that vast area, the viceregal government increasingly felt the necessity of establishing secure areas where Spanish culture, Spanish law, and Spanish control could be maintained. This meant colonization, but the Spanish (European) population itself was too small to provide for a sufficient number of colonists. Therefore, beginning as early as the Mixtón War (1540–1541), the Crown initiated a policy of establishing colonies of Christianized Indians in the troubled north. These sedentary Indians, established on the northern frontier of New Spain, were to have considerable effect on the culture of the region. Tlaxcaltecans, Aztecs, Otomí, Tarascans, and other central Mexican natives introduced not only Spanish culture, but many elements of the Mesoamerican "great tradition" as well. It is therefore worth examining this movement in order to develop an understanding of the modern culture of the frontier of northern Mexico.

The first massive intrusion of Mesoamerican Indians into northern New Spain actually was to the west and north of the later areas of major Indian resettlement. It came in 1539 with the Marcos journey to the Greater Southwest and – in the following three years – with the exploring and colonizing party of Coronado. The Marcos party was small and we know the name of only one of the Indians. This was a certain Marcos "whom I had brought from Mexico" (Pecheco, et al. 1864–1884; vol. 3, p. 347). The following year Coronado advanced on New Mexico with over three hundred Spanish soldiers and several hundred Indians (Riley 1971: 295). Some of the Mesoamerican Indians remained in the American Southwest, others perhaps in northern Mexico. Several have been identified by name; they come from Mexico City, from Guadalajara, from the Tarascan area, and from Tlatelolco (Riley i.p.). No Tlaxcaltecans are specifically mentioned – interestingly in view of their later role in colonization of the northern frontier. However, there are hints that such Indians may have been early in the southwest. In accounts of the Chamuscado-Rodriguez expedition (1581–1582), a large pueblo, likely Pecos, is described as Nueva Tlaxcala (Hammond and Rey 1966: 59–60). This could indicate that the Tlaxcaltecans were found here. The Espejo expedition (1582–1583), for example, found "a Mexican Indian of those with Coronado, bold and daring" (de Obregón 1924: 299), though there is no further identification of this man. Conceivably Nueva Tlaxcala could have been named by or for Tlaxcaltecan Indians in the party (Simmons 1964) or indeed, the site – in someone's eyes – may simply have looked like Tlaxcala.

At any rate, there were Mexican Indians a few years later with Oñate (1599),some of whom settled in New Mexico. The city of Santa Fe had a Mexican Indian *barrio* called Analco apparently settled shortly after the founding of Santa Fe (Simmons 1964: 108). The identity of these Indians is far from clear (Adams and Chávez 1956: 304, note 2), but Simmons thinks that a majority were Tlaxcatecans (Simmons 1964: 108–110).

Although the Spanish made an early penetration up the west coast of Mexico to the upper southwest, they were soon deflected by rich silver strikes to the northern interior of Mexico. Although this region (modern Durango, Zacatecas, Chihuahua, Coahuila, Nuevo León, etc.) was rich in mineral wealth and had great potential for cattle ranching, it also was the home of roving bands of "Chichimec" Indians. Dealing with these wild nomads presented a more difficult problem for the Spanish than the Mesoamerican peasants, who had been subjected with relative ease. Fighting the northern tribes was very frustrating to the Spaniards; they complained bitterly that the cost in life and property of the Frontier Wars greatly exceeded the losses suffered during the conquest of the Aztec empire.

The Spanish first tried to protect this northern settlement by sending military expeditions against the Indians and by guarding convoys. This effort proved very expensive and did not greatly diminish Chichimec raids. The Spaniards then initiated a policy of total annihilation, reminiscent of many campaigns carried out against the Indians of Anglo-America.

Even during this early period of intensive hostility, with little direct contact, the culture of the nomadic Indians of the north was modified considerably. Groups such as the Guachichil and Zacateco Indians settled their differences and united against the common enemy. The authority of the war chiefs and priests increased, and mounted warriors fighting as coordinated units appeared. Horses, cattle, arms, knives, axes, cooking utensils, blankets and clothing were eagerly sought as booty of war.

In these early stages, Indian auxiliaries from the civilized tribes of central Mexico saw extensive service in warfare, road building, and colonization. By 1585, the Marqués de Villamanrique, then Viceroy of New Spain, initiated a policy of pacification through the giving of extensive gifts, reminiscent of the successful practices of France and England in cementing friendships with North American Indians. This policy had the desired effect, because the nomadic Indian became increasingly dependent upon European food and trade goods, and it was cheaper to increase this dependence through gifts than to have continual warfare.

This process is well described in Philip Wayne Powell's book (1969) on the northward advance of New Spain. Powell lists such items as metal tools and cloth from far-flung places – London, China, and the Philippines – which were included in these shipments. Materials of Mesoamerican origin (bolts of cloth, blankets, shoes, and plain and fancy *huipiles*) are almost always included in the lists. *Comales* made of metal were also becoming quite popular (Powell 1969: 73).

We are also indebted to Powell for a detailed description of the circumstances under which Tlaxcaltecans were recruited for northern colonization (1969: 195). Also valuable is material collected by the Mexican historian Vito Alessio Robles (Alessio Robles 1931).

The eighth Viceroy of New Spain, Don Luis de Velasco, continued the earlier practice of settling Christianized Indians on the northern frontier by recruiting 932 settlers from the lordships of Tlaxcala to be settled in the vicinity of San Luis Potosí and Saltillo. The capitulations agreed upon by the Tlaxcaltecans and the viceroy show that the special privileges afforded the colonizing Indians were confirmed and expanded upon in order to get them to migrate to the north (Powell 1969: 196):

The Tlaxcalan settlers in the Chichimeca country and their descendants shall be hidalgos in perpetuity, free from tributes, taxes, and personal service for all time.
They are not to be compelled to settle with Spaniards, but will be allowed to settle apart from them and have their own distinct districts [barrios]. No Spaniard can take or buy . . . within the Tlaxcalan districts.
The Tlaxcalans are to be at all times settled apart from the Chichimecas,

and this distinction is to apply to all of their lots, pastures, wooded lands, rivers, salt beds, mills, and fishing rights.

No grants for *ganado mayor* are to be allowed within five leagues of the Tlaxcalan settlements.

No *ganado menor* is to be allowed pasturage on the grain lands of the Tlaxcalans without their permission or that of their descendants.

The lands and estancias granted the individual Tlaxcalans and the community as a whole are never to be alienated because of nonoccupation.

The markets in the new settlements shall be free, exempt from sales tax, from excise taxes, and from any other form of taxation.

The Tlaxcalan colonists and their descendants, besides being hidalgos and free from all tribute, shall henceforth enjoy all exemptions and privileges already granted, or to be granted in the future, to the province and the city of Tlaxcala.

The principales of Tlaxcala who move to the new settlements, and their descendants, shall be permitted to carry arms and to ride saddled horses without penalty. For the journey itself, they shall be provided with the necessary provisions and clothing, and this shall continue for two years. In addition they shall receive aid in the cultivation of their fields for the same amount of time.

The Tlaxcalans shall be given a charter of written guarantees and a royal provision commanding that these capitulations be observed.

The Tlaxcaltecans began their northern migration in July of 1591.[1] Much of the nobility of the ancient Republic of Tlaxcala went with the group assisted by Franciscan friars and Spanish officials. Diego Muñoz de Camargo (1892), who was the mestizo author of *Historia de Tlaxcala*, traveled north with the migrants to help apportion the Indian lands near the town of San Luis Potosí. The description of the founders taking up the new lands throws much light on the cultural interactions between the Tlaxcaltecans and the wild Indians of the north (Powell 1969: 214):

As the expedition neared the site of their new lands, the Chichimecas came out along the road to welcome them and escort them to the edge of the lands where the Chichimecas themselves had been settled. The Tlaxcalans and the Chichimecas camped together at this point. Here also Captain Miguel Caldera pointed out to the Tlaxcalans the lands that had been set aside for them, lying between the river to Tlaxcalilla and the main road to the San Luis Potosí mines.

On November 2, 1591, Padre Fray Ignacio de Cardenas of the Franciscan order, Don Francisco Vázquez Coronado, and other principales of the Tlaxcalans appeared before Muñoz Camargo and presented the viceregal order regarding their grants of land and asked that these instructions be carried out. Muñoz Camargo took the viceregal provision, kissed it, placed it on his head, and promised to obey it. He then had Juan Tensso and Miquel Caldera, Chichimeca chieftains, appear before him, and through an interpreter he explained to them why he had come to settle and found his new town with the Tlaxcalans. The Chichimeca chiefs replied that they were content to live with the Tlaxcalans, whom they considered welcome because they were

[1]   Alessio Robles (1931) published the list of the Tlaxcaltecans, all from the *barrio* of Tizatlán, who founded San Esteban de la Nueva Tlaxcala next to the Spanish villa of Santiago de Saltillo in 1591.

relatives, and they expressed gratitude to the viceroy for having sent the Tlaxcalans to live among them and for having granted lands to the Chichimecas. On behalf of their people, Tensso and Caldera expressed the wish to divide their lands, forests, pastures, watering places, lime pits, and livestock lands, and all of their own free will. Muñoz Camargo then reconfirmed the Guachichil titles to half their lands; the other half was given to the Tlaxcalans. This action was witnessed by Padre Fray Pedro de Heredia, guardian of the Franciscan convent at Charcas Nuevas, Padre Fray Juan de Cervantes, and Andrés de Fonseca, a soldier.

On the same day, immediately following this initial ceremony, Muñoz Camargo went to a point below the town of Mexquitic where there was an arroyo containing water. Here he gave to Vázquez Coronado, to the other Tlaxcalan chief men, and to the Chichimecas possession of the lands downward from the arroyo forming a watered valley more than a league long. This was divided equally between the Tlaxcalans and the Guachichiles. Symbolically, Muñoz Camargo took the leaders of both groups by the hands and led them to their new lands; then after certain other ceremonies, the Indians pulled up grass and threw rocks in sign of possession.

The Tlaxcalans were also given possession in perpetuity of half the lands in the jurisdiction of the town of Mexquitic, especially the town of San Luís and all other towns and districts within the jurisdiction, including the waters called Espíritu Santo and Las Salinas, and other sites where they could establish settlements. They also took possession of the Bocas de Maticoya, where some rancherías of Chichimecas had been recently brought to peace through the efforts of Juan Tensso, Pedro de Tores and other Chichimeca captains.

The rest of the group continued north to Saltillo and beyond to the Spanish villa of Santiago de Saltillo. Here the hard-pressed Spaniards accepted the Tlaxcaltecans and divided their lands with them under the direction of Francisco de Urdiñola. This time the land was taken from the Spanish settlement which had suffered severe depopulation due to the wars against the nomadic Indians who surrounded them on all sides. Alessio Robles had published the account of the foundation of San Esteban de la Nueva Tlaxcala (1931: 182–184):

The Tlaxcaltecan pilgrimage must have moved very slowly as nearly two months passed between their departure from Tlaxcala and September 2, 1591 when Urdiñola began to divide up the land among the new settlers. On that day Urdiñola presented his documents before Cristobal Pérez, Lieutenant of the Alcalde Mayor, Juan Nevarro and Diego Montemayor, Alcaldes Ordinarios, and Alberto del Canto, magistrate of the villa of Saltillo. These men let him proceed with the orders of the Governor and named as scribe, Gasper Duarte, a settler of this villa. They asked the municipal government to indicate the lands that should be given to the Tlaxcalans and the Guachichiles who were to live in the same town. They sent notice of these matters to the magistrate Miguel Muñoz who was gravely ill. The town council met in a house on the plaza where they made a survey and after consulting with the justice, council and municipality they told him that the best part for the new settlers was by two springs that were located below the houses of Santos Rojo and that they would cede three fourths of the water from the little falls (Saltillo) for the Tlaxcaltecans. They were notified that the Indians wished to see the lands

and springs in the company of Fray Juan Torrones, the town council of Saltillo and the leaders of the Tlaxcaltecans. They named Martín de Solis of Saltillo as interpreter. They accompanied Urdiñola to view the lands. . . .
They showed the best and most fertile lands to the Indians for their use . . . . In the name of the Viceroy of New Spain he set out the lands for the Tlaxcaltecans to the east of the villa of Saltillo, next to it on the high ground to the south. He named the places for the church, convent and houses of the Franciscans and to the South and extending in an easterly direction he indicated the site for the town of the Guachichiles and the other Nations that were at war, making known that the villa of Saltillo was the frontier between the Guachichil and Rayado Indians, who were at war with each other. The Guachichiles should not go beyond the villa to the north and the Rayados to the south. It was more convenient that they be congregated together under the tutelage of the Franciscans and the *political authority of the Tlaxcaltecans.* He gave the new town three fourths of the water from the spring that serves the villa and showed them the place for their plaza and market, for the royal houses, for the jail, hospital and for the communal houses . . . and the mill that is just below the falls by the spring.

This well-organized community of Tlaxcaltecan peasants prospered at Saltillo, as did the Chichimecs under their control. They grew famous for the transformation they worked on the hill above the Spanish town. Irrigation was developed and many fruit-bearing trees were planted as well as magueys brought from the south. The Indians also brought their traditional dances (Alessio Robles 1931: 189).

The Spanish community was under the jurisdiction of the *audiencia* of Nueva Galicia with its capital in Guadalajara, while the town of San Esteban de la Nueva Tlaxcala was directly under the authority of the viceroy.

This Tlaxcaltecan colony in the northern part of New Spain flourished. The question now arises as to how much influence this and other nuclei of Tlaxcaltecans had in the cultural development of northern New Spain and how long the Tlaxcaltecans were able to continue as a separate ethnic group. Because Powell's study is confined to the sixteenth and early seventeenth centuries, his information is understandably incomplete. His last reference to the Tlaxcaltecans states (1969; 215):

The Tlaxcalans maintained themselves as a separate entity until well into the next century. . . . Thus on April 27, 1622 the viceroy answered an appeal from the Tlaxcalans by ordering the justicia mayor of Tlaxcalilla and Mezquitic to bring an end to the harm being done the Tlaxcalans by the livestock of the Spaniards and the wagon and pack train robbers.

In attempting to fill in some of the cultural evolution of the Tlaxcaltecans, co-author John Hobgood consulted the Municipal Archives of Saltillo. One of the most useful documents to come to light during these investigations is a series of letters dating from 1799 to 1805 which deal with various matters relating to Tlaxcaltecan communities in northeastern New Spain.

A letter written for the Indians to Governor Germán Delgado and his council from the Tlaxcaltecan community of Santa María de Parras and the town of El Alamo,[2] petitioning a new protector for the Indians, indicated that this office was still in use at the beginning of the nineteenth century. The letter gives a list of complaints against the Spanish judges of Parras. The Tlaxcaltecans complain that

. . . the jail, the courthouse, and the residence of the Alcaldes Mayores when they are in office were built at the cost and sweat of the Indians, and that the Spanish justices had no right to take over these royal buildings for use as residences for themselves and their retainers.

The Indians also complained that they had loaned the building where they stored their archives for use as a courtroom and now they were having trouble getting back the use of it (Powell 1969: 215). The petition ends with a strong appeal for the appointment of a suitable protector and the redress of their wrongs. A second petition to the political and military governor of the province, Don Antonio Cordero, was also sent by the governor and town council of San Esteban, apparently in support of the Tlaxcaltecans of Parras, urging him to take action as "much time had elapsed" since their first petition was made. This second petition was dated December 9, 1799.

This indication of vigorously active Tlaxcaltecan communities at the turn of the nineteenth century needs to be balanced by the viewpoint of the Spanish authorities. In February of 1800 more information was requested concerning the expenses of the Indians and the public houses they laid claim to. Juan Antonio de Senusián, governor of Coahuila, and José Barela answered inquiries with a report that strongly attacked the "prideful, exaggerated claims of the Indians." Don Antonio Corderoy Bustamente was told that "the Indians wish to control these houses so they can continue to have whom they wish live in them." The report goes on to say that "the Indian Alcalde moved out on January 1, 1800 and since that time, except for a humble family of custodians, no one but the troops brought by the Governor to Parras had stayed there."

The report then covers some of the points raised by the Indians. The *Casa Real* of Parras is in bad condition because the Indians have not kept it in repair. As to the jail being built at their cost (*Legajo* 9 1799–1805: exp. 501–561):

Indeed it was built at the cost of the ancient Indians, but now it is falling to pieces and they do nothing. . .

[2] This letter has two sets of signatures, separated by the signature of Trinidad Delgado, the scribe from Parras who signed for those who could not write. The second set of signatures apparently represents Don Máximo Adriene and the Cabildo of El Alamo. Bictorine Curovedo was the second scribe. The name of "El Alamo" was later carried to the Mission of El Alamo at San Antonio, Texas, by a garrison that came from Parras.

The Indians want the "Casa Real" unoccupied so they can use it to house a protector that will defend them with much energy: and it is true if they get what they want it will not be so that they will live in peace, but they will become embroiled in more agitation. It would be better if the time they spent in this was instead dedicated to the vineyards that some of them own, and to the plantings on the commons. They give little or no care to these matters and they will never get a half reasonable harvest of seeds and their vineyards are much worse, and because of this each day their situation gets worse.

Apart from what has been said, it is well to reflect that there are not in this town perhaps three legitimate Indians by nature and these few do not ignore it because all that have parcels (of land) are mixed with mulattoes, negroes, lobos and the other castes; they exaggerate so much their exemptions and privileges that they should be very grateful that in the midst of this strife, the judges and the Spaniards [*vecinos*] in good faith defend their possession of the waters, and swear to this. . . . May Our Lord guard your life for many years. (Parras, February 1, 1800.)

This letter gives an idea of the racial mixing (*mestizaje*) taking place at this time, including an explanation of the gradual disappearance of blacks in northern New Spain by the end of the colonial era.

In spite of the report attacking the Tlaxcaltecans, Don Alberto de Noin, a resident of Saltillo, was appointed "Protector of the Indians" of the towns of San Esteban and Tlaxcala as well as Parras and El Alamo. Notice that the governor's wishes in this matter had been carried out was given to him on June 1, 1800. The speed with which the Indians' petitions were acted upon compares very favorably to the rate at which legal action in the field of civil rights is taken in the United States today.

However, in the Tlaxcaltecan settlement of Guadalupe (located near Monterrey) things were going badly. The Governor and Council of San Esteban, in their petition for a protector of the Indians, state that they should not have "personal service imposed on them as is happening in the town of Guadalupe, where they are demanding wood and hay and other necessities."

A cursory examination of the church archives at Parras indicates that local "wild Indians," after being civilized, tended to intermarry with elements of other recently reduced tribes settled at Parras. After a generation or two these mixed groups tended to be absorbed by the Tlaxcaltecans. This process can be observed through reading the baptismal and marriage records of Parras which often give the tribal affiliation of those involved.[3]

Several confraternities (*cofradías*) honoring various saints flourished in Parras over the centuries. Some of these associations were made up exclusively of Tlaxcaltecans. As these confraternities sur-

---

[3]   This information was called to my attention by Basil C. Hendrick, then Director of the Southern Illinois University Museum after he had catalogued the Parras archives in 1969.

vived through the latter part of the nineteenth century, it is possible to trace Tlaxcaltecan families long after they ceased being designated as such in church records.

Another document, in the Saltillo archives, dated 1793 (*Legajo 9* 1799–1805) is of importance for the entire north of New Spain. This report is a certified copy sent to the Governor of Coahuila of the transference of all the Franciscan missions in the northeast from the jurisdiction of Pachuca to the jurisdiction of the mother house of Chihuahua. This report was compiled at Montclova, so that the Indians would not "be cut short from the good administration and spiritual sustenance that they need." For the seven missions of this province, a complete census is given by age, sex and civil state. All livestock is listed, down to the last goat, and a complete inventory is given of the stores, down to the last axe and hoe (the census was completed in the year 1794). The only information wanting is the tribal affiliation of those occupying each mission but this information can be ascertained from other sources. This forty-five page document is well worth publishing in its entirety, but we will confine ourselves to the advice it gives on how Tlaxcaltecan Indians can be utilized in sustaining and expanding the Franciscan missions on the northeastern frontier. The role of the Tlaxcaltecans in developing the northern missions from Montclova to the Río Grande and beyond is described in this report (*Legajo 9* 1799–1805: 1):

The Missions of Nuestra Señora de la Victoria de Nadadores, San Bernadino de la Candela and even the Mission of San Miguel de Aguayo are united under the Mission of San Francisco de Tlaxcala populated by Tlaxcaltecans. It would be very bad for the Indians if the Missions were suppressed and they were put under the secular clergy.

The founding date for the Mission of Santa Rosa de Nadadores is uncertain but existing documents indicate a time around 1675. In 1732, because the Mission was reduced to only six individuals, one of whom was blind, and considering the importance of conserving this outpost, the Viceroy Marqués de Casa Fuerte agreed to the petiton of the Governor of this province, Manual Sandoval, to allow that fifty parcels of land with their waters and irrigation ditches be made available to the Tlaxcaltecans of the town of San Esteban del Saltillo who volunteered to move there. . . .

Because of his fear of the enemies [wild Indians] who continually overran these lands, Sandoval combined the Tlaxcaltecans from the above mentioned town with those of. . .Montclova, and 52 individuals of both sexes and all ages took up the offer to form a Pueblo of Nuestra Señora de la Victoria Casa Fuerte de Nadadores with a population today of 536 souls.

This Mission of San Bernadino de la Candela was founded in 1690. In 1774 by decree of the Viceroy, Don Antonio María de Bucareli, the few Indians who remained in the Mission of San Miguel de Aguayo were also incorporated, marking out the lands and waters to other Tlaxcaltecan families of the town of San Esteban del Saltillo, with whom they formed the town of Nuestra Señora of Guadalupe de la Candela (which today has a population of 596 souls).

The Mission of San Miguel de Luna, known today as Aguayo, was founded in 1675 and in 1690 they brought fourteen Tlaxcaltecan families from the town of San Esteban del Saltillo, with the object of instructing the local Indians in the cultivation of the land. Today the population is counted at 184 souls, that is from the fourteen original families, 418, or better said 955 adding to the 537 they have produced from the 52 that settled in Nadadores. . . .

With this you have the object of this procedure. We find that it hasn't merited the changing of this way of utilizing the Tlaxcaltecans for 115 years, just to get them to work the land so that it will bear fruit, but the land is always situated three or four hundred feet from the edge of the villa and even holdings of the Northern Indians were at twenty five paces before the Tlaxcaltecans were brought here. Thus they can emulate the sermons we give without the help of practical examples of people of the same quality, to inspire them with the necessary light to do good and to reprove the bad.

After describing the great utility of the Tlaxcaltecans in the past the report goes on to describe the lamentable conditions of the missions to the north, near the Presidio of the Río Grande and in Texas because of the incursions of the *indios bárbaros*. The writer then suggests that a chain of missions and presidios be developed to protect the northeastern frontier. Even in 1793 the utility of the Tlaxcaltecans for the establishment of new missions is stressed.

There is water enough for more towns and population than is needed for forming a string of settlements. Even if they do not entirely stop the raids of the barbarians, at least they will make it more difficult for them to make their horrible incursions if we have warning from Rio Grande and Aguaverde, which are situated in the best places to give the alarm. The formation of this chain of seven towns. . . but without including the ranches that are now abandoned, but which will have to be repopulated, nor the villa of San Fernando that will remain the base of operations.

It will not take more than 24 Tlaxcaltecan families from the surplus population. . . the towns of San Esteban del Saltillo, San Francisco Montcova and the Boca de Tlaxcala in the Kingdom of León [now the state of Nuevo León] encouraging them to settle with just incentives to improve their situation. Those incentives [for settlement will be] some gifts useful for working the land and the construction of some temporary huts as well as giving them permission to graze some cattle and horses in the Province of Texas without paying the royal tax of two reales per head. They should be given permission to leave the missions of San Bernardo and San Francisco de Nizarrón so that they can get new grants in the vicinity of the presidio of Río Grande, and locate them so they can guard the headwaters of the Santa Rita. I believe that this move will not have any bad results, as nothing remains but the material for building the churches and the house or convent of the Mission of Nizarrón. This material can be used at Dulce Nombre de Jesús and at San Bernardo. There will always be someone in Río Grande who will buy this material.[4]

Apparently there was some foot dragging in this matter on the part of the Tlaxcaltecans, for Galindo Navarro wrote from Chihuahua on

[4]   Dated November 3, 1793, at Montclova, by Miguel Joseph de Imparán, this report was addressed to the Señor Comandante General Don Pedro de Nova. Manuel Marino made the certified copy.

September 1 1796, of the "great inconveniences" that would be caused for Indians of the missions by such a move. Then on October 1, 1799, Antonio Cordero wrote the Comandante General of Coahuila from Montclova expressing his opinion of the move. He began by doubting the utility of founding more pueblos without "active and energetic troops who know how to obey orders." Concerning the Tlaxcaltecans, he stated:

The Indians that make up the four missions under discussion. . . will not look with indifference at migrating from the places where they were born, raised and educated, and where at the cost of their sweat have not only lands that they have cultivated but their own homes, convents for their ministers, and lastly churches where the bones of their ancestors lie. These remembrances are a part of them; they, like all Indians, have an attitude towards the dead that they consider the first of their obligations. So if you take them from the opportunity of making their frequent commemorations at the tombs of their fathers it would be a terrible blow for them to suffer. Considering that, and their violent feelings in this matter, it would be most difficult to persuade them that this move would benefit them. You might get a few, but I am persuaded that this would cause a general feeling of disgust that would strengthen their resolve not to dedicate themselves to the development of their new settlements, fearing that we will do to their descendants what we are doing to them.

The Lipan [Apaches] are beginning to be civilized. They have begun to depend upon us and have asked to settle near our towns and their petitions to the Captain General of Mexico to settle along the Rio Saldao are encouraging. Their character is not as barbarous as that of the other gentiles. The war they wage with the nations to the north creates a set of circumstances to give us hope that in a few years they will give up the rest of their barbarisms and surrender to the yoke of religion and vassalage.

When this happy day arrives, it would be well to place these neophytes in the missions offering them lands for the labor of their hands and the example of older inhabitants that they find living there, and under the direction of the religious who through their knowledge and piety know how to get them to embrace, without violence, a civil and Christian life, dramatically opposed to the errant and licentious life that they abandon. Because of this I am of the opinion that. . . if you go ahead and apportion the communities of the Indians of the four missions of this province without separating them from their present destinations, giving them the waters and lands that they can cultivate. . . you can show with time, the same surplus of population mentioned by the Spaniards of the jurisdiction of Río Grande. . .

A report dated May 13, 1800, at Chihuahua, sent to the Comandante General at Montclova by Antonio Cordero, gives the details of the founding of the new villa near the Presidio of Río Grande:

The settlers were 48. Twenty four Spaniards that could be included among those with land grants at Río Grande (not all of them were grantees) and others from towns of this province whose background, pure blood and willingness to work and good customs are vouched for. . . and the other twenty-four, Tlaxcaltecan Indians, pure and of good circumstances, and who presented themselves voluntarily from the towns of San Esteban del Saltillo, San

Francisco de Coahuilla, Nuestra Señora de la Victoria de Nadadores and San Carlos de Cardela. The water was divided into two equal parts and dividing each division into thirty days for irrigation (as is the custom) each settler has water for one day a month with an extra five days each term. . . . Both of these grants have not only the land and water necessary for the families who have them but they also have whatever would be needed by the whole Lipan Nation if they give up hunting and integrate themselves into civil life, where they can live without lacking anything from the land. . . It appears convenient to me to call these holdings the Lands of San Lucas, corresponding to the Mission of San Bernardo. They stretch for fourteen leagues of maize and other plantings and are only one league distant from the Presidio.

The Tlaxcaltecans were still colonizing and were still maintaining their identity on the eve of Hidalgo's Revolution. However, with the destruction of the Spanish power in Mexico, the special position of the Tlaxcaltecans ended.

The outline of changes undergone by the Tlaxcaltecan communities can be traced in broad outline. The Newbery Library in Chicago contains a document that proclaims the adherence of the Four Lords of Old Tlaxcala to Ferdinand VII during the Napoleonic troubles. In 1826, the year the Tlaxcaltecans of San Esteban were forced into union with Saltillo, Carlos María de Bustamante, a member of a prominent family from Guadalajara with close ties to the Mexican Presidency, wrote a book (1826) which utilized the Tlaxcaltecan experience as an effective source of anti-Spanish propaganda. This work outlines the decline of the Tlaxcaltecans in population and political influence under the reign of the Spaniards. Bustamante says very little about Tlaxcaltecan colonization and ends by lamenting that nothing remains of the glory that was Tlaxcala. This work and his book on the Mixtón War are mainly valuable for giving an Indian identification to the meaning of the term *La Raza*, which foreshadows the modern Chicano use of this term. The Mexican creoles began to adopt a somewhat idealized world view, while at the same time highlighting the special status of the Indians under the old Spanish colonial system.

We hear again briefly of the Tlaxcaltecans from a short article by George Gibbs (1863). Gibbs obtained his information from a William Alexander of Austin, Texas, who was well acquainted with Mexico. Alexander must have talked to Tlaxcaltecans, judging from the tenor of his report (Gibbs 1863: 99–100).

He states that while the Spaniards were ashamed to enslave their republican allies, they were yet afraid to leave so numerous and warlike a population in one body, and that they adopted the plan of dividing and dispersing them through different parts of the country, under various pretexts, granting them lands in perpetuity and inalienable. This latter character continued to exist until the liberals gained the supremacy under Juarez and others. Among the parties thus severed from the parent stock, was one, the descendants of which still inhabit the neighborhood of Saltillo, in the state of Coahuila, where they occupy a sitio of 4425 acres of land, embracing part of the city itself. Their lands are subdivided into small sections which are irrigated and well tilled, and they have fine orchards and raise corn, the small grains, vegetables and maguey. They all speak Spanish in addition to their native language, and are citizens, but until lately they had chiefs of their own besides the Spanish authorities. They probably number 2000 to 3000 souls. Another similar colony known as the Pueblo of Guadalupe, is situated in the immediate neighborhood of Monterrey. How much farther this dispersion may have been carried on in other directions, I have no present means of ascertaining.

It is not of course to be inferred that the entire nation of the Tlaxcaltexas was broken up. A large body of course remained behind. According to Humboldt there were in 1793 in the government of Tlaxcalla, in the Intendency of Puelba, 59,177 souls; whereof 21,549 were male and 21,029 female Indians who were governed by a Cacique and four Indian Alcaldes, and were under the dependence of an Indian Governor, himself subject to the Spanish Intendent. Still it would seem probably that enough were thus colonized apart to render this people no longer a terror to their "allies."

At the time of the reforms of Juárez, the Tlaxcaltecans seem to have lost the last of their official recognition, even at the municipal level. We have found no material relating to their fate until a short article appearing in Tlalocán in 1966. At this time the ethnologist Serjio Morales Rodriguez interviewed Don Cesareo Rayes, one of the last Nahuatl-speaking residents of the old Tlaxcaltecan *barrio* of Saltillo. By this time according to Rayes, "Those of one nation have inter-married with those of the other nation; since that time everyone became the same" (Morales Rodríguez 1949: 84–86).

In looking at Saltillo today, one finds that there are still some Indian influences in the old Tlaxcaltecan *barrio* on the hill. Some still call it the *barrio* of the *Tecos*, the nickname for any descendant of the Indian community. The gardens and trees are now almost all gone because of repeated subdivision of the old lots. Most of the homes are humble and new people have settled in among them. The parish of Ojo de Agua and that of Santa Ana still have *danzas tlaxcaltecas* where the dance of the *matachines* is performed at all of the important festivals. There are many individuals on the "Hill of the *Tecos*" who still consider themselves Indians or descendants of Indians.

This group has acted as a cultural broker in the past, helping the nomadic Indians of the north and the European and *mestizos* from the south to create the modern Mexican state. Today any study of the modern Mexican and his cultural identity is enhanced by a knowledge of the "*Tecos*" and their cultural impact upon Mexico.

REFERENCES

ADAMS, ELEANOR B., FRAY ANGÉLICO CHÁVEZ
1956   *The missions of New Mexico*, 1776. Albuquerque: University of New Mexico Press.
ALESSIO ROBLES, VITO
1931   *Francisco de Urdiñola y el norte de la Nueva España*. Mexico City.
DE BUSTAMANTE, CARLOS MARÍA
1826   *Necesidad de la unión de todos los mexicanos*.... Mexico City: Aguila.
DE OBREGÓN, BALTASAR
1924   *Historia de los descubrimientos antiguos y modernas*.... Edited by M. Cuevas, 299. Mexico City: Señoria de Educación.
GIBBS, GEORGE
1863   Note on the dispersion of the Tlascaltecas. *The Historical Magazine* 7(3): 99–100.
HAMMOND, GEORGE P., AGAPITO REY
1966   *The rediscovery of New Mexico 1580–1594*. Albuquerque: University of New Mexico Press.
Legajo 9, exp. 501–561
1799–1805   Unpublished letters and documents, Archivos Municipales, Saltillo, Mexico.
MORALES RODRÍGUEZ, SERJIO
1949   "El náhuatl de los tlaxcaltecos de San Esteban de la Neuva Tlaxcala," in *Tlalocán*, volume three: 84–86.
MUÑOZ DE CAMARGO, DIEGO
1892   *Historia de Tlaxcala*. Edited by Alfredo Chavero. Mexico City: Sec. de Poment.
PECHECO, JOAQUÍN F., *et al.*
1864–1884   *Colección de documentos inéditos relativos al descubrimiento conquista y organización de las antiguas posesiónes españoles de América y Oceania*, forty-two volumes. Madrid.
POWELL, PHILIP WAYNE
1969   *Soldiers, Indians and silver*. Berkeley: University of California Press.
RILEY, CARROLL L.
1971   Early Spanish-Indian communication in the Greater Southwest. *New Mexico Historical Review* 46(4): 285–314.
i.p.   Meso-American Indians in the early southwest. *América Indígena*.
SIMMONS, MARC
1964   Tlascalans in the Spanish borderlands. *New Mexico Historical Review* 29(2): 101–110.

PART FOUR

Painting, Hieroglyphs, Ceramics, and Mythology

Introduction

A tremendous amount of data is hidden in the artistic designs and motifs on the ancient Mesoamerican artifacts, relating both to the supernatural and the secular, which can be extracted if the correct questions are asked or if the proper methodological technique is applied. Most of the papers in this section deal with the variety of approaches toward reconstruction or explication, using as data a particular corpus of artistic motifs and symbols.

Kinzhalov's postulated reconstruction of the Olmec mythological system is particularly interesting and useful since it provides us now with a third major set of hypotheses to work with in attempting to reconstitute Olmec religious beliefs. One previous approach was that of Furst (1968), looking at a corpus of ethnographic data on were-jaguar motifs in the New World to generate a generalized model. A second approach was based on a reconstructed pantheon, assuming that the Olmec pantheon was a direct historical forerunner of the ethnohistorically known Aztec and Mayan pantheons, a methodology applied by Joralemon (1971), Coe (1972), and Grove (1972). Kinzhalov's is a third approach, predicated on the belief that the Olmec pantheon may not necessarily correlate with either the ethnographic or the ethnohistoric data; his methodology is to attempt to formulate a mythology consistent with the known mythological Olmec themes, but which in a sense is self-generating.

The Olmec mythology is seen to have sprung from a trilogy – a prime mover, a polysemantic, multifunctional "goddess with braids," embodying heaven and earth, life and death; her son, the "fat god," and an aged "bearded god," presumably the fat God's father. Kinzhalov believes that under the Olmec, these deities were given new images in a constrained functional framework; thus the goddess with braids breeds with the lord of the earth, a jaguar, giving birth to male were-jaguar twins, one of whom becomes the water god, and the other the fat god, maize incarnate. Later Olmec mythology is seen in part as a clash of ideologies between the bearded god and the fat god; the famous colossal heads are seen as icons in a cult of severed heads as monuments to the fat god as the deity of maize. Kinzhalov has thus presented us with a new set of postulates, starting from a different frame of reference, for reconstructing Olmec mythology, and thereby measurably enhances our possibilities of finally generating a set of rules replicating the actual Olmec belief system.

Quirarte deals with the sticky problem of Teotihuacán influence in the Mayan Petén area. Teotihuacán traits are clearly present, but the significance of the traits is debated. Some have argued that the vessels exhibiting these traits were produced by Teotihuacán artisans imported into the Mayan area; others have maintained that the vessels were trade goods, produced in Teotihuacán and traded into Mayan sites; and still others have suggested that the vessels were nearly exact copies made by Mayan artisans. Basic to the resolution of this question is an adequate definition of the ceramic vocabularies and morphologies of the potters involved. Quirarte defines the visual surface of the Mayan, the visual compartmentalization, and the spatial hierarchy of the designs. Through rigorous reconstruction of Mayan artistic spatial conceptions, Quirarte is able to demonstrate that, while the motifs, particularly the personages, are Teotihuacán in inspiration, the conceptualization and resolution are definitely Mayan, so that in the sample studied from Kaminaljuyu and Petén, there were no vessels fabricated by Teotihuacán artists; rather, these vessels were constructed from Teotihuacán models based on Mayan artistic perceptions. This kind of data allows us to proceed from the realm of speculation toward some firm hypotheses on the actual Teotihuacán-Mayan interaction; such studies provide new insight into the relative political and prestige relationships between the Mayans and the Teotihuacanos.

The contributions of Galarza, Corona Olea, and Landar focus on the proper interpretation and translation of Aztec or Méxica hieroglyphic symbols. Each author approaches the problem from a slightly different perspective. Galarza suggests starting from scratch, and offers an outline for a detailed and systematic methodology for the analysis of these hieroglyphs. Because Nahuatl is still spoken in Mexico, because traditional Aztec writing continued until the eighteenth century, and because there are transcriptions of some of the characters by early Spanish clerics, Galarza believes that a systematic approach will allow us to decode these hieroglyphic symbols quite accurately.

Landar takes a different approach. Using principles of lexico-statistics and glottochronology, he goes through a number of sources trying to reconstruct counting systems for Proto-Mayan, Proto-Uto-Azteca, and other protolanguage families at particular points of time, in an attempt to explain better the available hieroglyphic translations of Aztec day names and numbers. The approach is an interesting attempt to bring archaeological and linguistic data together, although the archaeological data is rather roughly handled. An interesting hypothesis generated is that the Toltec were archaic Aztec speakers, and that Toltec merchants reaching Gran Chichimeca about A.D. 750 spread the language and the culture, such that the Chichimecans were partly sedentarized and Toltecized prior to the invasions of the twelfth and thirteenth centuries.

Corona Olea's approach to the hieroglyphic meaning problem is one of attempting to translate a portion of a Mexicatl text from the *Codex Mendoza*, giving a literal translation, and then a reconstructed historical translation. The paper is useful not only in terms of Corona Olea's interpretation of the glyphic text, but also in terms of the chronological table which he constructed relating to the events in his translation.

Elliott's short discourse on the differences between painting and glyphic scripts is an attempt to further elaborate the problems that Quirarte, Galarza, and Corona Olea were struggling with in translating and interpreting the Mexican materials. His approach using examples from throughout the world made his paper more meaningful to many participants.

The final two papers deal with the artistic themes peripheral to the main Mesoamerican culture area, but in areas still crucial to its definition. Aguilar's study on the grave goods recovered from the Las Pavas site near San José, Costa Rica, is of importance particularly since it is one of the few sites in the country not vandalized (Heath 1973). The materials described appear to correlate with the Aguas Buenas and Catalina phases of Costa Rica (Stone 1972), dating approximately A.D. 0–300, thus making these shaft tombs the earliest yet reported for Costa Rica.

Bullen attempts the very difficult problem of seriation of petro-glyphs, a very frustrating task since in most cases they are completely without any cultural associations. Bullen argues that petroglyphs have too long been overlooked and that they should be studied to cast new light on the migration and origins of cultural groups, to show the spread of religious or ceremonial cult ideas, and to help reconstruct religious beliefs and pantheons. His seven groupings of petroglyphs from the Antilles include the cultural significance, ideas on origins, and the approximate time period which he believes each grouping can be assigned. Most of these are associated with Arawak or pre-Arawak inhabitants (rather than Caribs). He sees discrete correlations between both Venezuela and Central America for certain of the motifs.

REFERENCES

COE, M. D.
  1972   "Olmec jaguars and Olmec kings," in *The cult of the feline: a conference in pre-Columbian iconography.* Edited by E. P. Benson, 1–18. Dumbarton Oaks, Washington, D.C.
FURST, P. T.
  1968   "The Olmec were-jaguar motif in the light of ethnographic reality," in *Dumbarton Oaks Conference on the Olmec.* Edited by E. P. Benson, 143–175. Dumbarton Oaks, Washington D.C.
GROVE, D. C.
  1972   "Olmec felines in highland central Mexico," in *The cult of the feline: a conference in pre-Columbian iconography.* Edited by E. P. Benson, 153–164. Dumbarton Oaks, Washington, DC.
HEATH, D. B.
  1973   Economic aspects of commercial archaeology in Costa Rica. *American Antiquity* 38(3): 259–265. Washington, D.C.
JORALEMON, P. D.
  1971   *A study of Olmec iconography.* Studies in pre-Columbian art and iconography 7. Dumbarton Oaks, Washington D.C.
STONE, D.
  1972   *Pre-Columbian man finds Central American: the archaeological bridge.* Cambridge, Mass.: Peabody Museum Press.

Toward the Reconstruction of the Olmec Mythological System

R. V. KINZHALOV

Over the past two decades, archaeological excavations and accidental findings have considerably augmented the stock of monumental sculpture, clay and jade figurines, celts, and so on, belonging to the Tenocelome culture – the Olmecs. For the first time, specimens of Olmec murals have been discovered and numerous works concerned with Olmec archaeology and culture have appeared.[1]

However, there is a great deal of controversy among researchers regarding interpretations of the characters and themes depicted on the Olmec monuments. This study attempts to determine the pantheon of the Olmecs and reconstruct their principal mythological cycles on the basis of both Olmec iconography and the later Mesoamerican written sources in which Olmec myths are recorded. The author subscribes to the view that Olmec religious ideas were decisive in shaping the subsequent Mesoamerican mythologies, and hence the latter may be useful for reconstructing the former. Thus, as we see it, Aztec reports are incomparably more helpful for the understanding of Olmec mythology than, say, Maya material of the Classic Period. But the Olmec-Aztec relationship undoubtedly calls for special study.

It is common knowledge that the time when a given myth is written down or perpetuated by pictorial means has no direct correlation with

[1] The limited scope of this study has prevented me from substantiating my propositions fully and giving a complete list of references. We have drawn on the works of the following scholars: Y. V. Knorozov, W. Y. Propp, I. I. Tolstoy, J. M. Tronskiy, J. Bernal, F. Blom and O. La Farge, A. Caso, M. D. Coe, C. Cook de Leonard, M. Covarrubias, P. Drucker, D. Grove, R. F. Heizer, W. Jiménez Moreno, G. Kubler, A. Medellín Zenil, M. W. Stirling, T. Smith, G. C. Vaillant, C. R. Wicke and G. R. Willey, as well as on the collection *Dumbarton Oaks Conference on the Olmecs*, Washington, 1968; *Contributions of the University of California Archaeological Research Facility* 1–5, 1965–1968, etc. No references are given pertaining to the publications of monuments.

the phase of development of this myth. To put it differently, fairly late monuments can be expected to represent a very early version of a myth. For this reason one feels justified in drawing on folklore as well.

In a previous work (Kinzhalov 1970) I tried to define the principal stages in the development of Mesoamerican mythology and arrived at three main mythological systems. The Olmec system is, in my opinion, the second one. It will be useful, therefore, to characterize briefly the first system before passing to the Olmec material proper. (The systems in question are not to be confused with cycles of legends.)

In this mythological system, the most ancient of those represented by the archaeological monuments of Mesoamerica, the supreme and omnipotent deity is the "goddess with braids." This mythological figure is the product of the earlier ideas about the spirits of the vegetable and animal world. The goddess with braids is an embodiment of both heaven and earth, life and death; the milk of heaven – rain – flows from her breasts; she is the ruler of all waters; the flourishing of the entire vegetable and animal worlds depends on her. Maize, the staple crop of the population of Mesoamerica, is her gift to humankind, In the subsequent systems, this deity was fragmented into several functionally specialized goddesses associated with waters, the moon, childbirth, maize, cacao, agave, and so on.

This polysemantic, multifunctional mythological image is paralleled by the polymorphism of the goddess's iconography. The goddess is completely anthropomorphic in artistic representations, and the iconography of her image is extremely varied for the above reasons. She may prop up her breasts with her hands or hold a baby (in both cases the symbolism is clear). She may be depicted as a woman in her prime with emphasized attributes of sex (breasts, thigh, etc.) or as a slender girl with four long braids hanging down over her breasts in two pairs. Sometimes she is depicted as an old woman with sagging breasts. The three phases of a woman's development – youth, the prime of life, and old age – are thus likened to the three seasons of the natural cycle: the bloom of spring, fruit-bearing, and the autumn-winter period. There is a unique figurine which represents this concept the most graphically, with a triple torso (unfortunately, the head of the figurine is missing). The dual nature of the goddess is still rather primitively expressed: she is sometimes depicted with two heads. On stylized seals from Guerrero she is shown writhing like a woman in labor, there is a sun in her belly (cf. the late images of Huitzilopochtli).[2]

[2] The stone stelae of Manabi (Ecuador) offer an opportunity to observe the gradual transformation of this figure into a spider, a being also associated with the cult of the mother goddess.

However, non-anthropomorphic images of this goddess also occur on art monuments. The most frequent symbol of the goddess as the ruler of waters is the duck. A relic related to the next system – monument 9 from San Lorenzo (Tenochtitlán) – supports this idea fully. The goddess was apparently also visualized as a two-headed monster (the same duality of heaven and earth); later Aztec material bears this out.

The goddess with braids has a son, the "fat god," depicted as a plump infant devoid of any outward characteristics of sex, most often in a sitting posture with his hands crossed on his belly. His function is to mediate between his mother and the humans and to ensure the well-being of the community. In all probability, this god is an incarnation of both maize and the sun. (Later, this mythological image was fragmented into several individual deities: the young god of maize, the young god of the sun, the god of spring blossoming, like the Aztecs' Xipe-Totec.) It is precisely the plumpness of the infant that conveys the idea of fertility. His connection with his mother is stressed on a seal from Tlatilco, showing a duck's head crowning a spiral; the latter is surrounded by teeth symbolizing sumbeams. As a matter of fact, the same idea is expressed in some later monuments, such as the famed Tuxtla figurine and monument 5 from Cerro de las Mesas (the ithyphallism of the latter strongly conveys the idea of fertility). It still remains to clarify the connection of this image with the ritual ball game ard the monkey whose images occur on some monuments.

The pantheon of that time features one more figure: an aged, bearded man – a precursor, it is suggested, of the old god of fire and earthquakes. This god may also have been visualized as the old god of the sun and hence the father of the fat god but his connection with the goddess with braids in this system is not yet clear.

Olmec mythology, having sprung from the above concepts, reformulated them substantially. The reason for this should be sought in the further evolution of Mesoamerican society. As the Olmecs had mastered new, progressive farming techniques, they left all the surrounding peoples far behind in terms of sociocultural development (Kinzhalov 1971: 74–78). Accordingly, the chief accomplishments of the preceding epoch were relegated to the sphere of religious ideology, where they were transformed into a set of immutable mythological concepts which become "fashionable" and obligatory for the new ethnic groups arising somewhat later around the Olmecs.

Scholars have long noted that the cult of the jaguar was extremely widespread among the Olmecs. Yet two important points had been neglected: (a) why was it that the jaguar, and not some other animal, became the central figure of the mythology, and (b) could it be that the jaguar image was only a form disguising a variety of mythological phenomena? Both these points have been clarified today. Y. V.

Knorozov (personal communication) has suggested an ingenious theory explaining the original causes behind the association of the jaguar with agricultural cults: forest herbivora were the greatest source of damage to the crops raised by people who had taken up farming, and so the jaguar, the lord of the forest who scared away the animals and never touched the maize himself, was regarded as the protector of fields and farmers. M. D. Coe (1968: 111–114) has convincingly proved, on the other hand, that in the Olmec period several deities, not one, were ascribed the aspect of the jaguar.[3]

It should be noted in passing that during the period under discussion, the mythological images were particularly stable and each was fitted into a certain functional framework. This process found its reflection in iconography as well. The former polymorphism was replaced by certain canonical features (or features which were becoming canonical) in the images of deities.

In this new mythological system, the goddess with braids lost her former importance and omnipotence. She became the wife or mistress of the lord of the depth of the earth, depicted as a tapir or jaguar.[4] From their union (monument of Río Chiquito 1 and monument 3 of Potrero Nuevo seen to represent their lovemaking) sprang male twins, part human, part jaguar. (The mother's duality in this system is thereby transferred to her sons.) One of the twins represents the water element and by weeping invokes rain; the other, a transformation of the fat god, incarnates maize. In most cases these two gods are depicted as infants. Their iconography still remains to be developed in greater detail, for, in our opinion, scholars often fail to distinguish between them. Be this as it may, M. D. Coe's observation (1968) that some images on ritual celts portray at least two mythical beings seems indisputable. We believe that one iconographic type with a cleft in the head and the arms folded on the belly, represents the myth of the young god of maize,[5] which is why this god is often shown on

[3] This idea is supported by the jade figurines from Guanacaste (Costa Rica), depicting flying were-jaguars with bat wings.

[4] I have omitted the problems of the possible genetic connection of this image with the bear – the father of the twins in the mythology of Siberian and North American tribes. Painting 1-o in the northern grotto of Oxtotitlán cave offers an interesting version of the myth where the male element is represented by a man (Grove 1970: 44). We believe that this version is a relatively late one, reflecting certain changes in Olmec mythology.

[5] Gay's hypothesis (1966: 58) that this cleft is characteristic of female jaguar rites may be correct. In such a case, this Olmec deity is a precursor of Xochiquetzal of the Aztecs. The deity's coiffure consists of two knots, and in Codex Borgia 60 the goddess is depicted with two heads, in the act of childbirth. She is assisted by Quetzalcoatl (we shall come back to their connection). A V-shaped symbol is a customary ornament of her dress in the figurines. If this assumption is true, then the famous jade figurine from La Venta is a completely anthropomorphic image of the goddess. One should also remember that the later deities of maize (Cinteotl among others) had numerous female forms. Finally, is it just a chance coincidence that one of the twins of the Quiche epic is called Xbalanque which literally means "she-jaguar"?

engravings with a trefoil – the symbol of maize – growing out of this cleft. The other type of figure is depicted with the arms folded on the belly, one on top of the other. The various objects sometimes held represent some still-obscure details of the myth. Both these gods are depicted most clearly on the relief of altar 5 from La Venta (south side); characteristically, the personages carrying them differ in their headdress.

A number of art monuments, however, display vestiges of old beliefs or the side branches of the myth in which the goddess with braids was still supreme, e.g. rock relief 1 in Chalcatzingo which shows this goddess, as of old, an omnipotent deity. She sits on a throne placed in a cave depicted as a stylized mouth of the jaguar (which gives the idea that she rules over the earth). From the cave, volutes shoot up, symbolizing thunder and lightning; above are clouds from which beneficent rain is pouring down on the stalks of maize surrounding the cave. The goddess holds a bar bearing a symbolic image of a two-headed dragon (a precursor of the ceremonial bar of the Maya rulers). On stela 1 from La Venta, the goddess, rising from the depth of the earth, lacks all attributes of power. In all probability, the statues from La Venta (monument 44) and San Martín Pajapan depict the selfsame goddess, though the substance of the myth imprinted here has not been explained so far.

The unique clay figurine from Atlihuayan (Morelos) introduces a new version of the myth, unknown from other materials. It depicts an ordinary fat god slightly bent forward; the arms are in the customary position, the mouth is treated in the Olmec tradition. One is struck, first, by the peculiar eyelids shaped as tridents, and secondly, by the skin of an imaginary animal with four limbs, each ending in human hands thrown over the back and head of the god. The eyelids resemble a similar feature of the later Maya sun gods: hence we can safely assert that the main personage has a solar function which, it has been noted earlier, is characteristic of the fat god. The second detail – the skin covered with crosses (stylized stars?) – is more difficult to interpret. I am of the opinion that it represents a transformation of the heavenly dragon with the head of an iguana, i.e. the skin of the animal counterpart of the goddess with braids.[6] Hence this figurine shows the son under the aegis of his mother. Such a picture may be interpreted as a symbolic representation of the birth of the young god of the sun, yet it is also suggestive of an Aztec myth about two gods tearing down the goddess of the earth into two parts, of which one forms the heavenly firmament and the other earth ("Histoire du mechique" 1905: 30–31). In this case the figurine shows the god of the sun lifting the heaven.

One of the principal myths dominating the monumental sculpture

[6] See the Aztec and Mixtec images (Covarrubias 1957: 322–23).

of the Olmecs was the legend of how man had received maize. Most Mesoamerican myths of the Postclassic Period tell that the grains of maize were hidden in a mountain from where they were recovered by Quetzalcoatl. We believe that this myth is depicted in the main relief of altar 5 at La Venta: a god (the future Quetzalcoatl) carries an infant (symbol of maize) from the depths of the earth to pass it to the humans; the baby's quiet posture (which leads some scholars to assume that it is a dead offering) indicates that the grain has not yet sprung to life. The same myth, but in a somewhat different version, is treated in the relief of monument 19 at La Venta: "Quetzalcoatl" offers to humans a bag containing the previous seeds; behind him is shown his *nahualli* – a snake.

We believe that another group of monumental sculptures, colossal heads, is also associated with the cult of the deity of maize. While once the overwhelming majority of monuments were traced to cults and were invariably explained in religious terms (sometimes ignoring the patently different purpose of a monument), at present, in the wake of Mme. Proskouriakoff's work (see for example 1950, 1954, 1960, 1961), the other extreme is the case. The latest researches classify most monuments as historical, that is to say, created to meet purely political demands (the assertion of dynastic rights, glorification of ruler, and so on). It is not surprising therefore, that most scholars (Stirling 1965; Bernal 1969: 56–57; Benson 1968: 74–78, 134) consider the colossal heads to be portraits of Olmec rulers, i.e. a peculiar (or early) form of stelae – so much so that some have actually asked where the bodies of these heads are to be found.

It should be mentioned at this juncture that the subsequent history of Mesoamerica displays nothing like this sort of cult of rulers or warriors. We think that the missing bodies are absolutely irrelevant: nothing has been found so far, and nothing is going to be found. Nevertheless, there can be no doubt that here we are dealing, if not with portraits in the full sense of the word, then with depictions which definitely set out to convey the individual traits of real persons.

The most familiar instance of severed heads in ancient America relates to the preservation of the heads of enemies. But the assumption that the Olmecs perpetuated the heads of their enemies in stone, and on such a gigantic scale, is in our view effectively refuted by the fact that none of the heads has closed eyes or any wounds. On the contrary, all of the heads appear to be alive and bear no visible traces of battle; most of them, in fact, have affable expressions, and some are even smiling. All are young, so it would seem that youths were chosen as models for these sculptures. Incidentally, this is another argument against the hypothesis of their being either rulers or enemies, for one would be hard put to explain why one or the other should have died at an equally early age.

At the same time. we encounter the cult of heads in the later religious practices of Mesoamerican peoples. Apart from the Aztec custom of preserving the heads of sacrificed people by impaling them on a *tzompantli*, or the fact that a head adorned with maize served as a symbol of Cinteotl, one could give several examples from the Maya practice. It is well known, for instance, that the head of the god of maize is used for the Figure 8 in hieroglyphic writing: in the *Dresden codex* (63a), his severed head lies on the altar. Depictions of this kind are frequently encountered in the sculpture of the Classic Period (a relief at the Temple of Foliated Cross, stela 1 in Bonampak, and so forth).

That the Olmecs did have a cult of severed heads is proved by the relief in stela A in Tres Zapotes, where on the left of the central personage there is a man with a knife, and the man on the right holds a severed human head by the hair. A similar theme is conveyed by a figurine from the Leningrad Hermitage Museum: a sitting figure holding a severed head adorned with feathers (Kinzhalov 1954: 30–31).

The Aztecs are known to have sacrificed, during the Toxcatl festivities, a young captive who was believed to embody Tezcatlipoca. After the sacrifice, his body was not thrown off the pyramid, as was the custom, but was carefully carried down, and his head was solemnly mounted on a *tzompantli*.

One will readily see that in this case Tezcatlipoca was combined with some maize deity. Thus, according to Clavigero (1781), the symbol of these festivities was the image of a severed human head with a chain below to convey a garland of dry maize grains. The captive was at all times accompanied by eight youths (the Maya, as noted above, associated this figure with the god of maize). The four women given him as wives bore the names of the fertility goddesses: Xochiquetzal, Xilonen, Atlantonan, and Huixtochihuatl. Even the flowers which the impersonator carried in his hands were to suggest maize grains that had burst in the fire.

It should be noted in passing that a few days later an embodiment of Huitzilopochtil was sacrificed in a similar manner but with less ceremony. His head was also impaled on a *tzompantli*. This rite demonstrated its connection with the cult of maize even more graphically: a statue of the god was made of amaranth dough; a ritual of eating tamales was observed,[7] and so forth.

One is justified, we believe, in tracing this rite to the Olmec period and assuming that the Olmecs likewise had a ritualistic custom of choosing a youth to impersonate the god of maize who, having been sacrificed, was perpetuated in a monolith which was preserved during the fifty-two-year cycle as a token of future harvests. The youths who impersonated the god may have been chosen in some way during a

[7] On the cultic significance of the amaranth see Kinzhalov (1971: 82).

ball game; hence their headdress. As is evidenced by the hymns collected by de Sahagun (1950–1964), the ball game was associated with the maize deities. According to Aztec rules, the impersonators of Tezcatlipoca were to meet certain requirements with respect to their appearance. The Olmecs may also have chosen such impersonators by certain physical features (hence the so-called negroid traits of the colossal heads).[8]

In their subsequent cults, the people of Mesoamerica gave up stone monuments and began to bury the heads in the ground. Possibly, quality was made up for by quantity, symbolizing a mass spring sowing. The same idea was expressed in the later monuments of Golfo, the diminutive laughing heads. These exhibit an obvious Olmec tradition: (a) youth-age, (b) cultic laughing expression, (c) individual headdress, and (d) the custom of burying the broken-off heads and the bodies of the figurines in different places.

The myth of the bearded god was considerably developed by the Olmecs. New iconographic versions occur alongside traditional images of this god (La Venta, monument 40, altar 6; Laguna de los Cerros, monument 8) in a sitting posture and with the quiet position of the arms (which definitely carries a certain symbolic implication – the Aztec Xiuhtecuhtli was almost invariably depicted in a sitting posture).[9] An example of the new iconographic version is the famous statue of the "wrestler" from Santa María Uspanama whose hands are on the level of the chest. In this respect, stela 3 from La Venta is particularly interesting. It depicts a meeting or clash of the bearded god with the god of maize, whose corpulent torso reflects the iconographic tradition of the fat god. The combatants are surrounded by assistants, three for each side. The meaning of this stela is still obscure: the transfer of power from one social group to another protected by Xiuhtecuhtli, or the onset of a new unfavorable cycle?

The idea of opposition (and at the same time connection) of the bearded god and the young god of maize is expressed, in our opinion, even more graphically in relief 2 at Chalcatzingo where the bearded god, with his hands tied, fertilizes the earth. In front of him are three jaguar-like deities. The first figure on the left triumphantly carries away the result of this union – a maize stalk. Here we observe the same myth about the giving of maize to humans, but expressed more comprehensively.

[8]   Of course there is a possibility that Olmec rulers, upon reaching a specified age, themselves became the embodiment of the deity and were sacrificed. However, in this event, too, cultic considerations again prevailed over purely political reasons in monument erection.

[9]   In this respect the tradesmen's prayer to Xiuhtecuhtli is very indicative: "May thou sit in peace on thy throne, O noble lord, thou sitting in the navel of the Earth, the lord of the four cardinal points" (de Sahagun 1950–1964: vol. 9, p. 3).

The Olmec pantheon exhibits one more deity (judging by later parallels, an unfavorable one) with a human body and an owl's wings. The images of this god are comparatively rare; there are only the principal painting at Oxtotitlán and one Tlatilco figurine.

It may be assumed that the Olmecs not only originated the concepts of the cardinal points of the universe (symbolized by the so-called St. Andrew's cross inscribed in a rectangle), but also the legend of the Eras of the World. Particularly noteworthy in this respect is the statue from Las Limas. According to the Aztec myths, the finding and mastering of maize by man dates back to the fifth era (which was to be destroyed by earthquakes, i.e. by the old god of fire). Therefore, the god presenting humans with an infant – the incarnation of maize – is an auspicious symbol for the current era. But on the shoulders and knees of this god are carved the heads of four other deities which are, in our opinion, the symbols and protectors of the preceding eras. Of course, there is no reason why these deities should coincide with the Aztec gods, for both the protectors of the eras and their order may have changed. The same myth is expressed in the central picture on the so-called Humboldt celt, the sole difference being that hieroglyphics are here substituted for the heads of the deities.

The material presented here obviously makes no claim to covering the entire content of the Olmec pantheon and mythology. There is evidence that the Olmecs believed in seven or nine deities (higher and lower); still to be clarified is the role of the images of the snake, the bird, and the monkey, and the anthropomorphic seated figures holding a bar; the meaning of St. Andrew's cross in a rectangle as a symbol of a specific group of deities, and so forth. We can look forward to the archaeological investigations currently in progress clarifying many points and adding considerably to our body of knowledge.

REFERENCES

BENSON, E. P., *editor*
1968   *Dumbarton Oaks Conference on the Olmecs.* Washington, D.C.
BERNAL, J.
1969   *The Olmec world.* Berkeley: University of California Press.
CLAVIGERO, FRANCESCO JAVIER
1781   *Storia antica del Messica.* Cesana: G. Biansini.
COE, M. D.
1968   *America's first civilization.* Eau Claire, Wisconsin: E. M. Hale.
COVARRUBIAS, M.
1957   *Indian art of Mexico and Central America.* New York.
DE SAHAGUN, B.
1950–1964   *Florentine codex, general history of the things of New Spain.*

(Translated by A. J. O. Anderson and C. E. Dibble.) Santa Fe: University of Utah School of American Research.

GAY, C. T.
1966   Rock carvings at Chalcazingo. *National History* 75(7): 56–61.

GROVE, D.
1970   "Olmec felines in highland central Mexico," in *The cult of the feline.* Edited by E. P. Benson, 153–164. Dumbarton Oaks, Washington, D.C.

"*Histoire du mechique*"
1905   "Histoire du mechique." Manuscrit français inédit du XVIe siècle. *Journal de la Société des Américanistes* 2: 1–41.

KINZHALOV, R. V.
1954   Ol'mekskaia statuetxa Ermitazha [The Olmec figurine in the Hermitage Museum]. *Soobshcheniia Gos. Ermitazha* 6. Leningrad.
1970   Mifologicheskie sistemy Mesoameriki [Mythological systems of Mesoamerica]. *Kratkoe soderzhanie dokladov godichnoi nauchnoi sessii Instituta Etnografii AN SSSR,* 1969. Leningrad.
1971   *Kul'tura drevnikh maïja* [Culture of the ancient Mayans]. Leningrad.

PROSKOURIAKOFF, TATIANA
1950   *A study of Classic Maya sculpture.* Carnegie Institute of Washington Publication 558. Washington, D.C.
1954   *Varieties of Classic central Veracruz sculpture.* Carnegie Institute of Washington Contribution 58: 63–100. Washington, D.C.
1960   Historical implications of a pattern of dates at Piedras Negras, Guatemala. *American Antiquity* 25: 454–475. Salt Lake City.
1961   The lords of the Maya realm. *Expedition* 4 (1): 14–21. Philadelphia.

STIRLING, M.
1965   "Monumental sculpture of southern Veracruz and Tabasco," in *Handbook of Middle American Indians,* volume three, 716–738. Austin: University of Texas Press.

Maya and Teotihuacán Traits in Classic Maya Vase Painting of the Petén

JACINTO QUIRARTE

The designation of a painted vase as Maya rarely presents a problem for specialists. Several indices are used – presence of typically Maya glyphic notations, technique (type of ware, preparation of surface, shape of vessel), and form (easily identified "Maya configurations"). But what specifically makes Maya painting Maya? Or Teotihuacanoid? In order to arrive at a working definition several painted vases from the Petén sites of Uaxactun and Tikal as well as some from Kaminaljuyu and Teotihuacán will be examined for their "Maya" and non-Maya traits. (1) The visual surface will be used as a starting point for comparisons to determine whether the use of a rectangular as opposed to a square pictorial surface represents a significant difference in perception. (2) Thematic structures (double or mirror images, and continuous narratives or reentrant images) will be studied to determine how Maya or how Teotihuacanoid a particular vessel happens to be.

These morphological considerations will bring Maya painting into sharper focus. The study of the imagery as opposed to themes or motifs would clarify further the nature and extent of the central Mexican presence in the Petén during the Classic Period.

PROPORTIONS OF THE VESSEL WALL

Kidder, et al. (1946: 159) used an index of wall-height/orifice-diameter to determine whether a vessel was squat, medium, or tall. An index of 1 represented a height and diameter of equal dimensions. A height smaller than the diameter correspondingly gave an index that was less wall-height/orifice-diameter than 1, and so on. They designated vessels with an index of less than .65 as squat, .65 to .89 as medium, and above

Table 1. Comparison of some Maya vessels

Site	Vessel	Present location	Bibliographic source	Height Diameter (in centimeters)		Height-diameter index
Teothihuacá	cyl. tri.	Nat. Mus.	(Gaines, M.)	10.00	20.00	.50
				15.88	29.84	.53
				13.34	24.13	.55
				10.16	16.67	.61
				10.80	16.83	.64
		Dumb. Oaks	(K.J.S. 1946: 176b)	9.20	14.50	.65
		Nat. Mus.	(Gaines, M.)	8.57	12.70	.67
		Dumb. Oaks	(K.J.S. 1946: 176c)	10.00	14.50	.68
		Nat. Mus.	(Gaines, M.)	8.57	12.06	.71
Kaminaljuyu	cyl. tri	Gua. Mus.	(K.J.S. 1946: 204d)	12.80	16.40	.85
			(K.J.S. 1946: 205f)	14.40	18.00	.89
			(K.J.S. 1946: 207h)	19.00	20.00	.95
			(K.J.S. 1946: 207e)	14.60	15.20	.96
			(K.J.S. 1946: 205a)	16.00	16.00	1.00
			(K.J.S. 1946: 204b)	15.20	16.00	1.02
			(K.J.S. 1946: 204c)	15.60	16.80	1.03
			(K.J.S. 1946: 204a)	16.40	16.80	1.03
			(K.J.S. 1946: 204e)	17.80	16.80	1.06
			(K.J.S. 1946: 205c)	19.80	18.00	1.10
			(K.J.S. 1946: 205d)	20.50	18.00	1.14
Uaxactun	cyl. tri.	Gua. Mus.	(Smith 1955: 1a)	13.07	15.20	.86
	cyl. vase		(Smith 1955: 1f)	23.80	15.50	1.54
Tikal	cyl. vase	Tikal Mus.	(Coe 1965: 42)	26.50	16.20	1.64
	cyl. vase		(Coe 1965: 42)	30.50	17.10	1.78
Holmul	cyl. vase		(M.V. 1932: 30b, d)	34.80	25.40	1.37
			(M.V. 1932: 30a, c)	34.80	18.90	1.84
Yalloch	cyl. vase		(Gann 1918: 24)	27.90	15.20	1.84
			(Gann 1918: 25)	19.00	11.40	1.67
			(Gann 1918: 25-28)	26.70	10.00	2.67
Chama	cyl. vase		(Dieseldorff 1904: XLIX)	15.00	17.50	.86
			(G.M. 1925-1928: VII-VIII)	18.60	20.60	.90
			(G.M. 1925-1928: LIII)	16.70	15.00	1.11
			(G.M. 1925-1928: XXXVIII)	20.00	17.10	1.17
			(G.M. 1925-1928: IX)	19.00	16.00	1.19

ABBREVIATIONS:

Column Two	Column Three	Column Four
cyl.: cylindrical	Nat.: National	K.J.S.: Kidder, Jennings, and Shook
tri.: tripod	Mus.: Museum	G.M.: Gordon and Mason
	Dumb.: Dumbarton	M.V.: Merwin and Vaillant
	Gua.: Guatemala	

.90 as tall. This index, applied to Teotihuacán and Maya examples, will be used here for comparison purposes only (see Table 1).

Although it is difficult to say at this time how many Teotihuacán cylindrical vessels there are in public and private collections, we can safely take a small sample for this study, because they exhibit relatively uniform characteristics. Even a cursory glance will demonstrate that the vase painters dealt with a horizontal format. The orifice diameter, usually greater than the height of the vessel wall gives these tripods a squat appearance.

Two of the Teotihuacán vessels now in the Dumbarton Oaks Collection (Kidder, et al. 1946: Figures 176b–c) are definitely squat by Kidder's definition. They have indexes of .65 and .68. One particularly squat vessel now in the Rivera Museum has an index of .52, or twice as wide as it is high (Pellicer, et al. 1965: 153). Seven of the tripods from the extensive collection in the National Museum of Anthropology in Mexico City have indexes that range between .50 and .71. An eighth vessel, definitely in the tall category, has an index of 1.03 (Mary Gaines, personal communication).[1]

The Kaminaljuyu vessels presented a different problem to the painters. The shape of the vessel wall, although slightly concave towards the center rather than vertical, is almost square. Indexes hover slightly below or above 1. One of the eleven vessels found in burials A–VI and B–II has an index of .89 while the others range between .95 and 1.14 (Kidder, et al. 1946: 162; Figures 173h, a–g, and i–k).

Vessels from the Petén sites are on the opposite end of the scale. Although the few extant cylindrical vessels demonstrate close affinities to the Kaminaljuyu and Teotihuacán pieces, the vast majorities are definitely in the tall category. The proportions of a stuccoed tripod vessel found in burial A31 in Uaxactun (Kelemen 1946: Plates 128a and c) have an index of .86 while a much larger cylindrical tripod found in a grave in Tikal (University Museum 1960: Cover) has an index of .35! The latter may simply be an imported piece.

The Uaxactun vessel falls into the Kaminaljuyu format although its sides are vertical rather than concave. The Initial Series (IS) cylindrical vase found in Uaxactun chamber A-2 (Kelemen 1946; Plates 129a and c) differs in almost every respect from the Tzakol stuccoed tripod vase (burial A31), save for the glyphic and formal programs. The cylindrical vase has an index of 1.54 or a vessel height one and a half times the size of the diameter. Two cylindrical vases found in Tikal burials 196 and 116 have indexes 1.78 and 1.64 respectively (Coe 1967: 53, 102). A glance at height to orifice indexes in neighboring sites shows only slight variations.

Two vessels found in Holmul burials have indexes of 1.37 and 1.84 (Merwin and Vaillant 1932: Plate 30a–d). Four Yalloch vessels found in chultun burials have indexes that range between 1.54 and 2.67! This

---

[1] Mary Gaines, a graduate student in the art department of the University of Texas at Austin, has studied Teotihuacán cylindrical tripods in public and private collections in Mexico and the United States.

is a far cry from the horizontal, square, and vertical formats reviewed here, for this last example demonstrates a vessel height two and a half times the width (see Plates 1, 3 and 5).

THEMATIC STRUCTURES

Classic Maya artists were aware of the distortions caused by the constantly curving surface of a vase. Although one-half of the total surface of a cylindrical vase is visible at any time, only one-fourth (a quadrant) of that is free from distortion. The greater the angle at which pictorial parts are viewed on either side of that quadrant, the greater the distortion until the image is lost entirely toward the edges of the vessel. The artist could resolve this problem by breaking up the narrative program into several interrelated units. The earliest solution appears to be the double or mirror images depicted on opposite sides of a vessel. Whether this is Maya or Teotihuacanoid is difficult to determine at this time.

Perhaps better suited to the cylindrical surface – keeping in mind the quadrants which are free from distortion at any one time – are the continuous narratives or reentrant images. Each figure, whether seated or standing, is completely visible if viewed at right angles. That is, if the viewer positions himself or the vase in such a way that the figure is in the center of the visual field, then those adjacent to it on either side – within the contiguous quadrants – will be visible but distorted. The vase can then be turned so that each successive pictorial unit can be read. Thus the painter spaced the figures so that the viewer's attention could be focused on a single figure, and yet parts of the others would still be visible, thereby functioning as links to each successive stage of the continuous narrative.

Uaxactun and Tikal

The Uaxactun burial A31 stuccoed tripod considered here (Kelemen 1946: Plates 128a, c) was the only one with a predominantly displayed figural scene painted on its exterior wall. The painting is patently symmetrical. Pairs of seated figures facing each other are represented within two rectangular panels. The figures, gesturing in a manner which suggests conversation, are seated on cushions covered with jaguar skins. Head, neck, chest, wrist, and waist accessories worn by each figure are almost identical except for very minor details.

Eight glyphs, arranged in two columns of four glyphs each, take up the central portion of each frame. Four glyphs depicted twice as

Plate 1. (a, b) Two stuccoed and painted cylindrical tripods with lids from burial B-II, Kaminaljuyu, Guatemala. Both have *mirror images* – (a) index: 1.03; (b) index: .85. Courtesy of the Peabody Museum, Harvard University

Plate 2. Drawing of the unrolled design taken from stuccoed and painted tripod vessel with lid from burial A31, Uaxactun, Guatemala. *Mirror image*, index: .86. Courtesy of the Peabody Museum, Havard University.

Plate 3. Polychromed cylindrical vase from burial 196, Tikal, Guatemala. *Mirror image*; index: 1.78. Courtesy of the University Museum, University of Pennsylvania

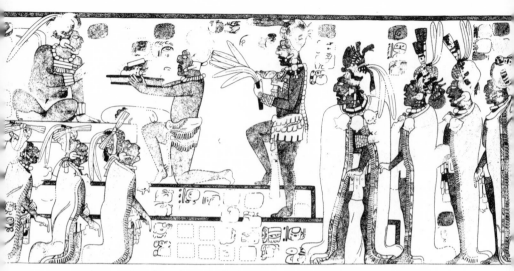

Plate 4. Drawing of the unrolled design of the stuccoed and painted cylindrical vase found in fragments in burial 116, Tikal, Guatemala. *Reentrant image*; index: 1.64. Courtesy of the University Museum, University of Pennsylvania

Plate 5. (a, b). Two painted cylindrical vases from burials in Ruin X and Building F, Group 1, Holmul, Guatemala. (a) *Mirror image*; index: 1.37. (b) *Reentrant image*; index: 1.84. Courtesy of the Peabody Museum, Harvard University.

Plate 6.   Courtesy of the Peabody Museum, Harvard University, Drawing of the unrolled design of the Initial Series polychromed cylindrical vase, Uaxactun, Guatemala. *Reentrant image*; index: 1.54. After Kelemen (1946; Plate 129c)

large and in two single columns take up the space on either side of each frame. These buffer areas, like the painted scenes, are back to back or 180 degrees apart. The latter are best described as mirror images, possibly depicting the same two individuals at different times (see Plate 2).

Whereas the Tzakol stuccoed tripod has two scenes, or mirror images, made up of paired figures, the Uaxactun IS vase found in chamber A-2, structure A-1 has one continuous scene taking up the entire length of the vessel (Kelemen 1946: Plates 129a, c). This is typical of the Classic Maya use of the continuous narrative or reentrant image (see Plate 6).

There are six figures facing a glyphic block divided into two columns and bearing the IS date. To the left of this block are two standing figures, similarly attired (with front cloaks, feathered headdresses, and back ornaments) and wearing black body paint. A jaguar sits between them. They look toward the right beyond the glyphic columns at the three figures facing them; one is seated cross-legged on a thin cushion placed over a spotted (jaguar) dais; the other two are standing.

The surface pattern of the painting is made up of a series of vertical units – standing figures with accessories (staff, back ornaments) and glyphic columns. The diagonal displacement of the parasol on the right draws our attention to the seated figure, obviously the most important in the painting. He is shown in frontal view with head in profile, while all the others are shown in profile.

The Tikal vessel considered here, found in burial 196, Structure 5D–73, demonstrates the use of a mirror image. Two thin black lines define the visual field of the vase, one below the rim and the other drawn an equal distance from the bottom of the vessel. A band of fourteen glyphs is displaced directly below the upper line, which partially overlaps the upper portions of the headdress worn by the seated individual portrayed twice (on opposite sides of the vessel).

In both cases he is shown seated on a thick cushion with back rest, which is covered with jaguar skins. On one side he is shown in profile with the sole of his right foot partially seen under his left knee. On the other his torso is represented in frontal position, with his right leg now crossed over his left in yoga fashion. Arms and face are shown in profile. He is depicted in an identical pose in both cases but with minor variations (see Plate 3).

Teotihuacán and Kaminaljuyu

With a visual surface restricted in a vertical direction, the Teotihuacán painter resorted to readily identified pictorial conventions. One of these stipulated that the profile figures placed within a quadrant should be half figures seen from approximately the waist up. Whenever a full figure is represented the results are not at all satisfactory as far as the placement within the visual surface is concerned. An example of this is found in the National Museum of Anthropology (Bernal 1968; 65). Like the Maya examples this, too, has mirror images. The figure's accessories are extended in front so as to fill in the quadrant.

Even when half figures were used the artist often extended feathered headdresses and attachments toward the sides of the quadrant so as to take up the allotted space. There are numerous examples of this type (Pellicer, et al. 1965: Kidder, et. al. 1946; Figures 176b, c). These are often placed next to the similar accouterments of the mirror image without any apparent visual break. It is often difficult to tell where one image ends and the other begins for there is no apparent boundary between the two.

The Kaminaljuyu painters had visual surfaces that were basically different from those used by the Teotihuacán painters. The more nearly square and often slightly vertical format allowed the artists a little more "head" room.

Kidder noted that these vessels demonstrated Teotihuacanoid and Mayoid characteristics. The most blatantly Teotihuacanoid of these is a vessel found in burial A-VI (Kidder, et al. 1946; Figure 205e). The artist represented a seated individual on opposite sides of the vessel with the speech scrolls taking up the buffer zones between halves. Instead of presenting the full figure the artist opted for the Teotihuacán convention and painted a half figure. However, unlike Teotihuacán examples, there seems to be some equivocation regarding the subject's position. In the central Mexican examples the figure is invariably overlapped or supported by a band going around the base of the vessel. The torso is occasionally obscured by a shield.

Whatever the case there is no question that we are seeing the upper part of a standing figure. Each figure in the Kaminaljuyu example has his own band that appears to function as a seat. So although these appear to be half figures they may be merely seated figures presented within pyramidal configurations. It is almost as if a Maya artist had been assigned a subject he did not clearly understand. On the other hand, it could just as easily have been a Teotihuacán artist who was not accustomed to using a vertical rather than a horizontal format. It is more likely that the former was the case for he has clearly placed the figures within their respective quadrants.

In another example (Kidder, et al. 1946; Figure 204a) the resolution is more clearly Maya even though the figure represented in mirror fashion is definitely a Teotihuacano. The placement and displacement of the figures within the vessel wall clearly point to a Maya conceptualization of the image. The theme or subject is Teotihuacán and the resolution is Maya. The seated figure fits within the quadrant as do most Maya examples demonstrating the use of the mirror image. The bag held in the right hand signals the entry into the next quadrant where the artist has depicted the speech scroll that interestingly does not emanate directly from the speaker's mouth (see Plate 1a).

Two other examples (Kidder, et al. 1946; Figure 204b found in burial B-II and Figure 205f found in burial A-VI) are definitely Maya thematically and morphologically. The artist had to squeeze the seated figures within the visual format (height slightly less than the width); still the resolution of the figures in both cases is basically the same.

SUMMARY

The Maya artist invariably used a vertical format in the painted vessels with or without supports (tripods or vases with slightly rounded bases). The Mayoid and Teotihuacanoid vessels found in Kaminal-juyu, although tall in Kidder's index, are more nearly square than the later Classic Maya vessels. Interestingly enough, the square format continued to be favored along with the vertical format in the Guate-mala Highlands. Chama vases have indexes of .86 to 1.19 (see Table 1). As is well known, this type of format lent itself to representations of full figures.

The Maya artist was very conscious that a complete quadrant as well as one-half of the two contiguous quadrants (one eighth of the surface) on either side is visible at any one time. The division of the visual surface into quadrants minimized this distortion. Thus the use of a seated or standing figure within each quadrant of a cylindrical vessel offered a maximum of visual legibility and a minimum of image loss (see Plates 4 and 5).

Compartmentalization – the breakup of the surface into two or three identical images spaced around the outer cylindrical wall – is generally considered to be Teotihuacanoid. But Teotihuacán examples demon-strate that although these conceptualizations may be in operation the breakup of the surface into distinct compartments is not usual. This is actually a Maya trait. In Teotihuacán examples, figures disappear toward the edges and merge with their companion mirror images on the other side without a clear break between the two. Thus we are often treated to details in front and behind an elaborately attired individual that may actually belong to the figure depicted on the other side. Only when we have studied the rolled out design do we see that this is not the case.

In contrast, the Maya artist was very conscious of the horizontal divisions. Even when he did not encase his figures within cartouches he still established their independent existence spatially by leaving blank spaces on the other side of the quadrant occupied by the figure. This spatial hierarchy is very definitely Maya. The Teotihuacán artist does not appear to have been as conscious of these spatial envelopes. Thus for the Teotihuacán artist the physical restrictions in a vertical direction are in sharp contrast to the seemingly unlimited extension of the images in a horizontal direction.

It is unlikely that Teotihuacán artists were ever in residence in Kaminaljuyu or in the Petén. There is no question that Teotihuacán-based peoples were there. Pictorial as well as actual models must have been used by local artists to deal with the themes at hand. For, although the personages depicted are definitely non-Maya, their *conceptualization* and *resolution* are Maya or very much closer to Maya than to Teotihuacán sources.

REFERENCES

BERNAL, IGNACIO
1968   *The Mexican National Museum of Anthropology*. London: Thames and Hudson.
COE, WILLIAM
1962   A summary of excavation and research at Tikal, Guatemala: 1951–1961. *American Antiquity* 27(4): 479–507.
1965   Tikal, *Expedition* 8(1). Philadelphia: University Museum.
1967   *Tikal, a handbook of the ancient Maya ruins*. Philadelphia: University Museum.
DIESELDORFF, ERWIN P.
1904   A pottery vase with figure painting from a grave in Chama (with remarks by Schellhas). *Bureau of American Ethnology Bulletin* 28: 635–670. Washington.
GANN, THOMAS
1918   The Maya Indians of southern Yucatán and northern British Honduras. *Bureau of American Ethnology Bulletin* 65. Washington D.C.
GORDON, G. B., J. A. MASON
1925–1928   *Examples of Maya pottery in the museum and other collections*. Philadelphia: University Museum.
KELEMEN, PAL
1946   *Medieval American art*. New York: Macmillan.
KIDDER, A. V., J. D. JENNINGS, E. M. SHOOK
1946   *Excavations of Kaminaljuyu, Guatemala*. Washington: Carnegie Institution of Washington, Publication 561.
MERWIN, R. E., G. C. VAILLANT
1932   *The ruins of Holmul, Guatemala*. Cambridge, Mass.: Peabody Museum.
PELLICER, C., R. RIVERA, D. OLMEDO DE OLVERA
1965   Anahuacalli Museo Diego Rivera. *Artes de Mexico* XII (64–65). Mexico City.

QUIRARTE JACINTO
  i.p.a   *Maya vase and mural painting.* Austin: University of Texas Press.
  i.p.b   "Murals and vase paintings of the southern lowlands: central zone (first century B.C. to ninth century A.D.)," in *Symposium on Maya art.* From symposium held April 15, 1972, New Orleans. Austin: University of Texas Press.
SMITH, LEDYARD A.
  1950   *Uaxactun, Guatemala: excavations of 1931–1937.* Washington: Carnegie Institution of Washington, Publication 588.
SMITH, R. E.
  1955   *Ceramic sequence at Uaxactun.* New Orleans: Middle American Research Institute.
UNIVERSITY MUSEUM
  1960   *Expedition* 2(2). Philadelphia: University Museum.

The Aztec System of Writing: Problems of Research

Those interested in the Aztec writing system have three great advantages over the specialists in the Maya writing system, namely:

1. Knowledge of the language transcribed by the Aztec signs, Nahuatl, a modern language which is still spoken in Mexico by one and a half million people.

2. Continuation of the traditional writing up to the eighteenth century. The survival of the written tradition produced abundant documents in various regions of Mexico.

3. Transcription into Latin characters of a fairly considerable series of phonetic signs (especially those used for names of persons and places) at the beginning of the Spanish Conquest.

But, in spite of these advantages and in spite of the research made in the sixteenth century and mainly at the end of the nineteenth century until today, we can observe that *scientific research* on the Aztec writing system is still underdeveloped in comparison with the study of other writing systems.

I. Excluding the very numerous traditional documents, which are still in the native villages, hidden and inaccessible, the *known* Mexican pictographic manuscripts are spread out all over the world and are preserved by various institutions. What we need are *workable resources*, such as complete inventories of these manuscripts, where the documents would be classified by country and by institution. The catalogs produced in libraries or other institutions are incomplete or out of date. (For example, in Paris, the great Fonds Méxicain has a nineteenth century catalog [Boban 1891]; in Mexico, only one institution has a complete catalog, which was only published in 1964 [Glass 1964]; in Chicago, in Texas, and elsewhere there are no catalogs.) It will be another year or two before the first catalog and the first general bibliography of the Mexican manuscripts will be available. This production, put together by a group of Americans formed by Glass, Cline, Robertson, Nicholson, etc., will be published in the final volumes of the *Handbook of Middle American Indians* (edited by Wauchope 1964).

II. Among the Mexican manuscript specialists, almost no one has dealt with seeking the development of a *scientific method of work*, based on *detailed and systematic analysis* of the various groups of manuscripts. Each researcher has worked individually, following his own ideas and his own criteria. The analyses of the manuscripts carried out up till now are rarely complete and stop at the interpretation of certain signs, most of these phonetic. Here too, we are lacking tools. In the first place, there are no exhaustive lists of anthroponymic and toponymic glyphs. In the second place, there are few complete lists of phonetic elements. Peñafiel's catalog of place names (1885), which has become a classic work of reference, is the only one of its kind and only covers part of a single manuscript: the "List of Tributes" of the *Codex Mendoza*. From this catalog, a very succinct, so-called phonetic dictionary was made by Barlow and MacAfee (1949); this only includes a short series of phonetic elements, without taking into account the pertinent variations (with changes of meaning) which are very numerous in this system.

The majority of the research carried out at present on the Mexican pictographic manuscripts is oriented toward obtaining elements, either historical, chronological, or religious, in order to better "illustrate" summary works on the Aztec history, calendar, or religion. The authors of these works are forced to follow the existing interpretations, regardless of whether they are incorrect, incomplete, or just out of date, because they do not have time to seek a new reading of the signs. We lack an analysis of the hundreds of pictographic manuscripts spread out in the Mexican and foreign institutions. That is, we lack research with regard to the *whole compass of the Aztec writing system*, in all its aspects, not only for the purposes of extracting certain data from it, but also for attempting to read the pictographic documents in full.

The Aztec writing system is a complex and curious mixture of pictorial expression blended with phonetic transcription. In this double expression of graphic art and writing, the drawing/painting scribe uses all the means of artistic expression combined with the signs of phonetic transcription in order to form his own writing system. A perspective very different from that used in Europe is employed: superimpositions of planes in space, which are then brought back to a single surface. On this surface, where phonetic elements blend with symbolic elements, the search for aesthetic balance is not disregarded by the writer-artists.

In the drawing technique, all graphic means are used to enrich the means of written expression. The variants of the phonetic signs are also expressed by graphic means (such as dimensions, position, orientation of the signs) along a plane and in space. This very complex expression was stopped, in the midst of its phonetic evolution, by the Spanish Conquest. Influences of the European drawing technique were added to the existing system and Christian symbols and attributes very soon blended with the traditional phonetic and symbolic glyphs, together with phonetic transcriptions of Spanish names with traditional signs.

Scientific research, in the field of Aztec writing, has reached a state where we must, above all, carry out an exhaustive survey of the Mexican pictographic manuscripts preserved in every institution; carry out a systematic and extensive analysis of each group of manuscripts; and obtain the census of the traditional phonetic signs and elements to form comprehensive lists – real dictionaries – which would enable us to carry out more satisfactory, methodical research. It is only along these lines that we will be able to discover the *valid scientific method* for deciphering Aztec writing. As a broad knowledge is essential, we believe in a working group in which the ethnologist-historian, the artist, the linguist, and the art historian can obtain positive results together.

III. One of the main difficulties in reading Mexican pictographic manuscripts is that each page is a real "graphic picture." To read each picture, you must take artistic expression into account, since it is a fundamental part of the whole. To find the solution to this reading is to be able to read alternately the pictograms, glyphs, phonetic and symbolic signs, and the elements which seem to be purely decorative but which form a part of the whole writing.

These various elements, however, have been drawn in the order fixed by the writer-artist, according to the laws and the conventions of the system. The way to read the manuscript, which is indicated by graphic means, is sometimes difficult to find; but it does exist, and the scribe-drawer has indicated it on each page and in each single document. Now, this preset way of reading, these laws, these conventions, this order – they exist; but we do not know them since we lack extensive analyses of hundreds of manuscripts and especially because we do not have a real scientific method of deciphering this complex system of art and graphic expression.

Another important problem is that of the training of specialized researchers. All those who have become specialists in Mexican manuscripts have, above all, other specialities. That is to say that, while studying Mexican pictographic manuscript, they are, foremost, archaeologists, ethnologists, linguists, historians, etc. Their isolated efforts only cover certain aspects of the manuscripts and they disregard nearly all the others. Now these individual aspects, combined in the research of a working group, would be very fruitful for the general study of the Aztec writing system.

This problem is even more striking when the researcher specializes in the study of classical Nahuatl. He gives preference to the translation of the notes in Latin characters. And unfortunately, very often, the pictographs are judged on European lines, as illustrations of a text written in Latin characters, and not as expressions having an independent existence and forming a whole complex of native writing. For example, in Mexico City, the Nahuatl Culture Seminar, which is comprised of well-known scientists whose work is outstanding, deals mainly with the Nahuatl language transcribed in Latin characters. Even from the standpoint of the Nahuatl language, one very rarely finds a "Nahuatlatologist" who has started to learn the *living* language before studying the *classical* language. Yet, this procedure would seem to be far more logical. The ideal case would be that of a group of researchers of Nahuatl origin, having Nahuatl as their first language, who would require a much easier training in order to comprehend the classical texts. These native researchers could become "decipherers" of Aztec writing. But up to now we know only one researcher, in Mexico City – L. Reyes Garcia – who possesses these qualifications.

Now a project could be developed, that of the creation of a kind of Nahuatl Academy, in a native village, where the teachers would be Indians or mestizos, whose first language would be Nahuatl. They would first of all be responsible for teaching this language to be loved in their own villages, by the young in particular. The new generations go to the towns for instruction and forget their own first language for the sake of Spanish, and then for English – which they learn badly at secondary school.

With such a group possessing a thorough training in Nahuatl, one can envisage an analytical study of all those documents which are sleeping in the records and in the villages. The Aztec writing system could then be studied more efficiently and more rapidly.

CONCLUSIONS

Scientific research into the Aztec writing system requires a knowledge of the majority, if not of the totality, of the traditional documents through the eighteenth century, and the extensive, methodical, and systematic analysis of all documents. Furthermore, as there are many of these documents and they form groups, the methods of analysis must correspond to each of these groups. The first step would therefore be to make an exhaustive survey of the manuscripts. The second step would be seek a scientific method of analysis of each group. The third step would be the analytic work itself, with a survey of the complex signs and of their elements. The fourth and last stage would be the comparison of the results within each group.

It is only when these analyses have been completed, following methods based on the same scientific principles, that we will be able to make comparisons between the groups and to obtain scientific conclusions on the whole system, that is to say, on the possibilities and limitations of Aztec writing.

REFERENCES

BARLOW, ROBERT H., BYRON MAC AFEE
  1949 *Diccionario de elementos fonéticos en escritura jeroglífica* (*códice Mendocino*), Publicaciónes del Instituto de Historia 9, serie 1, Mexico City: Universidad Nacional Autónoma de México.
BOBAN, EUGENE
  1891 *Catalogue raisonné de la collection de M. E. Eugène Goupil* (*Anc. coll. J. M. – A. Aubin*), deux volumes. Documents pour servir à l'histoire du Mexique. Paris: E. Leroux.
GLASS, JOHN
  1964 *Catálog de la collección de códices*. Mexico City: Museo Nacional de Antropología, I.N.A.H.
PEÑAFIEL, ANTONIO
  1885 *Nombres geográficos de México*. Catálogo alfabético de los nombres de lugar pertenecientes al idioma "Nahuatl." Estudio jeroglífico de la matrícula de tributos del códice Mendocino. Mexico City: Of. Tip. de la Sría. de Fomento.
WAUCHOPE, ROBERT, editor
  1964 *Handbook of Middle American Indians*. New Orleans: Middle American Research Institute; Tulane University. Texas: University of Texas Press.

The Deciphering of Glyphs Representing México Governmental Titles

HORACIO CORONA OLEA

The first section of the *Codex Mendoza* (Clark Cooper 1938), which refers to the group properly known to history as the Mexicatl, contains (among others) eight illustrations devoted to the Conquest and the period wherein it was completed. It also includes groups of glyphs connected by a line to the upper part of a figure representing a ruler.

Since the colonial period, these series of glyphs have been identified with the titles given at the time to the most outstanding figures represented in these glyphs, and have been arbitrarily assigned to México rulers. We have referred to them collectively as "governmental titles," as they would be more accurately described as conventional simplifications. That is to say, they are glyphs which have been inserted for the purpose of summarizing the most significant events in the history of this predominant group. These include their earlier history, the manner of their reappearance, development, domination, and expansion – events which, whether taken singly or in combination, illustrate and integrate the different periods in the history of México government.

The deciphering process must follow the same rules as are used to determine the meaning of conventional ʒlyphs. That is, it must take account of the fact that the significance of a figure is not by itself enough to decipher it, but one must also consider the voiced sound of the element to be deciphered which is contained in the word assigned to the glyph. This usually turns out to be the homophonic or homonymic apocope of the first syllable or syllables of the word in question, whose meaning is linked to that of the previous word. For example: Obsidian (ITZT-*etl*) on (IPAN) the head (TZON-*técomatl*). To confront (IXT*ia*) another person (IPAN*tilia*) in revenge (TZON*cui*). Synonyms: *Tlacopintli*, copy. *Tlamachioantli*, copy.

Homonyms: *Panuetzqui*, elevated, *Panuetzqui*, to gain fame.
Chalma, apocope of *chal(li)macpalmachiotl*, a sign made with the
palm of the hand.
Epyollotli, aphaeresis of *huitzilepyollotli*, pearl.

(Element denoting place)	(Element denoting meaning)
COATL, snake, serves as apocope of:	COATL*aca*, confederation.
MITL, arrow, serves as apocope of:	MITL*chimalli*, war.
HUECA*hua*, to prolong, localizes:	*tla*-HUECA*tenehualiztli*, prophecy.

DESCRIPTION

1. Bent over (*mochipichtlaliqui*) and in an arch (*cultic*), the de-
capitated (*tlaquechcontli*) snake (*cóhuatl*) is the figure (*machiotl*)
which supports, at the top (*panuetzqui*), a head (*tzontécomatl*) which
apparently (*motlatlaliqui*) is taking the place of the true (*neltiliz*)
image (*ixiptlati*), in view of the fact that a part of his body (*chico-
centlacol*), which is incomplete (*cocotic*) and flaccid (*tlaxacualtilli*),
is resting (*pachoa, nitla*) on the picture (*tzotzomatli*) of the ruler
(*nahuatileni*) (see Figure 1A).

2. From number (*tlanahualicuilolli*) one (*ce*) flint (*técpatl*) an
oblique (*tlanacacictecalli*), curving (*tlanolololli*) line (*tlaxotlalli*)
(*mixta:*) joins (*tlaaquiani*) and unites (*popotia, nitla*) one side to the
other (*tlanalquixtilli*) when it descends (*temo, ni*) from the other part
(*tlatepuzco*) separated by the space (*tlacauhtli*) which, as we have said
before, joins it (*tlaaquiani*) from the top (*icpac*) and is lost (*poliuhqui*)
in the girdle (*topitzahuavan*) of the governor (*nahuatileni*) (see Figure
1B).

3. From the knot (*tlalpiliztli*) of the mantle (*tlapatitli*) from down
below (*tlatzintlan*), it is connected (*popotia, nitla*) by means of a small
(*tontli*) line (*tlaxotlalli*), which does not reach either the top or the
bottom (*anonaci*); it joins (*tlaaquiani*) to the one which separates by
itself (*tlanononcuacequixtiani*), leaving large spaces (*tlacoyahua*) on
each side (*tzatzacutimanitne*), and consists of a forearm (*maxoxopachtli*) which with the fist strongly (*motzoltzitzquia, nitla*) grips
(*tzontepoloa*) two (*ome*) arrows (*tlacohctin*) of reed with a straight
stalk (*acahualli*) which form a (*ce*) small sheaf (*malpilli*) (see Figure
1C).

4. From the upper (*tlacpacpa*) end (*yácatl*) of the knot (*tlalpiliztli*)

of the mantle (*tlapatitli*), it goes up (*tleco*) and is joined (*popotia, nitla*) by means of a small (*tontli*) oblique (*tlanololli*) line (*tlaxotlalli*); underneath (*itzintlan*) it joins (*tlaaquiani*) the one which separates by itself (*tlanononcuacequixtiani*), leaving large spaces (*tlacoyahua*) on each side (*tzatzacutimanitne*), and consists of a forearm (*maxoxopachtli*) which with the fist strongly (*motzoltzitzquia, nitla*) grips (*tzontepoloa*) three (*yei*) arrows (*tlacohctin*) of reed with a straight stalk (*acahualli*) which form a (*ce*) small sheaf (*malpilli*) (see Figure 2A).

5. A short distance off (*huehueca*), there was placed below (*tlanitlalia*), aligned and in a row (*pantli*), a copy (*tlamachioantli*) of the ruler (*nahuatileni*) "*tequihua*", artificially (*tlachichiuhtli*), who is seated (*motlali*) pressing down (*pachoa, nitla*) on the small portable seat (*tzinicpalli*), which is matted (*petlatl*), which is connected (*tlaaquiani*) and delimited (*tepayo*) by the line (*tlaxotlalli*) which from one side to the other (*tlanaquixtilli*) and behind him (*tlatepuzco*) closes (*tzacua, nitla*) the space (*tlatlallo tiliztli*) which separated the two rows (*ompantli*) turning him inside out (*ixcuepa, nitla*), and in putting each thing in its place (*tlanononcuacaquixtiani*) links it loosely (*tlatotontli*) to the middle (*centlacol*) of the eighth (*chicuei*) cane (*ácatl*); after seven years (*ichiconxiuhyoc*) in the calculation which is made (*poa, nitla*) (see Figure 2, B and C).

6. From the picture (*tzotzomatli*) of the ruler (*nahuatileni*) there goes up (*tleco, ni*), apparently (*piqui, nitla*) to connect it (*popotia, nitla*), a smallish (*tlaconemi*) and oblique (*tlanololli*) line (*tla-xotlalli*), which from outside (*panipa*) joins it (*tlaaquiani*) to the fledged (*ihuiyotepehua*) head (*tzontécomatl*) of a humming bird (*huitzilin*) from which feathers (*ihuitin*) radiate (*pepetlacac*) around (*yahualoa*) and above (*ipan*) (see Figure 3).

7. There hangs down (*piloa, nitla*) from the top (*icpac*) of the cipher (*tlanahualicuilolli*) four (*nahui*) rabbit (*tochtli*), a long (*huetlatztic*) and oblique (*tzimpuztecqui*) line (*tlaxotlalli*), which links it (*tlaaquiani*) and connects (*popotia, nitla*) from one side to the other (*tlanalquixtilli*). In descending (*temo, ni*) it encloses (*tlatepuhtzacutli*) the area (*tlatlallotiliztli*) which was separating the two rows (*ompantli*) and connects (*cetilia, nitetla*) the cipher (*tlanahualicuilolli*) with the lower (*tlani*) point (*yacatl*) of the mantle (*tlapatitli*) of the ruler (*nahuatileni*) (see Figure 4A).

8. From the upper (*tlacpacpa*) end or point (*yácatl*) of the knot (*tlalpiliztli*) of the mantle (*tlapatitli*), there ascends (*tleco*) and is

connected (*popotia, nitla*), turning around (*coloa, nitla*), a smallish (*tlaconemi*) oblique (*ilacatziuhqui*) line (*tlaxotlalli*) over which (*tepan*) it joins to another (*tlanetechilpilli*) which it serves as a model (*machiotl*), that is, the glittering (*pepetzca* or *pepetlaca*) shield (*chimalli*). Enclosed (*toca, nitla*) within (*tlatec*) the circle (*yahualiuhqui*) and divided (*xexeloa, nitla*) by very twisted (*tetemmalina, nitla*) thin ropes (*macahuia, nitla*), in three (*yei*) rows (*pantin*), they form a ring (*maquizqui*) adding up to (*mocempoa*) seven (*chicome*) delicate and pleasing (*tlachcayotin-*) feathers which cover it (*-ehuahuia* or *ehuaquimiloa*) with a thin (*poxactic*) web.

Outside (*panipa*) there are four (*nahui*) (of its sparkles in the shape of) volutes (*poctin*) which are opposite each other (*ixnamictia, nitla*) and superposed (*ipanti*) (see Figure 4B).

9.   It is an amended (*melauhcaytoa*) copy (*tlamachioantli*) without modifications (*amoneneuhqui*) to which underneath (*itzintlan*) a smallish (*tlaconemi*) curved (*tlanonololli*) line (*tlacxotlalli*), while descending (*temo, ni*), connects (*popotia, nitla*) to the base (*tlatzintlan*) of the picture (*tzotzomatli*) of the inclined person (*mopacho*) who is sleeping (*nicochtoc*) as that personage who is representing (*ixiptlati*) the ruler (*nahatileni*) is pretending to be (*tlapictli*) (see Figure 5, A and B).

10.   At the girdle (*topitzahuayan*) of the inclined person (*mopacho*) who is dozing (*cocochtica, ni*) and is in the position of one "whose back is strained" (*tlatlacohuitectli*), since passing through him (*tlanalquixtilli*) horizontally (*melahuac* or *melaztic*) is an interrupted (*cahua, mo*) line (*tlaxotlalli*) which passes behind him (*tlateputzco*), closing (*tzacua, nitla*) the space which separated the (*tlatlallotiliztli*) two rows (*ompantli*) and connected him (*popotia, nitla*); upon doubling and bending (*chuitihutzi*) it goes up (*tleco*) and is under (*itzintlan*) the cipher (*tlanahuali cuilolli*) thirteen (*matlactliomey*) cane (*ácatl*) (see Figure 5, C and D).

11.   He has the nose (*yácatl*) of the obsidian house (*itzte-calli*) on (*ipan*) his head (*tzontécomatl*), which is doubled (*tlacueptli*), and is wearing a load of (*tlamama*) obsidian darts (*itzte-mitin*) on his curved (*coltic*) part of the incomplete (*cocotic*) body (*chico-centlacol*), the snake (*coatl*) which rises up (*tlamina, nino*) from the picture (*tzotzomatli*) which he holds extended (*patzoa, nite*) from the miter (*xiuhuitzoltla*TEC*tli*) of the ruler (*nahuatileni*) (see Figure 6).

12.   There will later be included (*tlapololli*) the beam to draw out the fire (*tlacuahuitl*) which had been smothered (*tlamamalli*) leaving

(*cahua, nitla*) as marks of evidence (*maxelhuia, nitetla*) on the other side (*cuepa, nino*) a small (*tontli*) oblique (*maxaltic*) line (*tlaxotlalli*), and for that reason there is omitted (*hualquixtia*) the one which is attached (*mocuazaloa*) to the "ome ácatl" (i.e. two cane), that is to say, the one which is fallen (*cenhuetzqui*) (see Figure 7A).

13. In the border (*teanyo*) of the writings (*cempantin*), five (*macuilli*) rabbit (*tochtli*) is the cipher (*tlanahualicuilolli*) which is in the corner (*tlanacaztli*) (see Figure 7B).

14. The red vermilion (*tlauhtlapalli*) picture (*tzotzomatli*) of the miter (*xiuhutzoltla*TEC*tli*) supports (*tzitzquia nitla*) and connects (*popotia, nitla*) to a smallish (*tlaconemi*) and short (*tzapatl*) line (*tlaxotlalli*) which in rising up (*tlamina, nino*) is inserted (*calaqui, ni*) under (*itzintlan*) the one which it joins to (*mopiqui*), that is to say, the sky (*ilhuicatl*) with the shot arrow (*minti*), since it has enclosed in it (*namictia, nitla*) the "point" (*mitl*) of the arrow (*tlacochtli*) which is suspended there (*piloa, nitla* or *pilcaticac*) (see Figure 8).

15. Behind (*icampa*) the miter (*xiuhuitzoltla*TEC*tli*) of the ruler (*nahuatileni*) is connected (*popotia, nitla*) a smallish (*tlaconemi*) line (*tlaxotlalli*), which goes up (*tleco*) obliquely (*ilacatziuhqui*); and on it (*tepan*) there is supported (*tzitzquia, nitla*) a (*ce*) silent figure (*nahuati, ani*) which is perspiring (*panuetzi*) from the head (*tzontécomatl*) (see Figure 9).

16. From the end (*yácatl*) of the knot (*tlalpiliztli*) of the mantle (*tlapatitli*), a small (*tontli*) oblique (*ilacatziuhqui*) line (*tlaxotlalli*) goes up (*tleco*) to connect it (*popotia, nitla*), where it inserts itself (*calaqui, ni*) underneath the (*itzintla*) arch (*tequiahuatl*) of the foot (*icxitl*) of the one who has a sharp pain (*tecococayutl*), since he is wearing thorns or prickly hairs (*ahuatin*) out of penitence (*tlamacehualiztli*) (Figure 10).

17. From the upper (*tlacpacpa*) end (*yácatl*) of the knot (*tlalpiliztli*) of the mantle (*tlapatitli*) of the ruler (*nahuatileni*) which holds up (*acoquiza, n.*) the head (*tzontécomatl*), there goes up (*tleco*) to connect it (*popotia, nitla*) an oblique (*tlanololli*) smallish (*tlaconemi*) line (*tlaxotlalli*) which from below (*itzintlan*) also supports (*quetza, nitla*) the one wearing the load (*tlamama-*) of drops (pearls) (*-huitzitziepyullotin*) of water (*atl*) on the surface (*ixtli*) of the skin (*tzontli*) (see Figure 11).

18. Below (*tlani*) is the thing which is represented (*tlamachiotlalilli*)

which appears similar (*quixtia, itlaipan, nino*) to the one which is found above (*tlacpac*) and is derived from the usual one (*noncuaquixtia, nitla*) (see Figure 12A).

19.   This figure is on a par with the other (*itloc*) which in addition wears by way of reinforcement (*toctia, nic*) a nose pendant (*yacac-uaztli*) (in the shape) of a flower (*xóchitl*), which remains (*huecahua, nitla*) held up in the air (*eheca-toctilli*) at the corresponding height with respect (*panitia, nechmo*) to the ear-plug (*nacochtli*), the hair (*tzontli*) and the head (*tzontécomatl*), since the principal ruler (*tlacatecuhtli*) could not stand the inclination (*mayana, nic*) to blow his nose (*tzomia*) (see Figure 12B, see also Figure 13).

MEANING

1.   Because of having withdrawn from the treaty which he had made (*moxiximiani*) with the Colhuas, against whom he had revolted (*tecuatihuetzi*), having induced others (*coconahuia, nite*) to change over to the opposition faction (*quetza, tehuio*), and as the former tried to subject him to the regime (*machiotlalilia, nite*), the latter was able to win fame (*panuetzi, ni*) by escaping from his town with great difficulty and risk (*tzomocquiza, ni*), owing to the fact that because of having been falsely slandered (*tlatlapiquilli*) they had entered his lands (*tlacxitoquilia*), stripping him of the same as an act of humil-iation. Which resulted as a consequence that the part (*chicotlapanqui*) of the group (*centlaca*) which had remained asleep were held as prisoners (*tzatzacua, nite*), with his very much regretting (*patzmiqui*) not having said good-bye to them because of having left suddenly (*nahuatia, nite*).

2.   This group (*centlaca*) could have gone to another place (*tlanahu-acnitlacuania*), according to a petition which it had made (*tepantlato-liztli*), in order to earn a salary or day's wages (*tlaxtlahuilo, ni*) and maintain itself by its diligence and work (*nacazcualtia, nicno*), if he had accepted or agreed to (*nonotza, tito*) serve as a mercenary (*tlaquehualli*), for which he would have been pardoned for the offenses which he had committed (*popolhuia, nitetla*) and conse-quently he would have been free from servitude (*tlamaquixtilli*). Although later they did not take any notice of them nor take them into account (*temoxictiani*) and the slave owners (*tlacahuaque*) left them abandoned (*tlateputzcualli*), because of their crime being hidden from them (*icpaltitlannitlaaquia*), the latter put aside their anger (*pololtia, nicno*) and the former were able to take leave of them in order to go

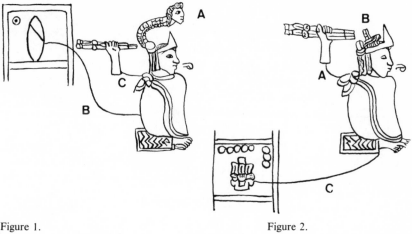

Figure 1.   Figure 2.

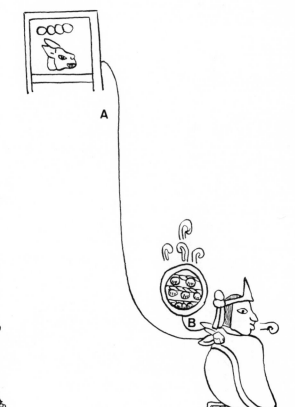

Figure 3.   Figure 4.

Figure 5.

Figure 6.

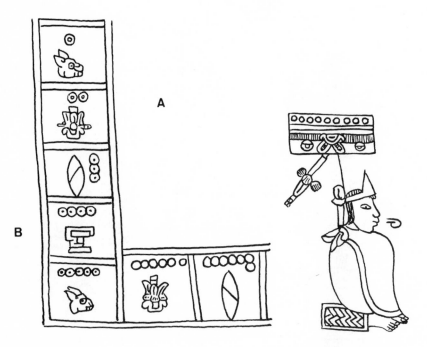

Figure 7.

Figure 8.

Figure 9.

Figure 10.

Figure 11.

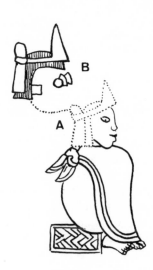

Figure 12.

to another place (*nahuatia, nite*) once they had discharged their duty (*tlapixpoloa, ni*).

3. As the prisoner of war which it was (*tlalpilli*), it would have to expiate the wrong it had done (*papatia, nitla*), and as a consequence the tribute which had been assigned (*tzinquixtia, nitla*) would be reduced for it; it would be pardoned for the offense which it had committed (*popolhuia, nitetla*), if this group (*centlaca*) should decide to go off tired and tormented (*tonehuatinemi*) bearing miseries and

Figure 13. A. *Zuma*, child, flies into a violent rage. B. *Tecuhtli*, head, etc. (Petroglyphs from *Horno de la mora*)

pains (*anonaci*), which it already was participating in (*tlanonotztli*); and in order to be able to fulfill its obligation (*quixtia, mohuicnino*), it would go to apprehend and imprison many people in different areas (*zazaca, nite*), whose inhabitants would have to pay tributes (*tlacahua, non*) in order to replace the amount which had been deducted from them (*papatla, tito*). This would be the only way in which freedom (*xoxouhqui*) could be obtained by the exhausted (*maca, ninote*) group (*centlaca*) which through cleverness (*mozcali*) managed to escape with great difficulty and risk (*tzomocquiza*), whom they later advised where to go (*omachtia, nite*) because of their having continued their very weary (*tlacochizololli*) way. And for that reason they lacked (*acanoyehuati*) a suitable place to settle (*hualmomaquixtia, ni*) and lands for sowing (*centemitin*), since they were in captivity (*mallotl*) paying for the crime which had been committed (*tlapilchiuhtli*).

4.   By way of salary (*yaoquizcatlaztlahuilli*) obtained by dint of considerable work (*tlapaliuhcahuia*), it had to deliver others into the hands of their enemies (*tlecoaquia*) in order to be reconciled with those (*tlazotlalia*) who had taken it out of prison (*toma, nite*). According to what was stipulated in the agreement (*nonotza, tito*), it was obliged to admonish or punish others (*itzticatltzitzicaztli*), for which reason it went off as mercenaries (*tlaquehualli*) to apprehend and imprison many people in different areas (*zazaca, nite*), whose inhabitants from that time paid tribute (*tlacahua, non*) in order to replace the amount which had been deducted from them (*papatla, tito*). So it was, that

freedom (*xoxouhqui*) was obtained by the exhausted (*maca, ninote*) group (*centlaca*) which had remained enclosed and isolated from the others (*motzatzacqui*) because of having escaped with much difficulty and risk (*tzomocquiza*), and who notwithstanding having continued fighting fiercely in the war (*yeccayaoc, nitla*) had been reduced to slavery (*tlacochihua, nite*).[1]

From that time on they did not any longer lack (*acanoyehuati*) a suitable place to settle (*hualmomaquixtia, ni*) or lands for sowing (*centemitin*), abandoning their captivity (*mallotl*) because of having paid for the offense committed (*tlapilchiuhtli*).

5. When the report (*huechihua*) was rendered in which they reported that they had humiliated and overwhelmed (*tlanitlaza, nite*) those who had incurred serious crimes (*tlanamiquini*), as for a pacifier of lands and towns (*tlamachtlatlatlaliani*) the punishment which they had been paying for (*nahuatitlaza*) was raised because of their having discharged their obligation (*tequiuhtia, nicno*), by which the others (*tlachialtia, nite*) were surprised.

Owing to the fact that their direct rulers (*tlapachoaque*) were obligated and compromised with them (*motlatlaliliani*), the latter wished to repent and extricate themselves from the arrangement they had made (*tzinquixtia, nino*) in order to hide their crime of (*petlatitlanicpaltitlaquiliztli*) incitement (*tetempacholiztli*).

The one who received a reward for his work (*tlaxtlahuile*) as recompense (*tlanamictilia, nite* or *tlanamictiliztli*) and who delayed paying his penalty (*tlateputzacuani*), in order to withdraw (*tlatlallo-tiliztli*) (from the Colhuas) and to leave (*ompahualiztli*) setting a good example (*ixcuitia, nite*) because of having remained united by way of friendship (*cetilia, tito*), all of them departing without anyone missing (*tontotquitihui*), they said good-bye to them to go away (*centlamitiuh*), depending on themselves (*noncuahuia, nitla*) to take possession (*ixcoyantia, nicn*) of what was going to be Tenochtitlan, in the year 1331, according to what this secret historical report (*ichtacatlapoalli*) asserts.

6. In order to test it (*tzotzona, nino*), it had been taken with caution and deceit (*nahualpoloa, nite*) to those places where it might be in danger of falling into the hands of its enemies (*tlecocaquia, nite*), but, showing calmness in danger (*pouhtiuh, ni*), this group (*centlaca*), in spite of being threatened with death (*tlaconixpiqui-xoxocpipil*) had

---

[1] The position at the bottom, *tlacxitlan*, is indicating to us that it should be taken as a correction of writing (*tlacxitocani*), which should be noted as: to correct writing (*tlacxitoca*), something opposite to what is put down (*tlacxitoctli*), the one who asks what they ought to be (*tlacxitocani*) and to refute an argument or what someone else says (*tlaxinioia, nite*).

been provoked to this (*tlacocolcuitolli*) by those who had agreed to accept (*nonotza, tito*), with entreaties and supplications (*tepantlatoliztica*), being mercenaries (*tlaquehualli*), and, with the purpose of taking revenge (*tzoncui, nino*) it was given that commission (*ihua, nite*), having come out victorious in the battles (*tepehuani*), reprimanding and punishing them (*huitztliomitltetechnicpacho*); at the same time it had to fight the enemies of its friends (*yaochihua, tehuicpanite*) who are now able to reign and govern (*icpalpanpetlapan, nica*) gently and peacefully (*ihuianyocoxca*).

7.   To discharge the duty (*pilchihua, nitla*) of ruling and governing others (*icpapanpetlapan, nic*) it would go out to all the villages looking (*tlanahuacniquiza*) for those it might come upon in the process of hearing their crafts and suspicions (*nahualcalaqui, ni*). For this purpose it hastened (*totoza, nite*) to satisfy itself (*tlaxtlahuia, nino*) and proceeded to choose (*hueltlatlattalli*) among those peoples it had taken (*tlatzintoquilia, nite*) as a mercenary (*tlaquehualli*) those who had previously defamed it (*tlamahuiz-pololli*); and had caused it uneasiness and anxiety (*temocihuiliztli*). Now as the victor (*tepoloani*), it would delimit them (*tzatzacuilia, nite*), keeping them apart (*tlatlallotiliztli*) from those with whom they had been linked (*cetilia, tito*) so that in this manner it would be able to order them (*tlanahuatia, ni*), control them (*yacana, nite*) as well as to humiliate them, humble them (*tlanitlaza, nite*), and reform them (*tlapatilia, nite*) with full authority (*nahuatile, ni*).

8.   To exercise control (*vacana, nite*) and rule others (*tlapachoa, ni*) it would have to take an oath at a special ceremony (*tlalcualiztli*) at which it would succeed someone else in command (*patcayotia, nite*) and its rank as noble (*tlapiltilli*) would be acknowledged.

The date (*tlecotia*) for the taking of possession (*pohui, tetechni*) was fixed (by) the Colhuas, who had admitted them into their faction (*ilacatzoa, tepanin*) and were sharing with them (*tlecoitta, nite*) out of gratitude (*tlazocamati*).

Notwithstanding having resisted this (*tlanehuia, nic*), it was going to discharge that office (*pilchihua, nitoa*) after having given a warning (*machiotlalilia, nite*) and devastated (CHICHIMaCA, *poloa*) the towns it had selected previously (*pepena, nite*).

The names corresponding to these towns (*tocayotia*) are: Chalco and Tequixquinahuac, its very strong (*tlatelchiuhque*) mockers and at all times gratuitous enemies (*teyauh*) who obliged it (*tlacealtilli*) to be awarded to them as their property (*mieccanquizqui*); and now that it considered the time appropriate (*yehualcan*) to overturn (*panahuia, nite*) those tale-bearers who were spreading the word (*chiquimolin*) that "it was worried (*mocihuitinemi, nino*) because they had escaped falling into the hands of the Confederation of Nations "(*maquiz-coatl*), through a pact of war (*tlachinolli-tehuatlpouhqui*) it obtained authorization (*nahuatia, nite*) to fight (*ixnamiqui*) and launch forth against the said enemies (*ipantilia, nite*).

9. Upon both parties (*tlamachilia, nite*) being judged, the complainant (*mellelmatini*) was not in agreement with the result of the judgment (*amoninocaqui*), and for that reason this ally (*tenonotza, ni*) pretended not to take notice (*iximatcanenequi*) for becoming reconciled (*tlazotlaltia, nite*) with those who had rejoiced at his trouble (*tlacominochihualti*), for which purpose passing over it purposely (*temoxictiani*) it subjugated (*popoloa, nite*) the towns previously mentioned which had remained peaceful and calm (*tzintlalteppachihui, ni*), in order in this manner to revenge itself for the offense which they had committed against it (*tzoncui, nono*) and to be able to rule and govern them (*pachoa, nite*), with the one who had been insulted (*tlapinauhtilli*) thus starting its government (*nicananotequiuh*), and, for whom by way of having regard for it (*ixitta, nite*), it had been granted authorization for this purpose (*nahuatia, nite*).

10. To accept the responsibility (*tlamixpoloa*) of ruling and governing (*pachoa, nite*), reducing others to the status of slaves (*tlacochihua, nite*) and so it might be able to take possession of his office (*tlatlacoltia, nicno*), it separated (*tlatlamantitica*) fairly from among the others (*tlatlamelahucachihualiztli*) when it exceeded and surpassed (*cahua, nite*) those towns which it had been awarded (*tlatzontequilicatlatquicahualtia, nite*), leaving them deserted (*tlateputzcahualli*) while detaining (*tzatzacuilia, nite*) and separating from these latter (*tlatlalotiliztli*) two (*ome*) which it had gained in his care (*pantlaxilia, nic*). In this manner it was accepted (*pohui, ni*) within the time period fixed (*tlecotia, nino*) as the successor of the other (*ixiptlati, nite*), and since that time it was acknowledged as lord (*cuitia, nite*), being dignified and honored by others (*tlamahuizomactli*) in the year 1375 (at 52 years of age, one century after the treaty made with the Colhuas).

11. (This group) had just appeared again (*yacatlicatlalia, nite*) because of having entered into another's pay (*calaquia, nitoa*), thus being able to face (IXTIA, *nite*) their enemies (IPANTILIA), for the purpose of taking revenge (TZONCUI) for the injuries and harm which they had caused it (paying them in this manner with the same coin) (TLACUEPCAYOTILIA, *nite*).

It also made efforts (*tlamatataquilia, nite*) to make up (*izquetza, nite*) a single family (*mixnamicticate*) with the Colhuas and the other part (*chicotlapanqui*) of the group (*centlaca*) which had received afflictions, worries and difficulties (*cocoteopouhquinicnottitia*) from the Confederation of Nations (*coatlaca*), which also slandered it (*tlatlamia, tetechni*), and for that reason had to escape with much difficulty and risk (*tzomocquiza, ni*), (that is,) this group which now rules (*pachoa, nite*) among the principal rulers (*tlacatecuhtin*) drawing up laws (*nahuatiltecpana*).

12.   The account (*tlapoalli* or *tlapoaliztli*) of the drawing out the fire (*tlamamali*) is suspended (*cahua, mo*) to begin again (*cuepcayoa*), succeeding in (*macehuia, ninotla*) replacing what was lacking (*maxiltia*), since with the inclusion (*tlaxtlahuia, nite*) of both (*tonehua*) one manages to double (*hualaquilli*) the "two cane" cycle (*mocacahua*) and an "old age" (*cenhuehuetiliztli*), that is, 104 years, is attained.

13.   By being too long (*tepanniquiza*) the sum of the calculation (*cempoa, nic*) is maintained behind (*toctia, nicno*) one hundred years (*macuilpoalxiuhtilizli*) and changes its direction (*tlanahuacnitlacuania*), going back or in reverse (*nacazpatilcaqui, nic*) (see Figure 7B).

14.   It drove away by means of arms (TEC*a*-NO*n*-TLAHUI*tzoa*), dislodging the territory of those intruders (*tzonquixtia, nitla*) who had been fleeing in retreat (*tzinquizcatlayecoa*) who, so trustingly (*poutiuh, ni*) were circling (*tlacoloa, ni*), who, when they realized, were intercepted (*tzatzacuilia, nite*) and later sentenced to death (TLAMI*quiz*-TLATZON*tequililli*) because of having entered into another's pay (*calaquia, nino*).

It also admonished and punished those towns (*itzticaltzi tzicaztli-tetec, nicpachoa*) through which they had gone with violence, going through them (*mopitzmamali*), as well as the neighboring towns which were invaded (*milxocoa, nite*) through which they had entered through a narrow pass and at night (*ilhuiz*), those who had incurred (*namiqui*) the death sentence (*miquiznahuatia*), to be hung (*piloa, nite*) or to be subjected to slavery (*tlacochihua, nite*).

15.   Because (of being) slanderers (*icanitoa, nite*) they were deposed and deprived of their dominions (*tecuhtlaza, nite*) and it made out a statement for them, hearing their cunning and wickednesses (*nahualcaqui, ni*), conquering them by means of war (*poloa, nite*), then because of being agitators (*tlacomonia, ni*) they deserved the punishment which had been imposed on them (*tlatzacuiltia, nite*), since they had praised (*tlatleyotiliztli*) and offered support to the other party (*ilacatzoa, tepannin*), on the one hand, and, on the other, they had discovered and publicly disclosed (*panitlaza, nic*) the motto (*tena-*

hualahualiztli) of the group (*centlaca*): "He who because of having escaped with great difficulty and risk (*tzomocquiza, ni*) has achieved fame" (*panuetzi, ni*).

16. Adversity arrived (*yacatia, nompammo*) when the territory became deserted because of plague (*tlalpolini*), bringing with it famine, a scarcity of provisions (*tlapatiotihua*) and sufferings (*tlatlematiliztin*) because of provisions (*popoloa, nic*) having diminished, for which reason it was necessary to increase the number (*tonacatilia, nitla*) of those who were called to work or be skilled in something else (*tlatzatzioiloni*), with messengers being sent forthwith to various districts to make it known (*tlayihualtin*) in every town (*calla*) to all tribute-payers (*tequitini*) who were paying in due proportion and moderately (*ixyeyecalhuia*) what was established (*tecpana, nitla*) in the new ordinances (*tlamanitiliztli*), in which there was included in addition the tribute which the residents of the city of Tenochtitlan (*ahuaquetepehuaque*) were to pay on that occasion (*ixotia, nitla*).

17. As soon as the epidemic (*yacatia, nompammo*) was checked (*tlapapatilli*) in the deserted territory (*tlalpolini*) and as a consequence the price of essential products was raised (*tlapatiotihua*), the ordinances which were in force (*nahuatilaza*) became null and void and by these work (*acoquetza, nitla*) was doubled, since the latter had been raised (*tzoncuilia, nitetla*) at the time (*tlécotl*) when the deferred tribute (*tlacxicahualli*) was exempt (*poa, itechnic*) and payment (*nonequixtil*) was reduced by half (*tlacoitta, nite*). With the aid which was hoped for so anxiously (*quetza, tehuio, nino*) being accepted with gratefulness (*ixitta, nitla*) it was considered that nothing better had existed (*atle*) which had so deeply touched the soul of the nation (*yollocomati*) than this excellent event (*tlamahuizolli*): "The reduction of the quota (*tzontla, nitla*) which had been assigned to them as a tribute (*ixotia, nitla*)."

18. Include only the other (*tlanehuia, nic*) instead of this replica (*tlamachioantli*), its likeness (*itlan*) in all its parts, (*ipanoc*) since it is omitted (*quixtia, nino*; or *quixtia, nitla*) because of having been previously discussed and examined (*tlacuecuepalli*), it remained in this way one on one side and the other on the other side (*nononcuaquixtia, nitla*).

19. The one who governed (*itqui, nite*) with ill-fortune had the name (*tócaitl*) Favorite (*iyacactlaantli*) Baby (*xochtic*), who because of having died (*huelomic*) was prevented (*eleltia, nite*) from having gone after those who fled to take refuge in another district (*tocaticalaqui, nite*), and in that manner he would have been able to conquer them

(*panahuia, nite*), notwithstanding the fact that he had preferred to heap honors upon them (*nachapanquetza, nite*) for no other reason than because they were fair-haired (*tzoncuztilia, nino*), having agreed only to (*tzomocyeyecoa*) the expulsion of those intruders (*teca-nom-mayahui*).

APPENDIX: DATES OF THE MOST IMPORTANT
EVENTS OF THE MEXICATL GROUP[2]

Para-graph	Period of time		Nahuas dates		Summary of the theme
I	c. 1298		1 tochtli		Captive of the Colhuas (43 years after having left *Zumpahuacan*). Shut up in *Mexicaltzinco* for 25 years.*
II	1323		1 técpatl		Proposal, agreement, and commutation of sentence because of war services.
V	1331		8 ácatl		Goes off to *Tenochtitlán*.
		c. 1344		8 técpatl	
VI	1345		9 calli		Mercenary of the Confed-
	1351		2 ácatl*		eration of Nations.
		1365		3 calli	
VII	1366		4 tochtli		Shares as an ally: merits, conquests, possession of lands and subjects, and taking revenge for previous offenses, as a requisite for ruling.
X		1375		13 ácatl	Is acknowledged and accepted as ruler.
XI	1376	1388	1 técpatl	13 técpatl	Heads the Confederation of Nations.
XII	1389		1 calli		In this long period of expansion and glory, he ejects invaders, succeeding
XIV	1403		2 ácatl		in ambushing them.

[2] *Translator's note:* By way of explanation of the terms used above and in the main text, the following may be helpful. The dates of the Nahuas referred to above reflect the counting system of the early Mexicans. Their years went in 52-year cycles, and were identified by the use of four key words: *técpatl* (flint), *calli* (house), *tochtli* (rabbit) and *ácatl* (cane). If year 1 of a 52-year cycle were *técpatl*, they would be identified as follows:

Appendix (continued)

Para-graph	Period of time		Nahuas dates		Summary of the theme
	1448		8 técpatl		Commemoration of the 125 years of the Colhua treaty and renovation of the
	1455		2 ácatl		main Temple.*
		1469		3 calli	
XV	1470	1481	4 tochtli	2 calli	Growing separation and differences between factions of the Mexicatl group.*
XVI	1482	1486	3 tochtli	7 tochtli	To remedy the catastrophe caused by the epidemic and famine which decimated the population, the "personal service tax" was doubled and a tribute imposed on residents of Tenochtitlán.
XVII	1487	1502	8 ácatl	10 tochtli	Ordinances on tribute are cancelled, the remainder is forgiven, and the amount in existence is reduced by 50%.*
XVIII	1503		11 ácatl		The "Quequetzalcoatl", the so-called "Favorite Baby",
	1507		2 ácatl		comes to power.*
	c. 1521			3 calli	This ruler dies, who because of having preferred and given honor to the Spanish did not conquer them and only was able to expel them.*

---

* The dates agree with the calculation which is carried in *Historia de los méxicanos por sus pinturas* (Pomar y Zurita 1941).

---

1 técpatl (flint)	6 calli	11 tochtli	
2 calli (house)	7 tochtli	12 ácatl	
3 tochtli (rabbit)	8 ácatl	13 técpatl	
4 ácatl (cane)	9 técpatl		
5 técpatl	10 calli		

then,
   1 calli
   2 tochtli, etc., until 4 cycles of 13 each have been completed.
Because of the repetition of the cycle, and the successive use of the same words, the position of the year in the 52-year cycle would be easily identifiable. For example, in the list above, "2 tochtli" (or "2 rabbit," as it appears in the main text) would be the 15th year of that cycle.

REFERENCES

CLARK COOPER, JAMES, *editor and translator*
1938   *Codex Mendoza*. London.

CORONA OLEA, HORACIO
1964   *Glífica criptográfica náhuatl*. Mexico City.

DE MOLINA, FRAY ALONSO
1571   *Vocabulario en lengua castellana y méxicana*. (Published in facsimile.) Colección de incunables americanos. Ediciónes cultura hispánica. Madrid.

POMAR Y ZURITA
1941   "Historia de los méxicanos por sus pinturas," in *Relaciónes de Texcoco y de la Nueva España*, 207–289. Mexico City. S. Chávez Hayhoe.

The Aztec Day Names

HERBERT LANDAR

Barriers to a full explication of the Aztec day names range from a lack of phonemic transciptions and other descriptive data (on the linguistic side) to a need for better ethnographic data. The meanings and implications of some of the Mexican day names are unknown. From contemporary ethnographers we need clues based on studies of native religious life, ethnomedical beliefs and practices, methods of divination, and canons of mythology and folklore. A broader perspective, which ties religious beliefs and symbolism to social needs and structures, is also needed. Almost nothing is available on the clans and *moieties* of Aztec and Mayan tribes. That the so-called totemism of the native astrological calendar should not be intimately linked with the structures counted as clans, by means of which delicate fabrics of social expectations and obligations are maintained, would be astonishing. Yet we have scarcely posed the question, how far and in what ways were clans linked to the calendar and the stars?

An even broader perspective is needed, in which areal analysis figures. We need to know not only how the calendar fits into a setting of religious and social customs, but also how the structures of each tribe fit into patterns ranging over all tribes in a linguistic family such as the Mayan or the Uto-Aztecan. And we need to know what, if anything, is pan-American as well as pan-family in the patterns which might seem idiosyncratic from the limited perspective of any one tribe.

The opportunity has passed, of course, for investigating any possible relationship of Mayan clans of the Colonial Period to the Mayan calendar. Mayan clans have been modified by modern conditions, have been fragmented and disguised, or so I suppose, from what little is available in published literature. The hope remains, on the other hand, that something interesting will turn up somewhere in the Mayan regions, or in those of the Uto-Aztecans, or in those of other tribes with calendrical histories, such as the Otomanguean, notably the Mixtecan and Zapotecan.

Linguistic materials on Mixtec and Zapotec day names are less satisfactory than those for the Aztecs and Mayans. For Mixtec, Caso (1956, 1967) gives: (1) *Quehui* 'Day' (?), (2) *Chi* 'Wind', (3) *Cuau* 'House', *Huahi, Mae,* (4) *Cuu* [not translated by Caso. Cf. *Coō* 'Snake' in Mixtec of modern San Miguel el Grande], (5) *Yucoco* 'Snake', *Yo,* (6) *Mahua* [not translated by Caso. San Miguel *Máá-yá* 'God' probably is not related], (7) *Cuaa* 'Deer', (8) *Xayu* 'Rabbit', (9) *Duta* 'Water', (10) *Ua* 'Coyote', (11) *Ñuu* [not translated by Caso. San Miguel has *Ñuū* 'Earth, Pueblo' and *Ñúú* 'Night'], (12) *Cuañe* 'Grass', (13) *Huiyo* 'Cane', (14) *Vidzu* 'Mountain Cat', (15) *Xayacu* 'Eagle', (16) *Cuij* 'Turkey', (17) *Qhi* [no translation], (18) *Cuxí* 'Knife', (19) *Dzahui* 'Rain', (*20*) *Uaco* [Caso proposed 'Flower' in 1962 but withdrew his proposal later. The meaning is unknown].

Seler (1904) analyzed the Zapotec calendar as preserved by Juan de Córdova late in the sixteenth century. Reconciling contradictions in translations of day names of Aztecs, Mayans, and Zapotecs (of Mitla), Seler traced the Mexican calendars to Oaxaca, where the Zapotec and Mixtec tribes flourished before the Conquest. Howard Leigh (1958a, 1958b) has identified calendrical symbols of stone monuments, idols, vases, and religious edifices, published with simplified linguistic forms in *Boletín de Estudios Oaxaqueños*. The Zapotec day names, in simplified form: (1) *Quiachijlla* 'Crocodile', (2) *Pexoo* 'Wind', (3) *Calicij* 'House', (4) [word unknown] 'Lizard' [seen on Estela 2, Monte Albán III, in the date or name 'Two Lizard', and on Lápida 1, Museo Nacional, Monte Albán II, in what is perhaps the name 'Eight Lizard'], (5) *Pelaa* 'Snake', (6) *Quelana* 'Death', (7) *Quiachina* 'Deer', (8) *Pillaloo* 'Rabbit', (9) *Quianiza* 'Water', (10) *Quiagueche* 'Dog', (11) [word unknown] 'Monkey' [on a stone, Museo de Arte Zapotecano, Monte Albán III, name 'Three Monkey'], (12) *Quiatella* (?) 'Twisted Grass', (13) *Quij* 'Reed', (14) *Pepeloo* 'Ocelot', (15) *Picixoo* 'Eagle', (16) *Peloo* 'Vulture', (17) *Xoo* 'Earthquake', (18) *Quiaguij* 'Flint', (19) *Quegappe* 'Rain', (20) *Quialoo* 'Flower'.

Proto-Mayan reconstructions have been published by Kaufman (1964). Some of these hypothetical forms might have figured in the religious system of the Proto-Mayans. In the absence of good grammatical and lexical studies of all Mayan languages, of course, the following vocabulary has to be considered as tentative and subject to revision. Other qualifications, which attach mainly to particular words, should be noted in Kaufman's essay (1964).

(1) **peqw'* 'dog' [a Zapotec loan?], (2) **bahlëm* 'jaguar', (3) **t'u'l*

'rabbit', (4) *chich* 'rabbit', (5) *'imul* 'rabbit', (6) *kooj* 'puma', (7) *kyehj* 'deer', (8) *ma'x* 'spider monkey', (9) *k'oy* 'spider monkey', (10) *batz* 'howler monkey', (11) *'oq* 'coyote', (12) *xo'j* 'coyote', (13) *mutw* 'bird', (14) *tz'ikwin* 'bird', (15) *jooj* 'crow', (16) *tuhkuru* 'owl' [a Uto-Aztecan loan], (17) *'ikin* 'owl', (18) *sootz* 'bat' [note the phonetic association with a storm symbol, *suutz* 'cloud'], (19) *mo* 'guacamaya', (20) *likw* 'hawk', (21) *t'iiw* 'hawk', (22) *xi(h)kw* 'hawk', (23) *kwot* 'hawk', (24) *kaab* '(honey) bee' [note the connection with the Bacabs, gods of apiculture], (25) *sanik* 'ant', (26) *'am* 'spider', (27) *xim* 'spider', (28) *tzek* 'scorpion', (29) *'wo* 'toad', (30) *peq/poq* 'toad', (31) *hos* 'eagle owl', (32) *'usej* 'eagle owl', (33) *k'uty* 'eagle owl', (34) *'aj-muuch* 'frog', (35) *pajtza* 'frog', (36) *ch'uch* 'frog', (37) *'ahyin* 'lizard', (38) *intam* 'iguana' [from a non-Mayan source, borrowed in the form *'in(V)tam*, etc., this reconstruction forces one to wonder about a possible external source of the high god *Itzam Na* 'Iguana House'], (39) *huuj/hiij* 'iguana', (40) *kan* 'snake' [Kaufman's reconstruction for 'yellow' is *q'ën*. While his reconstructions do not solve certain etymological problems of the Mayan day names or deities' names, such as the origin of the name *Kukulcan*, Kaufman's reconstructions do show that some cases of apparent homophony did not exist in the original Mayan homeland].

Information on animal names in Proto-Mayan is limited to what has been given above. There are other words, however, which concern the mythology in general and which help us to see pieces of names of gods and other figures. Here is a selection of nonanimal terms of the ancient culture: (41) *mam* 'grandfather; father', (42) *xiib* 'male', (43) *'ix* 'female', (44) *'aj-* 'masculine agent', (45) *'ix-* 'feminine agent', (46) *nan/na* 'mother', (47) *chuch* 'mother', (48) * mim* 'mother', (49) *me'/mi* 'mother', (50) *'winaq* 'person', (51) *q^wëb* 'hand; arm', (52) *ngi'/ngu* 'nose', (53) *tzwa'm* 'nose', (54) *'eh* 'tooth', (55) *wëty* 'eye; face', (56) *sat* 'eye; face', (57) *'oq* 'foot', (58) *ma* 'know; think', (59) *'utz* 'good', (60) *mul* 'bad action', (61) *mahk* 'bad action', (62) *'eleq* 'bad action', (63) *'ak* 'new', (64) *tz'ihb* 'write', (65) *hu'ng* 'paper', (66) *'ok* 'enter', (67) *ngah* 'house' [cf. item (38) above], (68) *'otyoty* 'house', (69) *lab* 'evil spirit', (70) *këm* 'die' [cf. the Mayan day name *Cimi* 'Death'. By coincidence if not by metathesis, the same consonants occur in the Proto-Uto-Aztecan root *muki* 'die', which lies behind the Aztec day name *Miquiztli* 'Death'], (71) *k'uh* 'god', (72) *way* 'nagual; witch; dream', (73) *'aj* 'cane', (74) *jalal* 'cane', (75) *'inup* 'ceiba', (76) *'i'm* 'corn' [Huastec; others have *'ix* with *i'm*; cf. the day name *Imix*], (77) *ngik* 'flower', (78) *'aq* 'grass', (79) *k'im* 'grass', (80) *kih* 'henequen agave', (81) *tyoq* 'cloud', (82) *suutz* 'cloud', (83) *muyal 'cloud', (84) *'asun 'cloud' [from Mixe-Zoque into Tojolabal, Chuj, Kanjobal, and Jacaltec], (85) *'ulew ' earth ', (86) *lu'm 'earth', (87) *ch'och' 'earth', (88) *q'a...q' 'fire', (89) *'uh/'uj 'moon', (90) *'iik' 'moon', (91) *poh 'moon', (92) *'ix-'ajaw 'moon', (93) *'aq'ab 'night', (94) *'aq'b-al 'night', (95) *ngab 'rain', (96) *kya'ng 'sky', (97) *sib 'smoke', (98) *'eeq' 'star', (99) *q'anal 'star', (100) *ch'umil 'star', (101) *'abaj 'stone', (102) *ton/tun 'stone', (103) *ky'e'n 'stone', (104) *q'iing 'sun; day', (105) *kyah(o)q 'thunder', (106) *hë' 'water', (107) *'iq' 'wind; air' [we note phonetic similarity, again perhaps by coincidence, of this Pan-Mayan form and Proto-Uto-Aztecan *heka 'wind'], (108) *ha'b 'year', (109) *ha'b-il 'year', (110) *tz'ihb 'year', (111) *k'aq 'black', (112) *'ejq' 'black', (113) *yë'x 'green', (114) *kyëq 'red', (115) *sëq 'white', (116) *q'ën 'yellow', (117) *'aj 'count', (118) *nah 'first', (119) *bah 'first'.

Prehistoric counting customs for Proto-Mayans and Proto-Uto-Aztecans who moved into southern Mexico perhaps involved the use of particles to classify the shape or nature of the counted objects. One of the deficiencies in our records of the ancient calendars is the lack of any indication of how the day signs were classed. That is, we do not have the number words written out, and we cannot always be certain of our reconstructions of the actual pronunciations of day names for this reason.

The Mayans when counting had to classify the object counted, according to an intricate, as yet incompletely reconstructed, system. If winik 'man' is classified as animate, the particle tul 'animate' had to follow the number, as in oštul winik 'three men'. The particle p'el 'inanimate' worked the same way: ošp'el na 'three houses'. We cannot at present conjecture how the prehistoric counting customs intersected with day-name usage, though we can speculate that particular numerological associations inhered in the number part of the day name. In the following list I have assembled number words in several kinds of spelling, from Thompson (1932), Tozzer (1921, 1957), Torresano (1754), and Kaufman (1964), with numerological associations: (120) *jun 'one', hun-, Hun, hun (hu-). [The forms are from Kaufman (1964), Tozzer (1921: 99), Thompson (1970) and (in Cakchiquel) from the manuscript of Estevan Torresano in the Bibliothèque Nationale, dated about 1750. The work is dated 1754; Tulane and Harvard have variant titles. This order is adhered to below as well.]

U or Ix Chel, moon goddess and the day Caban, (121) *ka'(ib) 'two', ka-, Ca, cay (ca), god of sacrifices or earth, day, Etz'nab, (122) *'ox 'three', oš-, Ox, oxi(ox-), Itzam Na, celestial dragon, Cauac, (123) *kyang 'four', kăn-, Can, cahi (cah-), Kin the sun, Ahau, spirit of the sun, and the day, Ahau, (124) *ho' 'five', ho-, Ho, voo, -oo (vo-), crocodile god, day, Imix, (125) *'waq 'six', wăk-,

Uac, *vakaki* (*vak-*), *Chac*, god of rain and germination, day *Ik*, (126) **huq* 'seven', *wuk-*, *Uuc*, *vuku* (*vuk-*), jaguar (*Akbal*/*Votan*), earth and night god, ruler of days *Akbal* and *Ix*, and the month *Uo*, (127) **waqxëq* 'eight', *wašak-*, *Uaxac*, *vakxaki* (*vakxak-*), *Ah Mun*, corn god, day *Kan*, (128) **beleng* 'nine', *bolon-*, *Bolon*, *belehe* (*beleh-*) *Chicchan*, snake god, ruler of the day called *Chicchan* [perhaps 'nine' is the sacred number of *Bolon Dz'acab*; 'nine' also means 'many'], (129) **lajung* 'ten', *la hun-*, *La Hun*, *lahuh*, *Cizin*, death god, day *Cimi* [Tozzer explains the form as *la* 'all' plus *hun* '(of) one (count)'], (130) **buluk* 'eleven', *buluk-*, *Buluc* [Tzeltal, Tzotzil, Chol, Chorti, Yucatec], (131) **jun lajung* 'eleven', Cakchiquel *hulahuh* [Kechi, Jacaltec, Mam], (132) **'us-luk* 'eleven' [Chuj, Kanjobal] – with 'eleven' are associated *Buluc ti Ch'abtan*, androgynous earth god, and the day *Manik*, (133) **laj-ka. . .-* 'twelve', *la ka-*, *La Ca*, (134) **kab-lajung* 'twelve', Cakchiquel *cablahuh* – with 'twelve' are associated *Lahun Chan*, Venus spirit, and the day *Lamat*, (135) **laj-'ox* 'thirteen', *la oš-*, *La Ox*, *Ox La Hun*, *Ox Lahun*, *oxlahuh*, *Oxlahun ti Ku*, sky gods of the sacred numbers, and the day *Muluc*; 'thirteen' also means 'countless', (136) **kw'al* 'twenty', *hun qal-*, (137) **taxb* 'twenty', (138) **'winaq* 'twenty', Cakchiquel *hu vinak*, total count of day signs. The numerals 'one' through 'ten' are pan-Mayan. Part of our interest in the numerals, of course, comes from the repetition of 'one' through 'thirteen' with each of the twenty day signs, for a total of 260 day names, one for each day of the ritual year.

While nothing is certain about the Proto-Mayan system or other reconstructed systems, it is useful to consider dates which have been proposed for these systems. McQuown suggests that the Proto-Mayans were in a homeland in Huehuetenango, northwestern Guatemala, by 2600 B.C., with a population of perhaps 5,000 (McQuown 1964; Vogt 1969: 21–29). Some of Kaufman's reconstructions perhaps go back that far; others do not, and the extent of his work illustrates the degree to which we are handicapped in attempting to etymologize the Mayan day names. We are in even worse condition with the Zapotec counterparts of the Mayan calendrical names, from lack of ethnographic and linguistic research. The Zapotec family is part of a larger group, the Otomanguean. Glottochronologists suppose that Chiapanec diverged from Popolocan about 4000 B.C., and Otomian diverged about 2900 B.C. The Amuzgo-Mixtec group was formed about 1900 B.C. The isolation of the Zapotec group was complete about 2500 B.C.

Within the Otomanguean area, Proto-Popotecan and Proto-Popolocan reconstructions have been published by Gudschinsky (1959). These reconstructions take us back much earlier, probably, than Kaufman's for Mayan, though the exact temporal relationship is in doubt. To show the limits on Zapotec day-name etymologies and to have data for Mayan-Otomanguean comparisons, I have listed selected reconstructions. As with the Mayan list, names of animals are given first. Prefixes and suffixes are arranged with roots. Possible developments are indicated with an arrow. I have gone further than Gudschinsky here, taking liberties for which she bears no blame. If no arrow is used, the form is Proto-Popolocan; otherwise, the first form or forms are Proto-Popotecan and the form or forms after the arrow are Proto-Popolocan.

(1) *ku-tʸu-kaha 'ant' [variant prefixes 'yu- and ču-. Here as with other names of animals we have a prefix ku- 'animate', which is used with inanimates too, if they are moved by spirits (e.g. 'star')], (2) *ku-ña-nku 'bat' [variant prefixes ya-, ni-, 'i-; the Ixcatec outcome, with something added at the end, is 'u⁴ñu⁴ngu³ řa¹t'i 'vampire'], (3) *pa→*ša 'bee' [I use thorn for Gudschinsky's theta, apostrophe for her glottal stop, and tilde for her nasal hook], (4) *ku-'pë→*ku-se/še 'bird', (5) *ni-n-kë→*ni-n-ke 'buzzard' [some words in this list contain ni- or na-, prefixes which indicate nominal function], (6) *ku-ša'-šĩ 'coyote' [a number of animals with prominent teeth may have been represented by this form, as daughter languages have glosses like 'lion' and 'tiger' as well as 'coyote'], (7) *ku-ntʸa'ha 'crow', (8) *ku-šĩ 'deer', (9) *ni-n-nya→*ni-n-ya 'dog', (10) *ku-š-ha 'eagle, hawk', (11) *ku-'kë→*ku-h-tʸe 'fish', (12) *ku-(n)či-se 'fly' [variant root *sẽ(')], (13) *ku-ce' 'hare, rabbit', (14) *ku-ntʸuhi 'opossum', (15) *ku-ši-kha 'skunk', (16) *ku-kʷu→*ku-kʷa 'snail', (17) *ku-nče 'snake', (18) *ky-ye 'snake ', (19) *ku-ča-hʷa 'spider' [variant ya-], (20) *ku-nɔ→*ku-hnu 'squirrel', (21) *ku-tu' 'toad', (22) *ku-n(t)a-hñu 'turkey', (23) *ša-'we 'wasp' [perhaps earlier *ku-ša-'we], (24) *ku-ntʸa(') 'wolf, fox'.

People, body parts, verbs, and some other words: (25) *ča-hmi 'person, man' [variant ču-], (26) *na-'ni 'man, witch, priest, male' [variant ši-], (27) *nta-wa 'man', (28) *ni-čihĩ 'woman', (29) *hũ 'mother', (30) *čã 'arm', (31) *t-hñi' 'blood', (32) *ntʸa 'bone', (33) *yi-'kĩ/kĩ→ š-ku/kũ (*p-'kĩ/kĩ→*t-ku/kü) 'face, eye, head', (34) *n-kahĩ (*s-kahĩ) 'face, head', (35) *ncahi 'foot', (36) *sahi 'foot', (37) *ti-hu→*tʸ-ha 'hand', (38) *pu-'wɔ→*cu-'wa 'mouth', (39) *(n)tʸi-tʸhũ 'nose' [earlier root *tʸu], (40) *ni-(')nyɔ→*ni-(')ñu 'teeth' [variant na-], (41) *xi-'ntĩ'→*hi-(')nta 'good' [variants 'i-, ña], (42) *yã 'bad', (43) *šu 'to blossom', (44) *š-kʷhẽ 'green, unripe', (45) *kʷha 'death', (46) *'me, *mi'i die', (47) *'kĩ, *čĩ'die', (48) *ni-hña 'dream', (49) *n(tʸ)i-'ya 'house', (50) *ni-h-ña 'mat (of straw)', (51) *š-kũ 'sharp tip' [also 'knife' (?)], (52) *ka-te 'cut' [variant wa-].

Plants and nature: (53) *hma' 'beans', (54) *šika-cu 'maguey cactus', (55) *na-nta 'nopal cactus', (56) *(n)t(a)-hi 'cane (sugar)', (57) *nya-x-me→*na-hme (*ñu-hme) 'corn', (58) *(')ni'→*'nihĩ

'corn (ear)' [perhaps *'*ni-hi* from *'*ni'-xĩ*], (59) *chu* 'flower', (60)
ka-lihi, *ka-nt*ʸihi* 'grass' [*ka-* is from *kʷa*' 'leaf'], (61) *ku-š-tahi*
'mushroom', (62) *š-hũ* 'saltwort', (63) *n(t)a(')*→*n(t)a*, *la* 'tree',
(64) *ya*'→*ya* 'tree', (65) *t-xʷĩ*'→*t-hʷĩ(*') 'cloud' [variants *š-*, *yu-*],
(66) *š-tʸhĩ* 'day', (67) *ngʷĩ*→*nki* 'earth; under', (68) *pĩ(*')→*ša*
'earthquake', (69) *'*we-š-ce* 'fire', (70) *šu-'wi* 'fire; light; sun' [vari-
ants *cu-*, *'li*, *'nti*], (71) *ča-sẽ* 'light, dawn', (72) *h-wa-te* 'lightning',
(73) *ni-tʸhu-sa* 'moon', (74) *n(č)i-thẽ* 'morning' [variant *či-*], (75)
hña' 'mountain, woods', (76) *n-'ka* 'mountain peak', (77) *kʷa-'ña*
'night' (?) [Gudschinsky's gloss is 'dusk', the root from *(')nu*], (78)
š-ci 'rain', (79) *'*nka-tʸ-hmi* 'sky', (80) *n-ti'i* 'smoke, vapor', (81)
š-ce 'star', (82) *ñu-ce* 'star', (83) *po(*')→*šu*' 'stone', (84) *ča-kũ*
'sun', (85) *ča-hũ* 'sun' [variant *ka-*], (86) *yu-hʷa* 'water' [older roots
xʷu', *xʷu/xʷë*', *xʷë*], (87) *ci-ntʸa'hu* 'wind', (88) *ha'i* 'year'.
    Colors and numbers: (89) *-'ma*, perhaps *x-'ma*→*hma* 'black',
(90) *ti-ye* 'black', (91) *yu-wa* 'green', (92) *kha-ce* 'red', (93)
tʸha-wa 'white', (94) *si-ne* 'yellow' [variant *sa-*], (95) *x-nko*
→*hnku* 'one', (96) *yuhu* 'two', (97) *pi*→*š-hõ* 'three', (98)
*'*ni*→*nihẽ* 'three', (99) *mɔ-xũ*→*ñuhũ* 'four', (100) *š-ño'o* 'five',
(101) *š-ño'o* 'five', (102) *n-ya-tu* 'seven' [root *yu*], (103) *š-hni*
'eight', (104) *te* 'ten' [perhaps *ku-te*→Ixcatec *u³-te⁴*], (105) *š-kahã*
'twenty'.
    Before comparing Mayan and Otomanguean protoforms (see Table
1), a word of caution is necessary. We can infer from written records
that borrowing of traits occurs if contact conditions are favorable.
There is indeterminacy, however, in the date of borrowing and in the
precise phonetic properties of the borrowed forms, where the traits
are words. We can identify interesting sets of protoforms, the set
Proto-Mayan *'*usej* 'owl, sp.' and Proto-Popolocan *kuse*, *kuše*
'bird', for example, without being able to infer safely that the Mayans
learned the word for the *buharro* or 'eagle owl' from Otomangueans
in prehistoric times. While there are a few interesting similarities in
the following comparisons, the list does more, I think, to show lack
of contact than anything else. Thompson (1932: 454) has suggested
that the Old Empire tribes perhaps had one calendar and set of
glyphs, but different words for naming them. If the ritual calendar was
used by prehistoric Otomangueans, the same situation may have
obtained by 2600 B.C., and the wrong schedule of comparisons (the
only ones we can manage at the present time) may follow. Eventually,
perhaps, Proto-Zapotec and Proto-Mayan reconstructions will be
available to match those for Proto-Uto-Aztecan which will be presented
in the final section of this essay. At the moment, however, I think
we have evidence here of an impasse.
    We are in better shape when we turn to the Aztec day names

Table 1. Comparison of Mayan and Otomanguean protoforms

	Proto-Mayan	Proto-Popolocan
1. Ant	*sanik*	*–kaha*
2. Bat	*sootz'*	*–nku*
3. Bee	*kaab*	*ša*
4. Bird	*'usej* 'owl, sp.'	*kuse, kuše* 'bird'
5. Buzzard	*'ikin* 'owl'	*ninke*
6. Coyote	*xo'j*	*ší*
7. Crow	*jooj*	*–nt^ya'ha*
8. Deer	*kyehj*	*kuší*
9. Dog	*peqw'*	*ninya*
10. Eagle, Hawk	*kwot* 'hawk'	*–ha*
11. Rabbit	*t'u'l*	*–ce'*
12. Snake	*kan*	*–ye*
13. Spider	*'am, xim*	*–h^wa*
14. Toad	*'wo', peq/poq*	*–tu'*
15. One Person	*'winaq* 'person'	*hnku* 'one'
16. Die	*këm*	*'me, mi'i*
17. Water	*hë'*	*–h^wa,* from *x^wë'*
18. Green	*yë'x*	*yuwa*
19. Red	*kyëq*	*khace*
20. Yellow	*q'ën*	*sine*
21. One	*jun*	*hnku*
22. Three	*'ox*	*šhã*
23. Five	*ho'*	*sño'o*
24. Seven	*huq*	*–yu*
25. Twenty	*kw'al*	*–kahã*

and possible etymologies than in our efforts to deal with the Mayan or Otomanguean day names, Proto-Uto-Aztecan reconstructions have been published by Hale (1958); Voegelin, Voegelin, and Hale (1962); Miller (1967); and others. While scholars disagree about the possible dates of these reconstructions, I find it convenient to work with this pattern: before 2000 B.C. the Aztec or southern section of the Uto-Aztecan group broke away, moving south, leaving the Utean or northern section behind (in southern Arizona). This northern section separated into a Sonoran and a Shoshonean group around 1500 B.C. Between about 1100 and 900 B.C., the Shoshonean group separated into two groups, the first producing the Plateau language type and the Kern River or Tubatulabal language type, and the second producing the Pueblo or Hopi language type and the Takic language type. For the former two types, the time of separation was 500 B.C.; for the latter, around 900 B.C. These dates are crude, and it must be pointed out that Hale has made more sensitive estimates; they serve here, however, to give us some perspective.

We can tell from these dates, for example, that the Mayans could not have come in contact with the Uto-Aztecans when each group was in its homeland, the Mayans in Huehuetenango about 2600 B.C., the Uto-Aztecans in southern Arizona before 2000 B.C.

Table 2. Aztec day names

Aztec day names	Comments
1. *Cipactli* 'Crocodile'	No etymology. Cf. *se* 'cold,' *pa* 'water'
2. *Ehecatl* 'Wind'	Reflects *hekā* 'wind'
3. *Calli* 'House'	Protoform *kali* 'house'
4. *Cuetzpallin* 'Lizard'	No etymology
5. *Coatl* 'Snake'	Root *ko(wa)* 'snake,' with the usual singular absolutive suffix
6. *Miquiztli* 'Death'	Reflects *muki* 'die'
7. *Mazatl* 'Deer'	Root is *mas–* 'deer'
8. *Tochtli* 'Rabbit'	Root is *to–* 'rabbit'
9. *Atl* 'Water'	Root is *pa–* 'water'
10. *Itzcuintli* 'Dog'	No etymology
11. *Ozomatli* 'Monkey'	No etymology
12. *Malinalli* 'Grass'	Reflects *meli* 'twist'
13. *Acatl* 'Reed'	Root is *paka–* 'reed,' perhaps with *pa* 'water' as the initial element; the Badianus manuscript shows that *akatl* means any water plant
14. *Ocelotl* 'Ocelot'	No etymology. Manuscripts show pumas as well as jaguars
15. *Quauhtli* 'Eagle	Root is *kwa–* 'eagle'
16. *Cozcaquauhtli* 'Vulture'	Metaphor: 'gem' plus 'eagle'
17. *Ollin* 'Earthquake'	Perhaps related to *'ol–* 'roll'
18. *Tecpatl* 'Flint Knife'	Possibly from *tek–* 'cut' and *pa–* 'hit'
19. *Quiahuitl* 'Rain'	No etymology
20. *Xochitl* 'Flower'	Cf. *se–*, *so–* 'flower'

We have no real date, on the other hand, for the invention of the 260-day ritual calendar with its thirteen numbers and twenty names in constant cycle. We have rough dates, however, for the start of the disordering of the calendar (assuming that at some time in Mayan history only one set of day names was used). The pristine pattern is distorted by the Quichean and Kekchian groups and the Tzeltalans as well. I find it useful (following McQuown, Vogt, and others) to set the date of 750 B.C. for the Tzeltalan migration, and about A.D. 1350 for the Quiche-Achi breakoff, with around A.D. 1700 for that of Cakchiquel-Tzutujil. In contrast, the Yucatec migration is dated at about 1600 B.C.

The Aztec migrations into Mexico might conceivably have predated the initial move of the Yucatecs, whose occupation of Yucatán was not completed until around 750 B.C. But we lack data on languages of the Nahuatlan branch, and we lack archaeological data to correlate with such linguistic data, so we are unable to make even crude guesses about early Mayan-Aztec contacts. Differentiation of Pochutla, Mecayapan, and Zacapoaxtla took place in the twelfth and thirteenth centuries, if we follow Hale's estimates. How Nahuatlan differentiation relates to a possible prehistoric calendar or to pre-Columbian diffusion of calendrical concepts, however, is a matter not yet worked out.

What we are reduced to, in the face of these unresolved mysteries, is the listing of the Aztec day names with such reconstructed elements as may pertain to them (see Table 2).

The surprising transparency of some of the Aztec names suggests, if anything, that we have relatively recent rather than archaic compositions. If we assume that the Aztecs, invading Mayan lands from the north, acquired calendrical lore from the Mayans of the southern lowlands when the culture there was at its peak, we would have to guess at contacts in the eighth century A.D., precisely when, glotto-chronologists say, we have the Chontal-Chol and Chontal-Chorti partitions.

There is, of course, the remote possibility that Proto-Aztecans reached Proto-Mayans around 2000 B.C. I think such contacts unlikely. Few vocabulary items of Proto-Uto-Aztecan and Proto-Mayan bear sufficient resemblance to support a theory of such early contacts. Such resemblances as Proto-Mayan *sanik 'ant' and Proto-Uto-Aztecan *'ane 'ant' may prove to be chimerical. And archaeologists do not speak, as far as I know, of Mayan contacts with northern peoples at the level of 2000 B.C. Indeed, the general belief, it appears to me, is that the Mayans were closest to Late Preclassic cultures of southern Mexico and Guatemala, and took culture (perhaps including class structuring) from central Mexican Teotihuacán in the Early Classic Period. It was then, for example, that Tlalocs were integrated into the culture, and finally flourished in Late Classic Mayan sculpture.

Since some scholars have proposed that Mayan culture went into decline around A.D. 790, with abandonment of Classic centers by about A.D. 950 (10.6.0.0.0) or some time thereafter (Uaxactun, Tikal, Altar de Sacrificios, Seibal, Piedras Negras, and Palenque being all but abandoned), and since the eighth century was a time of increased central Mexican contacts with Mayan cultures for whom calendrical ceremonialism had become as important as it ever would be, it is not beyond speculation that invading Aztecs adopted calendrical concepts including the meanings of day names from Mayan slaves acquired by conquest, slaves who were temple specialists, and who may have added refinements to a more primitive calendar already in Aztec hands, perhaps centuries old.

It is not within the means of a linguist to date the oldest calendar used by Aztec invaders of Mexico. The span of time from 2000 B.C. to A.D. 700 is so broad that it guarantees only mystery. Given incomplete records for various Uto-Aztecan languages, it is hazardous to speculate about the isoglosses of the day names, but some thoughts may be ventured in this connection. I had expected a different distribution of names than I found. My expectations were based on those of Robert Shafer, who had discovered for Sino-Tibetan languages an instability of names of animals and plants. Shafer (1967: 148) says:

Table 3.

Day name elements	Distribution
1. *se* 'cold'	Sho. Son. Az.
2. *pa* 'water'	Sho. Son. Az.
3. *heka* 'wind'	Sho. Son. Az.
4. *kali* 'house'	Sho. Son. Az.
5. *kowa* 'snake'	Sho. Son. Az.
6. *muki* 'die'	Sho. Son. Az.
7. *mas* 'deer'	Son. Az.
8. *to* 'rabbit'	Son. Az.
9. *paka* 'reed'	Sho. Son. Az.
10. *kʷa* 'eagle'	Sho. Son. Az.
11. *tek* 'cut'	Sho. Son. Az.
12. *pa* 'hit'	Sho. Son. Az.
13. *se* 'flower'	Sho. Son.
14. *so* 'flower'	Son. Az.

Sho. = Shoshonean
Son. = Sonoran
Az. = Aztecan

In many years of comparative work on Sino-Tibetan languages I have seldom found the names of animals and plants extending very far geographically. The instability of such names is reflected in the fact that Morris Swadesh, seeking stable terms, omits all names of animals and plants from his glottochronological lists, even the longest one. I thought of using my collection of zoological and botanical terms in Uto-Aztecan languages in an attempt to decide why the names extend over such short distances.

Instead of discovering that the Aztec day names, the list rich in names of animals and plants, were restricted in distribution, I found that the roots of perhaps half of the twenty day names were Pan-Uto-Aztecan, that is, they were reflected transparently in cognates in a plenitude of daughter languages. Where instability had been expected, a remarkable and surprising stability was found.

In Table 3, I show reconstructed elements of day names and the distribution of forms in major branches.

The stability of forms finds partial explanation, perhaps, in the extensive travels and great mobility of the Toltecs, whom I assume for the sake of argument (admitting no certainty in the assumption) were speakers of archaic Aztecan. I assume too, following Di Peso (1968), that Toltec merchants reached all parts of the Gran Chichimeca or northern frontier of Mesoamerica. The Toltec city of Teotihuacán was on phase IIa when the Toltec forts, which were designed to keep Chichimecans from penetrating the Tropic of Cancer, were built, about the time of Christ. By the time of the phase Teotihuacán IV, in the eighth century, 20 percent to 40 percent of the Chichimecans had become sedentary and Toltecized. In Di Peso's belief, Toltec merchants were in Sinaloa and Durango by A.D. 750 and perhaps in

Sonora and Arizona by A.D. 900. In this view, we notice, there were speakers of archaic Aztecan in central Arizona, the ohokam worshippers of Tezcatlipoca, at just about the time that speakers of the same dialect were coming into contact with populations of the area of Mexico City. In Stone's belief, Toltec influence reached Central America "possibly between 300 to 1000 A.D." (Stone 1966–1967: 336).

A case can be made, then, however tenuously, for a stability in the day names based upon mercantile as well as military activities of speakers of Aztec dialects. While the ceremonialism may have been structured in different ways in different places, the divinatory tokens used in the various structures persisted, just as the European signs of the zodiac have persisted in the face of variant interpretations in different times and locations over the course of centuries. It is not past surmise that wherever Toltec and, later, Aztec merchants traveled, some clients of divinatory ritual geared to the 260-day calendar were cultivated.

I can venture no suggestion on the date of the earliest Toltec calendar of 260 days. I assume that the Mayan ritual calendar was invented first, and that Proto-Aztecans adapted it after early contacts. Since the Zapotec day signs go back mostly to Monte Albán III or II with only one sign, Rain, dating as far back as Monte Albán I, on the face of present evidence we have to guess that the Zapotec ritual calendar was developed after Mayan contacts, starting perhaps 400 B.C., but was not in anything like the form recorded by Juan de Córdova until as late as A.D. 950.

Because archaeological records rarely are satisfactory, I hesitate to say that the Toltecs knew nothing of the ritual calendar before about A.D. 1000, when carved day signs first appeared in the area of Teotihuacán, according to Tozzer in his posthumous study of Toltec-Mayan relations (1957). Tozzer certainly was wrong, since by 1000, Teotihuacán had fallen and had been depopulated. The tenor of Caso's views (see especially Caso 1966), in fact, is that at Teotihuacán people were named according to their day of birth as dictated by the ritual calendar probably by the middle of the third century, when Quetzalcoatl appears. His ritual name, Nine Wind, was used at Teotihuacán, Caso believed, with the sign of the reptile's eye standing for Wind. When the Toltec and Zapotecan gods first had day names, of course, we simply cannot guess. It is easy to become lost in attempts to correlate uncertain dates with scraps of data on symbols, a case in point being the coincidence of Monte Albán I with its day sign for rain and Proto-Teotihuacán I, about 400 B.C., with its focus on Tlaloc as god of rain.

Recent discoveries at Tehuacán, with which Marco-Mixtecan

speakers have been connected, deserve a few words. The Abejas phase at Tehuacán is dated 3500–2300 B.C. The earliest Otomanguean divergences, some glottochronologists say, began before 4000 B.C. By 2900 B.C. the Otomians had moved off. The Amuzgo-Mixtec group was distinct by about 1900 B.C. Isolation of the Zapotecans, then, which was complete perhaps by 2500 B.C., took place in the late Abejas phase, and the Amuzgo-Mixtecan isolation took place about midway in the Purron phase.

Later phases at Tehuacán are the Ajalpán, 1500–900 B.C., a time in which Otomanguean farmers had villages, good pottery, and crops of corn, beans, and squash; the Santa María, 900–200 B.C., a time in which ritual life was complicated by such things as figurines and buildings designed for ceremonials, and in which irrigation was used; and the Palo Blanco, 200 B.C.–A.D. 700, a time in which priestly luxuries abounded, with obsidian tools, woven fabrics, orange pottery, new foods such as peanuts, and hilltop ritual structures designed for the very gods, some have supposed, who are pictured in the *Codex Borgia* (1963) and similar manuscripts.

The Palo Blanco phase was contemporaneous with the development of civilization at Teotihuacán, though it began somewhat later; the Santa María phase which preceded the Palo Blanco phase, however, gives priority in ritual structures and objects to the Otomangueans as opposed to the Mayans and the Toltecs. But there is no evidence, as far as I can see, that the Palo Blanco phase involved day names. Only in the next phase, the Venta Salada phase, A.D. 700–1540, do we find city states, forts, calendars, and hieroglyphic writing. Skimpy as the evidence is, it fails to discourage a guess that the eighth century was a time of fairly widespread currency of day names. Yet we must confess that while the Santa María priests and their contemporaries at Monte Albán may have had day names and relevant lore, we cannot offer positive evidence.

Chadwick and MacNeish (1967: 115) say: "...the Borgia and the Venta Salada phase are closely related. It seems probable that the *Codex Borgia* originated in the Señorío de Teotitlán, with the culture characterized as the Venta Salada phase, and quite possibly within the Tehuacán Valley itself." Written records, such as the Borgia, provide more positive evidence than we have from other early sources on the use of day names. We must remember, however, that day-name innovations could have been introduced by the latest copyist. Thus the date July 16, 790, just after noon, is given by Cottie A. Burland for a scene in the *Codex Vindobonensis* (1929) in which Venus is rising near the eclipsed sun nearly at zenith (see Caso 1950). This codex shows Toltec history among the Mixtecs up to A.D. 1350. We may conclude that at least in the fourteenth century people bore day names.

We would be less secure in assuming that they bore day names on July 16, 790, were it not for Mayan, Zapotecan, and Toltec carvings and paintings.

I see no good way, in sum, to support a claim that there were speakers of Proto-Uto-Aztecan who moved southward from the Gran Chichimeca possibly as far as the Tehuacán Valley in Puebla in its Purron phase, and who there learned to use day names. The evidence points, rather, in a different direction. A study of several hundred isoglosses for words of the protovocabulary of Uto-Aztecan shows (speaking impressionistically) many more similarities than would have been expected from the glottochronological estimates. The Germanic languages, separated after unity about the time of Christ, are much more diverse, and have more complicated sound laws than have been reported for Uto-Aztecan. If we dismiss the glottochronological estimates, it becomes easier to guess that Uto-Aztecan ancestors of the Toltecs, Aztecs and others invaded Mexico successfully only after Mesoamerican civilization had reached a point at which the invaders could take by conquest a culture they could not develop. There is no reason to credit the Toltecs with the construction of Teotihuacán in its early stages. They might have come along in the sixth or seventh century to acquire by conquest, among other things, the day-name system which by then was in its Late Classic Mayan phase and in its fullest flower in Monte Albán III and Teotihuacán IV.

REFERENCES

BURLAND, COTTIE A.
    1967   *Ancient Maya*. New York: John Day.
CASO, ALFONSO
    1950   "Explicacción del reverso del Codex Vindobonensis," in *Memoria de el Colegio Nacional* 5: 9–46. Mexico City.
    1956   El calendario mixteco. *Historia Mexicana* 5: 481–497.
    1966   "Dioses y signos teotihuacanos," in *Teotihuacán: onceava mesa redonda*. Edited by Sociedad Méxicana de Antropología, 249–275. Mexico City.
    1967   *Los calendarios prehispánicos*. Cuadro IX, facing page 84. Mexico City. Universidad Nacional Autónoma de México, Instituto de Investigaciónes Históricas.
CHADWICK, ROBERT, RICHARD S. MAC NEISH
    1967   "Codex Borgia and the Venta Salada phase," in *The prehistory of the Tehuacán valley*, volume one: *Environment and subsistence*. Edited by Douglas S. Byers, 114–131. Austin: Robert S. Peabody Foundation.
Codex Borgia
    1963   *Códice Borgia*. Facsimile edition of a pre-Columbian codex preserved in the Ethnographical Museum of the Vatican, Rome, three

volumes. Edited by Eduard Seler. Mexico City: Fondo de Cultura Económica.

Codex Vindobonensis
1929 *Codex Vindobonensis Mexicanus I*. Facsimile edition. Edited by Walter Lehmann and Ottaker Smital. Vienna.

DI PESO, CHARLES C.
1968 "The correlation question in general archaeological perspective for northern Mesoamerica and beyond," in *Actas y memorias del 37° Congreso Internacional de Americanistas* 3: 23–37. Buenos Aires.

GUDSCHINSKY, S. C.
1959 *Proto-Popotecan: a comparative study of Popolocan and Mixtecan*. Indiana University Publications in Anthropology and Linguistics Memoir 15. Supplement to *International Journal of American Linguistics* 25(2).

HALE, KENNETH
1958 Internal diversity in Uto-Aztecan: I. *International Journal of American Linguistics* 24: 101–107.

KAUFMAN, T. S.
1964 "Materiales lingüísticos para el estudio de las relaciónes internas y externas de la familia de idiomas mayanos," in *Desarollo cultural de los mayas*. Edited by Evon Z. Vogt and Albert Ruz L., 81–136. Mexico City.

LEIGH, HOWARD
1958a Zapotec glyphs. *Boletín de Estudios Oaxagueños* 2: 1–11.
1958b An identification of Zapotec day names. *Boletín de Estudios Oaxagueños* 6: 1–9.

MC QUOWN, NORMAN A.
1964 "Los orígenes y la diferenciación de los mayas según se infiere del estudio comparativo de las lenguas mayanas," in *Desarollo cultural de los mayas*. Edited by Evon Z. Vogt and Albert Ruz L., 49–80. Mexico City.

MILLER, WICK R.
1967 *Uto-Aztecan cognate sets*. University of California Publications in Linguistics 48. Berkeley and Los Angeles.

SELER, EDUARD
1904 "The Mexican chronology with special reference to the Zapotec calendar," in *Mexican and Central American antiquities, calendar systems, and history*. Bureau of American Ethnology Bulletin 28. Edited by Charles P. Bowditch, 11–55. Washington, D.C.

SHAFER, ROBERT
1967 A bibliography of Uto-Aztecan with a note on biogeography. *International Journal of American Linguistics* 33: 148–159.

STONE, DORIS
1966–1967 The significance of certain styles of Ulua polychrome ware from Honduras. *Folk* 8/9: 335–342.

THOMPSON, J. ERIC S.
1932 A Maya calendar from the Alta Vera Paz, Guatemala. *American Anthropologist* 34(3): 449–454.
1970 *Maya history and religion*. Norman: University of Oklahoma Press.

TORRESANO, ESTEVAN
1754 Arte de lengua Kakchikel del ussa de Fr. Estevan Torresano. Año de 1754. (Photographic reproduction of manuscript in Rare Book Room, Tulane University, New Orleans.)

TOZZER, ALFRED MARSTON
  1921   *A Maya grammar with bibliography and appraisement of the works cited.* Peabody Museum of American Archaeology and Ethnology Paper 9. Cambridge, Mass.: Harvard University Press.
  1957   *Chichen Itza and its cenote of sacrifice: a comparative study of contemporaneous Maya and Toltec.* Harvard University. Peabody Museum of American Archaeology and Ethnology Memoirs 11–12. Cambridge, Mass.: Harvard University Press.

VOEGELIN, CHARLES FREDERICK, F. M. VOEGELIN, K. HALE
  1962   *Typological and comparative grammar of Uto-Aztecan: I (phonology).* Indiana University Publications in Anthropology and Linguistics Memoir 17. Supplement to *International Journal of American Linguistics* 28(1).

VOGT, EVON Z.
  1969   "The Maya: introduction," in *Handbook of Middle American Indians*, volume seven, 21–29. Austin: University of Texas Press.

The Relationship Between Painting and Scripts

JORGE ELLIOTT

1. Peoples who have devised picture writing have tended to confuse painting and writing. The consequence of this confusion has been to inhibit their visual arts as independent "expressive" media.

Before proceeding any further, it is necessary to make clear that I do not contend that man has never devised scripts of nonpictographic origin. Indeed, it is believed by many that at least the lineal script once used in Crete was of nonpictographic origin and probably evolved from motifs, because it is known that motifs have always borne meanings, however vaguely. But the point is, that if any of these were once devised, there could not have been many, for none appears to have survived.[1] And, in any event, all ancient scripts pertaining to current ones, and thus to artistic manifestations relevant to us, are of pictographic origin – Sumerian, Egyptian, and Chinese.

The confusion between painting and writing has not always been perceived, and when it has been perceived nothing much has been made of it. Thus, Mallery (1913) makes no effort to distinguish between inscriptions that might be deemed paintings and those which are clearly pictographs. But the farseeing Boas did so, remarking: "A third example is to be found among the American Indians of the Great Plains. *Their representational art, in the strictest sense of the word, is almost entirely confined to a crude type of picture writing*" (1955: 67, emphasis added).

Again, many specialists in the arts of the pre-Columbian peoples

---

[1] Some specialists suspect that the scripts used in the Caroline Islands are not pictographic in origin. However, there is reason to believe they did not arise spontaneously but as a result of cultural diffusion from Malay and perhaps India (see Reisenberg and Kaneshiro 1960).

of Mesoamerica, Kubler[2] and Marquina[3] among then, have realized that the pictographs in Mixtec codices and the representations on Mixtec murals are almost identical, without attempting, however, to get at the significance of the confusion.

It is not easy to investigate this phenomenon, because even though the vast majority of Mesolithic and Neolithic peoples painted schematic descriptions, many of which could be deemed "incipient" picture writings, few appear to have organized their schemas and signs into even a crude picture writing. Moreover, wherever advanced scripts have been devised from original picture writings, little trace has been left of the picture writings. In point of fact, it is only in the Americas that examples of these have been found in sufficient number to be of use to us.

Naturally, I believe they *are* of use to us because I am convinced that there is such a thing as a "human psychic unity" – that is to say, similarities of thought and action among the most diverse peoples are not all due to cultural diffusion – and hence that "polygenesis" exists. In short, I agree with Boas (1966: 154) when he contends that Bastian was right in speaking "of the appalling monotony of the fundamental ideas of mankind all over the globe."

2. Let us begin our inquiry by considering the first known pictorial efforts of man – by discussing the paintings of Paleolithic man.

It is common knowledge that Paleolithic man painted abstract designs somewhat halfheartedly; they were either of a geometric character – freehand, of course – or of a meandering character. He seems to have preferred to paint representations. As far as we know, he seems to have preferred to paint realistic or true-to-nature representations (Plate 1) rather than schematic representations, although he *did* paint the latter. Why he should have chosen to paint realistically is a matter of conjecture, especially because it is now held that magical practices could not have been the reason.[4] However, it is not indispensable to our argument to seek an explanation for his preference, because we are more concerned with the schematic strain in representation than with the realistic strain.

It is significant that the one truly descriptive representation found

[2]   "Most closely related to Mixtec manuscripts are the paintings of the east side of the church court. They invite comparison with such manuscripts as the *Codex Colombine-Becker.*" (Kubler 1962: 99.)

[3]   "Las representaciónes son muy semejantes a los códices mixtecas" (Marquina 1964: 386).

[4]   "The brilliant naturalism of the admittedly magical Paleolithic paintings cannot be explained by their magic function. Any kind of scrawl or smudge would have served the purpose, if the neophyte, on approaching it, had been told it was a bison" (Collingwood 1958: 69).

in the well-known Paleolithic caves is schematic. We refer to the descriptive schema found at Lascaux (Plate 2). It tells a sad little story of a man – probably a masked magician – who was gored by a wounded bison. Now, it is important to underscore the fact that it cannot be proven that the realistic representations painted in the different known Paleolithic caves are organized into a well-composed whole, despite the fact that a number of art historians have of late taken to maintaining this belief. As they are most easily viewed, they appear as isolated images. They are certainly not *descriptively* organized.

Practical, everyday experience tells us that man is inclined to convey discursive ideas by means of graphic descriptions. Surely, when he is intent on doing so he can feel no need for absolute realism, for as soon as a sketch makes its point it need not be perfected further. When he does this his paintings are on the verge of becoming picture writing.

Because the mind naturally tends to follow the path of least resistance, it seems logical that man should always have been inclined to convey ideas by means of descriptive schematic paintings rather than by means of abstract symbols. This would explain why scripts of pictographic origin have survived rather than scripts based on abstract symbols.

All the evidence at hand indicates that with the passage of time man developed a descriptive urge and a somewhat weaker urge to record, in that painting from the Mesolithic Age onwards acquired a descriptive and clearly schematic character. Thus the vast majority of known Mesolithic paintings, particularly those discovered in Valletorta, Spain, are descriptive and schematic in character.

Some Neolithic paintings, especially those found at Tasili in Africa, are quite realistic, but they are exceptional. Commonly, Neolithic paintings are even more schematic and descriptive than Mesolithic paintings or of the type found at Çatal Huyuk in Anatolia.

Surely, from paintings of this kind, an easy passage might be made to picture writings similar to those devised in North America, for instance of the kind of picture writing used at one time by a people dwelling near Lake Superior. Naturally Mixtec pictographs are richer, more involved, and more detailed than any pictographs of the type we have mentioned so far. Moreover, they are considerably refined as representations.

It remains surprising, however, that so many peoples whose painting may be regarded as incipient picture writing did not actually develop a picture writing. This may be a consequence of wrong entries, or of premature attempts to combine schematic representations with abstract symbols in order to create a richer type of script than a crude picture writing. We get this impression not only from the petroglyphs studied by Heizer and Baumhoff in Nevada and eastern California (1962), but also from the very schematic and symbolic paintings made during the Bronze Age.

In any event, what really matters here is that post-Paleolithic man seems to have developed a descriptive urge, together with a vaguer urge to record, that led him to give preference to the schematic strain in representation. Indeed, it would seem that in his mind a "lock-in" occurred between the idea of a thing and a schema of its appearance: between, for instance, the idea of a tree and a schema of it – a vertical line with other lines jutting out from it at an angle.

The extent to which such an occurrence is a natural one, or a consequence of the characteristics of the human brain, is evinced by the fact that such a fixation or lock-in takes place in the mind of every child today, for our children's schemas are undeniably halfway to being picture writings. In point of fact, children soon settle for particular schemas and make them stand for houses, churches, ships, and, of course, the sun.

It appears also that, once this lock-in occurred, it affected sculpture as well – at least for a time. Thus the early figurines found at Eridu, Mesopotamia (see Plate 3), are extremely schematic. The universality of this occurrence is confirmed by the many figurines of the same sort found in other parts of the world, such as at Chupícuaro, Guanajato, in Mexico (see Plate 4) – naturally the Chupícuaro figurine must be considered a product of a retarded cultural formulation in respect to the Eridu formulation.

However, the fact that with time sculpture tended to become realistic before painting suggests that the lock-in had been generally resolved with some promptness and yet left undisturbed in painting either for functional or stylistic reasons. Thus, for example, the painted pots found at Mochica, Peru, are adorned with quite schematic, descriptive representations (see Plate 5), while the portrait pots found close to them are very realistic indeed (Plate 6). Occurrences in Egypt and elsewhere confirm this contention.

Finally, we must make clear that because Neolithic peoples were obsessed with "function" while they painted, confusing painting and writing, they failed to refine their schemas "artistically" so that their painting was, on the whole, "out of the style." Actually, because they were weavers and wickerworkers they were apt to design quantities of abstract motifs which dominated their styles, in that they were used for "overall" application on every kind of surface, as was the practice in Tierradentron, Colombia (see Plate 7). Yet when controlled scripts were in use, so that representational painting could acquire a measure of individuality, motifs were displaced from stage center, as among

Plate 1.

Plate 2.

Plate 3.

Plate 4.

Plate 5.

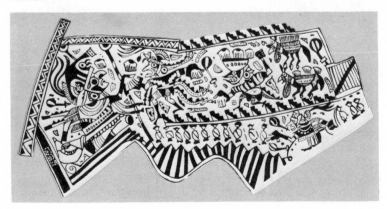

Plate 6.

Plate 7.

Plate 8.

Plate 9.

Plate 10.

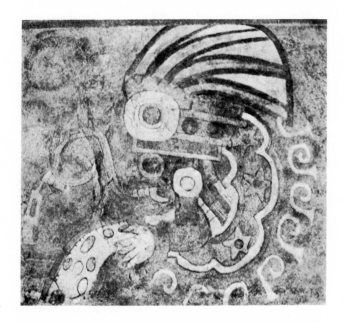

Plate 11.

Plate 12.

Plate 13.

Plate 14.

Plate 16.

Plate 15.

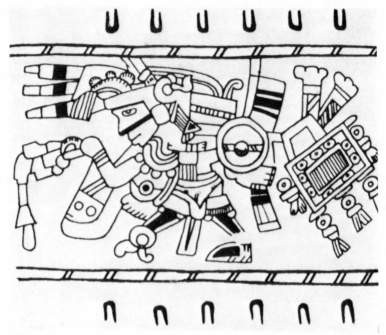

Plate 17a.

Plate 17b.

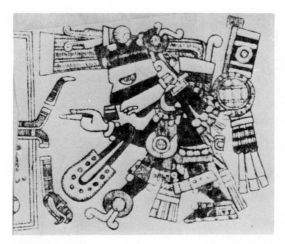

Plate 18.

Plate 19.

Plate 20.

Plate 21.

Plate 23.

Plate 24.

Plate 25.

the Maya, who decorated their pots with glyphs, representations, and motifs probably derived from the glyphs (Plate 8). This process could end by reducing the participation of motifs in the style to the mere role of framing representations, as happened in Greece (Plate 9).

In view of the fact that Neolithic schematic painting was generally "out of the style," its pertinence to art is slight. Hence, if we wish to discuss the place of picture writings in art we must turn to Mesoamerican picture writings, the only relatively refined picture writings which have come down to us from the past.

3. The use of pictographs in Mesoamerica seems to have begun mainly under Teotihuacán influence. The Teotihuacanos prospered near Lake Texcoco – where Mexico City now lies – from about the year 150 B.C. until the sixth century A.D., when they appear to have been disbanded by barbarian raiders. At that time their influence on the southern peoples of Oaxaca seems to have increased, for they certainly appear to have decisively influenced the rising people of Mitla, the Mixtecs. Certainly Mixtec pictographs are closely associated with Teotihuacán paintings. Thus if we compare a portion of the Mixtec *Codex Nuttall* (Plate 10) to a wall painting recently discovered at Teotihuacán (Plate 11), we are at once struck by their evident association. Indeed the rain god (Tlaloc) depicted in the mural is very similar to the surrounded pictograph in the *Codex*.

Further confirmation that a close relationship exists between the script of the Mixtec and Teotihuacán paintings – which might or might not be related to a Teotihuacán script, because no Teotihuacán codices have been discovered – is provided by the remarkable likeness between the figures in the bottom half of the Teotihuacán mural found at Tepantitla (Plate 12) and the pictographs in the Mixtec *Codex Vindobonensis* (Plate 13).

At all events, what really matters for the moment is the extremely close association between Mixtec paintings and Mixtec codices. Therefore, let us proceed to examine them.

Both at Mitla in Oaxaca and at Tizatlán in Tlaxcala, fragments of Mixtec wall paintings survive that are worth contrasting to the Nuttall and Borgia codices. Thus, if we compare another fragment of the *Codex Nuttall* (Plate 14) to a fragment of the mural at Mitla (Plate 15), it becomes immediately apparent that they are closely related, because the figures in both the *Codex* and in the mural are proportioned in the same way and are represented in profile, as is generally the case with glyphic systems. However, to underscore further their resemblance, we have placed a copy of a figure in the Arroyo North Mural at Mitla vertically alongside the *Codex* (Plate 16) so that it may be compared with any of the figures in it. Indeed, there can be little doubt that it is almost identical to the figure kneeling on the carpet in the lower segment of the *Codex* page.

The Tizatlán mural is not stylistically identical to the Mitla mural, but then neither are the *Codex Nuttall* and the *Codex Borgia*. This suggests that Mixtec scribe-painters arrived at personal styles without necessarily producing totally different forms.

Yet what really concerns us at this juncture is that the figure on the right side of the Tizatlán mural (Plate 17a) – the god Texcatlipoca – is practically identical to the pictograph for that god painted in the *Codex Borgia* (Plate 18). This confirms what we suggested initially: that the Mixtec scribe-painter barely distinguished between painting and writing. In point of fact, all he did when he was writing was to add calendric signs, placing signs and numerals by the representations.

It takes but a glance, of course, to realize that Mixtec representations are refined when compared to the rudimentary representations in North American Indian picture writings. Hence, it could not be said that they are "out of the style." Yet they did not coalesce into a sufficiently expressive script to displace motifs from stage center; rather, Mixtec art motifs and representations play an equal part in the style. We know that this was not the case where hieroglyphs were employed.

To come across hieroglyphic systems in Mexico one must move south to Oaxaca and even beyond, to the land of the Maya. In short, the Mixtec pictographic script was not the only one evolved in Oaxaca, for glyphs were employed at Monte Albán from an early date. Indeed, glyphs were employed at one time by a number of peoples in different parts of the world. Thus, in the Middle East not only the Egyptians but also the Hittites used hieroglyphs. However, in the space allotted to us we can hardly discuss every glyphic system in connection with artistic practices. Therefore we shall only refer, as we go along, to the Maya and Egyptian scripts, while stating that others, such as the Zapotec and the Hittite, will not be found to contradict our argument seriously.

4. Maya glyphs are obviously of pictographic origin, although no trace of the original Maya picture writing remains. Thus, the priestly Maya hieroglyphic script contains clearly representational elements such as might have been inherited from a pictographic script.

Hieroglyphs appear to have come about as people sought to increase the efficacy of their pictographs by devising homophones, using abstract forms as syllable symbols or symbols of consonants, etc. As they did this, their scripts often became less representational, and hence their painting could become somewhat independent from the script, though never totally so because the mind's penchant for association generally caused it to keep people from breaking the formal nexus between writing and painting. In other words, though painting became different from writing it was not actually permitted to become an independent medium, with full individuality. It was kept conceptual and handled as an extension of the script.

Surprisingly realistic – though conceptual and basically schematic – Maya paintings, glyphed as was to be expected, were discovered at a site in Chiapas, Mexico, where the temple city of Bonampak flourished for several centuries in and around the year A.D. 540. In those paintings the relationship between the figures and the glyphs is by no means obvious, yet it exists nevertheless, and sometimes quite obtrusively since occasionally we can successfully compare a glyph to a portion of a particular figure (Plate 19). Note how, in the example at hand, the individualized glyph suggests the configuration of a face in profile very like that of any of the figures near it. Moreover, the fact that the Bonampak paintings should be conceptual – faces in profile, bodies flatly painted in one color – tells us that in the minds of the Maya of Bonampak the two were kindred forms.

It is also worth noting in this example that the main figure, which apparently represents a hierarch being dressed, has a cloth hanging from both thighs. That cloth is obviously decorated with glyphic motifs, which suggests that glyphs came to be used so abundantly in decoration that they displaced geometric motifs from stage center, mainly through the agency of glyphic motifs. Certainly the fringe on the cloth appears to be geometrically decorated.

Maya paintings at other sites, such as Uaxactún, and on pottery, exhibit the same characteristics as the Bonampak paintings. However, it must be kept in mind that the Maya used at least two scripts, the quite abstract and very cursive script employed by the Bonampakans, and the more pictographic script known as the priestly script, used in relation to sculpture on stelae (Plate 20), and on reliefs in plaster (Palenque). This brings to mind the fact that the Egyptians developed two abstract cursive scripts – the hieratic and the demotic – without discarding their hieroglyph. Yet the Bonampakans related their two scripts formally so that there was no stylistic contradiction when they used one or the other in relation either to painting or sculpture and relief sculpture, while the Egyptians handled their advanced scripts "out of the style."

The Maya cursive script is more advanced than the Egyptian hieroglyphic script, though not more advanced than the hieratic script. Hence its formal nexus with painting is almost exclusively calligraphic. It allowed Maya painting to become pliant and gestural. However, Maya painting did not turn toward us and acquire tactile qualities or temperamental expressiveness. We shall see that not all the conditions necessary for that to happen arose in the Maya world.

The decorative language spawned by the Maya glyph and its extension, the Maya glyphic motif, pervaded Maya artistic style in general, contributed to its flowering, and even affected the mood of its architecture, whose surfaces were often adorned with glyphic forms. Indeed, in Tikal lintels were indented with them (Plate 21).

In contrast with the Maya glyphs, the Egyptian hieroglyphs are static and heavy. In an Egyptian mural decoration we always find them dwelling in harmony with painted or engraved figures (Plate 22). The forms have a great deal in common. The hieroglyph is as hard of line as it is static. When several are gathered in a cartouche, it is by means of a clear, unwavering line. The contours of the painted or engraved figures are also firm and clear, with a fusion of curvature and straightness suggestive of strength and perpetuity.

The extent to which the Egyptian hieroglyph came to constitute a formal gnomon in the Nile Valley is made evident by the degree to which it spreads over columns and walls at Karnak. Its form is in harmony with the strict, ponderous mood of the architecture.

Due to hierarchic pressures, the cursive hieratic script failed to displace the hieroglyph or to draw painting toward it so that it might develop into a more cursive art. In fact, when papyri were written in cursive hieratic, the illustrations to the script were separated and surrounded either by hieroglyphs or by archaic hieratic symbols, formally very close to the traditional hieroglyph, as is the case with the Pedin Imenet papyrus (Plate 23). Only on unimportant ostraca – entirely "out of the style" – were illustrations allowed to dwell alone by texts in demotic script.

5. Peoples who developed picture writings could skip the glyphic stage as they advanced their script. It appears, at least, that the Sumerians and the Chinese did so.

The Sumerians were unable to develop a paper-like material and hence wrote on clay tablets, which they subsequently baked in the sun. As it is hard to engrave representations on clay, they started to indent it and thus rapidly developed a very abstract cuneiform, syllabic script. It seems obvious that under the circumstances painting might have developed into an independent medium, separate from writing, but it did not. It appears that, when scripts were advanced rapidly, a period of obfuscation ensued wherein painting was neglected and left tied to the abandoned pictograph. Indeed, it took a long time for the representational arts to acquire a high degree of refinement in Mesopotamia, or until the rise of the Assyrians. But although Assyrian painting and relief sculpture acquired considerable expressive power, they remained conceptual and never became fully expressive on their own. As a consequence the Mesopotamians continued to use textile motifs regressively for overall application in architecture.

On the other hand, the Chinese appear to have skipped the glyphic stage also and to have left painting behind for a time, because the illustrations accompanying the ideographs in the oldest silk text known (500 B.C.) are extremely crude. Because they developed rice paper and silk and invented a fine painting brush, they were eventually able to retrieve the link they had abandoned and evolve their painting in formal harmony with their script. In doing so, they finally went much further in developing painting as an independent medium than any of the peoples we have come across so far. Their painting turned toward the spectator and acquired full individuality, yet never failed to keep subtly associated to the script, as is evinced by Mu Ki's delightful "Persimmons," now at Kyoto (Plate 24). Because this painting is but a fragment, there are no ideographs on it, but the small leaves and stems protruding from each persimmon, taken on their own, could be ideographs (Plate 25), which serve to demonstrate the relationship which concerns us.

Because Chinese painting did not acquire the characteristics we have been discussing until the late Taoist Han Period, we may conclude that once painting has been subjugated by a script it can only gain full individuality, however much the script is advanced, if an adequate naturalistic and individualistic philosophy arises, as it did in Greece and, indeed, in China. For there is common ground between Greek anthropocentrism, which regarded man as "the measure of all things," and Taoism's defense of individuality with its absolute rejection of all distortion and artificiality.

But to discuss Greek art would be to invade new territory, for the Greek used a phonetic alphabet totally divorced from an original picture writing. No true formal nexus associates their script with their representational art. Their art is tied to the content of their script or to their literature alone. What happens to the representational arts when the nexus we have brought to notice is broken, in relation to stylistic problems particularly, is most interesting, but is beyond the scope of this discussion.

The study of the association we have been underscoring is a fascinating one, related to how the mind feels it best apprehends meanings. In their penchant for association, so relevant to their solving powers and so enlightening, the arts are "cognitive" in nature, significant ingredients of the atmosphere of ideas prevailing at any given time.

REFERENCES

BOAS, FRANZ
1955 *Primitive art* (reprinted edition). New York: Dover.
1966 *The mind of primitive man* (reprinted edition). New York: The Free Press.
COLLINGWOOD, R. G.
1958 *The principles of art.* Oxford: Oxford University Press.
HEIZER, ROBERT F., MARTIN A. BAUMHOFF
1962 *Prehistoric rock art of Nevada and eastern California.* Berkeley: University of California Press.
KUBLER, GEORGE
1962 *The art and architecture of ancient America.* Baltimore: Penguin.
MALLERY, GARRICK
1913 *The picture writing of the American Indians.* Tenth Annual Report of the Smithsonian Institution. Washington, D.C.
MARQUINA, IGNACIO
1964 *Arquitectura preHispánica.* Mexico: Instituto Nacional de Antropología e Historia.
REISENBERG, SAUL, SHIGERU KANESHIRO
1960 A Caroline Island script. *Anthropological Papers* 60: 269–334. Bureau of American Ethnology Bulletin 173. Smithsonian Institution. Washington, D.C.

Petroglyphs of the Antilles

RIPLEY P. BULLEN

Both the Greater and Lesser Antilles are well known for the quantity and quality of their petroglyphs. There is no major island without one or more examples of this art form. Design variation is tremendous and sometimes variant forms are found on the same boulder, ledge, or wall of a cave.

Similarities and differences in certain designs permit studies of their distributions and associations, which can elucidate cultural processes. These studies may illuminate such problems as migrations and origins of cultural groups, cultural similarities or common ceremonial cults, and, if dated in various areas, may shed light on the rate of spread of cult ideas. When associated with a specific group, they may be correlated with their myths and legends or prove to be representations of their gods.

While many of the petroglyphs of the Antilles have been recorded in the literature, little interpretative work has been done except for a preliminary article by Frassetto (1960). The interpretations submitted below are now possible because of the availability of data presented at the Fourth International Congress for the Study of the Pre-Columbian Cultures of the Lesser Antilles held on St. Lucia in 1971 and published in the Proceedings of that Congress in 1973.

For the purposes of this paper, I have classified many of the petroglyphs of the Antilles into seven major groupings. This typology is presented below together with distributional data. Explanatory notes, discussion, and interpretation have also been included under most of the classes. There are, of course, other groups which are not discussed in this paper.

Type 1 – Abstract Geometric Designs

Abstract designs include involutes, concentric circles, concentric diamonds, frets, simple crosses with surrounding borders, and other simple geometric symbols (see Plate 1). Of these, involutes are the most common. Individual examples are found at Buccament Bay (see Plate 2b) on St. Vincent (Kirby 1969: Figure 9), at Caonillas in Puerto Rico (Frassetto 1960: Figure 7), Cotui (see Plate 1c) in the Dominican Republic (Veloz, et al. 1973: Figure 4c), Cueva de Ambrosio in Cuba (Núñez Jimenez 1964: 52), and, more plentifully, in Costa Rica (Kennedy 1973: Figures 13, 21). Concentric circles (Veloz, et al. 1973: Figure 4d), as far as the available data are concerned, are limited in the Antilles to Grenada (Bullen 1964: Plate 24), Santo Domingo (Morban Laucer 1970: Lam. 82), and Cuba (Veloz, et al. 1973: Figure 4d), but probably there are more than these three isolated examples. In Cuba they are found painted in fairly large numbers (Veloz, et al. 1973: Figure 4d; Núñez Jimenez 1964: Figures 36–38, 46) and have been reproduced on the two- and five-centavos postage stamps commemorating the thirtieth anniversary of La Sociedad Espeleológica de Cuba (*Emisión sobre las pinturas Rupestres* 1970). De Abate (1973) reports one for the Guri region in the Orinoco Basin of Venezuela, and Kennedy (1973: Table 1 and Figure 12) documents their presence in fair numbers in Costa Rica and Panama.

Concentric diamonds have only been noted for the Dominican Republic (see Plate 1c) and Cuba. In the latter case, they occur in red or brown paint (Núñez Jimenez 1964: Figure 21; Morban Laucer 1970: Lams. 34, 79). In one example, four concentric diamonds form the body of a male figure.

Frets seem to be limited to the Dominican Republic (Veloz, et al. 1973: Figure 4) but fretlike designs are found as pictographs in Cuba (Núñez Jimenez 1964: Figures 12–18, 37, 44; 1970: Figures 13–21). Associated with frets in the Sierra Prieta Cave of the Dominican Republic are four crosses with surrounding borders (see Plates 1b and 1c). Two others are known for the eastern Antilles, one at Reef Bay on St. John in the Virgin Islands (Hatt 1941: Figure 6), and the other at Mount Rich on Grenada (Huckerby 1921: Plate 3). A black-painted example from Isla de Pinos, Cuba, is reproduced on the five-centavos stamp mentioned above.

These simple geometric designs concentrate in the western part of the Greater Antilles. While involutes and concentric circles are found in the Lesser Antilles, their numbers are definitely limited. This distribution and the presence of similar forms in Central America suggest that geometric designs may have diffused to the Antilles from that region. Veloz, et al. (1973) have pointed out that abstract (geometric) designs, both pictographic and petroglyphic, occur in the western or nonceramic part of Cuba and may well date back to Pre-ceramic times. As these designs are not associated with the ball-court complex, which presumably came from Mexico or Central America in relatively late times, this survey would support the hypothesis of Veloz, et al. In that connection, it should be noted that the distribution of known Pre-ceramic blade-tool sites in the Antilles which have typological similarities with Central America – from Antigua westward to Cuba – agrees with the known distribution of abstract geometric petroglyphs except for one involute on St. Vincent, and concentric circles and a bordered cross on Grenada. These are separated from the other instances by a substantial distance, and they are so near Venezuela that possible diffusion from South America might explain their presence.

Type 2 – Colonarie (Capá) Style

"Colonarie style" refers to boulders or rock-shelter walls which are more or less covered by pecked or incised curvilinear lines which, however, do not form any designs meaningful to us (see Plate 2). I believe this is the same as that referred to as "Capá type" by Frassetto (1960: Figure 9) but, since I cannot see all the designs traced in her illustration, I am using the term "Colonarie" and substituting the petroglyphic boulder (see Plate 2a) at Colonarie, St. Vincent (Kirby 1969: Figure 10 on front cover), as the type specimen.

Perhaps twenty to a hundred individual petroglyphs may be present, but the types described below are never included. Abstract geometric designs (type 1 above), such as involutes and concentric circles, are sometimes present. At Colonarie one such design, resembling a short telephone pole, consists of one vertical line crossed by four horizontal straight lines (see Plate 2a).

Four Colonarie-style petroglyphs are known in the Antilles: the Colonarie boulder on St. Vincent (Huckerby 1921: Plate 8; Kirby 1969: cover); the wall of a rock shelter (see Plate 2b) at Buccament Bay, St. Vincent (Kirby 1969: Figure 9); the wall of the Icacos rock shelter in Puerto Rico (Frassetto 1960: Figure 9); and at Yuboa, Dominican Republic. Because of the inclusion of some abstract geometric designs, one is inclined to consider Colonarie-type petroglyphs as relatively early, but there is little factual reason for such an assumption.

Colonarie-style petroglyphs do seem to be related to some from Anamuya in the Dominican Republic (Morban Laucer 1970: Lams. 42, 46–48, 52–53, 56, 60–64). They are also reminiscent of boulders reported by Kennedy (1973: Figures 1b, 1d, 1e, 2a, 2b, 9) from Costa Rica and Panama (Kennedy 1973: Figure 3). However, the Costa Rica-Panama examples seem more highly developed. Somewhat similar arrangements are also reported by Haberland (1970: Abbs. 9, 13) for La Palma I and La Fuente in Nicaragua. These similarities are closer than those suggested by Goodland's illustrations of petroglyph-covered boulders in the Savanna of Guiana (Bullen 1973b).

Type 3 – Representations of Faces

Facial representations without bodies may be divided into three sub-types: simple, developed, and complicated (see Plate 3). These are sometimes referred to as "monkey faces." All type 3 petroglyphs have circular facial outlines. A fourth type with a larger trianguloid facial outline will be discussed later under the Utuado-type figures.

Simple faces consist of a circle surrounding three dots or small circles, one of which may be elongated to form a mouth (see Plate 3a). Such faces are ubiquitous in the Antilles and are known on Hispaniola (Veloz, et al. 1973: Figure 5; Morban Laucer 1970: Lam. 67), in Puerto Rico (Frassetto 1960: Figure 8 right), in the Salt River ball court on St. Croix (Hatt 1941: Figure 14), in Congo Cay, St. John (Hatt 1941: Figure 4), in St. Kitts (Laurie and Matheson 1973: 19), Guadeloupe (Clerc 1973: Figure 6), south of Soufriere on St. Lucia, St. Vincent (Kirby 1969: Figures 1–2), and Grenada (Huckerby 1921: Plates 1, 5; Bullen 1964: Plate 24). These simple faces are also found in Costa Rica (Kennedy 1973: Figures 4, 17).

Developed faces are similar to simple faces but noses, ears, and hair or "rays" may be added (see Plate 3b). They are also common and their presence has been noted on Hispaniola (Veloz, et al. 1973: Figure 5), in Santa Arriba, Puerto Rico (Frassetto 1960: Figure 6; Bullen 1973a: Figure 3), in Guadeloupe (Clerc 1973: Figure 3), on Martinique (Mattioni 1973: Figure 1), and on St. Vincent (Kirby 1969: Figures 4–5).

Complicated faces have added elements or a greater complexity but still no bodies (see Plate 3c). While fairly rare, they are recognizable as pictographs in the Dominican Republic (Morban Laucer 1970: Lams. 5, 8, 27, 29, 75) and as petroglyphs on Puerto Rico (Frassetto 1960: Figure 5 left), on St. Croix (Bullen 1973c: ball-court stone), on Guadeloupe (Clerc 1973: Figures 3, 6), on St. Vincent (Kirby 1969: Figures 4–6), and on Grenada (Huckerby 1921: Plates 2 upper and right, 4). This type blends into type 7 – stylized representations.

Before leaving this section, two comments should be made. The first is that all three subtypes of facial representations are found with bodies to form types 5 (see Plate 3d) and 6 (discussed below). It is possible, therefore, that they represent unfinished petroglyphs or, more likely, an example of the whole being represented by a part.

The second comment refers to petroglyphs found on Crooked Island in the Bahamas (Hoffman 1973: Figures 2–3). These rather sketchily drawn figures have well-made, pear-shaped heads and, in one case, rather realistic facial details. Pear-shaped faces, while rare in the rest of the Antilles, are found on two ball-court stones at Utuado, Puerto Rico (Frassetto 1960: Figure 14; Kennedy 1973: Figure 15) and on St. Kitts (Laurie and Matheson 1973: Figures 3e, 3f). These locations are relatively near the Bahamas.

Type 4 – Sun Symbols

By "sun symbols" I am referring to circular figures with "rays" which might be considered representations of the sun. Rayed heads as part of more complex figures are fairly common in the eastern Antilles but typical isolated sun symbols are extraordinarily rare. Only one dubious example can be cited (Fewkes 1903–1904: Plate 60d). It is on the Salto Arriba boulder on Puerto Rico and Frassetto's copy (1960: Figures 3–5) indicates the surrounding details are ovals and not rays. Judging from de Abate's report (1973: Figures 1–21) on the petroglyphs of the Orinoco, sun symbols in various forms are common in both Venezuela and Colombia.

Type 5 – Swaddled Figures

This class is comprised of complicated figures, each of which includes a recognizable head or face and a conventional body (see Plates 3d, 4a, 4b). The latter is more or less rectangular in shape and exhibits cross lines – diagonal, curved, or horizontal – which suggest wrappings (Frassetto 1960: Figure 7 right, Figure 8 left and right). Noticing the chubby appearance of the face of Puerto Rican examples, Frassetto (1960: 386) felt these petroglyphs resembled "swaddled infants."

As in most petroglyphs, there is a wide range of variation in the details and embellishments found on swaddled figures. Faces may be represented by three dots (Kirby 1969: Figure 7), ringed or broad eyes and mouth (Clerc 1973: Figure 1; Frassetto 1960: Figure 8 left), or with facial decoration (Frassetto 1960: Figures 7–8). Occasionally the face (see Plate 4b lower) is conventionalized (Kirby 1969: Figure 4). The head may support rabbitlike ears (Fewkes 1903–1904: Plate 60; Frassetto 1960: Figures 4–5), rays (Kirby 1969: Figures 4, 7 upper right), "waving hair" (Clerc 1973: Figures 1, 10), or other embellishments (Frassetto 1960: Figure 8). Wrapped bodies may be decorated with curving "hooks" (see Plate 4d) at sides (Frassetto 1960: Figure 8 center) or lower corners (Kirby 1969: Figure 4) and, sometimes, sinuous lines (see Plate 4b) at the sides (Kirby 1969: Figure 7).

Swaddled figures have an easterly distribution. They are absent on Cuba and Hispaniola but are found in Puerto Rico (Frassetto 1960: Figures 5, 7, 8), St. Johns in the Virgin Islands (Hatt 1941: Figures 5–6), on St. Kitts (Laurie and Matheson 1973: Figure 2), on Guadeloupe (Clerc 1973: Figures 4–6, 11), suggested on Martinique (Mattioni 1973: Figure 1) and on St. Lucia (Jesse 1973: Figure 1), and are present on St. Vincent (Kirby 1969: Figures 4, 7) and on top of the Mt. Rich petroglyph of Grenada (Huckerby 1921: Plate 2 lower left). Swaddled figures are one of the most important types of petroglyphs in the Antilles because they are also found in the eastern part of Guiana (Thurn 1967: 392). Diffusion of these swaddled figures (see Plate 4c) northward through the Lesser Antilles seems fairly certain, as the Guiana forms resemble those of St. Vincent (see Plate 4b) more closely than they do the more flowing and less angular forms of Puerto Rico (see Plate 4a).

Type 6 – Utuado-Type Figures

Two divergent human representations are included under Utuado-type figures. On the upright stone slabs bordering one of the ball courts or dance floors at Utuado (Capá) in the highlands of Puerto Rico are several distinctive female figures (Alegría n.d.: inside back cover). They appear to be lying on their backs with the arms bent upwards at the elbows and with the upper legs drawn upwards at the hips with knees flexed so that heels are below pelvis (see Plates 5a, 5b; Olsen 1973: Figures 16–17). At least four such figures are illustrated by Alegría for Utuado, while Olsen (1973: Figures 12–13) pictures remarkably similar figures in the round for Haiti and Puerto Rico (see Plates, 5c, 5d).

These figures on the ball-court slabs – and another unfinished on another slab (Alegría n.d.: inside back cover) – all have a circle in the stomach region surrounding the navel (?). Sometimes the stomach is clearly distended, suggesting pregnancy (Olsen 1973: Figure 11). This circle is repeated at other sites and may be interpreted as representing a fetus.

There is another figure represented at Utuado. Less well known than the female figures described above, I should think this other figure

Plate 1. Abstract geometric petroglyphs: a – c, Sierra Prieta Cave, Cotui, Dominican Republic; d, Punta del Este Cave, Isla des Pinos, Cuba (From Veloz, Pina, Ortega, and Vega 1973)

a

b

Plate 2. Colonarie-style petroglyphs: a, Colonarie boulder, St. Vincent; b, cave wall at Buccament Bay, St. Vincent (from Kirby 1970)

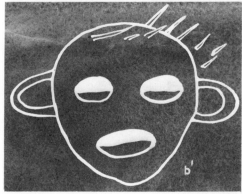

Plate 3. Representations of faces: a, simple; b–b', developed; c–c', complicated. a–d and b'. Trois Rivières, Guadeloupe (from Clerc 1973); c': Salto Arriba, Puerto Rico (from Frassetto 1960)

a

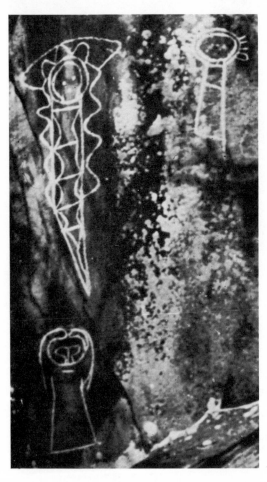

b

c

Plate 4. Swaddled figures: a, Upper Icacos, Puerto Rico (from Frassetto 1960); b, Petit Bordel, St. Vincent (from Kirby 1970); c, eastern Guiana (traced from Thurn 1967: 392)

Plate 5. Atabeyra figures: a–b, petroglyphs on upright stone slabs at Utuado, Puerto Rico; c–d, carved in the round, Haiti and Puerto Rico. a–b: photographs of Walter Murray Chiesa as published by Ricardo E. Alegría (n.d.); c–d: from Olsen 1970, 1973

Plate 6. Representations of Yócahu: a, on one end of stone three-pointer (*zemi*) from Puerto Rico (small legs at other end); b, as petroglyph at Layou, St. Vincent (both from Olsen 1971); c, as carved stone found in Kingstown harbor, St. Vincent (photograph by I. A. Earle Kirby, from Bullen and Bullen 1972)

a

b

Plate 7. Stylized representation: a, petroglyph at Barrouallie, St. Vincent (from Kirby 1970); b, sketch of Barrouallie petroglyph (from Olsen 1972)

represents a male although, as only the head is present, sex is not clearly indicated. In Mason's illustration (1941: Plate 7, Figure 2), this form consists of an oval face with large eye sockets and slit eyes, a prominent triangular area between nose and mouth, and thick or wide lips with the central groove of the upper lip well marked. There are some indefinite lines running off from the face, but ears, body, and limbs are not indicated.

Frassetto (1960: Figure 13) illustrates another large petroglyph from Utuado which has gross features like Mason's plus a concave line over the eyes which ends near the ears as circular ornaments. This concave line might delineate browridges which tend to be more evident on males than on females. The grossness of the eyes and mouths – mentioned above – might also be considered representative of males as opposed to females.

Olsen (1973: Figure 2) illustrates a large, three-pointed *zemi* (see Plate 6a) from Puerto Rico with a carved or picked face at one end that is surprisingly similar to those pictured by Mason and Frassetto. Characteristic of this *zemi* and of other petroglyphic representations of this figure is a curving line over the eyes which terminates in circular ends at or a little beyond the lateral ends of the eyes. This trait may be noted on many large, three-pointed *zemis*. Sometimes a similar curving line is found below the mouth but it curves upward instead of downward.

Olsen (1973), following Arrom's study (1967) of Herman Pérez de Oliva's 1525 document, correlates his *zemi* with Yócahu, the great Arawak male god – the giver of manioc. Arrom discusses this further in his 1971 article. I would extend this concept to the Utuado male heads which have similar artistic details. The female Utuado figures Olsen correlates with Atabeyra, the Arawak female deity who was mother of moving waters, of the seas, of tides and springs, goddess of the moon, and goddess of fertility or childbirth. Olsen makes a good case for the Utuado female figures as representing Atabeyra in the act of giving birth. I find these correlations very satisfactory.

Utuado-type figures seem to concentrate in the Greater Antilles although Yócahu is well represented in the Lesser Antilles. Sometimes what seem to be Yócahu and Atabeyra appear together. In the Cueva García Robiou in Cuba, there is a pictograph with upraised arms resembling Atabeyra, but on the head is the curved line ending in a spiral which I have taken as symbolic of Yócahu!

For Boda del Arroyo in the Dominican Republic, Hatt (1941: Figure 9) depicts a petroglyph which appears to be a simplified representation of Atabeyra in the act of childbirth. Elsewhere in the Dominican Republic, fairly similar figures are found (Morban Laucer 1970: Lams. 1–2, 9, 15, 26, 30–31, 76, 79, 84) in black and red paint or as petroglyphs. Similar pictographs, with the circle around the middle of the vertebral column, are present in Cueva de las Maravillas in the Dominican Republic. In one case (Veloz, et al. 1973: Figure 3) there are two adjoining figures, one with the central circle and one without. The first, following the criteria presented above, would be Atabeyra. The second has extra-large eyes and mouth. Could it be Yócahu?

After Puerto Rico, the next examples are found on St. Kitts. At the Wingfield Estate are two petroglyphs, side by side. The one on the viewer's left has a central circle interrupting the vertebral column. The other, with more prominent eyes and mouth, has an expanded, diamond-shaped body suggesting a corpulent male. Could these not be Atabeyra and Yócahu?

Proceeding down the Lesser Antilles, there are two interesting petroglyphs on Dominica (Mattioni 1973: 29–30) which have all the traits delineated above for Yócahu. These are large, prominent eyes, prominent mouth – in this case with clearly indicated upper and lower teeth – and a curving, concave, browridge line ending in upturned spirals at the ears.

Another representation of Yócahu is found on the petroglyphic boulder at Layou on St. Vincent (Kirby 1969: Figure 1). In this case (see Plate 6b), the face is triangular in outline like a three-pointed zemi, and the concave browridge line ends at the outside corners of the eye sockets which are countersunk, leaving raised eyeballs. The nasal area is also countersunk. The curved chin line ends in involutes at cheek corners to give a smiling impression. The most southerly representation of Yócahu is found on the top of the justly famous Mt. Rich petroglyphic boulder at Grenada (Huckerby 1921; Mattioni 1973: 30). It is a little cruder than those just described but it still presents prominent eyes, a wide, full or thick-lipped mouth, and the curving browridge line ending in a spiral.

Yócahu may also be represented by the large stone head (see Plate 6c) dredged in 1972 from Kingstown harbor, St. Vincent. All the features are gross and outlined with wide grooves, while the area between the nose and the full upper lip is well delineated. The mouth curves upwards in a smiling manner (Bullen and Bullen 1972: Frontispiece). It is evident from the above distributional data that, while both Yócahu and Atabeyra figures are found at Utuado in Puerto Rico, those of Atabeyra have a western Antillean concentration – from St. Kitts to Cuba – while those of Yócahu have a southeastern concentration – from Puerto Rico to Grenada. This is suggestive of the amalgamation of two cultural groups as typified by their respective culture heroes. It also seems probable that such an amalgamation (if one occurred) must have been at least started long before the date of the construction of the ball courts at Utuado.

During the reconstruction work at Utuado, post holes were found of which one, at least, contained the remains of a post in the form of charcoal. Radiocarbon analysis of this charcoal produced a date of A.D. 1270±80 (Alegría n.d.: 9–10). This date presumably applies to a phase of the construction of the ball courts. The cultural amalgamation, if one occurred, may have happened centuries earlier.

Archaeology tells us of two movements of peoples into Puerto Rico which might be correlated with Atabeyra and Yócahu respectively. First are the Pre-ceramic makers of prismatic blades whose debitage has been found from Antigua to Cuba. Because of the similarity between their chipped "daggers" and those of Central America, it is believed they came from that region via Pedro Cays, Bajo Nueva, Beacon Cay, and Cayo Gorda 3,000 to 5,000 years ago when the Caribbean Sea was much shallower and these cays were substantially larger than at present (Bullen 1962: 401). If these people were fishermen and hunters of large sea animals such as manatee, harbor seals, caymans, sea turtles, and sturgeon, they might have had a fertility goddess who also was in charge "of moving waters, of tides and springs, goddess of the moon." The other group were the first agriculturalists who, introducing Saladoid and later Barrancoid pottery, came from northeastern Venezuela via the Lesser Antilles. It is logical that their god might be "the giver of manioc."

Type 7 – Stylized Representations

There are various petroglyphs and pictographs in the Antilles which do not represent any of the types we have discussed with certainty, nor do they resemble any known feature of the natural or mythological worlds. Examples include at least one petroglyph at Layou, one at Indian Bay, and one at Barrouallie (see Plate 7), all on St. Vincent (Kirby 1969: Figures 1a, 2, 3), but others are known and they are sometimes found as pictographs in the Hispaniola and Cuban caves.

Olsen (1973: 36–37, Figures 4–5) would interpret the highly stylized example at Barrouallie (Kirby 1969: Figure 3) as a fertility symbol, possibly indicating copulation. If so, it is interesting to note that the upper or male part of the petroglyph has a concave line over the eyes which ends in circles (see Plate 7). This is similar to the symbol mentioned earlier as being present on Yócahu faces.

If this fertility idea is carried a bit further, it is possible to imagine that the "swaddled" figures represent babies. Considering them the children of Yócahu and Atabeyra might explain the "swaddled" effect. As magical or mythological children, they would be arrayed in fine clothes and liberally supplied with ornamentation befitting descendants of the gods. This ornamentation would undoubtedly also be present if they were conceived of as children of the sun god and the moon goddess. As a further extension, the type 3 (facial representations) might represent sympathetic magic tending to produce pregnancy.

CONCLUSIONS

In this article, some of the petroglyphs of the Antilles have been arranged into seven classes, which are described and discussed, and their distributions noted. As all seven classes are found in Puerto Rico and the Greater Antilles, where Caribs did not live, it follows that this art form is assignable to Arawak or pre-Arawak inhabitants and, even in the Lesser Antilles, was not used by Caribs. As a corollary to this, all petroglyph types, except possibly Atabeyra, were in existence before the ascendancy of the Caribs or before A.D. 1200. There are no similarities between petroglyphs of the eastern United States and those of the Antilles (Grant 1967).

Of Antillean petroglyphs, type 1, abstract geometric designs, and type 3a, simple faces, are found in Central America (Costa Rica and Panama). Simple faces are also found in Venezuela. However, these simple faces are almost ubiquitous and hence of little distributional importance. This statement may also apply to concentric circles.

The western distribution in the Antilles of abstract geometric designs and their presence in Central America suggest the latter as their place of origin. Archaeologically there are two known movements of people or of ideas from the Central American mainland into the Greater Antilles. The first is that of Pre-ceramic (Archaic) chippers of flint, the other the introduction of ball courts or dance floors and their accompanying accouterments. The earlier introduction seems the more likely for these figures.

Type 5 (swaddled figures) has a southeasterly distribution from central Puerto Rico to Grenada. The presence of nearly similar figures in the Guianas suggests that region as their place of origin, although it might be argued, based on their restricted distribution in South America, that their presence there was the result of diffusion from the Antilles. I would prefer the first alternative and would correlate them with the agricultural introducers of Saladoid ceramics who migrated up the Lesser Antilles around the time of Christ. This origin is supported by the lack of "swaddled" figures in Hispaniola and Cuba where ceramics are not found before A.D. 800–900.

The male and female Utuado figures present different problems. They are definitely associated with the ball courts and hence should date to around A.D. 1200. The ball courts, it would seem, must have been introduced from northern Central America or southeastern Mexico. Nearly similar figures in those areas are not known to me. There seems to be no similarity between Olmec heads and the Antillean representations of Yócahu, nor are the dancing figures on stone slabs at Monte Albán near Oaxaca, Mexico, similar to the Utuado representations of Atabeyra.

I would prefer to think that the ball-court complex was introduced from the west but that Yócahu and Atabeyra were local gods who absorbed the new cult or whose figures were used to legitimize or to authenticate the new ceremonies. It is quite probable the ball game – whatever its form – had ceremonial and religious overtones.

Yócahu as the giver of manioc seems to have been a benign father figure, but Atabeyra with her obvious fertility aspect was much more a participant in the everyday life of the people. One wonders if the Arawaks were not matriarchal. Most of the petroglyphs of the Antilles can be explained – perhaps incorrectly – in terms of family activities and the food quest.

Any consideration of this paper should keep two points in mind. The first is that we may not as yet have all the data. For example, M. Turenne of Cayenne, at the Fifth International Congress of the Lesser Antilles in July 1973, showed me pictures of petroglyphs from coastal French Guiana. One human figure, possibly female, had bent elbows and knees similar to those on St. Kitts. The Guiana figure did not have a circle in its midsection, but the position is similar to Atabeyra figures. The other point is that the concept of a great spirit and of a mother goddess is widespread. Possibly what we are dealing with is a local expression of a much more widely held concept.

REFERENCES

ARROM, JOSÉ JUAN
   1967   *El mundo mítico de los Taínos: notas sobre el ser supremo.* Bogotá: Instituto Caro y Cuervo.
   1971   El mundo mítico de los Taínos: notas sobre el ser supremo. *Revista Dominicana de Arqueología y Antropología*, 181–200. Santo Domingo. (Contains minor additions not in the earlier article.)
ALEGRÍA, RICARDO E.
   n.d.   *El centro ceremonial indígena de Utuado.* Publicación del Instituto de Puertorriqueña. San Juan.
BULLEN, RIPLEY P.
   1962   The pre-ceramic Krum Bay site, Virgin Islands, and its relationship to the peopling of the Caribbean. *Akten des 34 Internationalen Amerikanistenkongresses*, 398–403. Vienna.
   1964   *The archaeology of Grenada, West Indies.* Contributions of the Florida State Museum, Social Sciences 11. Gainesville, Fla.

1973a   "Petroglyphs of the Virgin Islands and Puerto Rico," in *Proceedings of the Fourth International Congress for the Study of the Pre-Columbian Cultures of the Lesser Antilles*, 13–16. Gainesville, Fla.

1973b   "Re: petroglyphs in Guiana," in *Proceedings of the Fourth International Congress for the Study of the Pre-Columbian Cultures of the Lesser Antilles*, 63. Gainesville, Fla.

1973c   "Further comments on Antillean petroglyphs," in *Proceedings of the Fourth International Congress for the Study of the Pre-Columbian Cultures of the Lesser Antilles*, 65–67. Gainesville, Fla.

BULLEN, RIPLEY P., ADELAIDE K. BULLEN

1972   *Archaeological investigations on St. Vincent and the Grenadines, West Indies.* Wm. L. Bryant Foundation American Studies Report 8. Orlando, Fla.

CLERC, EDGAR

1973   "Petroglyphs of Guadeloupe," in *Proceedings of the Fourth International Congress for the Study of the Pre-Columbian Cultures of the Lesser Antilles*, 21–24. Gainesville, Fla.

DE ABATE, JOHN

1973   "A key to the interpretation of the petroglyphs of the Orinoco," in *Proceedings of the Fourth International Congress for the Study of the Pre-Columbian Cultures of the Lesser Antilles*, 57–64. Gainesville, Fla.

Emisión sobre las pinturas rupestres

1970   *Emisión sobre las pinturas rupestres de los aborígenes de Cuba.* Havana: Museo Antropológico Montane.

FEWKES, J. W.

1903–1904   *The aborigines of Porto Rico, a neighboring island.* Bureau of American Ethnology, 25th Annual Report. Washington.

FRASSETTO, MONICA FLAHERTY

1960   A preliminary report on petroglyphs in Puerto Rico. *American Antiquity* 25(3): 381–391. Salt Lake City, Utah.

GRANT, CAMPBELL

1967   *Rock art of the American Indian.* New York: Thomas Y. Crowell.

HABERLAND, WOLFGANG

1970   Felsbilder von Ometepe, Nicaragua. *Tribus* 19: 97–116. Stuttgart.

1972   The Cave of the Holy Ghost. *Archaeology* 25(4): 286–291.

HATT, GUDMUND

1941   Had West Indian rock carvings a religious significance? *Nationalmuseets Skrifter, Etnografisk Raekke* 1: 165–202. Copenhagen.

HOFFMAN, CHARLES, A., JR.

1973   "Petroglyphs on Crooked Island, Bahamas," in *Proceedings of the Fourth International Congress for the Study of the Pre-Columbian Cultures of the Lesser Antilles*, 9–12. Gainesville, Fla.

HUCKERBY, THOMAS

1921   Petroglyphs of Grenada and a recently discovered petroglyph in St. Vincent. *Indian Notes and Monographs* 1(3): 143–164. New York: Museum of the American Indian, Heye Foundation.

JESSE, C.

1973   "Petroglyph and rock-cut basins at Dauphin, St. Lucia," in *Proceedings of the Fourth International Congress for the Study of the Pre-Columbian Cultures of the Lesser Antilles*, 33–34. Gainesville, Fla.

KENNEDY, W. JERALD
1973   "A comparison of certain Costa Rican petroglyph designs with those from adjacent areas," in *Proceedings of the Fourth International Congress for the Study of the Pre-Columbian Cultures of the Lesser Antilles*, 47–56. Gainesville, Fla.

KIRBY, I. A. EARLE
1969   *Pre-Columbian monuments in stone*. Kingstown: The St. Vincent Archaeological and Historical Society.
1970   "The Pre-Columbian stone monument of St. Vincent, West Indies," in *Proceedings of the Third International Congress for the Study of the Pre-Columbian Cultures of the Lesser Antilles*, 114–128. Gainesville, Fla.

LAURIE, C. KEITH, D. LLOYD MATHESON
1973   "The petroglyphs of St. Kitts, West Indies," in *Proceedings of the Fourth International Congress for the Study of the Pre-Columbian Cultures of the Lesser Antilles*, 17–20. Gainesville, Fla.

MASON, J. ALDEN
1941   "A large archaeological site at Capá, Utuado, with notes on other Porto Rico sites visited in 1914–1915," in *Scientific survey of Porto Rico and the Virgin Islands* 18(2): 209–272. New York: New York Academy of Sciences.

MATTIONI, MARIO
1973   "Communication sur les petroglyphes de la Martinique," in *Proceedings of the Fourth International Congress for the Study of the Pre-Columbian Cultures of the Lesser Antilles*, 25–32. Gainesville, Fla.

MORALES RUÍZ, CARLOS
1971   Informe sobre tres grupos petroglíficos. *Revista Dominicana de Arqueología* 57–80. Santo Domingo.

MORBAN LAUCER, FERNANDO A.
1970   *Pintura rupestre y petroglifos en Santo Domingo*, volume 147. Universidad Autónoma de Santo Domingo. Santo Domingo.

NÚÑEZ JIMENEZ, A.
1964   *Cuevas y pictografías*. Havana.
1970   *Caguanes*. Serie Espeleológica y Carsológica 16. Havana.

OLSEN, FRED
1973   "Petroglyphs of the Caribbean Islands and Arawak deities," in *Proceedings of the Fourth International Congress for the Study of the Pre-Columbian Cultures of the Lesser Antilles*, 35–46. Gainesville, Fla.

THURN, I.
1967   *Among the Indians of Guiana*. New York: Dover. (Originally published 1883.)

VELOZ, M., MARCIO, PLINIO PINA, ELPIDIO ORTEGA, FERNANDO VEGA
1973   "Antillean pictographs and petroglyphs: patterns and procedures which can be applied in the study of their location in time," in *Proceedings of the Fourth International Congress for the Study of the Pre-Columbian Cultures of the Lesser Antilles*, 1–8. Gainesville, Fla.

Contribution to the Study of Cultural Sequences in the Central Area of Costa Rica

In the face of the accelerated urban expansion of the area of Costa Rica, and united by the desire to improve its periodization and chronology, the Archaeology Department of the Universidad de Costa Rica has found it necessary to be on the spot for the occasional archaeological discoveries made during urban development on the outskirts of major cities in the center of the country.

THE PAVAS AREA

In the western part of the city of San José, starting west of the former airport of La Sabana, lies the district of Las Pavas. Its lightly rolling terrain has been cultivated since the middle of the nineteenth century with large coffee plantations. The fertility of its land is due to its deep organic layer and to its excellent drainage, toward the north by means of the Torres River and toward the south by the María Aguilar River.

The archaeological interest of this area began with the preliminary excavations in the Rohrmoser urbanization (see Figure 1). The grading of the land and the ditches excavated to extend the water lines uncovered a large quantity of archaeological material, mainly potsherds, in some cases constituting almost 25 percent of the displaced earth. This abundant archaeological material convinced us, as investigators of the Universidad de Costa Rica, of the importance of the find, and of the need to make a permanent collection.

Periodical visits to the area indicated that the archaeological material was to be found not only in the upper top layers, but lay as deep as three meters, in a kind of pocket formed by grayish earth, which differed by its color, texture, and content from the compact

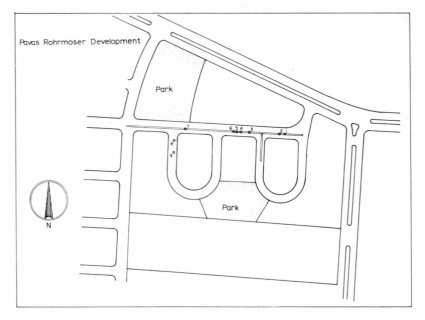

Figure 1.   Location of the tombs in a section of the Rohrmoser development

yellowish clay of the rest of the area. These pockets made the com-pacting of the earth in the streets difficult; they had to be excavated and later refilled with suitable material.

We were told that these pockets were numerous and that the best opportunity for obtaining an idea of their nature was to be present at the moment of the excavation of a deep trench. This opportunity presented itself during August, 1970. Professors and students of the Departamento de Ciencias del Hombre of the Universidad de Costa Rica were able to locate tombs 1 to 7 and to reclaim several objects, some *in situ* and some from the material taken out by the excavating machines. The heavy rains during the three days of excavation and the contractor's haste (once the trenches were made, the pipes were laid and the excavations again closed) did not permit exploration with the precision desired, but it was possible to discover that the tombs were bottle- or bell-shaped. Tomb 8 was destroyed by the work of the machinery, but tomb 9, in the middle of avenue 11, was barely touched by the excavating machine, and showed a very marked contrast between the yellowish clay and the dark earth of the tomb.

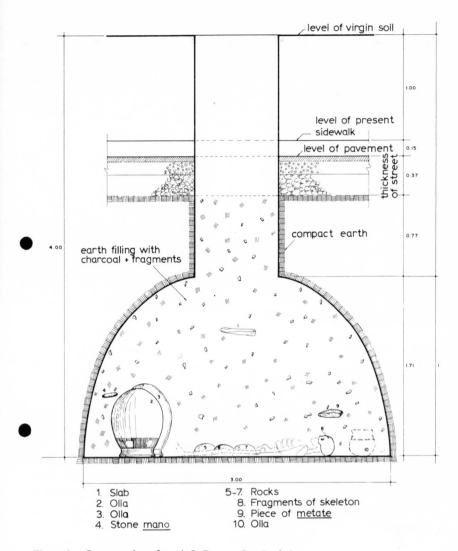

level of virgin soil

level of present
sidewalk
level of pavement

thickness of street

compact earth

earth filling with
charcoal + fragments

1.00

0.15

0.37

0.77

1.71

3.00

4.00

1. Slab	5-7. Rocks
2. Olla	8. Fragments of skeleton
3. Olla	9. Piece of <u>metate</u>
4. Stone <u>mano</u>	10. Olla

Figure 2.   Cross section of tomb 9. Pavas – San José site

THE EXPLORATORY WORK

We started the work of exploration in the upper part and to one side of the tomb (see Figure 2), in the section exposed by the excavations, close to the border of the sidewalk, on the street level about a meter below the natural level of the terrain. Here we found a cylindrical entrance of approximately 60 centimeters in diameter and 77 centimeters below the base of the concrete sidewalk. This cylindrical

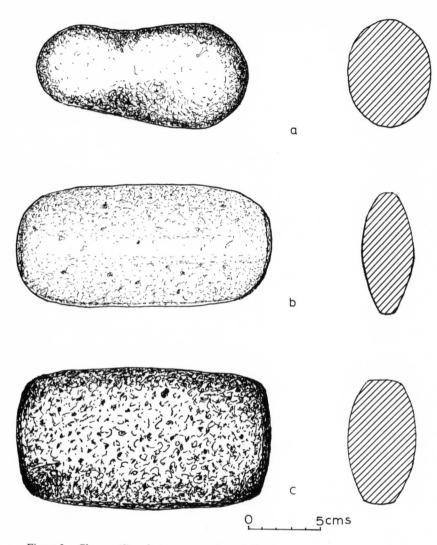

Figure 3. Chopper(?) and stone *manos* for grinding

portion had been refilled with dark earth and with numerous pots. Probably a little higher than the level of the sidewalk had been a layer of *coyolillo*, small stones from the river, and on top of these stones the layer of organic earth also full of potsherds.

Beneath this cylindrical portion, the tomb widened out, with curved walls, to a depth of 171 centimeters from the lower edge of the cylindrical entrance to the bottom of the tomb. This bottom had a more or less circular form with an approximate diameter of 300 centimeters.

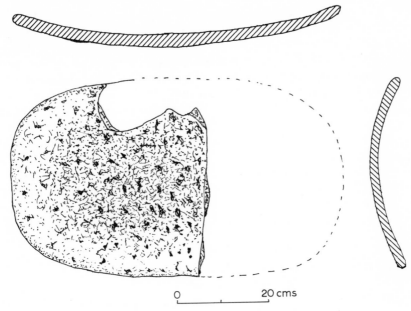

Figure 4.   Grinding stone in the form of a trough found in tomb 9

The tomb fill was formed by layers of very large and very compact potsherds, probably placed here intentionally. At about 30 centimeters above the bottom, we found a small slab and, beneath it, rather deteriorated remains of human bones. Because exploratory work at these heights should be carried on continuously, we had to work during the night, in rather difficult conditions. Nevertheless, we were able to locate some fragments of bones which seemed in a state of dispersion, probably the product of a secondary burial. A block of earth in which the upper jaw appeared, when cleaned in the laboratory, did not show the rest of the skull, confirming our suspicions that it was indeed a secondary burial.

Inside the tomb we found, on the north side, two large jars (*tinajas*) with wide mouths, one in the form of an ovoid 65 centimeters high and of a diameter of 51 centimeters, and the other 70 centimeters high and 55 centimeters in diameter, both with the mouth against the bottom and filled one-third with remains of an organic substance.

Among the potsherds we found a carbonized ear of maize, about 30 centimeters long, in a very bad state of preservation. On the side of the large jars, there was a stone *mano*, well polished with use (see Figure 3b), and on the opposite side two fragments of a smooth stone – a rectangle with a slightly raised edge and another oval without legs (see Figure 4).

As we have noted, the entire tomb was filled with potsherds, clay mixed with an organic material, and a fibrous substance, with short, fine fibers, very abundant, especially around the burial. Several fragments of carbon were found stuck to the jars, but what was most unusual was a kind of carbon and sand, about 3 centimeters thick, which covered the walls of the tomb.

It is very possible that two or three more containers had been placed inside the tomb, one of them could have been located, but it was impossible to tell the location of the others because of their state of fragmentation.

Finally, beside the potsherds and almost on the level of the floor, we saw the opening of a drain of about 20 millimeters diameter, in a horizontal position, the length of which was impossible to determine. It is possible that this duct was a communication between two tombs.

ARCHAEOLOGICAL MATERIAL

The material used in the Pavas area comes primarily from the earth removed by the machinery in the work of formation and, to a lesser extent, from tomb 9.

The level of archaeological interest consists of a thick stratum of organic earth of about one meter deep which is on a claylike layer of a yellowish color and which is more than three meters deep. In this formation there is no rocky layer, which makes us suspect that the lithic material had been brought from other regions.

LITHIC ARTIFACTS

The rock gathered from the earth removed by the tractors is made up of numerous fragments of rocks of a very fine grain, with angular cuts in chips or in simple flakes. Some portions of those materials, particularly of the first, seem to be refuse.

Several lithic specimens display a special chipping or flaking which permits us to consider them as useful implements; perhaps they are monofacial scrapers.

Perhaps we could consider as choppers a number of cores of approximately 10 centimeters in length which have chipped upper faces and, similarly, certain elongated river stones with an appropriate form for grasping by one end (see Figure 3a).

Among the most abundant materials gathered were some small, more or less round stones of approximately 5 centimeters in diameter. A layer of this material apparently sealed the entrance of some tombs.

Table 1. Stone *manos* for grinding (in millimeters)

	Length	Height	Width	State
1.	120	45	84	whole
2.	130	47	90	whole
3.	165	45	90	whole
4.	180	60	90	whole
5.	? (75)	50	95	fragment
6.	? (130)	45	80	fragment
7.	? (90)	55	70	fragment

A very similar material to this is found as a characteristic seal in the jade tombs of the plains of the Atlantic, known by the Huaqueros as *coyolillo.*

There was also an abundance of pebbles of approximately 10 centimeters in diameter, of a volcanic rock, round or slightly elongated in form, which present the larger surface with a slight abrasion, a characteristic which suggests, together with a size appropriate for holding in the hand, that they were used as hammers.

The characteristic type of grinding stone is the form of a bar of soap, in andesite, especially of a vesicular type. For the study of these grinding stones we have counted seven examples, of which four are whole and the other three are in fragments (see Table 1 and Figure 3b–c). It can be seen that the greatest length is 180 millimeters, height 60 millimeters, and width 95 millimeters.

We should also consider here a fragment of a stone *mano* in the form of a stirrup.

The simplest instrument for grinding is made of volcanic vesicular rock. This is a simple river stone, slightly smoothed, in which there is a groove made by the rubbing back and forth of another stone. The example we have (see Figure 5a), which was found in the discarded material, is a fragment of more than half of the original object. This fragment is 420 millimeters long, 300 millimeters wide, and 270 millimeters high. The groove is less than half of its height.

A more elaborate example is also made of porous volcanic rock in an oval form with very little distance between the upper and lower surfaces. The largest fragment of this type (see Figure 4) was found in tomb 9. It is very probable that this object was from 750 to 800 centimeters long. This *metate* takes on the form of a trough with the approximate depth of 40 centimeters. Although this *metate* has no legs, fragments, possibly of *metates* of this type, were found with curious feet with round ends, about 50 millimeters high and about the same width. The location of these fragments allows us to suppose that *metates* of this type had three legs.

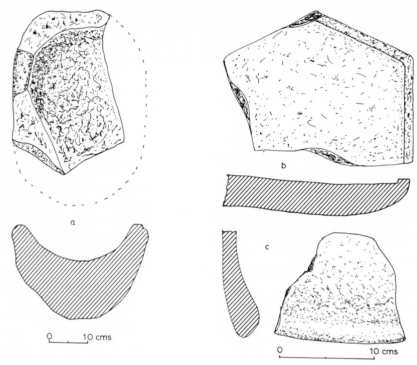

Figure 5.   Grinding stones

A fragment with a thickened edge seems to take on the form of ceramic circular plates (see Figure 5).

Five fragments of slightly smoothed rock approximately 30 millimeters thick have a border raised about 5 millimeters and are from 10 to 15 millimeters wide. One of these fragments has an exterior side which is straight and at an angle (see Figure 5a), the other side curved and adorned with little heads. A fragment of stone worked in the form of a prism seems to be associated with the previous ones, leading us to believe that such stones might form part of circular or rectangular tables, with perforated supports, now found very frequently in the Atlantic region of Costa Rica.

CERAMICS

Ceramic material which has been used in this study comes primarily from the earth removed by the excavating and leveling machinery, and also from tomb 9. Although we would have liked to have gathered all the ceramic material in this last tomb, unfortunately that was not possible because of the special conditions of this excavation. The fact that many of the large ceramic fragments in tomb 9 corresponded to complete vessels leads us to believe that the ceramic material of that tomb was very possibly the result of whole pieces which were carried to the burial and broken as offerings during the funeral ceremony.

The study of the ceramic material has permitted us to establish five well-defined types: Sabana bichrome, Sabana trichrome, Pavas bichrome, Virilla bichrome, and Crespo trichrome. All five types have a very similar paste. The most characteristic form is that of large periform vessels, then, in lesser numbers, small bowls with restricted mouths, bowls with unrestricted mouths, some with rims, and large plates. The exception to the former is Crespo trichrome, whose characteristic form is a globular, flattened shape with restricted mouth.

For all types, the slip is red or orange. The decorative elements consist of thick purple lines traced with the fingers or arranged in zones with painting of the same color.

Sabana bichrome is characterized by a contrasting band, generally of a uniform thickness from top to bottom, bordered at the top by the rim and at the bottom by a thin line. This band is the same matt color as the paste. In Sabana trichrome there is also a contrasting band, of either the natural color of the paste or covered with slip.

In Virilla trichrome, the purple stripes are vertical or horizontal. These stripes sometimes extend to the edge or are in zones with appliqué decoration.

In Pavas bichrome, the purple is in zones, sometimes bordered by thin lines.

Crespo trichrome is not only different from the other types in form, but also in decoration. The slip covers the entire vase, and the decoration of wide or narrow purple stripes may be vertical. The contrast between the bright purple stripes and the matt purple stripes is very marked.

The incised decoration in Sabana bichrome may be scarified (*debrochado*), roulette incised, or reed incised. In Sabana trichrome we also find reed incisions; in Pavas bichrome, simple incision. The unclassified jars have vertical, ridged lines at intervals of 5 millimeters.

The appliqué decoration in Sabana trichrome and Virilla trichrome is of buttons or knobs: in Pavas bichrome, it is of pieces of appliqué coil.

Modeling is characteristic of Pavas bichrome, particularly in the form of lizards or scorpions (?) back-to-back on the exterior surface.

Although we had considered that characteristic of the types we have established are vessels without supports (see Linares de Sapir 1971: 238), in the material removed we recovered about 45 supports. These solid, flattened, cylindrical supports were arranged in a radial fashion;

for the most part they were those of two paired sections or with a cleft in the front, but there were supports in the form of an angular loop, very difficult to identify precisely, although some fragments of unclassified ceramics, from bowl forms, have impressions where supports of this kind might have been placed. These latter, plus a small mammiform bell fragment and a sherd of Irazú ware with yellow lines perhaps may be considered foreign to the Pavas complex.

CONCLUSIONS

Although the work carried out in Pavas was subject to certain limitations due to the circumstances, the materials obtained have provided an understanding of a rather ancient cultural phase of the central area of Costa Rica.

In light of our present knowledge, we can say that the archaeological site in the Rohrmoser urbanization was apparently a locale dedicated primarily to burials; to judge by the great quantity of fragmented material, the number of tombs must have been very large and must have covered a time span of several centuries. Although the exploratory holes made in two or three places did not show any apparent change in the different levels, it is logical to suppose that the study of a greater number of burials would have permitted us to determine the specific transformations in time and space of a civilization such as the Pavas.

The supposition that this spot was used solely for burials is based on the apparent absence of utilitarian material: there are no vestiges of another nature which would permit us to suppose the habitability of the location (with the exception of some river stones which could have been part of a simple basement, perhaps apart from the Pavas complex). Similarly, perhaps one should consider the presence of a few slabs which could have been used in some sort of tomb different from those known on the site.

Although at the moment we have not made a C-14 determination to locate this culture more precisely in time, the type of burial, the lithic tools, and the ceramics permit us to suppose that the Pavas phase is before the Curridabat phase.

Shaft tombs are widely distributed in America. There are some data on such tombs in the west of Mexico. There are more abundant data from Ecuador, where they appear to be from around A.D. 400–500, and from the Valley of Cauca in Colombia, where they are apparently from A.D. 400–500, and they continue up to several centuries before Spanish contact (Evans and Meggers 1966: 259–260).

The abundance of fragmented ceramic material found in tomb 9, where many pieces corresponded to whole vessels, allows us to suppose that the burial ceremony was carried out by the breaking of ceramic pieces. An oval *metate*, also found in fragments, is a proof of this funeral custom.

The presence of sherds of a single plate, one of them sooted, may indicate to us that a fire formed part of the funeral ceremony and that the breaking was carried out before this. It is very possible that this is related to the smoked walls of the interior of the tomb; this smoking would be the result of lighting the fire prior to the deposition of the corpse.

Although our data are somewhat deficient in relation to the remains of the cadaver, there is no doubt that the presence of a single piece of the face and of the skull is an indication of a secondary burial. The bundle of bones was curiously wrapped, probably in organic material, judging by the abundant fibers found around the corpse.

The recovery of two scrapers suggests the continuation of a rather old technique in the Pavas phase. The large quantity of stone chips suggests active manifestation of the technique of percussion stone chipping in the production of tools, not only of scrapers, but of other types which we were not able to gather.

The most simple grinding stone, made of a volcanic vesicular rock with a deep cavity, was definitely used to grind roots, probably yucca; the same is true of a trough-shaped stone and of the plate-shaped *metates*. The fragments with a slight flange seem to correspond to a type of decorative *metate* or table which could have been part of a column-shaped fragment, characteristic of these lithic pieces. In our opinion the presence of this type of table, as well as the *metates* with characteristic legs from the Curridabat phase, may very well indicate that some of the tombs contained transitional material from the Pavas to the Curridabat phases. We can say the same with respect to the presence of a fragment of stone *mano* in the form of a stirrup, which is very characteristic of the Curridabat phase.

The stone *mano* in the form of a bar of soap has a wide distribution in Costa Rica in the area of South American influence; its form seems to have been little affected since the Cartago phase in the central area of Costa Rica.

The dominating forms in ceramics are the periform, primarily in the large vessels and the large, shallow plates. Secondary are the forms of bowls and *lebrillos* and the vessels of a globular, flattened type.

All types of ceramic are characterized by the reddish-orange color which covers the interior part of the rim and almost the entire exterior surface. The colored surface has been well polished, in many cases indicating the marks left by the polisher – vertical or slanted, crossed decorative motifs.

A basic characteristic of the decoration is its location in a band which includes the exterior part of the rim and an area of equal size or a little larger on the upper part of the body, except for the Crespo trichrome type. This band could have been totally or partially covered with the slip or could have been left with natural color of the paste and simply polished, giving a very marked contrast between the slipped surface and the band. This contrasting border is characteristic of the Sabana trichrome and Sabana bichrome types, and is also characteristic of the ceramic types of the Atlantic called "red lip ware" (Lothrop 1926: 11, 327) as well as those which have band decorations, comb incisions, scarified, and with appliqué decoration, in the form of superimposed figures or buttons. Given the similarity of the types of "red border" with Zelaya trichrome (Baudez 1967: 99), they have been considered as contemporaries, probably from the beginning of the Christian era. Nevertheless, we should realize that ceramics with red borders, "Guápiles with red borders" (Aguilar 1972: 71), are found in Guayabo.

The incised and appliqué decoration of the Pavas ceramics also permits us to credit to this site a great antiquity if we consider that wide-line incision is characteristic of the Valdivia type of Ecuador (Willey 1971: 276), and, on the other hand, that vessels with picked and incised decoration in a contrasting band very similar to Sabana bichrome appear in the Chorrera phase of the same country (Evans and Meggers 1966: 249).

With specific reference to Costa Rica, it should be noted that the scarifying is characteristic of the oldest phase of Chiriquí-Diquís. Reed incision is still important in types of the Curridabat phase (Chassaul site, University Cat. No. 79). We can also consider the small appliqué balls pressed on the surface of the vessels and painted with purple (Lothrop 1926: 335) as another decorative element which is continued in the Curridabat phase.

Although we had suggested in a preliminary report (see Linares de Sapir 1971) that the Pavas ceramic unit was characterized by an absence of supports, a more complete review of the material has, in fact, indicated the presence of solid, flattened, cylindrical or conical supports. Some of these latter have a small animal, probably a representation of a lizard, on the upper part or outer edge of the support. It is precisely these long, solid, flattened, cylindrical supports which demonstrate the transitional aspect between the Pavas and Curridabat phases. A tentative reconstruction based on these supports can lead us to the evolution of long, hollow, tripodal supports with a lizard on top. For these reasons, it is probable that the vessels with solid, flattened, cylindrical supports are from the final period of Pavas.

The extension of the Pavas culture is not well known; nevertheless,

Table 2. Archaeological sites according to the catalog of the Universidad de Costa Rica. Placement of terrestrial coordinates according to the maps of the Instituto Geográfico Nacional

Name of site	Catalog No.	Map			Latitude	Longitude
Pavas	68	Abra	3345	I	9° 56' 50"	84° 07' 15"
Cariari	3	Abra	3345	I	9° 58' 45"	84° 09' 30"
Castella	84	Abra	3345	I	9° 58' 14"	84° 08' 15"
La Paulina	80	Abra	3345	I	9° 56' 30"	84° 03' 30"
Alto del Zoncho	73	Istarú	3445	IV	9° 55' 45"	83° 59' 00"
El Molino	59	Istarú	3445	IV	9° 51' 30"	83° 55' 50"
López	66	Istarú	3445	IV	9° 55' 50"	83° 57' 30"
Córdoba	8	Istarú	3445	IV	9° 55' 30"	83° 53' 30"

in the ceramics collection of the Archaeology Department of the Universidad de Costa Rica, there are materials from various sites of the central area which bear great similarity to the Pavas wares (see Table 2). We believe these sites to be very important in the work of serialization which is reaching its conclusion and which will permit us to place the Pavas phase with greater precision within the archaeological context, not only of the central area but of all of Costa Rica. (See Appendix for a classification of the Pavas ceramics.)

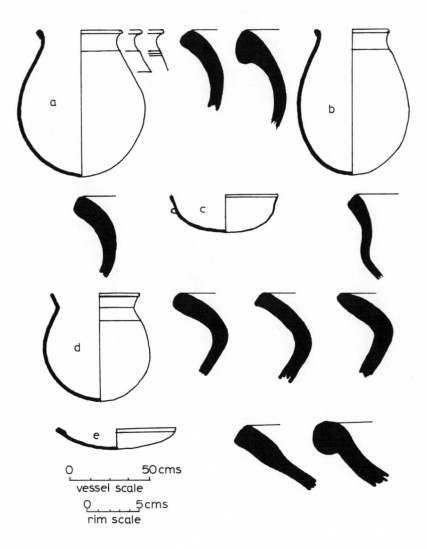

Figure 6. Ceramic types: forms and rims; *a*: Pavas bichrome; *b*, *c*: Sabana trichrome; *d*, *e*: Sabana bichrome

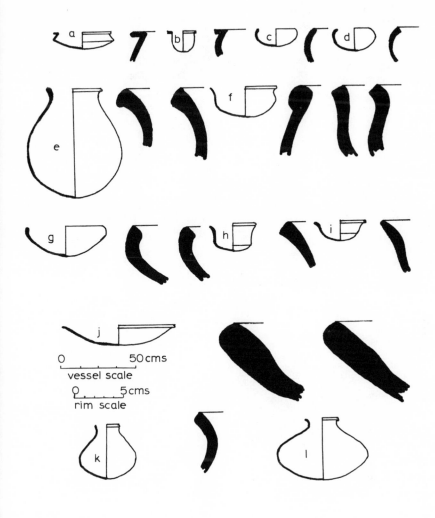

Figure 7.   Ceramic types: forms and rims. *a–d*: Sabana bichrome; *e–j*: Virilla bichrome; *k–l*: Crespo trichrome

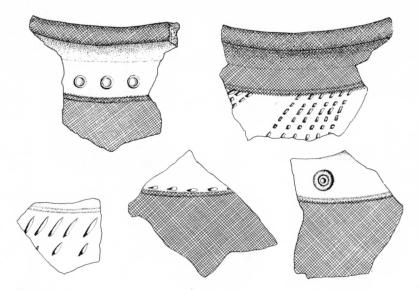

Figure 8.   Ceramic types: Sabana bichrome decoration

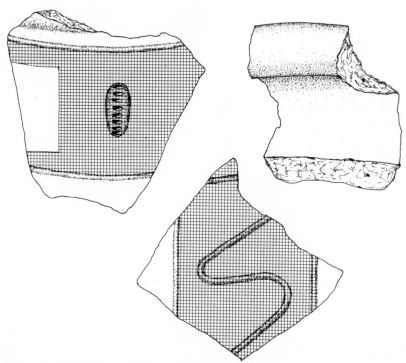

Figure 9.   Ceramic types: Pavas bichrome decoration

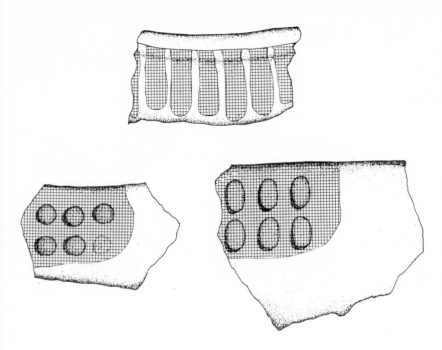

Figure 10. Ceramic types: Virilla bichrome decoration

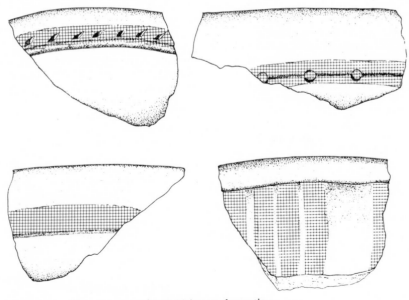

Figure 11. Ceramic types: Virilla bichrome decoration

APPENDIX* CERAMIC TYPES OF THE PAVAS SITE

Pavas Bichrome (see Figures 6a, 9)

DISTINGUISHING FEATURES: decoration of alternating zones of slip and purple paints. *Sample*: 2212 potsherds. *Method of manufacture*: by coils. *Paste*: same as Sabana bichrome.

SURFACES: *Treatment*: the interior surface is simply polished with conspicuous striations resulting from the dragging of the grains of temper during the action of polishing. The interior of the rim and the lip are polished. The external part of the rim is well finished. The decorative band, situated on the upper part of the body, is at times simply finished, or polished and finished in zones. The rest of the body is polished and burnished with lines. *Hardness*: 2.5 to 3, Mohs scale.

FORM: *Rim*: outcurved, simple as in Sabana bichrome. A lightly thinned rim is rare; in general it is reinforced on the exterior part. *Lip*: lightly rounded, with an arista on the upper part and another on the lower, producing a small curve on the lower part, so that it folds over the rim. *Neck*: concave neck 70 mm high, which starts with a small flange on the upper part of the body. *Body*: walls 10 to 15 mm thick. *Base*: curved. *Profile*: periform vase.

APPROXIMATE DIMENSIONS: *maximum diameter*: 600 mm; *Opening*: 400 mm; *height*: 700 mm.

DECORATION: *Painting*: the dark red or orange slip on the inside of the rim and the rest of the neck and body surface may be separated by: (a) a light flange 1 mm high; (b) a groove 10 to 12 mm wide and 1 mm deep; (c) two paired grooves of the same dimensions as (b). A band of decoration may be present on the upper part of the body and below the neck, sometimes up to 120 mm wide, and enclosed between: (a) two light, parallel flanges, one above and one below of equal dimensions with the ones already mentioned; (b) two channels, one above and one below, of the same dimensions as the ones already indicated; or (c) two paired grooves above and probably two equal ones below of the same size as indicated previously. The purple paint used in the decoration was applied on: (a) the exterior surface of the rim, in stripes 10 to 15 mm wide, sometimes paired to cover zones. These stripes, diffused and carelessly painted on the edge, were made with the finger; (b) the horizontal and vertical grooves of the decorative band. The purple paint on the band may be: (a) simple stripes in the interior of the collars; (b) zones of purple color, 4 to 150 mm wide, alternating with slipped zones of the same width; these latter are polished and decorated in a vertical direction or crossed on a slant.

INCISING: two rows of punctures in the deepest part of each canal. The punctures are more or less triangular, 5 mm long by 3 mm wide, and are spaced at a distance of 5 to 10 mm.

APPLIQUÉ DECORATION: decorative elements placed in the small, purple squares are: (a) lengthened coils placed vertically with horizontal parallel clefts. These coils may be up to 12 mm wide; (b) coils the same width as the former, placed horizontally with parallel vertical clefts; (c) smooth, vertical coils 8 mm wide, in the form of a bird's beak(?); (d) coils 8 mm wide placed in an inverted V and sectioned horizontally; (e) vertical, undulating flanges 2 mm wide which go from one side of the band to the other (serpent); (f) undulating, vertical coils 6 mm wide with reed-incised decoration.

MODELING: (a) appliqué scorpion with reed-incised eyes; (b) lizard? adjoining the surface of one of the purple-painted squares. Animal formed by the stretched-out body from top to bottom, with dorsal decoration of seven buttons in a row with reed incisions; two equal buttons form eyes and the paws are at an angle, the front ones towards the top and the back ones towards the bottom. Probably the vase to which this sherd belonged had two or more figures of this kind.

CHRONOLOGICAL POSITION: tentatively placed in the first centuries of the Christian era.

REFERENCES AND COMPARISONS: Ceramics similar to the types of the Pavas have been found in the sites of Cariari, Castella, El Alto del Zoncho, Córdoba, López y Molino (see Table 2).

Sabana Trichrome (see Figures 6b–c)

DISTINGUISHING FEATURES: decoration in three colors (paste color, sometimes smoked, red, or orangish-red, and purple). *Sample*: 1201 potsherds. *Method of manufacture*: by coils. *Paste*: the same as Sabana bichrome.

SURFACES: *Color*: the interior surface color of Form 1 is the same as the paste. *Treatment*: in form 1, the interior is smoothed with evident fluting, resulting from the dragging of the grains of the temper in carrying out the action of smoothing. The interior of the rim and the lip is polished. The external part of the rim is refined. The band of decoration situated on the upper part of the body is refined and polished in zones. The rest of the body is polished and burnished by lines. Probably in Form 2 the interior surface is also polished. *Hardness*: 2.5 to 3, Mohs scale.

FORM 1: *Rim*: outcurved, simple as in Sabana bichrome. The slightly thinned rim is rare; in general it is reinforced from the inside. *Lip*: slightly rounded, with an arista in the upper part and another in the lower, producing a small curve in the lower part, in such a manner that the lip folds over the rim. *Neck*: concave neck approximately 70 mm which starts with a small flange on the upper part of the body. *Body*: walls 10 to 15 mm thick. *Base*: curved. *Profile*: periform vase.

APPROXIMATE DIMENSIONS: *maximum diameter*: 600 mm; *opening*: 400 mm; *height*: 700 mm.

DECORATION: *Painting*: dark red or orange slip on the interior of the rim and on the rest of the exterior surface of the vessel. Only a few pieces show that the exterior surface of the neck and of the body are separated by: (a) a slight, thin flange 1 mm high. A band of decoration may be present in the top part of the body and below the neck, sometimes up to 85 mm wide, included between two light, paired flanges, one above and one below, of dimensions equal to those previously mentioned; this band emphasizes the natural color of the paste. The purple paint used in the decoration was applied on: (a) the exterior surface of the rim in wide, vertical stripes of 10 to 15 mm, sometimes paired to cover zones. Probably these diffused and carelessly painted stripes were made with the fingers; (b) the same stripes in the interior of the flanges of the decorative band; (c) vertical, or slightly slanted, equal stripes, sometimes four or five in number, in the interior of the band; (d) horizontal stripes in threes (?) on the decorative band; (e) in zones alternating with others of the same color as the paste, these last probably darkened by the use of an organic substance used in smoking, perhaps applied in a heating after the firing of the ceramics.

APPLIQUÉ DECORATION: these elements are located on the decorative band in the paste-colored, smoked squares. These elements are: (a) half-spherical knobs 18 mm in diameter; (b) knobs 15 mm in diameter with a cleft made with a reed; (c) conical knobs; (d) conical knobs in the form of stylized birds' heads.

FORM 2: *Rim*: outcurved, reinforced in the exterior part. *Lip*: slightly rounded, with an arista in the upper part and another in the lower, producing in the latter a small curve in such a manner that the lip folds over the rim. *Body*: walls 10 mm thick. *Base*: curved. *Profile*: shallow bowl with unrestricted mouth. *Accessories*: protuberance 55 mm long, 15 mm wide, and 10 mm high of a rounded form. One sherd has this type of solid handle which may well be a decorative element if there are more than two of them.

APPROXIMATE DIMENSIONS: *maximum diameter*: 520 mm; *height*: 180 mm.

DECORATION: *Paint*: red or reddish-orange slip on both surfaces, except on the contrasting band which forms the entire concave wall of the vessel, and which is of the natural paste color. Wide, vertical lines or zones of purple color alternating with the natural color in the contrasting zone.

CHRONOLOGICAL POSITION: tentatively placed in the first centuries of the Christian era.

REFERENCES AND COMPARISONS: Ceramics similar to the Pavas types have been found in the sites of Cariari, Castella, El Alto del Zoncho, Córdoba, López y Molino (see Table 2).

Sabana Bichrome (see Figures 6d–e, 7a–d, 8, 9, 12a–d)

DISTINGUISHING FEATURES: zone of color contrasting with the paste. *Sample*: 853 sherds. *Method of manufacture*: by coils.

PASTE: *Temper*: sand composed of grains of white feldspar and black andesite, both up to 1 mm, grains of iron oxide of less than 1 mm. Incrustations of feldspar and andesite up to 3 mm. Very fine grains of mica (muscovite) which are visible on the surfaces, which have only been smoothed. *Texture*: a not very successful mixture of laminar appearance with bubbles of air, sometimes quite large. Rims not brittle; slightly rounded. *Color*: light, uniform coffee. *Firing*: oxidizing. Only the very thick sherds have a gray nucleus. The black spots of some seem to be accounted for by the fact that they were containers used for cooking, and also because of the deficiency of the firing. The smoking of the contrasting zone, quite rare, could be intentional.

SURFACE: *Treatment*: the interior surface simply smoothed with obvious flutings resulting from the dragging of the temper grains to accomplish the action of smoothing. Sometimes it is possible to note the scarcely visible joints of the coils. In the slipped areas, the surface has been polished. *Hardness*: 2.5 to 3, Mohs scale.

FORM 1: *Rim*: simple outcurved. *Lip*: slanted. *Neck*: slightly rounded angle. *Body*: walls 8 to 10 mm thick. *Base*: curved. *Profile*: periform vessels of a wide, restricted mouth.

APPROXIMATE DIMENSIONS: *maximum diameter*: 420 mm; *opening*: 360 mm; *height*: 450 mm.

DECORATION: *Paint*: red slip on the interior rim and lip. The exterior rim and a band of approximately the same width on the top part of the body are both paste colored, separated from the rest of the painted surface of the body by a small arista 1 mm high. This contrasting band is characteristic of the type. The slipped areas display polishing marks, horizontal on the rim and vertical on the body. These marks are 3 to 4 mm wide. *Incising*: incised decoration has been employed on the lower part of the contrasting band, or on the upper section of the body. The decorative elements consist of:

1. Picked with instrument which leaves: (a) marks with parallel and sharply curved sides 1 to 2 mm wide, 5 to 8 mm long, and 2 mm deep; (b) marks with triangular sides with dimensions like the above; (c) marks with parallel and extremely straight sides 1 mm wide, 4 mm long, and 1 mm deep. All the incisions seem to have been made while the material was of waxy consistency and after the surface was finished, which is why the rims are raised. The decorative patterns of the incised elements consist of: (a) two horizontal series with a separation of 10 to 25 mm between each series and of 10 to 40 mm between each mark of the cut; (b) three horizontal series with 10 mm of separation between each series. The incised elements of the previous series seem to have sides in a horizontal direction, although more commonly they are inclined.

2. Cuts made with a roulette or comb: (a) in zigzag from top to bottom; (b) in a series of five inclined, curved lines from the top to bottom.

3. Grooved incision: (a) vertical strokes made with a comb which leaves marks of 3 to 4 mm in width and 1 to 1.5 mm deep.

APPLIQUÉ DECORATION: *Knobs*: (a) rounded, flattened knobs 10 mm wide, smooth or with four vertical clefts; (b) smoothed, elongated knobs with eight vertical clefts; (c) conical, knobs, smooth or with a reed impression at the center; stylized birds' heads with beak pointed upward; smooth heads or with deep horizontal cuts. The number of knobs may be four, eight, or sixteen. The birds' heads are four in number. The decorations of knobs and birds' heads are associated.

FORM 2: *Rim*: outcurved, reinforced from the interior or on both sides. *Lip*: smoothed or slightly rounded. In some pieces, the lip is folded over the exterior part of the rim. *Body*: walls 10 to 20 mm thick. *Base*: curved. *Profile*: plate.

APPROXIMATE DIMENSIONS: *maximum diameter*: 620 mm; *height*: 100 mm.

DECORATION: *Paint*: polished red or orange slip on both surfaces. More than half of the rims have, on the extreme and immediate area of the lip, a zone of contrast characterized by parallel channels, not very deep, with a variable distance between one and the other, probably produced by the action of polishing with grains of sand; for this reason the slip has been eliminated and a zone of contrast has been achieved. We have grouped most of the plates of this type according to this zone of contrast.

FORM 3: *Rim*: incurved, reinforced from the interior. *Lip*: rounded, or slightly flattened. *Body*: walls 6 to 8 mm thick. *Base*: curved. *Profile: lebrillo, escudilla*, incurved edge.

APPROXIMATE DIMENSION: *maximum diameter*: 230 mm; *opening*: 140 mm.

DECORATION: *Paint*: slip on both surfaces. The contrasting zone may take up the entire surface of the body of the bowl up to the collar or it may be a band 20 mm wide at the greatest diameter and without collar. *Pasting*: knobs from 5 to 8 mm turned over and placed on the contrasting zone: (a) in a horizontal line spaced 25 mm one from the other; (b) in zigzag from top to bottom with a contiguity of 1 to 2 mm.

FORM 4: *Rim*: incurved at an angle of 90° to 85°. *Lip*: slightly or entirely flattened. *Body*: walls 5 to 8 mm thick. *Base*: curved, forming an arista with the walls of the body, at least in one specimen. *Profile*: bowl with outcurved rim.

APPROXIMATE DIMENSIONS: *maximum diameter*: 300 mm; *opening*: 270 mm; *height*: 90 mm.

DECORATION: *Paint*: both surfaces with red or reddish-orange slip, except for the contrasting band which covers the whole surface between the rim and the collar. *Appliqué*: circular knobs of 12 mm with concentric reed incisions of 6 mm located in the zone of contrast.

CHRONOLOGICAL POSITION: tentatively placed in the first centuries of the Christian era.

REFERENCES AND COMPARISONS: this ceramic bears much similarity to Zelamaya trichrome of Guanacaste (Baudez 1967: 98), and the "red lip ware" of the Atlantic Drainage (Lothrop 1926: 327). Wares similar to the Pavas types have been found in the sites of Castella, Cariari, El Alto del Zoncho, Córdoba, López y Molino (see Table 2).

Virilla Bichrome (see Figures 7e–j, 10, 11)

DISTINGUISHING FEATURES: decoration of purple lines or purple zones. *Sample*: 1647 sherds. *Method of manufacture*: by coils.

PASTE: *Temper*: variety A: white grains of feldspar, black of andesite, both 1 mm with inclusions of feldspar and iron oxide up to 4 mm; variety B: same composition as A but with grains of less than 1 mm and inclusions of 1 mm. *Texture*: a somewhat irregular mixture with a rather laminar appearance in variety A. Homogeneous in variety B. Irregular fracture, slightly angular rims. *Color*: coffee or light coffee. *Firing*: reduced fire or oxidizing. Less than half of the sherds have a dark gray nucleus taking up one third of the thickness of the walls.

SURFACES: *Color*: that of the paste. A few sherds have dark spots which are the result of a defective firing. *Treatment*: both surfaces polished; in the wide-mouthed forms, the interior surface and the interior side of the rim are simply smoothed. Some edges also have a previously polished surface. On the polished surfaces, the marks of the polisher are readily visible. Sometimes made with fine decoration. *Hardness*: 2.5 to 3, Mohs scale.

FORM 1: *Rim*: outcurved, reinforced on the outside. *Lip*: lightly rounded with aristas at the joining of the interior and exterior sides of the rim. *Body*: walls 10 mm thick. *Base*: curved, pronounced towards the center. *Profile*: bowl with an edge at an angle of 1 to 4 mm in height, a little towards the bottom of the widest diameter. Less than half of the pieces do not have this rim.

APPROXIMATE DIMENSIONS: *maximum diameter*: 450 mm; *diameter of opening*: 440 mm; *height*: 120 mm.

FORM 3: *Rim*: simple, reinforced on the outside or thickened on the inside. *Lip*: slightly flattened or rounded. *Neck*: concave, very small, or no neck. *Body*: walls 5 to 8 mm thick. *Base*: curved. Some specimens have in the bottom series of hollows 10 mm in diameter placed in three rows of three hollows each, and with a distance of 15 mm between each row (strainers). *Profile: lebrillos* with straight sides or with slightly restricted mouth.

APPROXIMATE DIMENSIONS: *maximum diameter:* 180 mm; *opening:* 178 mm; *height:* 100 mm.

FORM 4: *Rim:* outcurved, reinforced on the outside, or thinned rim. *Lip:* slightly flattened or rounded. *Body:* walls 8 mm thick. *Base:* curved. *Profile:* bowls with flanges between the straight or inclined walls of the body and the base.

APPROXIMATE DIMENSIONS: *maximum diameter:* 260 mm; *height:* 150 mm.

FORM 5: *Rim:* reinforced from the inside. *Lip:* flattened or slightly rounded. *Body:* walls 8 mm thick. *Base:* curved. *Profile:* plate.

APPROXIMATE DIMENSIONS: *maximum diameter:* 600 mm; *height:* 100 mm.

DECORATION: *Paint:* slip on both surfaces, except in Form 1 with narrow mouth, whose inside surface is paste colored, which in more than 50 percent of the rims reaches up to the lip. In the rest of the pieces, the slip covers the inside of the rim. *Decorative elements:* purple lines 12 to 15 mm wide, traced with the fingers (thumb or index). This line is found in groups of four or five with less frequency in succession. These purple lines are placed vertically on the neck, particularly in the vessels of Form 1 and in some of Form 3 or as a single horizontal line towards the bottom of the collar of Form 1. It is also found as a horizontal line, but above the collar in the majority of the vessels of Form 2. In Form 4, plates, the purple lines are placed radially on the interior surface of the rim and fall on another line which is found in a circle on the interior of the rim. The purple color is also present in the rectangular areas up to 70 mm long and 40 or 50 mm wide, placed horizontally or vertically below the rim. This zone decoration serves as a background for the appliqué decoration. *Incising:* only three samples of Form 3 have incised decoration: incisions up to 10 mm placed in horizontal lines or slanted on the collars, each cut separated by a distance equal to its size. Only in one sherd is the incised decoration associated with the purple line on the collar. *Appliqué decoration* consists of: (a) round or elongated knobs 10 mm long, placed in a row at a distance of 20 to 30 mm between one and the other and on the collar; (b) round knobs of 8 to 15 mm, or elongated ones of 10 by 18 mm placed below the rim in groups of two horizontal rows of three knobs in each row, the elongated knobs on their vertical axis. These groups could probably be two or four. This decoration occurs in the Form 2 specimens without collar. These groups have a purple background which fills a rectangular zone which goes over that occupied by the knobs; (c) circular knobs of 10 mm with a reed incision placed below the rim in the form of a square. This decoration appears on one of the vessels of Form 3.

CHRONOLOGICAL POSITION: tentatively placed in the first centuries of the Christian era.

REFERENCES AND COMPARISONS: wares similar to the Pavas types have been found in the sites of Castella, El Alto del Zoncho, Córdoba, López y Molino (see Table 2).

Crespo Trichrome (see Figures 7k, l)

DISTINGUISHING FEATURES: decoration with purple stripes. *Sample*: 326 sherds. *Method of manufacture*: by coils.

PASTE: *Temper*: composed of white grains of feldspar, black grains of andesite of less than 0.5 mm with inclusions of feldspar of 1 mm and of iron oxide of 2 mm. *Texture*: good mixture, of a slightly laminar appearance, with very small air bubbles. Irregular fracture of slightly angular rims. *Color*: coffee, light coffee, or beige. *Firing*: in an oxidizing or reducing fire. Almost all the sherds have a gray or black nucleus of less than half of the thickness of the sherd and weighted towards the side of the exterior surface. *Surfaces*: the color of the interior surface is the same as that of the paste. None of the surfaces bear indications of defective firing. *Treatment*: the interior surface is simply polished. In some sherds, flutes are produced by the grains of the temper in the act of smoothing. The entire exterior surface and the lip are polished. *Hardness*: 2.5 to 3, Mohs scale.

FORM: *Rim*: simple or very slightly thickened rim. *Lip*: flattened. *Neck*: very short and concave. *Body*: walls 5 mm thick. *Profile*: globular, squat vessel with a very pronounced curvature in the center of the body. Some vessels have, located in the center of the body and equidistant from one another, four slightly indented portions of an oval form whose horizontal diameter is widest (40 mm long, 30 mm wide, and 4 mm deep).

APPROXIMATE DIMENSIONS: *maximum diameter*: 460 mm; *opening*: 115 mm; *height*: 220 mm.

DECORATION: *Paint*: the lip and the rest of the exterior surface have red slip. The decoration is made on the basis of purple stripes, which vary from 4 to 30 mm in width, of a thick appearance, made with the index finger and placed vertically or slightly inclined, as much on the upper part as on the lower part of the body or in a capricious form of stripes which are connected one with the other in different directions. When the stripes are vertical, there are two rings, one a little below the neck and the other in the curved central region of the body. These rings, from 10 to 15 mm wide, are also purple and contrast in their matt aspect with the briliant stripes; this purple was probably mixed with some organic substance (an acid) capable of penetrating the slip, producing an area of matt color. In other areas, such as the decorative concave surfaces, there are also purple lines of a matt color.

MODELING: in the upper part of the body there are two projections placed diametrically. In one specimen these bodies consist of a type of triangle with a base of 25 mm, 15 mm high, and 5 mm thick with the outside curve twisted towards the top. This type of appendix is similar to the stylized birds of the Sabana bichrome and trichrome decoration. In another specimen, it is a question of a sort of handle (from 20 to 25 mm width, height and length respectively) with a small horizontal hole of triangular form. This model has three coils in the upper part which make an angle towards the bottom.

CHRONOLOGICAL POSITION: tentatively placed in the first centuries of the Christian era.

REFERENCES AND COMPARISONS: wares similar to the Pavas type have been found in the sites of Cariari, Castella, El Alto del Zoncho, Córdoba, López y Molino (see Table 2).

Supports and Handles

SOLID, CONICAL SUPPORTS: *Sample*: 21 pieces. *Length*: 35 to 100 mm. *Diameter*: 20 to 40 mm. *Decoration*: one piece has a decoration of a stroked incision on the upper part. *Typological placement*: not determined.

SOLID, FLATTENED, CYLINDRICAL SUPPORTS: *Sample*: 16 pieces. *Length*: 200 to 700 mm. *Thickness*: 20 to 30 mm. *Width*: 20 to 60 mm. *Decoration*: one support has a small animal head in the upper angle. Another piece has a kind of lizard modeled on the external arista. Another piece has purple on the base. *Typological placement*: probably Virilla bichrome.

CONICAL SUPPORTS, DIVIDED IN TWO OR PAIRED: *Sample*: 4 pieces. *Length*: 200? to 500 mm. *Width*: 80 mm. *Thickness*: 50 mm. *Decoration*: one piece has an appliqué decoration which could be that of a stylized lizard. There is purple decoration on a section attached to one part of the vessel. *Typological placement*: probably Virilla bichrome. These supports seem to be the representation of the legs of a human figure which has the head in the upper part.

HANDLE SUPPORTS: we have a series of cylindrical ceramic fragments which seem to be handle supports. There are vessel pieces with two marks at the base which could correspond to these supports. This ware has not been typologically determined.

HANDLES: two pieces in the form of a tongue 80 mm wide by 50 mm long and 10 mm thick, with appliqué bands interspersed in the upper part, could be handles or supports.

REFERENCES

AGUILAR, CARLOS H.
  1972 *Guayabo de Turrialba. Arqueología de un sitio indígena pre-hispánico.* San José, Costa Rica: Editorial Costa Rica.
BAUDEZ, CLAUDE
  1967 *Recherches archéologiques dans la vallée du Tempisque, Guanacaste, Costa Rica.* Travaux et Mémoires de l'Institut des Hautes Etudes de l'Amérique Latine.
EVANS, CLIFORD, BETTY J. MEGGERS
  1966 "Mesoamerica and Ecuador," in *Handbook of Middle American Indians*, volume four, 243–264. Austin: University of Texas Press.
LINARES DE SAPIR, OLGA
  1971 Current research: Central America. *American Antiquity* 36(2): 236–239.
LOTHROP, S. K.
  1926 *Pottery of Costa Rica and Nicaragua*, volume eight (parts 1 and 2). Contributions from the Museum of American Indian. New York.
WILLEY, GORDON R.
  1971 *An introduction to American archaeology*, volume two: *South America*. Englewood Cliffs, N.J.: Prentice-Hall.

Biographical Notes

CARLOS H. AGUILAR P. (1917–) was born in Cartago, Costa Rica. He received his degree in Archaeology from the Escuela Nacional de Antropología e Historia de México in 1946. In the Costa Rican National Museum he has acted as the Director of the Archaeological Section. Since 1947, Aguilar has worked at the University of Costa Rica as Professor of Costa Rican Archaeology and American Archaeology, as well as Research Director in the archaeological laboratory. He is currently technical adviser in the Jade Museum of the National Insurance Institute. His most important publications have been: *Orfebrería en el México precortesiano* (1946), *Religión y Mágia entre los indios de Costa Rica de origen sureño* (1965), *Guayabo de Turrialba* (1972), and *Colección de objetos indígenas de oro del Banco Central* (1972).

FRANCES F. BERDAN (1944–) is currently Assistant Professor of Anthropology at California State College, San Bernardino. She received her B.A. in Geography from Michigan State University and her Ph.D. in Anthropology from the University of Texas at Austin. She has authored several works on Aztec culture and ethnohistory, and has coauthored a book on Nahuatl documents of the colonial period in Mexico.

RIPLEY P. BULLEN (1902–) is Curator Emeritus of Anthropology at the Florida State Museum, University of Florida, and Editor of the *Proceedings of the International Congresses for the Study of the Pre-Columbian Cultures of the Lesser Antilles*. He is especially interested in culture growth and change, including independent invention vs. diffusion in Southeastern United States and the Caribbean Islands. His publications include: *Excavations in northeastern Massachusetts* (1949), *Eleven archaeological sites in Hillsborough County, Florida* (1952), *The transitional period of Florida* (1959), *The archaeology of Grenada, West Indies* (1964), *The origins of the gulf tradition* (1972), *The orange period of peninsular Florida* (1972), and (with Adelaide

K. Bullen) *Archaeological investigations of St. Vincent and the Grenadines* (1972).

GEORGE W. BEADLE (1903–) attended the University of Nebraska and Cornell University where his major studies were cytology, genetics, and biochemistry. His primary research interests have been centered on genes controlling meiosis in maize, genetics and development of eye-color in *Drosophila*, biochemical genetics of the bread mold *Neurospora*, and the origin of maize. His research was accomplished at Cornell University, the California Institute of Technology, Harvard University, Stanford University, and the University of Chicago, while his botanical fieldwork, particularly *re* the origin of maize, has centered on Middle America. His publications include the following: *Genetical and cytological studies of Mendelian asynapsis in* Zea mays (1930, Cornell University Memoir 129); *A gene in maize for supernumerary cell divisions following meiosis* (1931, Cornell University Memoir 135); "Studies of *Euchlaena* and its hybrids with *Zea*, I: Chromosome behavior in *Euchlaena mexicana* and its hybrids with *Zea mays*; II: Crossing over between the chromosomes of *Euchlaena* and those of *Zea mays*" (1932, *Zeitschrift für Abstammungs- und Vererbungslehre* 62): "The differentiation of eye pigments in *Drosophila* as studied by transplantation" (with B. Ephrussi, 1936, *Genetics* 21); "The relation of inversions in the X-chromosome of *Drosophila melanogaster* to crossing-over and disjunction" (with A. H. Sturtevant, 1936, *Genetics* 21); "Teosinte and the origin of maize" (1939, *Journal of Heredity* 30); and "Genetic control of biochemical reactions in *Neurospora*" (with E. L. Tatum, 1941, *Proceedings of the National Academy of Sciences* 27). He is currently at the Department of Biology of the University of Chicago.

HORACIO CORONA OLEA. No biographical data available.

JORGE ELLIOTT. No biographical data available.

BILLY JOE EVANS (1942–) is Associate Professor of Chemistry at the University of Michigan, Ann Arbor. He received his undergraduate training in Chemistry at Morehouse College, earning a B.Sc. *summa cum laude* and a Ph.D. in Chemistry and Crystal Physics in 1968 from the University of Chicago. He served with the National Research Council of Canada as a Postdoctoral Fellow in Solid State Physics and Magnetism at the University of Manitoba and has been an Honorary Woodrow Wilson Fellow, an Alfred P. Sloan Foundation Research Fellow and consultant to the Metallurgy Division of the

National Bureau of Standards. His interest in archaeological artifacts made from or containing magnetically ordered iron oxides grew out of fundamental studies of the crystal chemistry and crystal physics of ferrites.

JOAQUÍN GALARZA. No biographical data available.

JAMES C. GIFFORD (1927–1973) was Associate Professor of Anthropology at Temple University, Philadelphia. He received his B.A. and M.A. from the University of Arizona, and his Ph.D. degree from Harvard University in 1963. His major interests included archaeology of the American Southwest and Middle America, and particularly ceramic typology that could lead to an understanding of prehistoric cultural processes. He was instrumental in establishing type-variety ceramic analysis in the Maya area and concomitantly he founded *Ceramica de Cultura Maya* and edited Numbers 1–8. Recent publications include *Prehistoric pottery analysis and the ceramics of Barton Ramie* (1976), "Recent thought concerning the interpretation of Maya prehistory" (in *Mesoamerican archaeology: new approaches*, 1974), and "The prehistory of *sapiens*: touchstone to his future" (in *Human futuristics*, 1971).

JOHN J. HOBGOOD (1931–) began his study of Anthropology at the University of the Americas in Mexico and received his B.A. in 1956, continuing for a Master's degree in Anthropology (1964) at Southern Illinois University. He did fieldwork on the ethnohistory of the Pilgrimage Center of Chalma in Mexico and received his Ph.D. in 1971 at the Universidad Interamericana with a dissertation entitled "Pilgrimage and the social integration of the Mexican people." He spent five years as a Human Relations Officer before joining the Social Sciences Faculty of Chicago State University. His main research interests are Mexican ethnohistory, North American ethnohistory, and the influence of Portuguese culture in India. He is the author of several articles on Mexican ethnohistory.

JEFFREY C. HOWRY (1947–) has conducted field research in both archaeology and social anthropology with a focus on the processes of social change evidenced by material culture and language. His graduate work at Harvard University encompassed both disciplines and culminated in a doctorate in Social Anthropology (1976) on the ceramic traditions and marketing system of the highlands of Chiapas, Mexico. His present research is centered on the problems of social response to rural development.

CYNTHIA IRWIN-WILLIAMS (1936–) is Professor of Anthropology at Eastern New Mexico University, Portales. She did much of her training at Radcliffe College and Harvard University, and received her Ph.D. degree from Harvard University in Anthropology in 1963. Her major areas of specialization are research on Paleo-Indian and Archaic cultures of the New World; the effects of environment of man; and the prehistoric Pueblo cultures of the American Southwest. She is the editor of *Eastern New Mexico University Contributions in Anthropology*; and is the co-author of *Excavations at the LoDaiska Site*, 1959; *Excavations at Magic Mountain*, 1966; *Climate Change and Early Population Dynamics in the Southwest United States*, 1970; and *Hell-Gap Paleo-Indian Occupation on the High Plains*, 1973.

ROSTISLAV KINZHALOV (1920–) was born in Michurinsk (U.S.S.R.). He studied classical philology and Americanistics in Leningrad State University (1942–1947) and continued his studies in the State Hermitage (Hellenism and Americanistics), where he received his *kandidat's* degree. He has been a member of the American Department of the Institute of Ethnography of the Academy of Sciences of the U.S.S.R. since 1957 (Leningrad). In January 1963 he became Chief of the American Department of the Institute and, since 1971, has been a Doctor of Historical Sciences. His numerous publications include works on art and history of Hellenism and Mesoamerica.

HERBERT LANDAR (1927–) was born in New York City. He received his B.A. from Queens College in 1949, an M.A. from Yale in 1955, and a Ph.D. in Linguistics from Yale in 1960. He has taught English, linguistics, and anthropology at Reed College, Indiana University, and California State University, Los Angeles. He has been Professor of English at California State University, Los Angeles, since 1966 and is currently Visiting Professor of Anthropology at Indiana University. He is the author of *Language and culture* and several dozen contributions to American Indian Linguistics.

JANE WHEELER PIRES-FERREIRA (1943–), studied at the American University (B.A., 1964), Cambridge University (Certificate in Prehistoric Archaeology, 1965) and the University of Michigan (Ph.D., 1973). She was a member of the Valley of Oaxaca Prehistoric Human Ecology Project, Valley of Oaxaca, Mexico, from 1967 to 1973, working primarily on Formative Period exchange networks. Her research includes the study of strategies of animal exploitation and the development of early farming villages in southwestern Iran, and the origins of domestication of the Camelidae in the Central Peruvian Andes. She has taught at the University of Illinois at Chicago Circle, the University of Chicago, and the Universidad Nacional Mayor de San Marcos, Lima, Peru, and has been an Assistant Research

Professor at George Washington University, Washington, D.C., since 1972.

JACINTO QUIRARTE (1931–) Studied art and art history at San Francisco State College (B.A., 1954; M.A., 1957) and at the National University of Mexico (Ph.D., 1964). He has taught art history at the University of the Americas, Mexico City (1962–1964); Yale University (1967); the University of Texas at Austin (1967–1972); and the University of New Mexico (1971). He is presently Professor of Art History and Criticism and Dean of the College of Fine and Applied Arts at the University of Texas at San Antonio (since 1972). Recent publications include *El estilo artistico de Izapa* (Mexico, 1973); *Izapan style art, a study of its form and meaning* (Dumbarton Oaks, 1973 [English version]); *Mexican American artists* (UT-Press, 1973); and articles and reviews on Izapan, Maya, and Mexican American art. His translations include Alfonso Caso's *Selden Codex* (Spanish to English) and articles by George Kubler (English to Spanish) published in Mexico and Venezuela. He is presently finishing work on a book on Maya vase painting (to be published by UT-Press).

CARROLL L. RILEY (1923–) did his anthropological studies at the University of New Mexico (A.B., 1948; Ph.D., 1952) and at the University of California at Los Angeles (M.A., 1950). Riley has taught at the University of Colorado and the University of North Carolina, Chapel Hill. At present he is Professor of Anthropology and Associate Director of the University Museum and Art Galleries, Southern Illinois University, Carbondale. He is author of *The origins of civilization* (Southern Illinois University Press, 1969; Arcturus Books, 1972); chief editor of *Man across the sea* (University of Texas Press, 1971, 1973); and coeditor of the multivolume *Southwestern journals of Adolph F. Bandelier* (University of New Mexico Press, 1966, 1970, 1975).

MALCOLM C. WEBB (1935–) was born in Wilmington, Delaware. He did his undergraduate work at the University of Pennsylvania and the University of Michigan where he received his Ph.D. in 1964. Most of his academic career since then has been spent in the Louisiana State University system, where he is presently Professor of Anthropology at the University of New Orleans. He has done archaeological fieldwork in Michigan, Illinois, and Middle America, but his principal research interest has been the rise of art motifs, stylistic links, and artifact distributions to produce synthetic studies in the political economy of ancient states. He has contributed chapters to *The classic Maya collapse* and *Ancient civilization and trade*, both published by the University of New Mexico Press for the School of American Research.

Index of Names

Index of Subjects